AFTER THE WALL

-◇-

Germany,
the Germans
and the
Burdens of
History

-◇-

MARC FISHER

Simon & Schuster
New York   London   Toronto   Sydney
Tokyo   Singapore

SIMON & SCHUSTER
Rockefeller Center
1230 Avenue of the Americas
New York, NY 10020

SIMON & SCHUSTER and colophon are registered trademarks of
Simon & Schuster Inc.

Designed by Jennifer Dossin

Manufactured in the United States of America

10   9   8   7   6   5   4   3

Library of Congress Cataloging-in-Publication Data
Fisher, Marc.
After the wall: Germany, the Germans and the burdens of his-
tory/Marc Fisher.
p.   cm.
Includes index.
1. Germany—History—Unification, 1990. 2. Germany—Ethnic relations. 3. Jews—Germany—History—20th century. 4.
Germany—Social conditions—1990– 5. Social
integration—Germany. I. Title.
DD290.29.F57   1995
305.8'00943'09049—dc20   95-3892
                                                          CIP

ISBN 0-684-80291-0

TO JODY

CONTENTS

◄○►

Prologue   9

PART I

The Wall Within

1. Fault Lines   *19*
2. Verboten   *43*
3. The Bloody Flag   *66*
4. Helmut Kohl and the Lust for Normalcy   *85*

PART II

The Wall Between Germans East and West

5. The Ossietzky School   *107*
6. First Train Out   *125*
7. Wall-Mart   *141*
8. Survivors   *162*
9. Carpetbaggers and Scallywags   *177*

PART III

The Wall Between Germans and Others

10. Germans and Jews   *203*
11. A German Pendulum: Father and Son   *225*
12. Fire and Ash   *238*
13. Ausländer   *255*
14. "How Ugly Are We Really?"   *273*

PART IV

The Wall Between Germans and the Past

15. Lost and Found   *293*
16. Back in the Middle Again   *311*

Notes on Sources   *323*
Acknowledgments   *333*
Index   *335*

PROLOGUE

EVEN BEFORE I moved to Bonn in 1989 to become bureau chief for the *Washington Post*, I knew Germany would captivate me. Any country with such a rich and tangled history would have to. But I was puzzled: In the newsrooms and living rooms of my own country, Germany had a gray reputation. This was no accident. A boring image was precisely what the people who rebuilt West Germany sought. If they had transformed their land from the core of global evil into a nonthreatening technocracy wrapped in a European flag, that was something to take pride in. And that is how the West German story had played in the American press since the economic miracles of the 1950s. Scouring newspaper archives and book catalogues, I found thoughtful reporting about the stationing of nuclear weapons in West Germany, the ups and downs of German automakers, the delicate minuet performed by the two German states and their superpower choreographers. But there was curiously little about the people who had struggled with the past and created a new society in such a short time.

After Germany's break with civilization in 1933, the country was, in relatively quick order, devastated by war, occupied by foreign powers, divided by concrete and barbed wire, and finally reunited in a peaceful revolution. I wanted to tell the story of a society that had taken pains to remodel itself even as outsiders examined it for traces of evil. My instinct was to look beyond the politicians and business leaders, the elites who make most of the news around the world, and focus on everyday Germans, families who had seen their world change so powerfully, so quickly. The German story, I thought, was one of generations, of families who had witnessed not evolutionary change but painful spasms of political and social upheaval.

In the months before I moved to Germany, I talked to diplomats, historians, political scientists both German and American. I was struck by the strong undercurrent of fear and doubt about Germans and what they wanted. What would happen if the postwar division of Germany were to end? "I fear you would have to intervene eventually to save us from ourselves," Egon Bahr, one of West Germany's most prominent postwar politicians and political theorists, told me four months before the Berlin Wall fell. "To say there is any realistic chance of my country uniting is a lie. Our neighbors would never accept it, and I don't know that we really want it." How could someone so widely admired be so wrong? Bahr was not alone.

Hardly anyone foresaw the events of 1989 and 1990; an entire country misjudged itself. My idea for a book on generations of Germans was overrun by history—the Wall, unification, the vacuum left by the end of the Cold War, the movement of millions of migrants across Europe. I realized that events had wiped out my plan on November 9, 1989, when my wife and I, then studying German in the little Rhine Valley town of Boppard, returned from dinner to the house where we rented a room from a kindly old couple. Herr Gödert stood in the stairwell as we entered. He had been there for some time. He knew no English and so had gleaned only the essentials of the message from my office in Washington: "The Wall is gone," the old man said in the simplest German he could muster. "You must work." My studies over, I made for Bonn, then Berlin.

Writing about eight hundred newspaper stories between 1989 and 1993, I became absorbed in the tension and novelty of unification. But as jarring and stirring as the fall of the Berlin Wall and the reunification of a divided land were, Germans reacted to these changes only in the context of the other great upheavals that had rocked their lives and those of their parents and grandparents—the loss of two world wars, the Holocaust, the shame and guilt submerged under a viscous postwar layer of affluence and democracy in the West, deprivation and repression in the East. To understand the events of the five years after the East German revolt, I had to learn how Germans had dealt with, repressed and accepted the past. And to understand that past, I had to see that the ongoing family tussle between Germans east and west is more than a clash among cousins.

The aftermath of German unification—the absorption of communist East Germany into democratic West Germany—is the story of a turning inward to face deep divisions that were either caused or exacerbated by the fall of the Berlin Wall. Germany today remains an unexpectedly divided country. It is divided against itself, east from west. It is divided against the "other," its own 6 million foreign residents as well as the hundreds of thousands of new migrants who arrive each year. Most of all, it is divided against its past, the continuing psychological and political aftershocks of this century's great traumas—old wounds ripped open by the readmission of 16 million East Germans to the country and the lifting of half a century of taboos. This book explores those divisions, how they are expressed in daily life and how they restrain Germany after the Wall.

The Germans used to be much easier to figure out. The Wall made life simple: capitalists here, communists there. The past was bad, the present eager to please. Business boomed, affluence leached through society, erasing class borders. Then everything seemed to change. The end of the Cold War and the fall of the Wall brought the promise of a new Germany, along with assurances that there would be no new Germany. This was not going to be easy. In the former East Germany, three generations of dictatorship left torn psyches and shattered confidence—a difficult foundation for the trying task of uniting with their comfortable cousins. In the west, where people had spent forty years shaping a new normalcy for themselves, the fall of the Wall bared the weaknesses of the system that had seemed so firmly rooted. The unification of 1990 put basic questions back on the table: Who are the East Germans to us? What should this new Germany be? Who are we?

The successful, efficient, unobtrusive West Germany that America took for granted and molded in our own image is now a society in transition— economically troubled, politically divided, and socially riddled with self-doubt. This book begins in the West Germany that Americans thought we knew—a seemingly satisfied place, a trusted ally, an efficient technocracy. I start with a focus on everyday German life, because it was there, where they least expected it, that western Germans found themselves wallowing in discontent and doubt in the years after unification. Western Germans suffered an emotional reversal after 1989, falling from euphoria to pessimism without quite understanding why. The fall of the Berlin Wall had exposed the Wall Within—the traumas of the past and rigidities of the present that threaten Germany's future. Western Germans suddenly were asking basic questions about their identity, questions about patriotism and normalcy, blood and brotherhood.

In Part II, I return to my original idea of watching and exploring the Germans through the eyes of families caught in the storms of change. The saga of the eastern Germans and their struggle to crawl out of the ruins of communism is dramatic in its own right, but I focus on the story of eastern Germany for another purpose as well: Their forty-year history was a controlled experiment, an enforced separation from their countrymen that enables us to ask basic questions about what binds and divides a people. The easterners—the German slang is "Ossis"—were heavily marked by their years under Soviet domination, but in a sense they were the "purer" Germans, free of the American influences of pop culture and individualism that had so sharply altered western German life.

The eastern Germans who shared their lives with me in that extraordinary period of change after 1989 did not have impressive titles or important positions. They were not, for the most part, the people who made revolutions or redesigned the country's institutions. But like all Germans in these years, their daily effort to hold a family together and make ends meet forced them into the country's political squalls. I found Egon Zeidler, an eastern Berlin shopkeeper, when I stopped into his store for something to eat. Zeidler took me under his wing and devoted countless hours to the thankless task of explaining the communist system to an American. Zeidler would be double-crossed by the very political change he had dreamt of for decades, but he never lost his passion and his humor—the characteristics that made his story so essential to my sense of the new life in the country's east.

I found some of my other guides to Germany by a less random process. Bärbel Bohley is an artist who had her fifteen minutes of fame, and a bit more, as the "Mother of the Revolution," a courageous East German dissident who helped organize the revolt of 1989, and then found herself discarded by a people eager to leap into the inviting waters of the west. And Ekkehard and Elke Hotz found me, responding to a classified ad I had placed in their local newspaper seeking eastern Germans who had migrated to the west and then back again. The Hotz story is a bittersweet affirmation of the tribalism that divides and unites the Germans even on the eve of the twenty-first century.

In Part III, as the paths of eastern and western Germany merge, I examine the fault lines in German society by returning to the generational approach. Günter Althans and his son Ewald belong to a German family that has experienced pendulum swings from one extreme to another, from Nazi to socialist to neo-Nazi. Half a century after the war, they struggle with Germany's nagging, embarrassing reality: Antagonism toward the "other," those who are somehow not German even if they and their ancestors have lived in Germany. Few Germans are neo-Nazis. But reunification forced many Germans to confront the root question of what it means to be German.

Throughout this book, I focus not on groups but on individuals, and on the basic unit of organization in any society, the family. Part IV tells the story of Gabriele Yonan and her son, who were separated for nearly two decades by the Berlin Wall and reunited only when their countries were. As a direct result of the country's division, the son grew up apart from his mother. That mother and son remained divided even after they were reunited was a family tragedy intertwined with their country's history. Theirs is a story of Germany east and west, of wrongs that cannot be righted, and of lives that nonetheless must be led.

Alone, these stories and others in this book tell of individual lives, a few ways of coping with the promise and terror of historic change. Together, their lives illuminate more than political events or diplomatic developments describe. These people—like nearly every German I met—were able to discuss the issues of the day only to a point, before they stopped, either to tell me of their own pasts and those of their families, or to say that they could not do so, it was too hard. Germany's burden, and its hope, lie in how its people deal with a history of anguish and glory.

At the dawn of a new millennium, a rich culture seems strangely stunted. As colonial empire, feudalism and slavery have proven to burden generations of other peoples, the Germans can be expected to wrangle with the legacy of dictatorship, genocide and repression for years to come. In Germany, as elsewhere in the world, there are people who propose to forget, to move beyond the traumas of the past. But the new Germany—finally free to begin writing its own story—is learning that concrete walls are easier to remove than the yoke of history. Two generations have not accomplished the purging of this century's excesses that so many seek. Neither affluence nor democracy sufficed. It is neither fair nor simple, but honest Germans have learned it is inescapably true: To grow toward normalcy, Germans, like all of us, must deal with the realities of their parents' and grandparents' world. They must accept the burdens of the past as their own.

When I decided to spend four years in Germany, my father said I was committing an incomprehensible act of aggression. In a way, he was right. Living in Germany fulfilled my professional dream to work as a foreign correspondent. But it was also a challenge, a break with my own past. Germany, like no other place in the world, was an idea I had let others define for me. Now I would have to consider it for myself.

My parents and teachers had strong views about the Germans. What I heard about Germany and the Germans as I grew up in New York City in the 1960s and '70s ran the emotional and political gamut from A to B. Germany was the Holocaust and the Nazis. Somewhere along the way, I had settled down as a Germany agnostic. That by itself was something of a rebellion. Any place that could elicit such overwhelming condemnation deserved a closer look, I figured. But I had not felt compelled to take that look. Before I moved to Bonn, I had managed, without quite realizing it, to visit most of Europe without setting foot in Germany. A map of my travels would have shown pins sticking out almost in a circle around Germany.

Surely, I told myself, this was unintentional. I was not one of those Americans who declared Germany off-limits because of its history. (I would later learn, to my great surprise, that fully 29 percent of Americans tell researchers they would never set foot in Germany.) I knew no Germans. Neither had I ever known a Holocaust survivor. My family was not directly affected by World War II. No one served in the military.

When it came time for me to move to Germany in September 1989, I read generational studies of German families. I pored over survey material documenting the shifting sands of German attitudes. And I resolved to stay closely aware of my biases and expectations. It was, I told myself, the best a reporter could do: To find out what is really happening, first know who you are.

PART

I

◄◦►

The Wall

Within

THE *Post*'S HOUSE in Bonn was a jewel, a postcard-perfect gingerbread cottage directly on the Rhine. We looked out our living room window at the Drachenfels, the ruins of a medieval castle that faded in and out of view as clouds swept over the hilltop. The house, a splash of red, blue and white along the river promenade, had been built a few years into this century, supposedly by a Rhine shipping captain who had carved an outline of a riverboat into the back wall of the fireplace, so that the vessel would rock and shimmer through the flames of a well-made fire.

Our tidy neighborhood seemed to be the Germany I'd read and heard about—the prosperous, quiet, hard-working West. But from our first weeks in the country, a time of turbulence and thrills, I began to see a Germany that had managed only a cosmetic makeover, a people still wondering who they were and where they fit in.

Even our charming cottage, a delightful house we will always recall as our daughter's first home, turned out to be something other than it appeared to be: Friedhelm Kemna, a former resident of the house and ex-editor of Bonn's daily paper, the *General-Anzeiger*, told us of the wartime days when our house, still under a thatched roof, served as an informal brothel, a safe house where SS men could take willing women for a waterfront rendezvous.

In Germany, history is everywhere, and nowhere. If you want to see it, you have to look. I wondered in those first days whether it would be fair to look. From my first moments in the country, I was struck by the euphemisms and circumlocutions many people used to reach around the past, to ease the present. "In former times," many a sentence began. "Of course, we have our special heritage," said a friendly fellow in the Foreign Ministry.

Far from Bonn, even in small villages in the Rhineland and the Hunsrück, I noticed that some Germans decorated their flagpoles not with the banner of their own country, but with a blue flag festooned with a circle of stars—the symbol of the European Community. In the coming years, I would see that banner on official buildings throughout the twelve west European nations that belong to the economic and political alliance. But only in Germany would I see that flag fly in front of the homes of ordinary citizens. The flagwavers seemed anxious to prove they were good Europeans; they were also none too eager to announce their own nationality.

Even before the fall of the Wall, West Germany was a bundle of contradictions, a nation suspicious of itself.

Fault Lines

No one is a Nazi. No one ever was. There may have been some Nazis in the next village, and as a matter of fact, that town about twenty kilometers away was a veritable hotbed of Nazidom. . . . Ah, how we have suffered. The bombs. We lived in the cellars for weeks. . . . It should, we feel, be set to music. Then the Germans could sing this refrain and that would make it even better. They all talk like this. One asks oneself how the detested Nazi government, to which no one paid allegiance, managed to carry on this war for five and a half years. Obviously, not a man, woman or child in Germany ever approved of the war for a minute, according to them. —Martha Gellhorn, reporting from Germany in April 1945, in her book The Face of War

AT THE DEUTSCHES Museum in Munich, an exhibit tracing the history of the country's railroads stops abruptly in the 1930s and picks up with the phrase "After the war. . . ." A survey of German cinema history at Frankfurt's German Film Museum slides right over the war years. Down the street at the Architecture Museum, there is no mention of Nazi design save a single house designed by Albert Speer. At a magnificent museum of modern art in Cologne, paintings from the twenties give way to works from the fifties, with nothing in between. In 1990, the Berlin newspaper *Der Tagesspiegel* managed to print an article about efforts to dig up Hitler's bunker without once mentioning the dictator by name. In 1992, when the Berlin government published an informative booklet on world religions in the city, it included eleven pages on Judaism, its history, holidays and synagogues. But there was only one sentence on Kristallnacht, one mention of concentration camps—not a word on gas chambers, Aryanization, or the daily oppression of the city's Jews during the Nazi years.

Once you discover the Gap, it is hard to stop noticing. When Jody and I met our landlady in Bonn, she told us some of her life's story, starting with her hometown and continuing with a recitation of her husband's postings as a diplomat. She listed each of his assignments up to his experiences in Central America in the 1920s. "And then," Frau Albers said, without skipping a beat, "in 1950, after the war, he helped to create the new Federal Republic." In one interview after another, business people and government officials of a certain age slid over those twelve years as if they had been excised from time. There was no smile, no nod to concede what they had just done. It was simply the way to behave about a time on which few wanted to dwell.

Some people had no choice. Museum curators who might have wanted to display Nazi-era art could not: Virtually all works from that period remain locked up at the Munich Customs Office and the Army Museum in Ingolstadt, where they have sat since the U.S. military, which confiscated the art in 1945, returned its holdings to the Germans in the mid-1980s. The paintings and sculptures, like Nazi books, films and symbols, are taboo in modern Germany. Allowing the public to view them is simply too dangerous, politicians and art historians argue. They contend that the far right could use these symbols to win new recruits, that the average German might not be able to withstand the emotional power of Nazi propaganda. But a few curators say enough time has passed, that if Germany's democracy has taken root, its people must be trusted to see the art of the Third Reich and decide for themselves if it is banal tripe or alluring evidence of a better way. The campaign to open the vaults has made little headway. In 1994, Munich's City Museum courageously exhibited hundreds of portraits made by Heinrich Hoffmann, Hitler's personal photographer. The show was a huge success. When I went, the longest lines were not for entry into the exhibit, but for a chance to read and write in the comment book, a remarkable document that displays the broad spectrum of German thought. Some said the pictures—power-packed views of the Führer as superhuman, tender scenes of Hitler as wise man, father figure, and dog-lover—were too dangerous to be seen in public. "We have millions of unemployed again and there is another quest for a strong man. With this exhibit, you are only helping to feed this desire!" a man from Munich wrote. A woman from Berlin responded, "As a member of the postwar generation, I am glad to see that finally we are beginning to recognize that this episode did not consist only of Auschwitz and Dachau." And a young student from Leipzig added, "These are pictures of a corrupt politician, that is all. When you break the taboo, he is only a man, no longer a mysterious evil god." But the taboo could not be broken: The Munich museum tucked the Hoffmann pictures in a hard-to-find corner. No postcards from the exhibit were sold. And the show's next stop, at the German Historical Museum in Berlin, was canceled because the leader of the city's Jewish community complained that the pictures would generate new support for neo-Nazis.

Nazi symbols, anti-Semitic writings, and even artifacts of the 1930s and '40s are illegal in Germany. (But Nazi military decorations, party membership cards, and all manner of swastika-emblazoned items—radios, medallions, books—are routinely sold from beneath cloth covers in the back corners of flea markets.) Hitler's *Mein Kampf*, a standard assignment in many American high school and college classes, is banned in Germany; you can be jailed for owning a copy. Six times a year, government censors—the Federal Office for the Examination of Youth-Endangering Publications—issue a list of about 3,000 records, movies, videos and video games that minors are prohibited from seeing. The list includes all Bruce Lee movies, the *Friday the 13th* series, *Rambo: First Blood, Part II,* and dozens of neo-Nazi video and computer games (One, "The Nazi," includes questions such as "Which is the stupidest animal? (a) the guinea pig, (b) the ape, (c) the Jew"; and "Who won World War II? (a) Germany, (b) Germany, (c) Germany.") Some videos and books are banned because they are pornographic or violent, others because they are "race-baiting" or include Nazi symbols or messages. The index of banned items includes recordings on the CBS and BBC labels.

Robert Zank is a Berlin music producer and record importer, a nervous young fellow who scratches out a living selling LPs and CDs of the latest New York and London techno, industrial and hip-hop sounds. He publishes a small catalogue of German, Japanese, Dutch and American experimental music, some of it political, most not. Without thinking much about it, he ordered from a distributor in Massachusetts thirty copies of a record by a New York band called Women of the SS. The band's music has zero political content, but, rockers being rockers, they decided to spice up their album cover with swastikas and the SS symbol. The songs had titles such as "Oh, What Fun We Shall Have." When the records arrived at customs in Germany, agents called Zank and told him they would allow the albums into the country because they were artistic expression rather than political agitation.

But within days, three plainclothes police officers showed up at Zank's home with a search warrant. They tore apart his apartment, confiscated the Women of the SS records, and charged Zank with importing Nazi material. Zank was livid. He thought the police in his democracy were acting just as the Nazis had, declaring art they didn't like to be degenerate. "It's a bankrupt declaration that they can't trust their own people," he said. "This banning mentality creates exactly the feelings they're trying to avoid."

In the early nineties, as the Bonn government sought to prove it was taking a hard line against right-wing extremism, it heaped new taboos on the censorship pile. Neo-Nazi gangs sidestepped the ban on the stiff-armed *"Heil Hitler"* salute by raising three fingers into the air instead of the proscribed four. So the government responded by adding the three-finger position to the blacklist. The slightly altered swastikas and SS symbols used by the far right also were added to the index.

Any effort to eradicate or repress twelve years of history is, of course, hopeless. Germans' fear of the Nazi period, the rawness of an experience that lies half a century in the past, is exposed by the Gap and the awkward euphemisms so many Germans use to refer to "those times," or "our difficult past." Even those who can bring themselves to give the Nazi years a name often brand the Third Reich and the Holocaust as the work of a single person. They were "the Hitler years," "the time after Hitler took over," as if he were an alien force who arrived in 1933 and vanished twelve years later, leaving behind a society clean of responsibility.

The Nazis are ubiquitous. In eastern Germany's first free political campaign in 1990, the citizens movement Democracy Now distributed a poster asking voters "Do you want total imitation" of the west?—a reminder of Nazi Propaganda Minister Joseph Goebbels' infamous rallying cry as the Nazis sank into defeat: "Do you want total war?" Language poses a maddening Catch-22 for Germans. Some cases are easy: A writer advocates in a newspaper article that Germany offer to buy back some of its old territories in Poland and the Czech Republic because the country needs more *"Lebensraum"*—consciously using the Nazi term for the extra living space Hitler said the Germans needed. But some cases are not so simple: When the government of Chancellor Helmut Kohl decided to house refugees in mass, central camps instead of in small shelters around the country, the official name for the sites was *Sammelunterkünfte.* Literally, that translates as "collection lodgings," but since that phrase makes no sense in English, my fellow reporters and I translated the name as "collection camps." The Bonn authorities went ballistic: They had created a new word expressly to avoid any overlap with *Konzentrationslager,* German for "concentration camp." Anyone who heard or read the government's careful coinage thought immediately of concentration camps. No one was fooling anyone. But what should they have done? They couldn't very well use the Nazi term. Of course, they didn't have to create such camps, and after the fierce, shocked reaction to the proposal (mostly from abroad), the plan was quietly downgraded and eventually all but dropped.

When taboos ease, when the past breaks out into the open, the public hunger for a useful, living past is palpable. In 1992, at the request of Washington's Kennedy Center, two German musical theater veterans, Jürg Burth and Volker Kühn, put together a cabaret based on the classic show tunes of the Nazi-era UFA studio musicals—songs personally approved by Goebbels. Burth and Kühn spent months wrestling with the script: They knew the songs were gems that, despite the unstoppable advance of American pop music in the postwar years, had managed to outlive the Nazis and find a place in the humming repertoires of millions of Germans. But Burth and Kühn were aghast that audiences might come to their show to wax nostalgic about songs once used to cement bonds between Germans and their repressive regime. So the writer and director suffused their show with powerful scenes and disturbing settings designed nearly to smother the songs under illustrations of the perversion and allure of Nazi rule. A love song called "The World Becomes Beautiful Through You" takes on a new flavor when it is sung while athletes from the 1936 Berlin Olympics show how the Nazis glorified the Aryan body and spread the myth of racial superiority. Burth and Kühn tried to force their audiences to confront the fact that they were tapping their feet to tunes once used to buck up the spirits of Wehrmacht soldiers on the Eastern Front.

The show was a fascinating mix of old Nazi propaganda and the acerbic commentary of contemporary cabaret. When I watched the show in rehearsal, I thought Burth and Kühn had broken the taboo in a way that would achieve exactly the confrontation with the past they sought. But then I went to see the show with a Berlin audience consisting largely of old folks bused in from around the country to hear the songs of their youth. Nostalgia reigned supreme. All around me, men and women grew teary as they hummed and even sang along with the old tunes. Burth and Kühn's overt displays of Nazi brutality, even an assault by a muscular Aryan on a withered Jew—none of the modern overlay weakened the emotional punch of the rediscovered soundtrack of a repressed youth. When the same show ran in Washington, the powerful scenes of Nazi terror left audiences drained and silent. But in Berlin, nothing the director put on the stage could compete with the roaring force of memories finally liberated from decades of evasion and taboo.

Memory assaults at every corner in Germany. Every old war-pocked building in Berlin and every new concrete apartment block obviously built to fill a bomb crater, every old person, every exclamation point on a government document, every encounter with an old woman shouting lustily at someone who dares cross the street against the red light, every pedestrian who hears a foreign language and mutters loudly about "damned foreigners"—they brought rushing back to me a war and a time I had never experienced. In the same way, the songs of the thirties brought back to Germans who had been there the good times, first loves, and lost fathers; the miracle of radio, the brilliance of flags fluttering along broad boulevards. Only now, half a century after it all happened, are Germans taking the next step after the angry 1960s confrontations between teenagers and their parents ("What did you do in the war?"). So many of those angry accusations ended in silence and distance that it took another generation before the country was ready to try again. And when it did, the memories emerged finally as grief and self-pity. Germans as victims. A 1993 war movie, *Stalingrad,* subjected audiences to more than three hours of unrelenting carnage—young German boys being sent out to die in a hopeless suicide mission born of Hitler's monumental stubbornness. Older audiences wept; young people sat agog at the very notion of young German soldiers being portrayed as innocent victims. And when German television produced a five-part series on the fiftieth anniversary of the battle that left 250,000 German soldiers dead, producers were stunned by the reaction: A single press report notified the public that TV producers had obtained from Soviet archives a few hundred undelivered letters from German soldiers at Stalingrad. Within a few weeks, more than 50,000 Germans had contacted the network in the hope that one of the letters might be from a relative who had never returned.

After fifty years of pretending that life had started anew in 1945, Germans watched with satisfaction, fear and disbelief as the past pushed up new shoots. Margarete Mitscherlich, a German psychoanalyst, wrote in the influential 1967 book she coauthored, *The Inability to Mourn,* that her country had swept the Nazi years under the carpet, choosing instead to rebuild life without memories. A quarter of a century later, Mitscherlich said nothing had improved: "If you don't go through this process of mourning, grief always remains as a deep-seated depression in a nation and in individuals too. The normal process of mourning—and this has to do with remembering—lasts a lifetime. With respect to collective mourning for historic guilt, this will continue throughout the course of German history."

The country might not be ready for collective grief, but in the Bavarian town of Passau, Hitler and Himmler's boyhood home, one nasty girl made damn certain that no one would escape the past. From a head full of frosted curls to her fluffy pink bunny slippers, Anna Rosmus looked like anything but a nosy, know-it-all Nazi hunter. She was approaching middle age, but she still giggled like a school kid. It was hard to imagine that she could inspire her own mother-in-law to say that because of people like Anna, Germany needed another Hitler. Hard to imagine Passau's mayor, the local priests and many of her family's friends deciding that Rosmus was so evil she deserved to be "gassed, chopped up and pulverized."

Rosmus, an eternal graduate student in her mid-thirties, was the inspiration for German director Michael Verhoeven's *The Nasty Girl,* the film version of Anna's decade-long battle with her hometown and its hidden history. Passau takes pride in being a normal Bavarian town, its medieval city center restored to fantasyland colors, its new downtown boasting a chrome-and-glass indoor mall. Growing up, Anna accepted her home as the city fathers portrayed it. She knew nothing about Passau's secrets. The house where Hitler lived as a child became a museum to the Führer during the Third Reich. American occupation forces closed the museum in 1945 and gave the house to the Passau Jewish community. Later, the building reverted to private hands, and, oddly enough, no one seems to know where it is. When I arrived, I asked passersby, the tourist information office, even the mayor's office. Somehow, no one was quite certain. Perhaps you'd like to see the lovely cathedral instead.

Rosmus was still in high school when her favorite teacher suggested she enter an essay contest that could win her a trip to Paris. She wrote "Freedom in Europe." Nice milquetoast topic. No one was offended. When she won the top prize, the whole town cheered her on. There were ceremonies at City Hall, parties, proud feelings all around. The next contest beckoned. This time, Anna decided to write "My Hometown in the Third Reich." Yes, well. Very good to show interest in history, the town librarians and teachers told Anna. Surely you'll want to write about Passau's resistance movement against the Nazis. Rosmus didn't quite know what she wanted to write about. She isn't Jewish, but she was curious about her town's treatment of Jews. Mostly, she wanted to see the old newspapers and other archives tucked away in a locked cabinet in the city library.

The city refused her access. It would come to regret that move. Rosmus began a four-year legal effort to pry the records out of the hands of city officials who, it turned out, had good reason to resist Anna's research. As Rosmus pushed harder and harder, learning to enlist the aid of out-of-town newspaper reporters, the town turned against its child with a venom that betrayed Passau's placid storybook facade. With the distance of time, the whole campaign against Anna seems impossible: She is unremittingly cheerful, optimistic beyond all cause, trusting despite years of betrayal. But Anna Rosmus had been stubborn since she was a toddler. The more she was rebuffed, the more certain she grew of her cause.

Anna discovered that her town had been home to concentration camps, that everyone, even her own grandmother, knew where they were, but chose to forget. She learned that a Passau clergyman once denounced a local Jewish businessman, sentencing him to death at the hands of the Nazis. She discovered that the brother of the local newspaper's editor had been a Nazi sympathizer. The editor responded by banning Rosmus' name from the paper; for five years while Anna battled every level of city bureaucracy, the *Passauer Neue Presse* published not one word about the controversy. "It was really just a little girl writing a school report," Hermann Schmidt, cultural editor of the *Neue Presse,* told me when I visited Passau. The paper eventually came under new management, which lifted the ban against Rosmus and even printed a complimentary review of her third book on Passau's past. "What she did was fine," Schmidt said, "but I don't like the way she did it, seeking publicity, beating a good thing to death."

When she finally won access to the city archives, Rosmus discovered that the editor of the local Catholic newspaper, who had passed himself off for four decades as a resistance member, had actually written pro-Nazi articles in which he urged Passauers to pray for Adolf Hitler, a good man. The Catholic editor sued Rosmus for slander and invasion of privacy. He wanted $300,000. When the case went to trial, the judge told Rosmus she would have to sign a declaration stating that the editor was not a committed Nazi, that he did not want to murder Jews, that he only expressed anti-Semitic beliefs.

"OK, he wasn't really a strong Nazi," Rosmus said. "I was willing to say that, but I must also have the right to say he was no resistance fighter either." She refused to sign the declaration. Instead, Rosmus, by then a pro at using the press, invited British, Swedish and Israeli reporters to attend her trial. Within moments after the judge was informed in chambers that his courtroom was packed with the vipers of the press, the court clerk announced that the trial was canceled because the judge had fallen out of an apple tree. Rosmus laughed, relishing the moment even in the retelling years later. She walked out without having to retract anything. In the years since, ten Passauers have taken Rosmus to court. None has won anything.

Outside the courthouse, Anna had grown accustomed to life with bomb and murder threats. Her husband finally left her, saying he could no longer stand the pressure. Neo-Nazis recognized Rosmus in a Munich restaurant and attacked her, smashing tables and chairs and leaving her unconscious. Police caught a man with a butcher's knife running toward the tent where she and her family were camping on vacation. She was spat upon on the streets of Passau. Strangers walked up to her and asked, "Are you working for Wiesenthal?"—the Austrian Jewish Nazi-hunter.

"People in town smelled blood and they created a martyr," Schmidt said after Rosmus achieved local celebrity status. But if the editor had come to terms with Rosmus, on the narrow medieval streets of the town where Adolf Eichmann was married, the name of Anna Rosmus was still enough to draw sputtering rage.

I asked a group of young men just released from their year and a half of mandatory military service what they thought of her. "The Nazi time is over and you should forget about it," said Hermann Haydn as his friends cracked jokes about "Anna the Jew-lover." "If you think about it always, you get very depressed and that's no way to live. Anna Rosmus overdoes it."

"Those were hard times for the older people and they shouldn't be forced to live it again," said a young stock clerk, Franz Heidner. "Times have changed. This stuff is always coming up, stories about the Nazis and concentration camps. They should just leave it alone. You should remember, but not always."

When the movie *The Nasty Girl* opened in Passau in 1990, the town fathers were invited. One of the few to show up, Vice Mayor Fritz Abelein, soon sank deep into his chair and at the end of the screening ran to the rear exit of the theater to escape the inquiring press. There was even talk of banning the film from Passau, but after years of bad publicity, the authorities were wise enough not to present Rosmus with another such lovely gift. Instead, they declared obscene and banned the movie's poster, which depicted a bronze statuette of a nude woman. (Rosmus was ready for that move; in her typically cheeky manner, she offered to pay for Pampers so the city could cover up hundreds of nude angels in the Passau cathedral.) A city councilman, H. P. Heller, told me Passau had completely mishandled the Rosmus affair. "They should have cooperated with her, such a nice, blonde little girl. The general opinion here is that we have no connection to those times. It's not interesting anymore."

Rosmus kept researching and writing. She published three books—on Passau's Nazi past, on Jewish life in the town before the concentration camps, and, using the National Archives in Washington, on the slaughter of Soviet prisoners by civilian mobs in the Passau area after American troops pushed through lower Bavaria in the last days of the war. For twelve years, Anna stayed in Passau, long after her friends had found it easier to steer clear of her, long after her marriage had dissolved. Always, she pushed the town to remember.

When she was researching her second book, she wrote to Passau's Jewish former residents in America. Struck by the homesickness many of them described, Rosmus approached her old nemesis, the mayor, and asked him to invite the former citizens to return for a visit, at Passau's expense. "The mayor told me, 'I didn't send them away, so I won't invite them,' " Rosmus recalled. She went right ahead and sent an invitation to New York painter Robert Klein, inviting him back to Passau on behalf of the city. After Klein accepted, Rosmus returned to City Hall, this time with a friend posing as a reporter, microphone and all. Suddenly, the mayor decided to invite Klein to give an art exhibition in Passau. Some weeks later, when Klein was about to arrive, Rosmus went once more to the mayor. She wanted an official city welcome for Klein at the train station. The mayor refused. The day before Klein was to arrive, Rosmus called the local newspaper and informed editors that the mayor would be at the station to receive the returning Passauer. The paper printed the information. "The next day," Rosmus said, "I was at the station with my daughter, a rose, a sign saying SHALOM, two hundred people who wanted to see a real Jew—and the mayor. Mr. Klein wrote me later saying what a great feeling it was, especially to be received by the mayor." Rosmus offered a feline smile, basking in the brilliance of her own tactics.

Rosmus has the soft, plump look of a woman who has known little hardship. Her big, sparkling eyes reveal no mean streak, no zeal for historic vengeance. She never wanted her parents to spend countless hours defending their rebellious child. Her goal was only to put history in its proper place. "The film, the research I have done, it all breaks a taboo," she said. "You can only change what happens now or in the future if you understand what happened here. We couldn't prevent Nazism; maybe we can't prevent the next war. All we can do is make people more sensitive." Her third book completed, she accepted an offer to spend a couple of years in the United States, finishing the dissertation she kept putting aside to focus on her hometown. But Anna Rosmus plans to return to Passau and its libraries, back to the search for a past even her friends prefer to consider in small doses. "I'm not proud to be one of the few," she said. "I'd rather be the normal case."

In so many ways, normal life since World War II in Germany has been defined as whatever Nazi life was not. A country anxious to prove to itself and outsiders that it had discarded the old ways simply banned them. If the Nazis corralled children into spying on their own parents, postwar Germans made it illegal to have phone extensions in your own home. If the Nazis persecuted Jews, the postwar Germans made it illegal to utter anti-Semitic words. Parents tried to dress and raise their children differently. Language changed. Life became more American. TV, democracy and economic boom times made the nightmare seem distant and dim. The Germans became the reliable ally, the well-behaved, quiet, pliant state perfectly situated to bear the brunt of the Soviet attack, whenever it came. In our eyes, at least, they had become more or less normal. We visited, we drank their beer, we praised their new democracy. But we never pried, we never asked whether such a complete change was really natural. Most Germans didn't bother with such questions either. There was enough good news to focus on: affluence, the wealth of leisure time, a social welfare system that seemed a perfect mix of capitalism and socialism. Then, the fall of the Berlin Wall forced basic questions about the postwar push to change everything.

When right-wing extremists warped the country's well-tended foreign image, criticism centered on German judges who consistently let off fire-bombing thugs with the lightest of sentences. What flaw in the justice system let these kids get away with murder? The question requires a look back at the creation of the West German system: Because the Nazis were so repressive, because they so cynically abused the court system, West Germany followed a different, opposite philosophy. Betting on rehabilitation rather than punishment, West Germans devised a system so lenient that they would open themselves to waves of criticism when terrorists were released and neo-Nazis slapped on the wrist. The criminal justice system was also hampered by another reaction against Nazi abuses: Because the Nazis spied on their own citizens, West Germany barred its police from using basic investigative tools such as wiretaps and electronic surveillance.

Hitler's emphasis on conformity and public spectacle—"mass, ritualized festivities that changed people's consciousness," as biographer Joachim Fest wrote—left Germans with a gnawing fear of any government invasion of privacy. And so, in West Germany, every effort was made to revive that inner life. Once again, the pendulum swung to the other extreme. Germans withdrew into their homes; streets became devoid of public life, shutters were closed tight after work hours, and privacy became one of the country's cherished values. A vast code of "data protection" laws created a fire wall between the individual and the state. Businesses were blocked from joining the consumer revolution under way in the rest of the west: Privacy laws prevented them from asking even a customer's address or age. Health officials were unable to join other countries in research because statistics on illnesses and causes of death were legally confidential. Epidemiologists are routinely denied access to death certificates, stymieing basic research.

Similarly, German scientists have been excluded from many avenues of research because of another ban that stems from Nazi abuses: a taboo against experiments involving embryonic cells. "If I did the same research that has won foreign scientists a Nobel Prize, I would get three years in prison," said the chairman of a gynecology department at a major German hospital. Because the Nazis subjected their prisoners to unspeakable medical experiments, German law half a century later prohibits the use of fetal cells in genetic research and the use of fertilized eggs anywhere but in the mother. The result is that many German women with fertility problems must go abroad for help. Those who cannot afford foreign travel are told to forget about having children.

Large families were so important under Nazi ideology that the state gave out cash prizes and the Cross of Motherhood, awarded to women who bore at least four children "for the Führer." In reaction to that mentality and the aftershocks of the Holocaust, the floor dropped out of the West German birth rate in the 1960s. Moralistic young people confronting what their parents' generation had done were in no mood to bring children into a world they considered cruel, a society they considered dishonest. *Kinderfeindlichkeit,* a German word meaning "antipathy toward children," became a social problem. The German League for the Child concluded that the war and its aftermath had poisoned relations between the generations. (East Germany basically continued the Nazi approach to childbearing, paying big bonuses to mothers and providing comprehensive day care and paid parental leave.) The West Germans tried to boost the birth rate with financial incentives for mothers, but many young women considered self-fulfillment more important than family (in one academic study, two-thirds of western Germans aged twenty-five to forty-five). Christa Meves, a child psychologist who wrote extensively on her country's treatment of children, called the reluctance to reproduce "a German problem. Nineteenth-century Germany was very child-friendly. But because Hitler was so adamant about honoring mothers, it came to seem so unmodern to us." The Bonn government did what it could to change attitudes, plastering subway stations with soft-focus photos of a cuddling, nude couple sharing lonely, forlorn looks, staring out over the caption "One plus one is three. We want a child!" The ad campaign had little impact; even in the early nineties, Germany's birth rate was the world's lowest.

National Socialism infected every stage of life. The Nazi takeover of the education system, the bureaucracy and the military tainted and trampled on Germany's traditional talent for producing creative and efficient elites—the university professors, businessmen, media figures and politicians whose leadership is essential, especially in an authoritarian society. Nazism left a legacy of deep mistrust for elites. Again, West Germans reacted by going to the other extreme. They adopted a false, rigorous egalitarianism that has left the country dangerously short on innovation and leadership. Afraid of allowing power to concentrate in one city again, West Germany's founders dispersed the country's major institutions, tucking the politicians away in the small town of Bonn, placing the press up in Hamburg, the banks in Frankfurt, and leaving Berlin—symbol of what went wrong—to draft-dodgers, bohemians and the avant-garde.

Similarly, the postwar university system was set up with no mechanism for identifying the country's best and brightest. There were to be no private universities. Elites were taboo, so there would be no Harvard or Princeton, no Oxford or Cambridge, none of the institutions whose graduates dominate government, business and education in other western countries. The country's leaders would not know each other from their youth. The result was an alienation from power, a discomfort with leadership and, again, a situation that drove many Germans abroad, to study, to teach, to research. Finally, in the early 1990s, there was talk of fostering new elites, creating a private university, easing the taboo on genetic research.

These cracks in the postwar permafrost came in the last days of the Nazi generation. The Nazi-hunters and the hunted Nazis, the judges who had been given second careers (not one judge in the west was imprisoned for carrying out Nazi justice), the small-town shopkeepers whom everyone knew had been concentration camp guards, the old women who had once hidden Jews in their attics—all were dying off. The federal war crimes prosecutor, Alfred Streim, was down to a caseload of just more than 100 alleged war criminals. There had been more than 100,000 cases in the previous four decades, although only 6,200 Nazis were ever sentenced to prison. The Nazis' last twitches still occasionally made news. I wrote a few articles about Hans Sewering, a seventy-six-year-old lung doctor in Dachau who was elected president of the World Medical Association even though he had signed an order dispatching a fourteen-year-old tuberculosis patient to a Nazi euthanasia center, where the girl was murdered with an overdose of barbiturates. Public pressure eventually forced Sewering to quit his post, but the German Medical Association supported the old man until the end, and the doctor went kicking: He blamed his forced resignation on a "defamation campaign" by the World Jewish Congress, even though more than fifty German physicians had joined doctors around the world in demanding his ouster.

The Sewering case demonstrated a deep desire to let old Nazis live out their years in undisturbed quiet. When Hermann Abs died in 1994 at age ninety-two, German newspapers wrote glowingly about the longtime Deutsche Bank chief. Abs thrived on the postwar business scene even though he served on the advisory council of the Reichsbank and was a leading manager of Deutsche Bank when it helped the Nazis confiscate Jewish property and assets. Tributes to Abs were a classic example of the Gap: Although Abs was controversial enough to land on the U.S. Justice Department's watch list of undesirable aliens, many German newspapers made no mention of the banker's activities between 1933 and 1945.

The same week Abs died, the most prominent publisher of neo-Nazi newspapers, Gerhard Frey, revealed that another recently departed West German elder statesman, the legal scholar Theodor Maunz, had long led a secret double life as a right-wing extremist. Through all the years when Maunz served as a leading interpreter of the postwar constitution and as

mentor to Germany's new president, Roman Herzog, the scholar had been
writing anonymous articles for Frey's nationalist newspapers and meeting
weekly with the publisher. A report on Maunz' secret life ran on page 11 of
the *Süddeutsche Zeitung;* most other papers ignored it. There was, an editor
of one major newspaper told me, really no reason to stir up such issues.
Everyone knows what people did back then, he said. Remember, of course,
but let the old folks die in peace.

Down in the postcard-perfect Bavarian town of Garmisch-Partenkirchen,
the people Bruno Ritter lived with, his tennis partners, his neighbors, they
all thought that way. Let it be already, they said. And so Ritter had for all
his adult life.

When his pals in the U.S. Army asked, Ritter said he was from Kansas
City. When they wondered about his foreign accent, he changed the subject.
Many years later, when his German wife asked about his family, Ritter said
they had died when he was young. Then he said he didn't want to talk about
it, clammed up tight. When his only child, his daughter Monika, asked
about her grandparents, Ritter said, "Oh, they passed away." The questions
continued, but he would say no more. On July 22, 1953, Bruno Ritter had
his number, 85229, removed from beneath the soft skin on the inside of his
arm. "Patient wants tattoo removed," it says in medical records of the U.S.
Army Outpatient Service in Bad Kreuznach, Germany. "Not that I was
ashamed," Ritter told me decades later. "But people were asking questions." For fifty years, Ritter said nothing, a skill he learned from his tor-
mentors, the people who taught him to be what he would proudly call
himself, "a man like a stone."

Then, on the evening of June 3, 1991, Bruno Ritter, a retired U.S. Army
sergeant, was reading the paper at home in Garmisch, where he had lived
for more than twenty years. A headline on page 3 of *Stars and Stripes,* the
military daily, said, "Holocaust survivors to testify Tuesday." In the second
paragraph, Ritter saw the name of Josef Schwammberger, the onetime Nazi
officer under indictment for murder. "I know that guy," Ritter told himself.
"I know that name. Then I hear in my mind my mother hollering at me.
'Stay,' she says. 'You'll survive, you'll see your brother.' " For the first time
in his adult life, Ritter, then sixty-three, found himself weeping.

The next morning, Ritter got in touch with the prosecutor in Stuttgart,
where Germany's last major Nazi war crimes trial was about to begin. He
left a message and waited a week. Then he called again and talked to a
lawyer, who said he would send someone to Garmisch to talk to Ritter. "No
way," Ritter said. "I'm coming to you." He closed up the one-room office
where he sold insurance to U.S. soldiers, went to Stuttgart and told two

lawyers what he had never told the people he worked with, the people he shared a home with, the people he loved. He told them what he knew about Schwammberger, the man responsible for the destruction of Ritter's town and the deaths of his family. When the prosecutors showed him an array of photographs, Ritter immediately picked out Schwammberger's face. "Such a good-looking face, not at all mean," said the man who had been silent.

How could you remember the face after so many years? the lawyers asked.

"I said, 'Look, he had a face like an angel, his name was Josef, like Jesus and Joseph. All the people in my village, we always talked about that face. How could someone with that face be so bad?' "

Strolling through Garmisch's pristine little downtown, Ritter looked like the stereotypical German businessman—richly tanned, proud, dressed like a man who has enough money and no reason to flaunt it. He drove a splendid, shiny Mercedes of the same silver tone as his thick, brushed-back hair. He nodded greetings to the shopkeepers on Olympiastrasse. He knew the woman guarding the entrance to the town park, a breathtaking rainbow of flowers in meticulously maintained grounds. Ritter seemed as far as could be from the confused, even tortured lives led by many Holocaust survivors. If others held their money and their opinions to themselves in a constant search for security, Ritter was confident and assertive. If others felt an obligation to keep the memory of the Holocaust alive as a lesson for future generations, Ritter presented himself as a living argument for purposeful forgetting.

I have no fear, no hate, he told himself. My friends are Germans, I married two Germans. They've changed, I've changed. Ritter even founded the local Kiwanis Club, where he would chum around with the good men of Garmisch. Create a new life. Put the horrors in the closet, lock up, melt the key. You live only once, so for God's sake, don't wallow. It was a startling argument and one that begged for opposition. What about your obligation to the young? What of history and memory? What of neo-Nazis on the march? What of those who deny the truth of the millions burned in Nazi crematoria?

Yes, yes, Ritter said, historians must remember, but those of us who lived it suffered enough. We deserve another life. Ritter certainly tried. His insurance office was barren but for plaques and photos commemorating his military successes. He had a briefcase filled with papers documenting his finest moments in the U.S. Army. He brushed off questions about his dreams, his night thoughts, lingering images of his lost family. "That's all gone," he said. "Another life."

When scenes of concentration camps came on television, Ritter turned off the set. "Why should I watch it? I know it." When a German friend said something about how the Holocaust wasn't as terrible as some say, or about how Hitler did good things, too, Ritter would wander away or change the topic. "Maybe I'll say I don't think the survivors would lie," he said, "but usually the conversation just ends."

And yet . . . After he volunteered to testify against Schwammberger, Ritter removed his name from his office door. "I don't want those old Nazis finding me," he said. "You never know what they're going to do." When I interviewed him for the *Post,* Ritter refused to be photographed in front of his car; he didn't want anyone to become jealous of his top-of-the-line Mercedes. As we walked through the town center, Ritter pulled me into a corner to answer a question about antiforeigner sentiment among teenage Germans. "I have a good life here," he said. "They don't need to hear this."

Bruno Ritter was thirteen years old when the Nazis pushed through Przemysl, Poland. The town's Jews were rounded up and placed in a ghetto. Soon thereafter, part-Jews, like Ritter's family, were identified by local informants and forced into the ghetto. Bruno was assigned to the Arbeitsdienst, a slave workforce that cleaned streets and shoveled coal. Mass arrests followed quickly, led by the local SS commander, Schwammberger.

One day in June 1941, Schwammberger and his men rounded up Jews to fill a cargo train headed for Auschwitz. The Jews of Przemysl knew where the trains were headed; word had filtered back from escapees and neighbors that those who were packed into the cars would never return from a place where people were burned to death. Bruno, the youngest of five children, was out in his white uniform, sweeping streets, when the Nazis came for his family. Standing near the rail station, he watched as his father, mother and three of his siblings were herded toward the train. It was his entire family except for his oldest brother, who was in Russia serving with the Polish Army. As Bruno's mother drew closer to the cargo car, she saw her son across the way. Between them stood the SS chief, with his omnipresent German shepherd, Prince. "Schwammberger was shouting at people, they must move fast or the dog eats you," Ritter said. "The dog was biting people's arms. I stood there crying. I'm all by myself, and the mother hollers across to me, 'Don't get on the train. Stay. You'll survive. You'll see your brother.' "

"The mother," Ritter said. In German, children often say not "my mother" but "the mother," as if there were only one in the world. Bruno's was a beautician, his father a barber. Simple people who had managed to teach their older children their trades even amid the insanity. They were Austrians originally, gone to Poland looking for a better life. Part-Jews, foreigners, they were alien poison to the Nazis. But a boy knew nothing of that. He knew only that the mother was leaving and instructing him to stay.

Bruno stayed. He never saw his parents or siblings again.

The boy lived in the ghetto and swept streets. One day, he saw Schwammberger walk over to a young woman, bark an order, and hold the gun to her head. "I hid in an entry to a house," Ritter said. "Everyone hid when they saw him come down the street. We would run and hide, he was so terrible." In the couple of seconds it took the boy to duck into the entryway, he heard a shot, then peeked out to see Schwammberger putting his gun back in his holster. Later that day, after the local Jewish council's work crew came through to pick up the killed and injured and bring them back inside the ghetto, Bruno found out that the woman who had been killed was Luisa Kleinmann, his sister-in-law, wife of his brother serving in the Polish Army.

Schwammberger was born in Austria, joined the Nazi party in 1933, and became a member of the elite SS four years later. He served as a lieutenant commanding labor camps in Poland, including concentration camps at Przemysl and Mielec where Jews were used as slave labor to repair German Army uniforms and build aircraft. Of the 28,000 Jews who lived in Przemysl before the Nazis arrived, about 100 are believed to have survived. After the war, French soldiers found Schwammberger carrying eight sacks packed with gold tooth fillings and diamonds. The Nazi was arrested and admitted killing 27 Jews. But in 1948, he escaped from a train transporting him to U.S. military authorities for a war crimes trial in Austria. Schwammberger made his way to Argentina, where he lived under his own name, working at a petrochemical plant near Buenos Aires. In 1965, he obtained Argentine citizenship. In 1973, West German prosecutors, encouraged by Nazi-hunter Simon Wiesenthal, who had placed Schwammberger on his ten-most-wanted list, requested his extradition.

Years of appeals finally ran out in 1990, when the thin, bald man with bushy eyebrows, a stern, thin-lipped mouth and big, gentle eyes was flown to Stuttgart and placed in a high-security prison. He was seventy-nine years old and claimed to be too ill to stand trial, a notion doctors and judges rejected. Unlike many accused war criminals, Schwammberger mounted no defense of mistaken identity. He admitted he ran the camps. After his 1945 arrest, Schwammberger had signed a statement admitting that he was ordered to shoot "all Jews who fled from my camp." In court forty-six years later, Schwammberger said he signed under duress.

"I cannot just go and kill thirty-five Jews, boom, boom, boom," Schwammberger testified. His new story was that he shot one labor camp inmate "because of special circumstances." He denied the murder charges against him, which included allegations that he personally killed at least 50 Jews and assisted in the murders of at least 3,377 others from 1941 to 1944.

Wiesenthal and the prosecutors found 73 witnesses to testify against Schwammberger, including Americans, Germans, Canadians and Austrians. The trial, meeting only twice a week because of Schwammberger's health, lasted eleven months.

Witnesses testified that Schwammberger threw 800 men, women and children into a bonfire, that he shot Jews in the neck, that he smashed children's heads against a wall, that he hanged Jews, that he pulled Jews' gold teeth out of their mouths with pliers, that he stood by and watched them bleed to death after they were torn to shreds by his dog Prince. An Israeli man, Max Millner, testified that Schwammberger shot a rabbi dead on Yom Kippur because the rabbi asked prisoners to observe the commandment to fast on that holiest day of the Jewish calendar.

The trial received minimal media coverage in Germany. A group of neo-Nazis attended the opening of the trial and disrupted the session with shouts of "Lies! Lies!"

Bruno Ritter managed to avoid the train that took his family to be burned, but he could not hide from the Gestapo for long in an emptying ghetto. He was caught and shipped to Krakow to join a Jewish labor force building a concentration camp on the site of a Jewish cemetery. While Bruno was sweeping the SS barracks one day, an officer ordered him to shine his service pistol. The officer left the room and another SS man walked in and saw Bruno with a pistol in hand. Despite the boy's protests, the SS man rushed over, whipped out his own pistol and slammed the back of it against Bruno's forehead. "Bury him," the SS man told the other prisoners. Bruno was left with a deep scar over his eye, but the beating became an opportunity. Left for dead, he sneaked out of the SS barracks and away from the camp, undetected.

He returned to Przemysl, where he found a secret room in a ghetto cellar stocked with plenty of food, a hiding place left behind by someone who never got the chance to hide. The boy smelled burning flesh from the concentration camp above the town. He heard Nazis hunting for the ghetto's remaining Jews. Still, he could not stand the loneliness of the cellar. After a couple of weeks, he climbed up and got caught.

Ritter was crammed into a cargo car equipped with barbed wire over narrow windows. On the way to Auschwitz, he and a few other youths decided to jump the train. They pried off the wire. The first boy jumped and hit a telephone pole, collapsing into a lump below. The second boy suffered the same fate. Ritter went next, carefully calibrating the distance between poles. "I knew I was going to die, either way," he said. He made it. He stayed in the woods for several days, but had no idea where to go. He went back to Przemysl. "I was a boy. It was the only place I knew."

There was no one there when Ritter reached the ghetto, only buildings. Nazi soldiers patrolling with dogs caught him quickly; this time, he landed on the selection ramp at Auschwitz. Old people, children and many women went off to one side, filing into the building from which no one emerged. Ritter got directed to the other side, to cold showers and living hell. "I always said, I'm going to get out of here. So many didn't want to live. They'd just go to the fence and be shot. I always remembered my mother and what she said."

Ritter has no idea how long he spent at each camp. He was assigned to the I. G. Farben electrical works at Auschwitz, building telephone equipment for the Reich. He worked side by side with Jews and "Germans whose crime was they just wouldn't say 'Heil Hitler.' " He survived by getting work peeling potatoes for SS officers, a job that allowed him to eat the peels. During sixty-four months in the camps, Ritter buried hundreds of people, spent weeks spreading lime on piles of corpses, lining up the dead so they would fit neatly in mass graves. "If any of our prisoners cried, bang! Shot," he said. "You had to be silent. That's how I learned how to be strong, tough."

As the war drew to an end and Soviet troops approached Auschwitz, the Germans panicked and tried to eliminate evidence of the death factories. They shipped Ritter and thousands of other slaves to camps inside Germany. Ritter was sent to Flossenbürg in Bavaria. As the train made its way through Germany, local people threw bread to the prisoners. At Flossenbürg, Ritter chiseled stones for street paving. But once again, the Allies approached, this time the Americans. The German command ordered the prisoners loaded onto trains and taken deep into the woods, where they were to be shot and dumped into mass graves.

But as Ritter's train made its way out of Flossenbürg, U.S. reconnaissance planes appeared overhead, dived and began firing. The SS men fled in one direction, the prisoners in the other. Ritter spent a week alone in the woods, at first hiding high in a tree, then on a farm, where he stole civilian clothes and the pigs' potatoes. He weighed seventy pounds. Ritter soon found a friendly old farmer who gave him work. Toiling in the field one day in May 1945, he saw U.S. planes dropping leaflets directing Germans to put up white flags or face attack. The local Germans ignored the order, but Ritter took a sheet from the farmer and hoisted it high. U.S. tanks rolled into the town and sought out those who had put up flags of surrender.

The first American Ritter met asked him if he was a Nazi. "I said I'm a displaced person, and they found a Polish-American soldier who could talk to me," Ritter said. Bruno made himself useful to the Americans, first as a shoeshine boy and then as a Polish-German interpreter. He soon met

Arthur Williams, a captain who befriended him, taught him English, and showed him how to drive a Jeep. When Ritter told Williams the story of his family, the captain, taken with the teenager's great drive and need, let the boy stay in the officers' quarters, then helped him get an Army job. A photo of Captain Williams and Ritter from that time shows a chubby officer in a too-tight uniform squeezing out a thin heartland smile while he drapes a short, thick arm around the shoulders of a slight young man with sunken eye sockets. Bruno, seventeen, basked in the strength and goodness of this captain from Kansas, this man who would make him an American citizen.

The two worked closely together in Germany. In 1947, when Williams was going home, he became the boy's legal guardian. The captain sent Bruno to Kansas City to live with his parents and attend Shawnee Mission High School, from which he was graduated after one intensive year. It was in these months that the boy who grew up in the camps decided to erase that portion of his life. "I decided my life started in Kansas City, a new life in my adopted country," Ritter said. "I didn't want to think about what happened to me and my family. That's why I took off my prison number. I decided no one would know about my old life." After school, he joined the Army out of gratitude—and because a judge told him it would cut the waiting time for U.S. citizenship from five to three years. To complete his makeover, Ritter converted to Protestantism, Williams' religion. Although Ritter was Jewish only on part of his mother's side, the family had not denied its heritage and the Nazis had certainly treated him as a Jew.

"But I said to myself, I don't want my kids to go through what I went through," he said. "By reading the Bible, you see if you're Jewish, you're going to suffer. Now nobody knows I'm part Jewish. Not that I'm ashamed of that religion. I went through the camps as a hundred percent Jewish." Later, when Ritter married a German woman, he converted once more, to her religion, Catholicism. "Religion here, religion there, what you believe yourself is the only thing," Ritter said.

Ritter spent the next twenty-one years in the Army, with stints in Maryland, Colorado and Hawaii. But he spent most of his career in Germany, serving as an interpreter (he speaks Russian, Polish, German, Ukrainian, Czech and English). He claimed he never minded living in Germany because "the Nazis were not all the people, and no one here ever mistreated me." Throughout his military career, only Bruno's commanding officers knew of his past. When Ritter retired from the Army in 1969, a reporter for a military newspaper wrote, "Today Sergeant Ritter refuses to discuss concentration camp life, and when questioned on the subject, his eyes glaze and his face assumes a stony aspect."

In 1947, Ritter asked Williams if he could visit his hometown in search of some trace of his family. An Army pass brought Ritter to Przemysl, where he found a stack of letters from his brother Joseph in Russia, asking if anyone was still alive. Bruno and his brother stayed in touch by post for years. In 1963, Joseph, who had married a Russian woman and, like his father and siblings, had become a barber, got permission to emigrate to America under Bruno's sponsorship. The brothers met in Paris after more than twenty years apart. Bruno bought his nephews their first ice-cream cones. Not a word passed between the brothers about Bruno's experience under the Nazis. "I didn't talk about it," Ritter said. "He never asked me. He didn't want to hurt me." Even in Joseph's last years at an old-age home in St. Louis, Bruno's past remained a taboo.

In Germany, where Ritter enjoyed a second career as manager of the local U.S. Army PX, he felt accepted and accepting, comfortable with Germans who had never met a Jew, comfortable with himself, the man who decided to forget everything. Ritter did not mention the camps to his German wife, Inge. Inge's father had been killed in the war, and she had told Bruno all about it. But he always insisted on silence about his family. He would say only that they had died when he was young. "She understood I didn't want to talk about it. She had figured out the truth, but she never said a word because she didn't want to hurt me." When Ritter finally sat Inge down one night to tell her the details, he did so only because he had decided to beef up his retirement package by applying for German government compensation money available to Nazi victims. The application was a complicated process and his wife would have found out about it. "Otherwise, I would never have told her," Ritter said.

His wife sat and listened and soon began to cry softly. "She just cried and cried," Ritter said. "She said all the money I can get I should get." After Bruno unburdened himself to the prosecutors, Inge kept asking him if he was OK, if he was sleeping well. "I sleep good," he would tell her. "I did what I had to do."

"Sometimes I wish I never bought that newspaper," Ritter told me one day. In all the years before, he said he had never dreamt about his imprisonment, never told a friend, never wished he had confided in his wife or Army buddy. "Nothing, until I read about that stupid guy in the paper. Then I hear my mother hollering, 'Stay. You'll survive and see your brother.' I never found my mother's ashes. They're all mixed up with other people's. I never had a childhood. When I see a child with a bicycle and enough to eat, I just . . . I was treated like a dog. Working at age eleven. I saw women already dead, the Germans put their knives inside them to look for hidden gold and diamonds. Beasts." He stopped for a long while. Then, "I'm grateful I had the chance to forget and forgive."

In Stuttgart, prosecutors challenged Ritter because he could not recall the dates of his arrests and transports. "If you want dates," Ritter told them, "look up my tattoo number in the Nazi records. I told the prosecutor, 'I'm here because I owe this to my family. I read where this man denies everything, he says he can't remember. How can he not remember? I remember." After he told his story, Ritter agreed to repeat it in open court if he had to. The judges later allowed many witnesses to submit their testimony in writing.

"When I left the court, I felt like I dropped a hundred pounds," Ritter said as we ate cheesecake in the blissfully pretty town gardens, the strains of the Garmisch-Partenkirchen Spa Orchestra competing with the buzz of bees flitting from one flower bed to another. "I felt I did my part, for my family. They didn't do nothing. Why'd they get killed?" When Ritter left the courthouse, he told himself once more, I'm going to forget this. When Ritter sees camp victims filled with anger or sadness, when he hears about them returning to their villages, trying to keep the memories alive, he does not understand. " 'Don't live with it,' I'd tell them. 'Forget.' I guarantee you I'm the coolest witness they ever saw in Stuttgart. The others all cry. That's because they didn't live another life. They're still back there. They're sick, suffering, thinking constantly about fifty years ago. I see them and I know I was right. I told the prosecutors, I give you my story, you do the prosecution. This guy is seventy-nine years old. Even if he only gets two years, he'll probably die in prison. You do the judging."

The confident gent telling that story stared across the garden and set his eyes on a small boy. "I never had softness as a child," he said, quietly now. "What you remember of yourself as a child is from when you're thirteen, sometime like that. When I was thirteen, I was eating grass in the woods and jumping from a train. In wintertime, melt the snow against my warm body and eat it. I'm glad I forgot that. Tonight, when you leave, I play tennis, six o'clock, singles. I get in the car now and my mind goes click. I go into my other life. I see some friends, have a couple of beers and don't think about it for a second." He leaned back, pushed his chest forward. A small smile crept across his face. "Hard as stone." Bruno Ritter turned away. His eyes, the pretty, gentle green of a Caribbean basin, were clouded with tears.

In May 1992, Josef Schwammberger was convicted of murdering twenty-five people and ordering the deaths of hundreds more. Before the judge pronounced sentence, he asked the Nazi if he cared to comment. Schwammberger mumbled, "About what?" He was sentenced to spend the rest of his life in prison. He was eighty years old.

• • •

Just as Bruno Ritter wanted to, more Germans than ever before want to say *"Schluss"*—finished, put an end to it, call it a day. They are not historical revisionists. They are not neo-Nazis or anti-Semites. They are thinking people who say it is time to move on. They are relieved that November 9, the anniversary of Kristallnacht, the 1938 night on which 267 synagogues were burned and 7,500 Jewish stores plundered, is now also the anniversary of the fall of the Berlin Wall. They are pleased that the Nazi records at the U.S.-run Berlin Documents Center are finally being returned to stricter German control, not to prevent genuine researchers from doing their work, but to stop the sensationalism of journalistic thrillseekers hoping to expose some old man as a teenage brownshirt. They shed no tears when the Berlin city government, complaining of budget problems, delays construction of a Jewish museum. They cheer on the chancellor when he rejects calls for a Holocaust museum in Germany, saying that existing concentration camp memorials are sufficient. They welcome the new willingness of politicians to say—even in the face of outraged criticism from the left—that "taboos must be broken" and "Germans must not be put in a special position for the rest of time," as Kohl's failed candidate for president, Steffen Heitmann, said. There is some relief that a nationally respected newspaper, *Die Welt*, makes its pages a forum for a new intellectual nationalism, a place where historians can argue that the Third Reich should be seen from a "proper historical distance," as Rainer Zitelmann wrote.

Even in the political center, some of those who believe strongly in the unique evil of the Nazi crimes argue that it is time "to shunt aside the famous German focus on guilt for the 12 years of Nazi rule," as Thomas Kielinger, editor of the Bonn weekly *Rheinischer Merkur*, said. "This is the end of the chapter of exclusively looking at our guilt. Germany has been on probation. Is Germany ready for parole? You've got to eat your rhetoric and recognize the German democratic revival."

Of course, many Germans resist any such shift in emphasis. Manfred Stolpe—a leading eastern German politician himself under fire for hiding his secret cooperation with the Stasi secret police when he was a church official in the communist era—once buried his face in his hands and told me of his frustration that so many Germans refuse to accept that "the Nazis were supported by all the German people. The fathers and grandfathers may all have some excuse, but everyone was involved." And historians throughout Germany protested against the meager resources devoted to setting the record straight at Buchenwald and Sachsenhausen, the eastern German concentration camp sites where the communists presented their own distorted version of history. The historians' cries have been largely in vain; there is plenty of money available to document Soviet crimes against the German public in the aftermath of the war, but little to remember the victims of the Nazis.

No two pasts are the same. Forgetting and remembering are both caricatures. What matters is honesty. It is easy to say that Germans are obliged to recall the Nazi years. But I cannot tell German parents what to say when their child asks, as so many do, "Why do the Germans always have to lose?" or "Why are the Germans always the bad guys?" Luckily, some Germans do know what to say. My friend Jochen Thies was born in 1944 in East Prussia. His father was a prisoner of war in Colorado. Before the Soviet troops moved into Prussia, Jochen and his mother escaped to Denmark. When he was at university, Jochen completed his thesis, "The Last Aims of Adolf Hitler." Jochen's chosen topic was a rarity: In all of Germany, only about a dozen history professors focus their work on the Nazi period. Most university students no longer study those years. Late at night, when he is driving home, Jochen flips his favorite cassette into the tape deck. It is the songs of the Comedian Harmonists, an a cappella group of German Jews who recorded in the early 1930s. The singers were lucky enough to flee Germany later that decade. "They were never successful again," Jochen told me. "This is how you see the true tragedy of Germany, the loss of Jews in society and culture. For us growing up, for me as a young boy, those twelve years were the Himalayas. You couldn't see beyond them to the past or the future. My generation was the most European, searching for something else. My daughter Nora and her generation will be more German, more comfortable." And yet Nora attends a French school, joined with a group of German students who presented a theatrical show in Israel, and thinks of herself as European. Sometimes, the invisible walls are the strongest.

Verboten

AFTER A VACATION in the United States, we arrived back in Berlin on a typically dark, wet winter's morning, the kind of January day in the far north when dusk arrives before the light has even had a chance to stretch across the sky. So when a German friend called to welcome us home and immediately asked, "Isn't it awful being back?" my wife tried to be diplomatic.

"Well, it's always hard to leave family and friends when we know we won't see them again for a year," Jody said.

"No, I mean, isn't it awful to be in Germany again?" our friend, a research psychologist, persisted.

"It is very dark this time of year," Jody offered.

"No," the friend said. "I mean Germany itself. Whenever I come back from another country, I feel the oppression from the moment the plane lands. The frowns, the rules, the impolite people. It just saps the life out of you."

Our friend, whose studies had drawn her into the fascinating if dangerous work of comparing national characteristics, was adamant: Something about Germany itself had produced the cold, inflexible, bureaucratic life about which foreigners and Germans alike complain. In four years of living in Germany, no other question came up so frequently. No other topic seemed as gripping to German friends and acquaintances: Are we different? How? And why? German views were as diverse as any foreign insights into the question: They ranged from extreme defensiveness to a perplexingly common self-criticism so virile it could only be described as self-loathing. But the questions never stopped coming, especially from Germans who had spent time abroad as students, tourists or employees. The contrasts were just too sharp to ignore. Like Germans who resist the notion of national differences until they've lived abroad, many Americans arrive in Germany believing that Germans are "just like us." They soon find themselves cataloguing the peculiarities of a society that is, in so many areas, *verkrustet*—stuck in its ways, paralyzed by rules, laws and traditions. After the Wall fell, eastern Germans, pounded by change, looked at their western neighbors and asked the same question, sometimes longingly, sometimes with boiling frustration: How could a country with such a powerful economy and such a successful democracy saddle itself with so much ritual, so much rigidity, so much obedience, such hunger for authority? Monika Maron, an eastern German novelist, said Germans suffer from an "irrational love of order and security because Germany was born out of war and insecurity, and periodically insecurity turns to panic and then the Germans go crazy." Maron saw Germany as imprisoned by history, a long and straight line of anxiety and instability stretching from the Thirty Years War (1618–1648) to Auschwitz. In 1920, Germans traumatized by the shame of their loss in World War I won public support for the creation of private armies with campaign posters that said WE WANT QUIET AND ORDER! Hitler promised order and stability. In 1994, both major parties stressed order and stability in their campaigns. Two generations of Germans since 1945 have sought to change themselves and their divided society, to preach and practice an openness and informality that would have made their parents shudder. Yet a root fear of disorder held fast. Would history relax its hold? Could it?

A German day often begins at the bakery, where tradition and strict laws protecting bakers against competition combine to guarantee a rich, delicious selection of fresh breads, rolls, cakes and strudels. (For many months after returning to America, my young daughter called rolls, difficult to find at all in Washington, by their German name, *Brötchen*.) A long, silent line of customers may stretch out into the street, as sales clerks, graduates of four years of schooling in baking and bakery sales, sing out their morning mantra: "Who gets? Next! Who gets?" Rarely is a pleasantry heard, except for a cursory *"Auf Wiedersehen!"* as the customer departs. No chitchat, no comments about the weather. Germans often roll their eyes at the elaborate minuet of polite chatter that Americans require of strangers they encounter in their morning rounds. In German shops, you are far more likely to be rammed in the ankles with a shopping cart by a scowling old lady than to be asked about the events of the day. Your crime, you will discover, was failure to inch up immediately to the heels of the person in front of you in the cash register queue. A middle-aged woman in a Bonn supermarket once belted me between the shoulder blades with her umbrella because I had left three feet of space separating me from the woman ahead. When I protested, the assailant replied, "Who do you think you are? You think you're better than everyone else in line?"

One of the most startling discoveries a newcomer in Germany makes is the unending willingness—eagerness, even—of everyday citizens to correct the actions of complete strangers. The day my wife and I took our daughter home from the hospital in Bonn, we were chastised for not putting a hat on her—even before we had reached the lobby of the building. I cannot count the number of times I was reprimanded—often in a loud, angry shout—by strangers for crossing an empty street against a red light. As I drove in the center lane of a six-lane autobahn north of Cologne one day, I suddenly saw a Mercedes ahead of me brake and slow from about 120 miles an hour to 50. I hit the brakes to avoid a collision. Then I watched as the Mercedes driver drifted off to the right lane, let me pass, then pulled in immediately behind me. He began flashing his headlights at me, pulled up nearly to my back bumper, fell back again, and repeated the whole process. Then he pulled around my left side and began gesturing wildly at me to get off the road. He deftly maneuvered me into the right lane, then onto the shoulder. I was convinced I was about to be the victim of Germany's first drive-by shooting. As soon as I came to a stop, Herr Mercedes was out of his car and at my window.

"Did you see that Audi pass me on the right side?" he said, frantically.

I had indeed seen an Audi pass the Mercedes in the center lane while my excited friend drove in the left lane. I nodded.

"I have his license number and I am bringing charges against him," Mercedes said. "You are the witness. You will follow me to the police station."

Having no great desire either to spend the afternoon fulfilling Herr Mercedes' autobahn revenge fantasy or to incur his wrath, I said, *"Jawohl"* (Sure thing), and followed him for a few hundred yards to the next exit ramp. Then, as he left the highway, I peeled off back onto the main road, zooming ahead to the next adventure.

No such escape was available some weeks later, when I drove into a downtown Bonn parking lot a little before 2 P.M. I had an appointment at two, but wanted to stay in the car for an extra minute or so to hear the hourly news bulletin on the radio. To do that in my primitive Peugeot, I needed to keep the motor running. As I sat listening to the news, I was startled by banging on my window and an angry shriek. I looked up and saw a woman, about thirty-five years old, struggling to hold her baby and a grocery bag in one arm while she pounded on my window with the other hand. "You must turn off your motor," she shouted. "You are polluting the air my child has to breathe. You are killing my child."

I was not polite. I recall that I referred, disapprovingly, to her country's tradition of imposing its will on others. Then I turned off the engine and got out.

When I told this tale to a member of Chancellor Kohl's staff, he said: "Germans like rules. They need them. And when they don't have them, you get the autobahn mentality or the old ladies in the supermarket shoving you with the carts because there's no rule against it." In a country with more than 100,000 regulations governing behavior, if you can find something that is not specifically prohibited, there is a temptation to go ahead and do it— to the max. Yet what is most impressive about Germans' reaction to their highly regulated lives is not their protest against it, but their happy compliance with it. Far from feeling oppressed, many Germans are quite comfortable with a degree of regulation that Americans and other foreigners often find suffocating. Germans find it perfectly reasonable that the law forbids them from telling off an arrogant or incompetent civil servant. It makes sense to them that it should be illegal to toss an obscene gesture at another motorist. (Although I must admit this one is rarely enforced. With apologies to my colleagues who may still be trying, it's only fair to reveal that I and several other foreign correspondents in Bonn tried for years to get caught doing this so we could write a story about it. Neither the cops nor any German citizens took the bait.)

In a society that still sees itself as homogeneous (even with 6 million foreigners among the population of 80 million), there is a strong consensus that the state should enforce a single standard of behavior. The result may seem like a stranglehold of conformism to outsiders, but it also produces a level of stability, comfort and trust unknown in most other western societies. When my wife bought a coat at a Frankfurt department store, only to find that the store (like most German establishments) accepts no credit cards, the saleswoman assured her there was no problem. The store happily sent the coat to our local post office, where we could pick it up in exchange for cash. Similarly, when I stayed at an expensive hotel and learned at checkout that the place took neither credit cards nor checks, the desk clerk offered to send me a bill in the mail. She asked only for my address—no identification, no collateral of any kind.

After suffering through wars and regional rivalries, wild inflation and economic want, political hysteria, shifting borders, and tyrants great and small, Germans understandably are eager to embrace promises of order and stability. The slogan "No Experiments" has repeatedly led the Christian Democratic Union to victory at the polls. "No surprises," Kohl often said during his speedy but orderly march toward unification. So it is in daily life, even in the most mundane ways.

A German who goes home for a midday snooze is guaranteed quiet. From 1 P.M. to 3 P.M., no lawn mower's growl will rouse him, no playing child's shout will pierce his nap. (Mowing the lawn on a Sunday afternoon could violate not one, but three laws—those banning work on God's day, noise during the afternoon siesta, and lawn mower noise above a certain decibel level.) A British friend freshly arrived in Bonn came home from work one day to find an envelope containing a handwritten white card: "We welcome our neighbors," it said. "We wish to inform you that according to the laws of the State of North Rhine–Westphalia, the use of lawn mowers is forbidden during the following times: 1 P.M. to 3 P.M. on workdays, on Saturday afternoons, Sundays and public holidays." The card was not signed.

Quiet is sacred in German law. Agents of the local order offices *(Ordnungsamt)* patrol playgrounds, sports fields, and city streets to assure that rules are observed. A physician in Düsseldorf was fined $65 in 1990 for taking a shower after 10 P.M. on a humid August night. His neighbors accused him of noise pollution, and local laws supported them, banning baths, showers and sometimes toilet flushing between 10 P.M. and 6 A.M. An appeals court reversed his conviction, but ordered the man to limit his late-night ablutions to thirty minutes.

Regulations govern not only when children can make noise, but when adults can beat carpets, shovel snow or put out garbage. Trash generates extraordinary regulation—in Bonn, each resident gets an annual eighty-page book from the city detailing what must be done with every conceivable form of garbage. Trash also provides recreation for the entire nation—the popular participant sport of inspecting the neighbors' trash. When I lived in Bonn, my landlady called one day to report that one of our neighbors, Hannelore Erbe, had phoned to tattle on our violation of refuse rules. We were using the wrong color garbage bags, the neighbor reported, and what's more, "Ever since they had that baby, the Fishers have been producing altogether too much garbage." Our landlady, Frau Albers, politely asked us to use brown instead of blue bags.

A couple of years later, in Berlin, I received a letter from Herr Hahnenkamp, the self-appointed lord of the trash in our apartment building. "On Sunday, July 4, 1993, paper, including newspapers and catalogues, from your household was placed in the gray trash bin instead of the blue paper container," the letter said. "Please assure that you and your family members, employees and coworkers sort and correspondingly dispose of your trash." When I complained that someone had apparently been pawing through my garbage, the building superintendent responded that I was lucky I had not been fined.

In the name of order, Germans accept the use of law to regulate behavior other countries might consider private or beyond the reach of lawyers. In East Germany's dying weeks, westerners were shocked to discover that eastern orphanages were sheltering dozens of children who had been taken from middle-class families not because of abuse or neglect, but to punish parents for failing to follow rules. For example, several children were removed from their homes because their parents had not shown up to state-required Health Department lessons on child care.

Laws require Germans to tell police when they move and to inform the government of their religion. When I declined to tell a clerk in Bonn my religion, arguing that it was none of the government's business, she hauled out the law book and showed me that I was nonetheless obliged to do so. When I still refused, she called in a supervisor, who argued, then grabbed the form and in the space allotted for religion, wrote "R-8," a notation he refused to define. If ever I challenged such rules, I was either lectured on the need for order to avoid a repetition of the horrors of the Weimar Republic or presented with bulky law books (one customs agent at a post office in Beuel plopped a four-foot-high stack of loose-leaf binders on the counter in front of me when I questioned his demand that I rip open a carefully wrapped surprise birthday gift for my daughter before he would let it leave the office).

I should have recalled those lectures the day the hallway buzzer rang at my office in Bonn. A man announced himself as being from WDR, a German TV station. So far so good: German journalists often stopped by to get a comment from a foreign correspondent on a breaking story. Moments later, my assistant, Lolita Klavins, came into my cubicle making strange gestures, indicating that someone odd was about to enter. The visitor sauntered in behind her, removed his hat, and turned his back to me.

I stood up, approached the man and said, after some seconds, "May I help you?" Silence. Slowly, he rotated, casting his eyes above my file cabinets, across my desk, along the windowsill, occasionally glancing down at his clipboard.

"Yes?" I said.

Finally, he spoke. "*Alles klar.* Everything's in order. One television, one radio." I was mystified, but my assistant got it. She rushed down the hall to the Reuters newsroom to warn our friends at the wire service of the man's impending arrival. Secretaries and clerks leaped from their chairs, stuffing radios into drawers.

Our visitor was—though he would never say so—from the German broadcast police. His mission: scope out unregistered radios, TVs, baby monitors or other telecommunications devices. Germany's government-owned broadcasters are funded through license fees charged on every radio and TV in the country, and every device must be registered with the government. Enforcement agents make surprise visits like our friend's. They also cruise city streets in vans equipped with exotic antennae that can detect the presence of radios and TVs in your house. The detection vehicles supposedly do a better job than our visitor, who missed four radios in plain view in my office. In Berlin, the local broadcasting authority, SFB, had twenty agents, called controllers, who worked mostly at night, snooping around houses and in apartment stairwells, listening at doors for the telltale sounds of blaring newscasts or sitcoms. Controllers may not enter people's homes without permission, but most citizens are gracious or frightened enough to let the broadcast cops inside. Violators can be fined up to $600, but punishment is rare; most scofflaws, once caught, pay their fees.

Most German rules are not quite that intrusive. Yet they are more than societies with a stronger sense of individual rights might tolerate. Hidden cameras make certain motorists don't jump the light at traffic intersections. You must fill out applications to get government permission to have a fax or an answering machine (and the law then requires that you use the words "automatic telephone answering machine" in your outgoing message.) Germans are prohibited from touching fruit and vegetables in public markets. Nor may they wash their cars on Sundays.

The government even gets to approve your choice of a name for your child—and names that do not appear on the government list can be, and are, rejected. The Frankfurt city clerk nixed the name Schroeder, arguing that even if it is good enough for the Beethoven-obsessed young pianist in the *Peanuts* comic strip, it is not sex-specific, and therefore illegal. Same for Woodstock, Pushkin, Hemingway, Martinlutherking and Möwe, the German word for seagull—all rejected for failure clearly to designate the child's sex. Other officials axed Pumuckl, the name of a German cartoon character, and Stechpalme, German for "holly," because other children might find the names unfamiliar. And still other bureaucrats have vetoed foreign names because they didn't pass the official test: If a German (often one married to a foreigner) wants to use a foreign name for a child, the government contacts the embassy of the country in question. If diplomats confirm that the name exists in their country, everything's *in Ordnung* (OK). If not, tough luck for the parents.

Until 1994, married women were prohibited from retaining their maiden names. They could adopt their husband's last name or combine the two in a hyphenated version. Then, the legislature revised the name law, aiming to eliminate tongue-twisting double names such as Herta Däubler-Gmelin and Heidemarie Wieczorek-Zeul, both parliamentarians. The new law prohibits hyphenated names. The law still says married couples "should" carry the same name, but women may now elect to keep their own names. Children of marriages involving two different last names may no longer be given both names. The parents must choose one name to pass on to their offspring. If the parents can't or won't pick, the court will.

Government officials are accustomed to such responsibility. They already require citizens to complete training courses before they may sail a boat, ride a horse, hunt or go fishing. Potential fishermen spend three months in night school preparing for an exam that includes questions such as "How much roe does a roach (a small fish) produce?" and "What fish has a dark spot just behind the first backfin?" The applicant must also pass a practical test, proving to examiners that he can put together a rod and reel. Winning a driver's license requires six months of classes in driving theory and expensive on-road lessons. The state even provides bicycle-riding lessons and licenses for children, who can be found circling charming little tracks in city parks, practicing hand signals and yielding techniques under the watchful eyes of professional traffic police.

In general, all this makes for a remarkably orderly society. Drivers flash directional signals not only when they turn, but even when the road curves sharply. Trains really do run on time. Even good friends can get genuinely worried about your health if you show up twenty minutes late to an appointment. And mail posted anywhere in the country by 6 P.M. reaches its destination the next day.

A society deservedly proud of its reputation for precision and order must be organized down to the minutest detail. And so, laws govern how late employees may show up to work in the event of heavy snow and exactly how long workers may take for their *Pinkelpause*—the bathroom break. In 1990, negotiations between postal workers and the federal Bundespost were stalemated for four days over the touchy question of whether two minutes and seventeen seconds was sufficient time for a visit to the toilet. Although postal workers had already nipped their work week down to a leisurely thirty-three hours, the government conceded an hourly four-minute-and-nineteen-second relaxation break along with a guaranteed two-minute-and-seventeen-second *Pinkelpause*. Customers around the country immediately felt the change: Postal workers, like many other German employees, are not the least bit shy about putting down their work, no matter the circumstances, the second their break begins, even if a customer is midtransaction.

I was once in the magnificent food halls of Berlin's finest department store, KaDeWe, shortly before the Saturday 1 P.M. closing time, collecting bread, cheese and sausages for a picnic lunch. After waiting my turn at the salami counter, I reached the head of the line at 12:55 and placed my order. The shop clerk was almost finished slicing the meat when a gong sounded throughout the store and an announcement asked all customers to leave. At that instant, the clerk replaced the cellophane wrap on the salami, put it back in the refrigerator case and walked away. As he left, I called, "What about my salami? Can't I have at least what you've already sliced?"

"It is one o'clock," he replied. *"Wir haben Feierabend.* Quitting time."

"But the meat you've cut will spoil over the weekend," I said.

"We are closed," came the answer as the clerk disappeared behind the door, already halfway out of his white uniform.

German regulators have a penchant for literalism. Bicycles have the right of way on the paths that run between sidewalks and streets in many German cities. Bicyclists, therefore, will not necessarily stop for pedestrians who wander onto the wrong piece of pavement, a fact some visitors do not discover until they have been knocked to the ground or spat upon. Visitors are also stunned to discover that buses will stop to pick up only passengers who are standing within one meter—three feet—of a bus stop. In the western town of Wolfenbüttel, several residents sued the city to shut down the local playground because children were playing there during the afternoon quiet time from 1 P.M. to 3 P.M. A panel of judges mercifully threw out the suit, noting that the sun sets so early in the winter months that strict adherence to the siesta tradition would leave children with no daylight time to play outside after school. (The German school day usually ends around noon.)

My favorite example of literalism run amuck came in a 1992 case involving a family from the western town of Flensburg. The family booked a three-week vacation at a seaside resort in Turkey. The travel agent who made the hotel reservation promised a pleasurable experience. So when the family discovered in the final week of their stay that handicapped people—confined to wheelchairs!—were also visiting the hotel, the family sued the travel agency. And won.

The court ruled that the sight of "10 severely disabled persons, some of whom were confined to wheelchairs, . . . was nauseating and impaired the well-being of the plaintiffs and their children." The family, whose name was not released by the court, was the victim of "defective travel services," the judge said. "The unavoidable sight of the disabled persons at close quarters during every meal caused nausea and was an incessant and unusually strong reminder of the possibilities of human suffering. Such an experience is not what is typically expected from holidays. The average tourist would avoid it if he could. Dining at leisure at a hotel is generally regarded as the essence of holiday recreation." The judge ordered the travel agency to refund 10 percent of the cost of the three-week vacation, plus interest and court costs.

That kind of case explains why foreigners in Germany sometimes feel compelled to mount renegade actions. When I had to renew the registration of the *Washington Post*'s car in Bonn, I asked my assistant to call the Traffic Office three times and get three different people to give her the complete list of documents I would have to bring. My assistant scoffed at my precautions, but they proved to be not nearly rigorous enough. Armed with a thick portfolio of papers detailing the car's relationship with the government back to its birth, I entered the Traffic Office, waited until my number was called, and approached the clerk with a generous smile. That always seemed to unnerve sour-faced bureaucrats. She took my folder and told me to have a seat. About fifteen minutes later, I saw the clerk carrying several large books into a glass cubicle, where she was joined by two very serious-looking men. There they sat with my folder and their books, poring over one sheet after another for half an hour. Next, I was summoned back to the counter and informed by one of the men that we had submitted everything properly, but that the *Washington Post* was somehow not listed in the directory of German corporations.

"Of course," I replied. "It is an American company. It wouldn't be on your list."

Well, then, the official said, the registration must be denied.

We went back and forth for a while, and it eventually emerged that I could get the registration renewed if I could prove I was the *Washington Post*'s official representative in Germany. No problem, I said, producing a letter from my editor saying exactly that.

No good, the official said. Such a letter must come from the *Geschäftsführer*—the managing director—of the company. I pointed out that American corporate hierarchies often include no such title. No go. Managing director or nothing. Desperate, I said, "That will be no problem. I have such a letter in my car. Would you be kind enough to wait five minutes while I go get it?" The official agreed and I ran to the garage, found a muddied piece of *Post* stationery, and wrote by hand a letter from one Lardly Rogins, whom I had just appointed managing director of the *Washington Post*. I brought the creased, dirty piece of paper to the official, who looked at it, nodded, and, with a flourish of rubber stamping, renewed the registration.

That was fun, but it couldn't hold a candle to the legendary bit of revenge against German order that two British tourists achieved at a resort in Italy. Each morning during their stay, the Brits awoke to find that every chaise lounge around the swimming pool had been claimed by Germans who arose at five-thirty, placed their towels on a lounge chair and retired to the breakfast room. Tired of having to sit on concrete, the Brits one morning waited until all the Germans were inside having breakfast, removed all of the towels from the lounges and tied them together. Then the Brits went inside for breakfast.

The outraged shouts of dozens of Germans indicated that the prank had had the desired effect. But then, the Italian hotel manager marched over to the Brits and accused them of having committed this gross insult. The Brits made a considerable show of appearing wounded by the accusation. "How can you know it was us?" they asked.

To which the hotel man replied, "Because the last time we had British guests here, they laid the towels out in the shape of a giant swastika."

All of which may say as much about the Brits as about the Germans. But Germans have their own form of protest against the micromanagement of daily life. German society has left a few areas of life free of regulation, and woe to anyone who seeks to tinker with those zones of freedom. When Lufthansa, Germany's largely government-owned airline, announced plans to ban smoking on domestic flights (the longest of which is just over an hour), the country's most popular newspaper, *Bild,* led a campaign to halt such an imposition on smokers' rights. On the eve of the new rule's introduction, the airline backed off, saying it could not risk either the boycott that travelers had threatened or the physical confrontations that Lufthansa executives feared. "Stewards are not policemen," Lufthansa executive Peter Höbel told me. In hopes of saving the no-smoking rule, the airline had turned to the government Health Ministry, seeking a word of support. The ministry, not inclined to offend half the population, wouldn't comment at all. (Lufthansa had previously caved in to the demands of smokers by arranging the seats on some flights so that the division between smoking and nonsmoking sections ran up the center of the plane, which is to say, the entire plane is filled with smoke. Smokers had protested against being relegated to the rear of the cabin.)

With no rules against smoking, Germans light up wherever they please. Hospital waiting areas are notorious for trapping clouds of smoke in often windowless rooms. At the Chancellery in Bonn one day, a delegation of American politicians met with Kohl's chief of staff, Friedrich Bohl. When Bohl offered his guests a selection of cigars and cigarettes from a lovely mahogany box, one of the Americans politely asked how a government leader could justify offering tobacco products in a government office. "Back home, we'd get killed for doing that," he said. Bohl, who has an excellent command of English, was so perplexed by the question that he asked for a translation before sputtering that anyone who does not smoke is not required to do so.

As passionate as Germans may be about protecting their right to smoke, their true love is the absence of a speed limit on the autobahns. When a two-hundred-car pileup killed ten people in 1990, the government proposed to impose a thirty-mile-per-hour speed limit in severe fog. German motorists and their lobby went into overdrive. "It is a basic desire of man to feel this emotional stress of acceleration and speed," said Andreas Kippe of ADAC, the German AAA. "It's a kind of escapism, a compensation for life's limitations. The greater your sexual problems are, you know, the faster you like to drive." That one is probably best off left alone, but there are other theories about the power and popularity of Germany's "Free Driving for Free Citizens" movement (one of whose supporters is Kohl, who told a German magazine that his favored driving speed is 130 miles an hour.)

"We drive fast because we are allowed to—no other reason," said Wilhelm Lautzbach, director of the Traffic Institute in Karlsruhe. Stefanie Rosenkranz, a reporter for *Stern* magazine, thought there was something more to the country's fascination with pedal-to-the-metal driving. She drove her Citroën 2CV, an awkward, waddling, 27-horsepower tin can nicknamed "the Duck," across the country extremely slowly to gauge her fellow Germans' reactions. She was subjected to insults, flashing headlights, and after her article about the adventure appeared, physical threats and hate calls. "The essence of democracy in Germany is not free speech but free speed," she told me. "Is it rational to drive two hundred ten kilometers an hour [130 mph] in fog? No, it's asinine. But in a country where everything is regulated and you need to fill out ten forms to do anything, this is the outlet for all aggression. Germans are so orderly in their daily lives, but on the road, they are out to kill. You even see people speeding up just to frighten old ladies."

If the anarchy on German roads is an escape from a life of obedience, discipline and order, it is also important to note that even the lack of a speed limit is a result of government policy. This is no blind spot in the law: Higher authority tells German drivers they are free to go as fast as they can. The craving for guidance from above is not violated.

As far back as the 1950s, Ludwig Erhard, the architect of West German economic success, said, "The wealthier we get, the louder the cries will be for security." Indeed, Germany's self-image has remained remarkably constant, even during the decades of affluence and peace in the west. The country's political and intellectual elites portrayed Germany as a nation surrounded, in need of protection from and by outsiders. West Germans overcame the physical traumas of war and destruction, but even as they settled into lives of comfort and leisure, the passion for security conversely grew. Even the gradual disappearance of class distinctions—a proud achievement of an economy that until the late 1980s seemed capable of indefinite growth—proved to trouble some Germans. Sociologists and business experts called it "verbal cocooning:" Germans spurned the 1960s trend toward relaxed use of the informal *du*, preferring to return to the traditional *Sie* form of "you" that maintained clear distances between levels of society. Secretaries and professionals alike boasted of being so formal that they didn't even know their coworkers' first names. In the east, where communist etiquette had required all comrades to address one another as *du*, some people, especially among the young, switched quickly back to *Sie*, saying they felt more assured when they could set the proper barriers in their relationships.

On a trip I once took with eight German reporters, nearly all of whom had been covering Foreign Minister Hans-Dietrich Genscher for many years, I was surprised to hear the men all speaking formally, addressing each other as "Herr This" and "Herr That." These reporters spent every workday together, year in and year out, traveling around the world, waiting endlessly in hotel lobbies, airports and meeting halls for politicians to emerge from closed-door talks to emit the day's news. Yet their conversation was limited to the weather, their latest vacations and the sights of the city, in this case Geneva. When I asked some of the reporters privately about each other, they had no idea whether their colleagues were married or had children, no sense of their lives away from the Foreign Ministry. "It's better this way," one reporter said. "No one knows enough to be uncomfortable around anyone else. Everything is kept on an even level. Just work. And if one of us is a nudist at home, or a gun collector, or a wife-beater, or the world's most boring man, it doesn't matter, it's no one's business but their own." (In a series of studies over the past thirty years, psychologists comparing German, American and Japanese societies found that social distance is closely related to authoritarianism, and that societies with strict social rules tend to be quicker to divide the world into in and out groups.)

But if affluence only bolstered German traditions of distance and reserve, the desire for stability was on a collision course with an essential element of success in the modern age—new technologies. In one institution after another, resistance to the modern encumbered the country's ability to compete globally. By 1993, Economics Minister Günter Rexrodt complained that "in German society, there are disturbing signs that people are not interested in high-tech issues. People want to feel secure in their old ways, to be a little bit lazy." A poll by the Allensbach Institute found only 36 percent of western Germans agreed that "technology is a blessing," down from 50 percent in 1976. Luddite attitudes exist everywhere, but in Germany, they have been allowed to set corporate and public policy. At bank offices, computers sit unused while tellers used carbon paper, pencils, and the old abacus to keep records and do their figures.

One day at a Deutsche Bank office in Bonn, I stood behind a woman who grew more impatient with every second she was forced to wait. When it was finally her turn, the clerk made her wait further while he made a show of stamping each copy of each form several times, then wrote out her request in longhand. "The computer is right there," the woman said. "Why don't you use it?"

The bank clerk stood up straight and in a righteously offended tone responded, "Madame, there is absolutely nothing automatic about Deutsche Bank."

Credit cards, long rejected as suspicious because of the well-grounded German phobia about debt and inflation, made few inroads into the country. Even in department stores and major urban shopping districts, credit cards remained largely unwelcome. Eighty-five percent of all transactions in Germany are still in cash; it is routine to see bank customers withdraw 1,000 marks (about $650) for their weekly purchases.

By resisting the computer revolution, Germany's airlines (where tickets are still often filled out by hand), telephone monopoly (still firmly rooted in the analog age, with little progress toward the business revolution achieved by touch-tone phones), banks (whose lack of computer connections has made branch banking nearly impossible), and retail sector (scanners are almost unknown) have burdened themselves with heavy disadvantages. German bankers say the country has virtually disappeared from the global electronics industry; only the country's superb training programs and fine tradition of apprenticeships have kept its machine-tooling, automotive and other successful industries in the ball game. Foreign competitors who found themselves boxed out in the sell-off of East Germany's state enterprises at first fumed that they were being excluded for xenophobic motives. But later, many foreign companies, including a number of American firms in the telecommunications, electronics and construction sectors, concluded that they were victims of a protectionism designed to fend off technologically advanced competition. U.S. diplomats tried to help some American companies enter the market, arguing to the Germans that reunification offered an opportunity to change how Germans live. A 1991 report to the chancellor by McKinsey & Company consulting recommended using unification to revolutionize the country's stagnant economy. Let old East German industries die, the report said; don't subsidize practices with no future. Instead, concentrate on massive, Japanese-style investment in "creative islands," bringing new technologies to microelectronics, traffic systems, fisheries and other sectors where Germany has good potential. But the Kohl administration let itself be paralyzed by the rigid western bureaucracy, which resisted loosening rules for the east. The government spent hundreds of millions on

subsidies to outmoded industries. Training money was used to keep easterners occupied learning skills with little future: Small villages in the east
found themselves with forty people retrained to cut and style hair or sixty
people reeducated in the fine points of being a baker's assistant.

Lee Boam, commercial officer in the U.S. Embassy office in Berlin,
tried to persuade Germans to use the east as an opportunity to change. He
used the example of home building: Instead of gluing carpeting to the
floors, a slow, smelly and labor-intensive process German companies had
always used, Germans could turn to U.S. companies offering the American
system of tacking carpets along the wall. Similarly, Boam suggested, Germans could change building codes to allow U.S. manufacturers of prefabri-
cated housing to introduce hollow-wall construction. That could have
saved eastern Germans enormously in housing costs, and it would have
permitted developers to include closets in their home designs, sparing
hard-pressed easterners the cost of the freestanding wardrobes that stand
in every room of most homes. Such ideas were rejected. Although its membership in the European Community prevents Germany from invoking its
own tariffs against foreign competition, Germany has erected nontariff barriers to trade, in the form of more than 40,000 technical rules governing
how products must be made and more than 25,000 norms dictated by DIN,
the national standards agency. These rules keep out everything from Oreos
(most packaged cookies do not comply with German food laws) to answering machines.

Germany's resistance to technology is not generational, as it tends to be
in other countries. A surprising number of young people display a strong
skepticism of technological progress, for two major reasons. The first grows
out of the country's strong Green movement, which argues that automation
and improved productivity are unnatural and destructive to the environment. Michael Mertes, a speechwriter for Kohl, dubbed this "anticiviliza-
tion fundamentalism." The other major source of antimodernism is a
widespread, heartfelt belief that modern society's attempts at labor-saving
unfairly infringe on the average person's right to a job. That last idea, which
many Germans sum up as "fairness," is used to justify the continued strict
limits on shopping hours. This concept holds that it would be unfair to require any workers to spend evenings or weekends on the job when other
Germans have that time to spend with their families. A German friend who
spent several years in the United States said the thing she would miss most
about American life was the ability to step out to a 7-Eleven at midnight to
pick up some milk. But when I asked her whether Germany would or should
change its closing-hours rules, she said: "Absolutely not. I will never forget
how miserable I felt when I was a child, and my family could not go away on

weekends like the other children could, because my parents had a shop and they had to stay in town to open on Saturday morning."

That belief in fairness also extends to public support for the country's Rabattgesetz, a law that prohibits stores from holding giveaways or discounting wares outside biannual, federally mandated sales periods. Even though it makes their country frightfully expensive, many Germans support the system because they know it guarantees jobs. Far from lamenting the lack of competition in the country's retail sector, many German consumers say rules against price-chopping allow sales people to maintain their dignity and relieve consumers of having to shop around "like Arabs in a bazaar" or "Americans driving through their mindless suburbs," to repeat two similes I often heard at dinner parties. Fairness, the basis of much of the country's social and economic thinking, insists that individual concerns be sublimated to a generic, blind equality. German fairness certainly eases some of the inequities and miseries that exist in other, more competitive western societies. But sacrifices demanded in the name of fairness—such as policies that discourage mothers from working—also demean and repress the individual, contributing considerably to what Thomas Mann called the "lachrymose German personality."

As the country struggled through recession in the early nineties, many industrialists and bankers joined with intellectuals and politicians in blaming their own culture—how Germans deal with one another and their problems. Some people reacted to that diagnosis by falling deeper into that depressed state Mann described. Others grew defensive about the German way of doing things, denying structural problems. The economic woes of the nineties, they said, were simply a matter of adjusting to unification. To be sure, Germany did not need the east economically. Whatever expansion of production facilities has taken place there has been largely symbolic. The east is a small-enough market that it could be served quite well from existing western German plants. But unification has contributed something to the economy: It has revealed underlying problems, the coming confrontation between the forces of retrenchment and the country's deep sense of entitlement.

"Industry and the economy are stuck in a cost and innovation crisis, labor in an employment crisis, the political class in a credibility crisis, and society in an orientation crisis," President Weizsäcker told industrialists in 1993. "We have to be more open to structural change. We have to dismantle many structures that run counter to innovation and investment." More than 30 percent of Germany's GNP went to pay for social benefits, more than anywhere but Scandinavia. And the nineties brought to an end Germany's long-standing position as world champion in exports. East European markets collapsed, while Germany priced itself out of U.S. and Asian markets, and held its own in western Europe mostly through protectionism. The world's highest labor costs sapped whatever advantages German companies had over the competition. Germany has the world's shortest work week (37 hours), most vacation time (an average of 42 work days off each year), highest industrial wages (about $27 an hour), most leisurely education (average age of college graduates is 29), and youngest retirees (average age at retirement, under 59). Most workers get an extra month's pay at Christmas, and another bonus intended to ease the burden of paying for a vacation. Liberal social and medical systems pay for vacation cures at health resorts, subsidize childbirth and child care, keep many young people in college for more than a decade, and encourage patients to take days off from work for the slightest ailment. (Without fail, every time I visited a German physician, no matter how minor the illness, the doctor offered to write me a *Krankschreibung*, a note that would get me off work for a week, or in the case of the flu, two.) The result is a populace that occasionally grumbles about its hefty tax burden, but also has grown happily dependent on everything its taxes pay for, and then some.

Kohl, who had long dismissed suggestions that Germany was getting fat and lazy, began sprinkling that idea into his speeches. "A successful industrial nation, a nation with a future, does not allow itself to be organized like a collective amusement park," he said. But his rhetoric came after industry had discovered the problem and begun to take painful corrective steps. In 1993, companies laid off half a million workers, despite contracts requiring employers to pay compensation of up to $36,000 per worker. By 1994, major companies had announced plans to export nearly half a million jobs, mostly to the new cheap labor sources of Poland, Hungary and the Czech Republic, but also to "Third World locations such as South Carolina and Alabama," as a director of Deutsche Bank expressed it to me. German companies and unions began talking about the unspeakable, a rollback in benefits.

"All western democracies are troubled, but Germany is especially encrusted," said Stephanie Wahl, a sociologist at the Institute for Economics and Society in Bonn. "Unification has made it necessary for us to show flexibility and openness to change, but we are more encrusted than ever. Our wealth and security in the past few decades created a laziness and an attitude that we are owed something." Sir Ralf Dahrendorf, the German scholar who went on to become warden of St. Antony's College at Oxford, estimated that half of all Germans depend on the public dole in some way. Even without unification, West Germany would have faced the Swedish dilemma of a social system that no longer made political or actuarial sense. (In 1994, the

German social welfare system consumed 40 percent of the total wages paid to the country's workers.) Unification only pushed the problems to the front burner.

Despite all this rigidity and regulation, despite the largess of Father State and the dependencies of a people accustomed to looking up for solutions, Germany's economy remains Europe's engine, and the country seems in many ways still to operate efficiently. How can both realities be true? Dahrendorf pointed to the benefits of the German apprenticeship system and the advantage of a homogeneous society with a strong work ethic. But he was not happy with his own explanations. There must be something more. Work style is a good starting point. When Germans work, they do work hard. And craftsmen and factory workers are often highly skilled. In addition, German companies are, by western standards, fairly lean in management, and more willing to devote resources to long-term planning than their American counterparts, if not quite as future-oriented as the Japanese. Like Japan, Germany has organized its economy with a degree of cooperation unthinkable and impractical in the United States. Like the Japanese *keiretsu*, the leagues of corporations and banks that work in tandem, Germany's largest banks have woven interlocking relationships with major industries and their suppliers. When bankers have significant ownership and directorship relations with companies that rely on them for capital, the two sectors work together in a way Americans might find suspicious. It is, however, highly effective, both for the big German conglomerates and for the *Mittelstand*, the midsize businesses that are the heart of German success.

But what really made the German economy hum in recent decades was the country's system of creating consensus. After the turbulent extremism and destructive factionalism of the first half of the century, West Germans were intent on crafting a social engine that would purr as smoothly as a Mercedes sweeping down the autobahn. In politics, labor relations and business practice, West Germany molded a culture of cooperation designed to avoid the recurrent confrontation that defined market economics in other western countries. Germans put workers in the governing bodies of their corporations. They invited unionists into the boardroom to help make decisions. In the health system, doctors and insurers quietly agreed to reasonable rates, keeping customer costs relatively in check. Germans created an unofficial form of governance in Bonn where, instead of banging heads in parliamentary showdowns, members of opposing parties gathered at the chancellor's office to settle tricky issues behind closed doors. In the face of authority, even journalists suppress their profession's natural antiestablishment bent: When high-ranking officials ask that certain topics not be broached, reporters often honor the request. That's how Kohl for many years managed to keep out of public view the fact that he sent his sons to college in the United States, a tidbit that might have reflected poorly on Germany's own university system.

The consensus system, pride of West Germany after the war, was a natural tributary of a historic stream in German thought. It combined the utopianism of German romantic nationalism and socialism with the country's long tradition of subordinating individual rights to the collective good. Like those other German political movements, the consensus system sought to minimize conflict by putting the interests of the people, the *Volk*, first. The price for the social peace and egalitarianism that bound trade unions, corporate directors and politicians was sometimes freedom of the individual, who was usually glad to give up some liberty and choice in exchange for personal security and stability.

But in the early nineties, the consensus system began to break down— labor and management clashed more frequently, the health system ran into trouble, recession seemed to dig in, and politicians stalemated over the country's global role, the immigration crisis, the future of the military, and reconstruction of the east. Many Germans wondered why the system that had carried them out of desperation in the 1950s seemed to run out of gas in the nineties. Many blamed the stress of unification. But coincident with the fall of the Wall, a generational revolution was under way. Older Germans who grew up with the old virtues of discipline and obedience were comfortable with the consensus system. According to German sociologist Werner Schiffauer, Germans look toward authority figures to define their goals, in sharp contrast to the English, French and Americans, who cherish a more individualist approach. The German ideal, Schiffauer argues, is the "experts' republic," in which politicians, academics and others who presumably know better determine what is right and good. The rest of society then adapts. The classic example is an institution called the Five Wise Men, a group of economists who tell the chancellor each year what wage increases should be. The Wise Men's figures form the framework of negotiations among government, labor and industry, none of whom stray far from what the experts ordain.

Younger Germans, products of post-sixties cynicism and a powerful push toward individualism, seem less willing to accept the word of the experts. The nineties brought a new kind of political crisis in Germany, called *Politikverdrossenheit*, a deep disaffection with politics, a Perotism without Perot. There was much wringing of hands in academia and the press about the failure of the "political class" to provide creative leadership. President Weizsäcker went so far as to call for a smashing of the consensus taboo. Instead of looking to experts, to Bonn, for all answers, Germany needed to develop alternative solutions from new sources. The people need to do for themselves instead of having everything done for them, he said. Others expressed the same idea differently: Werner Hoyer, a leader of the Free Democratic party, lamented Germany's lack of a "civil society," the network of volunteers, private universities, think tanks, foundations, grass-roots groups and lobbies that generate so many of America's ideas and initiatives. Germany's paucity of individual involvement in public life extends to the most basic level of society: Jochen Thies, foreign editor of the daily *Die Welt,* was in San Francisco during the 1989 earthquake and was astonished to see Americans taking it upon themselves to direct traffic after the power failed. "That is impossible in Germany," he said. "You wait for the police and you have a general halt until they arrive."

German medical culture provides another window onto the hierarchical way of thinking. The country's senior and often most-talented physicians are accorded a status no American doctor would dream of. The German "Herr Professor Doctor" behaves like royalty, has his name inscribed in foot-high letters on the wall of his hospital offices, expects his staff to shuffle before him, and brooks no skepticism or sharp questioning from a mere patient. "The differences in medical culture between Germany and other western countries are huge," said a German physician who has practiced in the United States and England. "In your country, the patient is an important part of the process. The interview is essential to the diagnosis. To us, the patient is a specimen to be examined, but not heard from."

I could never quite get used to the idea that I was not supposed to tell the doctor my symptoms. "Do you want to hear the history of the problem?" I asked one Berlin internist.

"Not necessary," he replied. "I will take blood."

At one introductory consultation with a Berlin pediatrician, after my wife and I had asked five questions about the doctor's approach and techniques, he stood and said, "Is that all?" It wasn't. Three questions later, he pushed his chair back from his desk, closed his file folder, and said, "You Americans certainly ask a lot of questions, don't you?"

The tradition of leaving initiative and control in the same hands—those of the state—served West Germany well in the postwar period of limited sovereignty, a time when the whole country needed to present the world with a pastoral, inoffensive face, the face of consensus and solidarity. But now, the combination of a new generation perhaps less willing to be led by the same old experts, along with the social and economic problems bared by the end of the Cold War, required Germans to make hard choices. Would they hand back some of their lush benefits or simply stand by and watch the decline of their country's economic prowess—and with it, some of their cherished stability? Some German unions surprised even themselves by swallowing their pride and rolling back the perks. In one company after another, the gravy train slowed as workers gave back rights to Christmas bonuses, subsidized lunches, profit-sharing payments, and company help with home mortgages.

It was only the start of a painful process. "Ever more people have evolved from citizens of the state to clients or customers of the state," said Bohl, Kohl's aide. The postwar welfare state—the extent of which surprised many eastern Germans who had believed communist propaganda about the west's ruthless capitalism—was the counterbalance to the post-Nazi rejection of authoritarianism. Even as the student rebels of what Germans call the '68 generation confronted their parents, uncles and aunts about their failure to stand up to National Socialism, even as one institution after another sought ways to spurn the legacy of *Gehorsamkeit* (obedience), West Germany's success lulled its people into accepting a new dose of hierarchical, authoritarian rule.

"Despite everything we have done to the contrary, we remain more hierarchical than the rest of the west," said Karl-Heinz Stahl, a professor of cultural and media studies in Berlin. "Look at our television news. It is a formal bit of theater, read from a stack of papers [without TelePrompTers] pronounced in officious tones as if it were a government edict, a message from above." Beginning with the Persian Gulf War, when German television was caught flat-footed and had to pluck CNN's pictures off the satellite, many news executives and politicians reacted with revulsion to what they saw as the trivialization of news by American "show business" networks. News in Germany is only credible if it has the aura of government authority. Journalists generally do not seek the views of ordinary citizens. Nor is the public nearly as attached to the device of communicating local and world events through the prism of the feature story—how news affects random individuals. That stems from a very different concept of privacy—something highly valued in Germany—but it is also explained by the tendency to look for an authoritative version of events. According to a study of German and American journalists by researchers at Dresden and Syracuse universities, German reporters are far more willing to cede control of the news to politicians than their U.S. counterparts, who believe they themselves determine what is news. German reporters say their job is to represent and advocate the values and ideas of their particular political party; American journalists decisively reject that notion.

"We have different cultural rules," said Stahl. "It is unimaginable that a German reporter could question a politician or a business figure as sharply as the Americans who tried to determine if Vice President Quayle was really so dumb. People still honor our cultural traditions and we lurch from extreme to extreme, from beating and burning foreigners to taking to the streets by the hundreds of thousands to prove we love foreigners. We value order over everything else. We will even accept injustice before lack of order in our private lives or in public."

None of this is to say that Germans will follow the directives of any demagogue who might happen to come along. But there are differences between cultures, and there is a desire for regulation and directive in the German tradition. Even in confrontations, the German passion for order emerges victorious. How else can one explain the ballet that occurs each Saturday night in the streets of Berlin, where police and hundreds of kids dressed in black clash in carefully choreographed confrontations over nothing? Every weekend, and in much grander fashion on May Day each year, Berlin's anarchists—bands of self-righteous punks who express their rage at everything by rampaging against the police and any other convenient symbol of authority—stage riots so intricately organized that the black-clad kids and their green-uniformed opponents know precisely when and where the other will assemble, what will ensue, and how it will end. It's never quite clear what the anarchists want, other than the opportunity to vent their collective spleen and demonstrate that they have the power to spoil official functions. Nonetheless, the ritual continues year after year. In my first spring in Berlin in 1990, I got instructions about exactly where to go to see the bloodiest part of the May Day conflagration, and indeed the events took place just as scheduled. The police place wire mesh over their windshields, put on armor for protection, and charge onto the turf claimed by the anarchists, whose impressive organization—including press releases, sound equipment, and instructions to demonstrators on how to deal with arrest—would seem to disqualify them for their chosen ideology.

The West German postwar consensus was dissolving, and a new generation was taking center stage, a generation still defined by the war, but one step removed from the experiences of dictatorship and battle. Germans who grew up during the economic miracle of the 1950s, free of the taint of the Nazi years, prepared to accept the reins of power in a society deeply disturbed by the very notions of power and leadership. This was the generation postwar West Germany had bet its future on. In all the ways that Germans had decided their parents were wrong, this generation would be different. It would have the civil courage to stand up against immoral acts by its leaders. It would be tolerant, open and warm. It would reject nationalism, elitism and authoritarianism.

But of course, it could not do this, any more than any generation in any nation can collectively change itself according to a checklist of demands.

Indeed, German leaders of the new generation were in some ways more confused and troubled by their own identity than those who came before them. For as good as their intentions had been, and as diligently as individuals had sought to be something new, they were who they were brought up to be. A study by members of the psychology department at Trier University in 1993 sought to measure the willingness of Germans to behave unreasonably simply because they are directed to by an authority. Students posted signs on public telephone booths saying FOR MEN ONLY and FOR WOMEN ONLY. They then observed the reactions of passersby. Nearly all the women and more than three-quarters of the men complied with the signs. A mother was heard telling her whining child, "We're not allowed in that one, it's just for men." The one woman who disobeyed the sign turned out to be a young Frenchwoman, who looked at the MEN ONLY sign and told the researchers, "Only the Germans could have such an idea."

3

The Bloody Flag

I have never believed I am German. We are beyond that. We are citizens of the world. —Marius Müller-Westernhagen, western German rock star, to a cheering crowd at a concert staged to rally Germans against hatred of foreigners, December 1992, in Frankfurt

We Germans like to think we are better than anyone else or that we are worse than everyone else. In the end, I think, we are neither. We are only human beings. —Wolf Biermann, eastern German poet and folksinger, at another concert against hatred of foreigners, January 1993, in Hamburg

ON ONE OF our first weekends in Germany, my wife Jody and I spent a Saturday night at the Tapetenfabrik, a hulking former wallpaper factory alongside the railroad tracks across the Rhine from Bonn. The place had been converted into a semichic performance space for artists of all sorts. Upstairs, the American jazzman John Zorn played to a larger, more appreciative audience than he ever could have prayed for back home. In a barren concrete room below, a couple of hundred young people danced listlessly to techno, disco, and the tinny Europop that sounds like jewelry-polishing machines. Along a long hallway of artists' studios, young Germans presented visions of life in their confused country. We wandered among installations of hanging metal objects and sharp-edged rocks. A photo display showed a row of erect penises and fried German sausage, all emblazoned with the West German flag and the logo used in celebration of West Germany's fortieth anniversary. Subtlety, we could see, was not to be the coin of the evening.

We blundered into the studio of a performance artist named Marie-Lu Leisch. She was a frail, slight woman covered from neck to ankles in tightly taped white bandages. She stood on a white dropcloth in front of billowing white bedsheets, holding her arms out, silently beckoning to twenty-five or so visitors. Leisch picked up a stiff, starched white dress and gripped it tightly, caressing it with love and admiration. Slowly, a faint, familiar tune grew louder. It was a string quartet playing an excruciatingly slow version of the German national anthem, the hauntingly beautiful Haydn tune known to fans of Nazi war movies as "Deutschland, Deutschland über Alles." Forlorn, reluctant, Leisch placed the stiff white dress in a wash pail at her feet. The rigid cloth immediately fell limp, to Leisch's heaving sorrow. She tried to revive her cherished dress, to recapture its firmness. She washed it repeatedly, but was never satisfied. As the music grew louder—menacingly so—Leisch recoiled from the very dress she had held so tenderly moments ago. Wracked with guilt, overcome with sadness and fear, she could not bear to embrace what she had once loved. She crossed her arms against the fear. Then, ever so slowly, her right arm lifted—involuntarily, it seemed— into the "Heil Hitler" salute. Again and again, she tentatively approached the washed, bleached Germany. She could not face its new clothes. Finally, she made one last approach, reached for the dress and suddenly pulled back, as if bitten. Some unseen force threw Leisch against the rear wall. She turned away from the wash basin, but something drew her toward it. The anthem grew painfully loud.

This mimed encounter with nation and past turned violent. First, the pristine white setting—confirming the old theatrical rule about never introducing a prop unless you plan to use it—was splattered with blood. Then, as Leisch fell victim to the false promise of a different Germany, her virginal setting was saturated in an astonishing flood of carnage. Performed in installments, Leisch's little drama drew her through ever-more-savage stages of violent confrontation with her Germanness. It was a bloodbath. We stayed only long enough to get the point. About two hours later, when we happened to pass Leisch's performance studio once more, we saw the artist leaving her space caked with stage blood from hair to feet. Germany's future, it seemed, had gotten considerably worse.

Four years later, another artist, Katharina Sievering, papered Berlin with 500 billboards. The words "Germany Is Becoming More German" were superimposed over the bandaged face of a woman staring through half a dozen daggers that pierced the wall behind her. In most other countries, such a slogan might be advertising hype for a tourist agency or the tagline for a dreamy political candidate. But in Germany, the very use of the word "German" as an adjective raises existential doubts. The Sievering poster assumes Germans have a bad conscience about themselves, that Germans associate themselves with an exclusionary nativism. "You will never know how hard it is to be German," a young friend in Bonn once told me. The mysteries of national identity and the pain of defining membership in one of Europe's youngest nations have become a cottage industry in Germany, spawning countless academic studies, conferences, TV talk shows, opinion polls, and awkward personal accounts. At least half a dozen times during my years there, German reporters called me to ask for a foreigner's view on "What is typically German?"; "Who are the Germans?" or "Can a German be patriotic?" (In a 1991 survey by the Allensbach Institute, Germans were asked whether the phrase "typically German" was a compliment. Only 15 percent of western Germans said it was.)

In the months after the two Germanys officially became one, everything was fair game. Politicians and journalists debated what their country's name should be and which anthem its people should sing. Kohl and Weizsäcker eventually decided to stick with the West German anthem. Set to Haydn's melody, the "Germany Song," a poem written by Heinrich Hoffmann von Fallersleben in 1841 in honor of the unification of the German-speaking lands, was no Nazi invention. But the National Socialists had turned the first line, "Deutschland, Deutschland über Alles," (Germany, Germany above all else) into a nationalist battle cry. That first stanza was banned outright in the postwar constitution. West Germans instead sang the poem's third stanza, which begins "Unity and law and freedom." But many Germans continue to use the old words, and they still have the power to divide. In 1992, teachers, parents and school administrators faced off in Bavaria over the wisdom of exposing children to the forbidden lyrics even as part of a history lesson. When parents learned that some schools were teaching the first stanza, the teachers' association argued successfully against any utterance of the banned words, for fear they would feed neo-Nazi sentiment among the young.

The excesses of the past have blurred the distinction between nationhood and nationalism in Germany. Pride in country has come to be seen as the first step toward the rabid national fervor that too often has led Germans to trouble. No symbol of nationhood remains untainted. A group of Berlin high school students debating whether a German may properly be proud of his nation proposed to their teachers that they hang German and European flags in their classrooms. The teachers, products of the postwar generation that most abhors expressions of nationhood, were aghast that their own country's flag might be displayed in a school. One teacher at Clay High School said if the German flag were flown, students would soon seek to fly a swastika. The students cried foul: After all, when Iraqi and Turkish students had displayed their country's flags on school premises, no teacher had complained. But the gold, red and black of the German banner was too hot to handle. "We advised the students that the German flag can create misunderstandings," said the school director, Detlef Schikorr. "We agreed with the class that the flag can remain hanging while they are in the classroom, but it must be removed when other classes use that room."

The omnipresence of American flags in the United States often bewilders or amuses Germans. Flagpoles attached to old houses in Germany usually stand naked, except when they fly the circle of stars on a blue field that is the symbol of the European Community. All of western Europe has lived through decades of propaganda for European unification, but no one took the idea as seriously as the Germans. They saw a single Europe, a Europe beyond the nation-state, as an escape route, a respite from the burdens of history. What a contrast with the days I spent in Prague during the November 1989 revolution, when thousands of Czech flags appeared on Wenceslas Square. People clutched their flags, waved them and wrapped them around one another—a swatch of cloth became patriotism, rebellion and togetherness, all captured in one symbol. (The German attachment to a united Europe never quite crossed over to the east. In 1990, the European Community wrote to East German grass-roots groups that had led the 1989 revolt, asking easterners to "Please use the European flag" in addition to the German banner at their rallies and meetings. Hardly anyone did. The fantasy of one Europe was a peculiarly western form of sublimation and transference. Easterners didn't need it. To them, West Germany's flag symbolized the good life.)

German aversion to nationhood is not simply a symptom of post-sixties political correctness, nor is it merely a reflection of a post-Nazi allergy to tainted concepts such as power, leadership and national identity. Germany has struggled with the very notion of nationhood throughout history. As early as 1796, Goethe chided his fellow Germans, warning that "your hope of shaping a nation" would remain forever "in vain." Germany did not evolve from religious state to nation-state as Britain and France did. Rather, the German lands were long divided between Catholic and Protestant principalities. Nor did Germany emerge from the Enlightenment with an intellectual class bent on realizing grand ideas of personal liberty and egalitarianism. Germany remained stuck in feudalism, its lands divided among warring princes and barons. There was no colonial empire where soaring myths of national destiny could be developed. Until 1871, the Germans were bound not by nationhood in the modern sense, but by far more slippery ties, of language and culture, literature and tribal roots. Germans came from all over: French Huguenots hoping for a better life, Poles looking for work, Jews seeking tolerance. They found a place considerably more diverse than later proponents of a German "race" or ethnicity would ever admit. That diversity left Germany in search of definition. The late-nineteenth-century Prussians found identity—and thus unity—in the kind of power politics and militarism that had served their European neighbors for centuries. Adolf Hitler marched farther down that road, creating a Germany defined by blood. It was perhaps precisely because of the great differences among them that Germans were so ready to accept a racial definition of themselves. Divided by dialect, culture, personality and even ethnic background, split Protestant from Catholic and north from south, as well as east from west, Germans at various stages in their history have settled for a negative definition of themselves—a German is someone who is not an *Ausländer,* or foreigner. Germans seem to ask, "Who are we, if not those who are not 'them'?" (Intriguingly, that kind of self-definition does not survive abroad. Germans, the single largest component of the United States population, are nearly invisible as an ethnic group in America. Although they account for about one-quarter of the U.S. population, they retain almost no separate identity politically, culturally or socially in the crumbling fruitcake of American ethnicity.)

After the Nazi debacle, the two German states defined themselves once again in the negative: East Germany was the nonfascist, noncapitalist state working toward a just, socialist utopia. West Germany declared itself the legal successor to the Third Reich. Morally, it reached further into the past to assume the legacy of German democracy, as botched by the Weimar Republic. But West Germans during the Cold War also defined themselves as the noncommunist Germans wedded to the west. They were ashamed of their nondemocratic past and contemptuous of their communist cousins.

Already before the revolution of 1989, both Germanys found their defining myths insufficient to sustain the popular support and satisfaction that make for successful states. Eastern leaders knew that if they dared to open the borders, millions, including many of the best and brightest, would bail out. And western politicians increasingly worried that the postwar alienation from nationhood had left a yawning hole in their society's heart. "Some identification with the nation into which a person is born is one of the natural needs and desires of most people," Roman Herzog, then a judge on the high court and later Germany's president, told Bonn's parliament in 1988. "Where such identification is denied or fails, other, more dangerous substitutes may fill the emotional vacuum," added a former government minister, Erhard Eppler, a year later.

Reunification gummed up the works: Both German states lost the identities they had molded during decades of division. Germany could no longer hold itself above others as the postmodern state that had outgrown the national form. The end of the Cold War brought not the European utopia Germans had dreamt of, but a revival of the nation as the most emotionally powerful and logistically plausible method of organizing societies. The European ideal lost its cachet, especially after it became clear that in a united Europe, Germany would lose the independence of the Deutsche mark—symbol of the country's greatest postwar achievement, its emergence as an economic power. Between 1991 and 1993, the percentage of western Germans supporting a European Community "with priority over national independence" dropped from 43 to 32, according to surveys conducted for Kohl's party. By 1993, the chancellor realized he had vastly underestimated the emotional bond most Germans felt with the mark. "Saving the mark is now our party's main political mission," said one of Kohl's closest aides. "That probably means kissing the idea of European currency union goodbye."

A drive to write a new German constitution after reunification faltered. Pride in their constitutional democracy was one thing; risking a rewrite of the American-influenced West German Basic Law seemed fraught with danger. After all, Germany had existed as a unified nation for only seventy-four years (1871–1945), and plenty of reminders of that unhappy experience remained quietly embedded in German law and tradition (citizenship is still defined by blood, for example). Few were eager to inspect the integrity of the foundation.

Hardly a month seems to go by in Germany without some pronouncement that the country is suffering from one crisis or another. It might be the future role of the German military, or how the country should deal with immigration and citizenship, or how to treat former members of the East German communist party. Whatever the issue, intellectuals, politicians and journalists resolve that nothing can improve until Germans get a handle on who they are. It's slippery stuff, this talk of identity and purpose. The debate tends toward morose, piercingly rational discussion about matters so abstract that solutions are hard to imagine. Yet at bottom festers a real problem, one that begins with shame and guilt and ends in a political and social paralysis that endangers Europe's future. Fear of the worst strains of German history—self-loathing, antidemocratic instincts, and self-image as victims and scapegoats—lurks behind the identity crisis.

"A German child is never taught pride for a flag or an anthem," said Jochen Thies, a former aide to Chancellor Helmut Schmidt. "A German is brought up in private, almost without consciousness of his state. It's a result of forgetting history. When you see two American travelers meet in a foreign country, they talk like longtime friends. When two Germans meet in a foreign hotel, they do their best to avoid each other. To talk to each other would be to admit that you have something in common, and that something is being German." Even among the most aware Germans, emotional connection to nation seems unwise at the least, downright criminal at worst. When President George Bush told German reporters at a 1989 news conference that he "prayed for Germany," the assembled hacks guffawed at the very notion. "There is a general refusal to accept that emotion plays a role in politics," Thies said. "Everything is overrationalized for fear that if emotion seeped into it, we would somehow revert to the Nazi time."

Some politicians sought to eliminate the pride taboo. Finance Minister Theo Waigel, leader of Bavaria's right-wing Christian Social Union, in 1993 urged his countrymen to "learn once again to feel like a nation, to trust in our national strengths. . . . No American, no Briton, no Frenchman and no Italian is ashamed of his nation. We do not have reason to be either." On the left, a former leader of the 1968 student revolts, Daniel Cohn-Bendit, accused his fellow leftists of failing to recognize the basic human need for belonging: "You cannot say to a 10-year-old child, 'It's your rotten luck that you are a German. You must live your entire life with a bad conscience.' Germany cannot be penned permanently in an anti-fascist quarantine."

"German intellectuals, who in good measure do not love their own people and cannot bear them, err if they believe that because they themselves can do without the nation, therefore the other 98 percent of the German people should do the same," said ex-Chancellor Helmut Schmidt. "There is no other people in Europe other than German intellectuals who are prepared to renounce their nation."

There was increasing talk of promoting "healthy patriotism." But such rhetoric set off warning bells. PATRIOTISM—NO THANKS! said a headline in the left-liberal weekly *Die Zeit*. "I have problems with people who need identity as such," Karsten Voigt, a leading Social Democrat in parliament, told me. "I have no problem saying it: We have a certain degree of power and influence in Europe and the world now. But that doesn't mean I want to return to a politics of flag-waving."

In 1993, Kohl's office tried to find out what Germans and Americans thought of each other. While 77 percent of the Americans thought Germans were patriotic, only 61 percent of eastern Germans and 42 percent of western Germans described their countrymen so. Whenever I met with young German students, I asked how they describe themselves when traveling outside Germany. Almost invariably, they steered clear of the word "German." "I would never say I am from Germany," said Marina Sprick, sixteen. "It just reminds people of Hitler." Katrin Sobczynski, seventeen, added, "People hear 'Germany' and automatically think 'Nazi.' There's nothing we can do about it. So we just say we're from Europe." The sad words were said with shrugs and uncertain smiles; the facts pained even teenagers with no memories of the war years.

Despite Germany's increased influence after unification, many Germans, and particularly the young, remained captivated by an image of themselves as embattled victims. The early nineties brought a familiar mix of victimization and self-assertion, partners in the same psyche. Since the 1968 student movement, western German youths have identified with Palestinians (the Arafat-style headdress is the scarf de rigueur on German university campuses) and American Indians (whose plight is at the core of any young German's critique of U.S. imperialism). These and other such downtrodden groups are seen as soul mates, misunderstood victims also punished by history. (That mind-meld with the Palestinians and American Indians came together in the virulent burst of anti-Semitism and anti-Americanism preceding the Persian Gulf War. Hundreds of thousands of Germans demonstrated against "U.S. militarism and imperialism" in those weeks. My office in Bonn was inundated with threatening phone calls, both anti-American and anti-Semitic. "Go home, imperialist pig Jew," a caller said. Another popular refrain was "How many Iraqis did you kill today?" available in German or English.)

If *Wessis* (slang for western Germans) felt victimized by unification, *Ossis* (easterners) believed their country had been conquered and colonized by western Germans. That new victim status only added to an already damaged self-image: At the Albertinium, one of Dresden's spectacular museums, curators placed in the honored position at the center of the entrance hall a painting called *The Death of Dresden*, a 1945 work by Wilhelm Lachnit. The figures of Death and a mother sit side by side, their heads collapsed into their hands, the ruins of the firebombed city stacked behind them in the spoiled light of a powerless sun. The mother's son stares out from the picture, his small hands draped over his mother's lap, his palm facing weakly outward, toward what remains.

The fall of the Wall did spark a fleeting revival of national spirit. The remains of Frederick the Great, removed to the west at Hitler's order when the Red Army was approaching Berlin, were exhumed and reburied with great pomp at the royal palace in Potsdam in 1991. With the chancellor in attendance and a nationwide TV audience watching the midnight ceremonies, "Old Fritz" was carried on nineteenth-century imperial rail cars and horse-drawn carriages to his original resting place at the Sanssouci Palace. Germany, Kohl said, "needs to stand before our entire history" instead of demonizing its past. But each attempt to build respect for German history led to new arguments about the light and shadows of the past. A citizens' movement fought for years to restore to the prominent point where the Rhine and Mosel rivers meet a controversial statue of Kaiser Wilhelm I that celebrates the German victory over France. The Prussian iron cross was returned to its perch atop Berlin's Brandenburg Gate, despite protests that it was a nationalist symbol. Weizsäcker delivered a speech praising the same Prussian virtues that postwar generations of Germans had been taught to renounce. News reports suddenly began using old German names for towns and cities in Poland, the Czech Republic and throughout central Europe. The German Railway introduced weekend nostalgia trips to Kaliningrad (Königsberg to the Germans), the formerly German, now Russian, city sandwiched between Poland and Lithuania. And some politicians felt liberated to say things that would have been unacceptable before 1989. Wolfgang Schäuble, Kohl's parliamentary leader and heir apparent, called in 1994 for a constitutional change to let German armed forces be used domestically, to protect borders against immigration or to combat urban crime. This was necessary, he said, not because of any pressing demand for extra enforcement, but because too many Germans had come to perceive the state as weak. Germany needed to demonstrate strength, and the best way to accomplish that was to make the military uniform a common, comforting sight.

The public didn't rush out to buy the new brand of national pride. The pain of unification undermined even the single unblemished symbol of all that was good and right—the mark, Germany's version of the Pledge of Allegiance, the "Marseillaise" and the Union Jack rolled into one. *Bild*, the country's most popular newspaper, served up a front-page love song to German money, crooning to "You beautiful, strong mark." But public awareness that the golden age of affluence was ending went well beyond fear of a European currency. Economists forecast a stagnant economy well into the nineties. The export king was trapped in a slow but inexorable process of dethronement. Germany had fallen dangerously behind in innovation; while the United States and Japan competed in the worldwide patent sweepstakes, the Germans fell ever further behind. German companies had failed to recognize the importance of marketing and sales techniques in getting consumers to buy quality products. "Made in Germany," concluded an analyst for the U.S. consulting firm of Arthur D. Little, was coming to mean "too expensive, too little innovation, too late on the market." Economic decline had far more than economic impact. Kurt Kasch, Deutsche Bank's top man in Berlin, bemoaned the loss of the "economic miracle" as the single object of national pride. "We never gave our people the national monuments, the symbols of pride that even the Japanese did after the war," he said. "We have allowed the far right to steal control of our national symbols."

The search was on for culprits in the loss of confidence. Some in the west blamed unification and the diversion of vast resources to rebuild the blighted region. Kohl's top political aide, Wolfgang Gibowski, said, "The Wall was security. The Red Army protected us from asylum-seekers and other foreigners. Now we all feel the paradise is gone."

Eastern Germans, too, felt the alienation wrought by economic drift. Identity, like so much else in the traumatized east, was a raw problem. Easterners wore their doubts plainly. In 1989, they chose the mark and western consumer society. Now they, too, suffered from its troubles. In their wisdom, communist urban planners, infatuated with broad boulevards and plazas empty but for hulking chunks of socialist realist art, had rendered city centers impassable by pedestrians. In the eastern city of Halle, the fix was a system of underground tunnels, broad, harsh, dark concrete passageways bereft of street life. But unification turned the tunnels into an urban bazaar: Vietnamese street merchants hawked cartons of bootleg cigarettes. Chinese women sold lace tablecloths. Gypsy mothers sat against cold stone walls, their babies asleep on their laps while Mom held out her palms for charity that seemed never to come. Entrepreneurs lined the three-hundred-yard tunnel from end to end, and not one of them was German. Easterners trudged along, wearing the same old cheap vinyl coats and unsmiling faces they had before the revolution. Even at eight in the morning, sour-lipped stragglers swigged from beer bottles as they reeled through the passageways—men in their twenties and thirties as well as older discards of a society rocked by the aftershocks of revolution.

Four years after the Wall fell, I made my way through the tunnels and on to one of Halle's old sections, a marvelous neighborhood of mansions and Victorian homes with towers and turrets, playful rounded corners and oversized, majestic windows. A few houses were in mid-restoration, their peeling paint and crumbling facades succumbing to bright yellow brick, orange roof tiles, fresh white paint, sturdy new windows. I was headed for a session with the east's shrink, Hans-Joachim Maaz, a psychotherapist who had illegally studied Freud during an era when communist psychology was limited to the organic—medical functionaries shuffling along white-tiled corridors at nerve clinics, administering electrical shocks to lunatics and healthy nonconformists alike. Maaz's attempts to work as a therapist had brought the Stasi secret police down on him; he was accused of antisocialist behavior and threatened with imprisonment. But he persisted, eventually finding refuge at this clinic run by the Lutheran Church. With help from west European therapists who brought him books and guidance while they were supposedly in Halle to visit "relatives," Maaz saw patients who revealed to him their fears of the repressive state. Many of his patients were later targeted by the Stasi for surveillance or harassment; under Maaz's tutelage, his patients had grown more self-confident and less malleable by the state apparatus. The regime did not take kindly to that, but Maaz gained important evidence of the psychic impact of a repressive state.

After unification, Maaz continued studying easterners as they struggled
to deal with their new identities—or failed to do so. A gentle man with the
requisite gray beard and soft blue eyes, Maaz became a staple on western
television, the Ossi who explained these strange new Germans to the rest of
the nation. But when Maaz began to say uncomfortable things about the
westerners themselves, the western press turned on him. All Germans, east
and west, he said, suffer from an identity crisis, a struggle against authoritarian upbringing. In the east, the repression was open, the punishments
clear. In the west, authoritarian structures were more hidden, enabling
westerners to seem more confident, stronger. But Germans both east and
west suffered from a collective pathology brought on by child-rearing techniques that were still arbitrary and often violent. Both Germanys had suc-
ceeded in their own ways in defeating the surface manifestations of fascism,
but what Maaz called an inner fascism survived. A nation of children
brought up to repress their anger and obey those above them was not ready
to create its own liberation; that had to be imposed by the occupying forces.
No inner democracy had grown in postwar Germany; instead, the east replaced one form of repression with another, while the west papered over the
guilt of unlived lives, covering genocide and their own war losses with the
soothing gloss of the economic miracle. "We remained an obedient people,
and the more obedient you are, the more likely you are to exhibit violence in
some way, sometime," Maaz said.

Unification, he argued, was a chance for all Germans, an opportunity to
resolve their own guilt, to confront the past and come to terms with their
sadness about the years they or their parents had devoted to the war,
Nazism, or communism. But easterners, their authoritarian anchors cut
away, were obsessed with making their way in the new sink-or-swim society.
They soon realized that their fantasies about the west were naive. And westerners, invested in the security of their postwar success, were determined to
avoid change, to deny that they, too, had reached a personal and societal
watershed. "We knew our system was sick," Maaz said. "The Wessis did not
know, and did not want to know, about what lay beneath their success." The
division Maaz saw in his daily practice eventually became obvious to all. An
Allensbach Institute survey in 1993 found that only 22 percent of westerners and 11 percent of easterners felt a common German identity.

The identity crisis emerged in soaring rates of depression, alcoholism,
and suicide, and plummeting indicators such as marriage and childbearing
rates. Those in the east who sought to break out of the crisis took refuge in
nostalgia for communist days or tried to muster enthusiasm for a new kind
of eastern pride. Ad campaigns for eastern products urged Ossis already
disillusioned by the west to come back and "Kost the Ost," or taste the east.

Billboards for the eastern Club Cola shouted "Hurrah! I'm still alive!" Eastern companies were no longer shy about calling their brands "our beer" or "the newspaper for us." When western TV produced a sitcom series about a grouchy westerner named Motzki who railed against stupid Ossis and their pathetic personalities, eastern producers came up with Trotzki, an equally angry easterner who mouthed off against western Germans, albeit in a far more amateurish manner.

One of the few western institutions to take the eastern search for identity seriously was the military, which assumed the task of merging two formerly enemy armies with gusto. At the Inner Leadership Academy in the western city of Koblenz, officers of the Bundeswehr, the German military, showed me how eastern officers trained together with their western counterparts. Wessis took Ossis around town to teach them the mechanics of daily life—banking, choosing insurance, finding a car, ordering wine. "The eastern men are developing a story of their life for their children," said Admiral Ulrich Hardt. "And that story cannot be one entirely of failure." The Bundeswehr tried not to run a conversion course for enemy officers, but to give Ossis a chance to fit in, at their own pace, without having to renounce their former lives.

Some western arrogance inevitably seeped into the relationship. Few eastern officers made the grade at the end of their probationary period, and several western officers I talked to attributed the failure to a lack of character in the east. After all, the Wessis said, the communists had taught their officers only Soviet military history; they had denied the successes and traditions of German militarism. Eastern officers lacked even basic knowledge of the great military thinker, Clausewitz, or the achievements of Frederick the Great or Bismarck. But the east's National People's Army, for all its faults and crimes, had ended its existence with a display of moral courage. Eastern military men refused orders to turn their weapons against their countrymen demonstrating against the government in 1989, a crucial turning point in the autumn revolution. For all the Inner Leadership Academy's emphasis on imbuing soldiers with the strength to stand up to their superiors' immoral commands—a direct and heartfelt attempt to reverse the authoritarian legacy—no one at the academy could give me an example of a German soldier who had done just that. (The Bundeswehr has not participated in any military action since its inception in 1955.)

That lack of experience illustrated another crucial aspect of the identity problem—the untested seclusion of West Germany's postwar democracy. Behind nearly every reiteration of Germany's quest to find its soul lay doubt about the society's belief in its own democracy. Academics such as Wolfgang Benz of Berlin's Technical University concluded that West German democracy flat out "would not have developed independent of the U.S. and the west forcing it on the Germans." Benz believed many Germans wanted neither dictatorship nor democracy, but a resumption of the benevolent authoritarianism symbolized by Frederick the Great. Life under a system imposed by foreign forces was a perfect recipe for self-doubt, and even some high-ranking politicians wondered whether the artificial nation of West Germany could ever be transformed into something natural. Good times, the Cold War and the U.S. military presence granted West Germany political stability, but now German democracy faced its first real test. Since 1949, power had not changed hands in Bonn even once because of a popular election, but only because of shifts in the ruling coalition. The impetus for change always came from the political elite, not the voters.

Many Germans wondered whether theirs was a fair-weather democracy. From 1991 to 1993, popular satisfaction with democracy dropped from 81 percent to 70 percent in the west, and from 72 percent to 53 percent in the east, according to polls by the Konrad Adenauer Foundation, the think tank of Kohl's party. To some extent, those numbers reflected hard times and increasing frustration with a government paralyzed with indecision. But other countries drifted in and out of recession without questioning the validity of their basic political system. In Germany, stress sowed the deepest of doubts.

Postwar West Germany took great pride in its dull, odorless political life. If its leaders were dry and boring, all the better. Contrast with the dark past was the goal. The measures of political success were continuity, consensus and compromise. "Stability über alles" had served both domestic and foreign audiences well. Germany sat comfortably as the object of other countries' foreign policies. Bonn's own foreign policy was a moralistic irrelevance, symbolized by the empty rhetoric of the longtime foreign minister, Hans-Dietrich Genscher, who, as former Kohl security aide Horst Teltschik told me, "was always in favor of peace and arms control. So of course he was always the most popular politician. Who's against peace?" Over the years, many Germans grew accustomed to denying their country's own interests. The writer Günter Grass had gone so far as to say that after Auschwitz, the Germans had no right to have their own country again.

Suddenly, after unification, the Germans lost their alibi. No longer restricted by tensions between Moscow and Washington, no longer required to judge every policy through the prism of east-west relations, Germans found themselves called upon to act their size. Kohl promised that the new Germany would be a more responsible player on the world scene. And the Germans tried: They pumped more aid into Russia than the other western powers combined. They pushed Europeans to recognize the breakaway Yu-goslav republics of Croatia and Slovenia. The Germans insisted they were going to remain good Europeans, but, as Foreign Ministry official Hanns Schumacher told me, "One thing has changed: The times when Bonn was carrying out the so-called convoy role of following others is over."

As could have been predicted, the slightest ripple of German muscle produced gasps of horror—feigned and real—among other Europeans. Kohl found himself lampooned as Hitler in British and Spanish newspa-pers. Poles and Italians worried aloud about a new German hunger to es-tablish hegemony in central and eastern Europe. German companies invested heavily in Czechoslovakia and Hungary, raising suspicions about Bonn's purpose, especially when German industrialists publicly called the east "our natural market" and "our cultural hinterland." Czechs and Poles discovered on the letters pages of the main German newspapers their worst nightmares: proposals to buy back Silesia, Kaliningrad, the Sudetenland and other formerly German territories in Poland, Hungary and the Czech Republic. Of course, the Bonn government rejected such notions and sought to prove its clean hands by boasting that while Germany might be an economic giant, it remained a political dwarf.

Despite Kohl's promise to accept more international responsibility, most Germans were having none of it. They preferred to live in a country that minded its own business, a big Switzerland or Sweden. Germans were not eager to give up their culture of reticence, the pacifism and antinationalism that many considered a proud legacy of the post-Nazi period. Then came the Gulf War and the Bush administration's scavenger hunt for foreign sup-port in its crusade against the archnemesis in Baghdad. The war against Iraq was a smack in the face of Germans who grew up believing in the mantra of "Never again war." To think they could be criticized for failing to take part in a military adventure was inconceivable to many Germans. They cried foul over the west's unfair expectations, and refused to send troops. Even those who believed the Gulf War was a just cause felt paralyzed by the conflict it posed: "We had learned never to use military force again," said Karsten Voigt, the Social Democratic defense expert. "And we had learned never to do anything again that could threaten the Jews. Suddenly, the two were in conflict." Every Scud attack on Tel Aviv ratcheted up the anguish. Just as they were beginning a national debate over the German role in the world, along came a crisis that forced them to take sides. The government's response was to search for a neutral path. In truth, Bonn was damned either way: Sitting it out was cowardice and irresponsibility, a refusal to help the allies who had protected Germany for forty years. Sending in the military would violate every tenet of the pacifist philosophy that the west had drilled into the Germans after 1945—not to mention raising inevitable, if hypocritical, foreign fears of German militarism.

German politicians breathlessly sought to set a course. Foreign Minister Klaus Kinkel compared Germany to "a St. Bernard in the living room who runs the risk of breaking the china every time he shakes his tail. This does not mean we cannot represent our national interests like anyone else. Normalcy . . . must be our goal. But please remember, dear Germans, that we are not alone, that especially because of our history, we have a special responsibility." Acting as one with the other Europeans was the easy way out, and the most popular rhetorical device in Bonn. But Germany could no longer find refuge in wishful thinking about the demise of the nation-state. There was no unanimity of policy in Europe, not on the Gulf War, not on civil war in Bosnia, not on the threatening events in Russia. Germans would have to decide what was right for Germany.

When they weren't trying to hide behind the European flag, German leaders sought solace from their constitution. Kohl long insisted that the German Basic Law (the country's Constitution) forbade the Bundeswehr from taking part in U.N. military actions or in international coalitions such as the one that fought in Iraq. The constitution actually said nothing of the sort. Rather, as the country's high court affirmed in 1994, German forces were specifically permitted to join in "collective security" ventures with other countries. Kohl eventually shifted strategy and sent a few medics to Cambodia to augment U.N. forces in 1992 and a few troops to Somalia in 1993 to give technical support to Americans there. Frustrated by the parliamentary stalemate, Kohl was eager to follow the teachings of his mentor, Konrad Adenauer, West Germany's first chancellor. Over the strenuous objections of fresh-baked pacifists, Adenauer had rammed through the creation of the postwar military, the Bundeswehr, in 1955 because, as he later wrote in his memoirs, "Rearming is the path toward achieving the full sovereignty of the Federal Republic." Kohl, too, hoped to find German identity and stature through uniforms and arms. When the first contingent of Bundeswehr soldiers landed in Somalia, the German commander stepped off his Luftwaffe plane, strode over to waiting microphones and announced, "We are back in the family." Foreign criticism did subside, at least until the next military adventure.

Many German leaders did not share Kohl's appetite for a place at the global military table. In my last conversation with Willy Brandt before his death, the former chancellor was exasperated by American demands that Germany act its size militarily. "For someone of my age and experience," he said, "I have experienced things much more serious than young Germans liking peace." Similarly, President Weizsäcker told me, "The Germans are a European nation without a world role. We do not have it and we do not want it. We are liberated finally from the Mittellage [being caught between east and west] and from the temptations that marked our history. We will not become very global in outlook."

Inside the Bundeswehr, even senior officers were not prepared to give up their pacifism. The Bundeswehr was a Cold War army, structured and trained only for the great tank battle with the Soviets that was never going to happen. When officers in the Pentagon and NATO pushed their German counterparts to get involved in other world hot spots, they were surprised to find some Bundeswehr officers reluctant to help out. Just as only one-third of the German public favored joining NATO operations outside of Germany and even fewer supported participation in U.N. actions such as the Gulf War, many German officers believed their task was to protect German territory and nothing more.

After the Gulf War, when I visited Major General Helmut Willmann, commander of the 7th Tank Division, in the northwestern town of Unna, he was putting his men through a drill in which they practiced house-to-house combat in a small village. The scenario was modeled after a U.S. Army training exercise based on guerilla warfare against Islamic terrorists in Beirut. But no German soldier could imagine ever being sent to a place like Lebanon, and Willmann knew it. "For thirty years," he said, "we told ourselves, 'We are soldiers, but war will never come.' In our army, we have forgotten the reality of war. Young conscripts come to us not to defend Germany, but to become driving instructors or radio technicians."

The Bundeswehr is an army in which no one, not even the most senior officers, has ever commanded in battle. No one has taken a life or lost a buddy in combat. After unity, after the embarrassment of the Gulf War, Willmann's American, British and French colleagues glared at him. The general itched to prove his allegiance to the allies. "I cannot accept that American, British and French soldiers come home in body bags and we sit on the sidelines," Willmann said. "We must not create any more mistrust. We must fight for the dignity of our country."

Bravely said; not so easy to achieve. "The normal reaction of the normal German mother is, 'OK, my son has to defend his country, but I didn't raise him to die in Saudi Arabia,' " the general said. "My own wife, mother of my son, argued that he shouldn't have to go to Somalia or Yugoslavia. She'd only give up her son to defend her own country. It will never be politically acceptable in Germany to use draftees in operations outside of NATO territory. We would have mothers protesting in front of the barracks."

Even as the country's political elite struggled to expand Germany's military role, the army was shrinking under tight budget constraints, and the people seemed ever less certain that their country needed a military at all. The Defense Ministry's own polls showed that the percentage of Germans who thought their country could get along without an army soared from 15 percent in 1984 to 42 percent in 1990. The Gulf War made some Germans question their security, but pacifists hardened their positions. Four of five Germans considered the Gulf War morally wrong, according to an Infas Institute survey, and the attack on Iraq set off blockades of military bases, mass demonstrations, silent candlelight vigils, teach-ins, school cancellations in solidarity with the Iraqi people, and, above all, threats against American institutions and individuals. Ordinary Germans were so shocked by the destruction and carnage they saw on TV that doctors reported a surge of illness. The daily *Bild* printed tips on calming down from the trauma of the war reportage (the paper suggested long walks in the woods and yoga exercises). The *Frankfurter Allgemeine Zeitung,* the daily that serves Germany's establishment much as the *Wall Street Journal* does the American elite, finally erupted at its own countrymen. "What distinguishes the Germans from other peoples is not that they fear war, but that they fear war more than they love freedom."

I was ready to dismiss that as exasperated editorial hyperbole until my final round of interviews in Bonn at the end of my four years in Germany. I visited members of parliament, aides to the chancellor and the usual array of policy experts. Only later did I realize that nearly everyone I had seen belonged to what Germans call the successor generation, people born too late to have experienced Nazism, people who grew up during the postwar boom, amid the silence and guilt of a defeated land. They are the generation after Kohl, the people who will rule Germany at the dawn of the next century. These are the people who had taken pacifism and passivity to heart, the generation that fancied itself European rather than German. Norbert Gansel, fifty-two, deputy parliamentary leader for the Social Democrats, was a powerful but depressed man, a personality type that simply does not exist in American politics, a combination of morose pessimism and reflective self-pity that plays quite well to the fears and tensions of the postwar generation. Gansel chain-smoked, poured himself some brandy and stared out his office window onto the Rhine River. The lights in his office were off; the fading day was gray and damp. Gansel wore the casual uniform of Social Democratic politicians, a flowery sportshirt, open neck, jeans. I asked him about his party's failure to offer any vision of the country's future, any answer to the identity question.

"We lack the strong personalities with the will of leadership and the readiness to run a personal risk," Gansel said. "My party and my generation are not prepared to fight things through. The problem is, German politics cannot appeal to a national dream like yours can. There is no German dream. There is only German nightmare. People talk about returning to normalcy now that the Wall is down. What does normalcy mean in German history? And what does return mean? The German capacity to adapt is a problem. We suffer from a lack of mobility and risk, a lack of enterprise. Two world wars brought not only enormous territorial losses but millions of Germans who lost everything to bomb raids, like my family. The little pieces of jewelry, the china, all blown away by a bomb. And then, the terrible inflation at the end of the war. It all changed German society enormously. There is a German desire for security now. And we live in a time of insecurity. Insecurity never helps people live with insecurity. It only makes them more determined to maintain their security."

Gansel turned toward the river and spoke to it, sucking on his Lord Extras, his gravelly voice getting deeper and softer. "I've been in politics twenty-five years, in the Bundestag twenty years. I've never experienced a situation like this. We are not sure of anything. We have really no new ideas. We are Roosevelt's children. We live not in the world that Roosevelt wanted, but the world he left us, which is how it always is with fathers and children. We still have the Iron Curtain in our heads, because without it, we do not know what we are."

Gansel and his age cohort in the Social Democratic Party were dubbed the Tuscany Faction—stylish, richly tanned politicians who spent their leisure months in Italy and could not bring themselves to express a vision for the country they were supposed to rule. (Their party suffered from an aversion to power and leadership with roots extending back to the Weimar Republic, when the Social Democrats voluntarily ended their rule rather than work with the communists.) Kohl's generation, in contrast, was driven by the horrors and pain they experienced as children. Herbert Schnoor, interior minister of the western state of North Rhine–Westphalia, told me he went into politics in part because at age ten he watched the synagogue burn in his hometown on Kristallnacht in 1938. Those who came after the war had to go through the anguish of being German without the anguish of having been there. The successor generation suffered only a reflected guilt and the approbation of a world incensed by the acts of their parents. The burdens of history forced them—once again—to define themselves in the negative. They knew Hitler and Goebbels were charismatic leaders, so charisma was out. Leadership was intrinsically suspect. Power was to be avoided. The protected cocoon of postwar Germany provided few challenges to the postwar generation; times were good, the Allies took care of the rest. These young people were not inert; they tested their elders, revolted against established mores in a student rebellion that shook their society. But as they got older, this generation stayed true to its deeply ambivalent attitudes toward power and leadership. The very word for leader, Führer, had been poisoned by Hitler.

By the time unification presented them with new opportunities and responsibilities, the generation of Germans who will be in authority over the next two decades had taken the tradition of cultural pessimism to heart. They had made it through the Cold War with a timid, inoffensive ideal: the successful manager who aims for compromise and consensus, disdaining personal vision or charm. But an era of confrontation and confusion lay ahead, and the country needed a new sense of itself, a new model. Its leaders were, like their broken nation, incomplete and insecure. And yet they had no choice: If they were to save their country from a dangerous flirtation with extremism, Germany's elites would have to embrace the very symbols they had been taught to shy away from. They would have to seek a middle ground between the historic extremes of pacifism and militarism. They would have to master the honest balancing act of national interests with the postwar pledge to avoid going it alone. It would not be easy, but it had to be done. The alternative was instability and insecurity, and that prospect violated everything that Germans had been, as well as everything they had become.

Helmut Kohl
and the
Lust for Normalcy

ALL OF THIS—the chanting protesters, the cacophony of slogans on bed-sheet banners hoisted aloft by opposing factions, the parents who held children high so they could glimpse the men in suits—it was all so new that many among the thousands who lined the streets of Dresden watched with wonder. Blank faces lined the open field around the ruins of the Frauenkirche, once a majestic cathedral, now, like so much in this royal city, reduced to rubble by the raging, wild revenge of American and British firebombing in 1945. There were none of the pained smiles or forced waves of the old communist demonstrations. Everything being played out before the people of Dresden this cold December morning in 1989 was too fresh, too fragile to be worthy of the old expressions, the trained gestures of life under a regime that demanded public displays of assent and satisfaction, even—no, especially—when conditions warranted nothing of the sort.

But now he was coming, the big man himself, that impossibly round figure with the trenchcoat that seemed to have been cut at a carpet factory, a huge expanse of material wrapped around the Father of German Unity, the lisping, mumbling politician who was suddenly being greeted in these parts as something of a savior, a visionary, a cool calculator who had stared down the communists and seemed on the verge of unthinkable victory. The chant started as a low rumble in the back of the crowd, as the real ones always do. "Helmut, Helmut, Helmut," it began. The sounds echoed off the bombed-out shells of the palaces of the Saxon electors, the fire-blackened towers and cupolas of Baroque masterpieces, the landmarks of the Paris of the east, the dazzling city long since rotting away under the neglect of communists who declared their air pollution-free and then watched as buildings that once made adults teary with pride now crumbled from the most insidious of chemicals. "Helmut, Helmut, Helmut," the chant grew louder, more insistent.

Angry young kids dressed in black distributed handbills equating the conquering West Germans with Nazis, picturing the pols in Bonn as fat robber barons hungrily devouring East Germany, the latest addition to their empire. A couple of hundred people gathered around an oversized cartoon that won murmuring approval: "May I eat from your trough?" the little pig (East Germany) asked the great big pig (West Germany) as they both fattened up on a tankard full of a sloshing gruel labeled "Third World." Everyone could hear the chanting as it swept across the field now, but off on the fringes, the confused voices of a society in trauma were loud and clear. A couple of dozen skinheads rehearsed lines they would perfect in the coming years: "Germany for the Germans!" "Foreigners Out!" *"Heil Hitler!"* One middle-aged man, his brown fisherman's cap pulled snugly over his forehead, approached the new Nazis politely and said, "You are not permitted to say such things."

"Fuck off, old man!" came the reply. Such things simply hadn't happened before, weren't permitted. But now, suddenly, you could do things you would never have dreamed of a few weeks ago. People just stepped off the sidewalk wherever they liked and crossed, whatever the light, and no one stopped them. Some people called for all the communist leaders to be thrown in jail, and others shouted the kind of slogans no one had dared speak aloud in many years. And here in the center of town, hundreds now waved the West German flag as if it was their own.

Then, suddenly, there he was. The man they had seen on TV all those years, the embodiment of capitalism, direct descendent of the Nazis themselves—that's what teachers and factory bosses had always said about Helmut Kohl. But all of East Germany watched him for themselves on TV the night after the Wall fell: Kohl standing on the steps of West Berlin's City Hall, singing the national hymn even as the rude western kids booed him. In the east, Kohl was not the symbol of politics as usual, but a true hero. As he wiped tears from his broad, fleshy face on that historic November night after the Wall fell, he was ready to lead the easterners into an era of prosperity and freedom. Two weeks later, they watched him again, the West German chancellor, speaking to the nation as one, going on TV to announce a revolutionary ten-point plan, a timetable for the unspeakable—German unification. And now, just three weeks after that, he was here, in the east, on enemy territory, and the crowd felt the situation changing before their eyes.

As Helmut Kohl walked across the field, tens of thousands of people clapped hands rhythmically, chanting "Deutschland, Deutschland," and "Helmut, Helmut," and "Take us!" and "We are one people!" and even that most German cry of respect and honor, *"Sie leben hoch, hoch, hoch,"* a kind of "Hip, hip, hooray" reserved for royalty and other fine folk. As the crowd peacefully parted so that Kohl could make his way through what he would call his "bath in the masses," the two Germanys, ripped asunder by history's greatest of crimes, divided so long, so hopelessly, so bitterly, were united once more. Months of negotiations would follow. The Soviets would bluster, fake, cave and fade. The Brits and the French would toil busily behind the scenes to heap all kinds of debris onto the tracks, but nothing could derail this express, not now. On this day in Dresden, Kohl and the decent, dour man who had the misfortune to be East Germany's last communist prime minister, Hans Modrow, agreed to create something called a "treaty community," to remove all remaining barriers between their countries, and to present the country with a Christmas gift, the reopening of the Brandenburg Gate, Berlin's most majestic symbol. There was cautious, diplomatic talk of the "German question" and of taking "our neighbors' interests" into consideration, as Kohl said, but what really happened this day, to the German people and to Kohl, was not recorded in the annals of diplomacy nor in the voluminous texts released to the snarling pack of reporters. It happened on the streets and the plazas of Dresden, where, even as East German politicians continued to act as if they represented someone other than themselves, the people had decided otherwise. It happened on the makeshift platform at the foot of the jumble of stones that had been the magnificent Frauenkirche, the Church of Our Lady, a cathedral so beloved that even the godless communists had not dared clear the site, a place where piercing white TV lights now cut through the late afternoon haze. Kohl addressed 100,000 East Germans as "Ladies and gentlemen, my young friends, dear countrymen." With those words, the whole city erupted. As it would again a few moments later, when he promised, "We won't leave our countrymen in East Germany in the lurch."

They gladly and freely put their lives in the hands of a politician who seemed to understand them. Even if he didn't, he was the one man in a position to give them what they wanted, which was, in a word, out. "The revolutionary restructuring of East Germany is a continuing process," Modrow said that day. No, it was over.

"This is, if you will, a new experience for the Germans in their history," Kohl said at a press conference that day. Yes, but reporters clamored for more. Will you go down in history as the chancellor of German unity? Kohl talked about "confederative structures" and the East Germans' "right to self-determination." Yes, but when will change come? And finally, Kohl released his thin, wide smile, and said, "With such rapid change, you can't expect things to go too orderly. In West Germany, things may be too orderly."

There is a smile that stretches across Helmut Kohl's face in moments of triumph, a great, involuntary grin that bears no resemblance to the tight, practiced smile flashed by politicians worldwide. It is a child's smile, honest, infectious and pure, and beginning in the autumn of 1989, Kohl enjoyed a time in which he had more reason than most other world leaders to show his satisfaction. The smile was there in Dresden that December day when the Easterners called his name and begged for shelter. It was there a few months later, when Kohl returned to Bonn from the Soviet Union with Mikhail Gorbachev's acquiescence to German unity in hand. It was there in October 1990, when the first all-German parliament since World War II convened in Berlin's Reichstag. And it was there at the end of that year, when Kohl campaigned for reelection as the "chancellor for Germany," a sentinel of optimism who rejoiced that "after the Nazi time, war, total destruction, the Soviet occupation and forty years of communist East Germany, we are together, free citizens in a free country."

Kohl, an American diplomat told me then, "is parading around like a hunter who just shot a lion. He's insufferable, but it's delightful to watch." Kohl's success masked what he considered his weak spots, the kind of work he had always eschewed—symbolic politics and the rhetoric of emotion. The 1990 campaign was the first in postwar history to rely largely on emotion—that most feared of political forces in a traumatized land. Kohl and his opponent, the Social Democrat Oskar Lafontaine, faced off over whether it was proper to refer to Germany as the "Fatherland." The term made Lafontaine shudder with dread. It reeked of nationalism and stormtroopers, Lafontaine's campaign aides said. Kohl loved everything about the word: He used it to show that even a German could be patriotic. He recited it repeatedly because his father did. Above all, he savored it to enrage his opponents.

Kohl ordered up a campaign song that year, produced by a Hollywood studio. The opposition ridiculed the ditty, comparing it to "Tomorrow Belongs to Me," the chilling number sung by Hitler Youth members in the film Cabaret. But Kohl's men were pleased with their anthem, "Touch the Future." "Feel the power, touch the future, reach the heart," the choir sang in English. "See the moment, get the feeling, touch the spirit. Let the future turn to gold. It's our time. The future starts with today." But Kohl did not limit his emotional rhetoric to the bright and trite. When he spoke of his

visit to Auschwitz, a terrifying yet defining moment for any German politician, Kohl said simply, "You cannot say anything; there is only silence."

The chancellor's 1990 campaign was to be the beginning and the end of
his post-Wall honeymoon with the voters. He promised no new taxes and
then raised taxes; to many Germans east and west, that made Kohl a liar.
He promised a "blooming landscape" in the east in three to five years, and
when that didn't happen, many said he had betrayed them. He promised a
new, more active, more responsible international role for the larger, fully
sovereign Germany. When that didn't happen, some of Germany's allies
spoke of cowardice and broken promises and wondered whether the Germans really thought they could go on writing checks instead of shipping
their young men off to fight. In the years after unity, Kohl described to his
countrymen a place they no longer recognized, a country of tolerance and
hard work, a successful economy with a strong, stable democracy. The
chancellor's optimistic vision clashed with TV pictures of Turks and other
foreigners dying in fires and bombings set by young Germans. Kohl said
this was not Germany, this was not the country his generation had set out to
recreate. And so he would not go to the funerals of the children, or speak at
their memorial services. That, he let it be known, would be "condolence
tourism."

In those months, well after the euphoria of unity had worn thin, Kohl
once again became what he had been in his early years in office, the tough,
combative, vengeful pol who ran his party with an iron fist, schemed bril-
liantly to remain in control, and testily blamed the country's woes on dun-
derheaded industrialists, undisciplined teenage extremists and world
events beyond German control. No, he insisted, his dream of European unification had not been spoiled; it was merely going through a necessary period of retooling. No, he snapped, the Germans were not growing apart; it
was just taking longer than expected to complete the "inner" unification of
two peoples who had grown apart. And later, when he had hit bottom in the
polls and his optimistic tones were convincing no one, Kohl turned on his
own countrymen, insisting in one speech after another (quite courageously,
actually) that Germans had grown lazy and careless after decades of the affluence and success that his Christian Democratic party had bestowed upon
them.

This was a remarkable turnabout for a politician who had been toasted as
King Kohl and the sun chancellor back in the heady days after the Wall
opened. As ever, the climate could be read on the chancellor's ample face.
In place of the smile, Kohl frequently wore a tight-lipped grimace. His
Palatinate dialect grew thicker. "I am the federal chancellor," he would re-
mind insolent reporters and uppity opposition parliamentarians, as if there

had been some doubt. He developed phrases that he used like flyswatters to extinguish pesky criticism. Shouldn't German citizenship law be more liberal? "Germany is not an immigration country." Isn't violence against foreigners getting out of hand? "Germany is and will remain a foreigner-friendly country."

It had taken Kohl the better part of a lifetime to reach this point, to become the first chancellor to rival Konrad Adenauer in length of tenure, to become the unquestioned, unquestionable boss of his party, sole survivor of a generation of western leaders erased from the world scene with the end of the go-go eighties. He was not going to let a few policy problems derail him. If the reunited Germany was something new, a sovereign country preparing to stake out its own identity and its own interests in an increasingly complicated Europe, it would be Kohl's Germany. And that was no political slogan. In postwar Germany, so dominated by the past and the feverish desire to overcome it, your generation determined who you were and what you wanted your country to be. Kohl had long since pronounced himself "absolved by the mercy of late birth." His was the first generation that could, without guilt, claim credit for the economic miracle and the comfort it had brought its long-suffering people.

Kohl was born in 1930, in Ludwigshafen, a Rhine River city forty miles from the French border. In later years, Kohl would adopt the common habit of thinking of the Nazis as an alien force, referring routinely to them as if they were outsiders whose "will to exterminate was, in the end, directed also against our own people," as Kohl said in a 1989 speech. Kohl's was a Nazi childhood, even if his parents felt uncomfortable with the regime. One of Kohl's earliest, fondest memories was his family's acquisition of its first radio, a *Volksempfänger*, the propaganda machine's toehold on each German home. Kohl was nine when the war began and he went through several steps of the system's youth indoctrination programs. At age twelve, he joined the other boys of Ludwigshafen in a fire brigade that sought to limit damage from the 124 Allied firebombings of the city, a rain of flames in which 800,000 bombs were dropped between 1940 and 1945. At age fourteen, Kohl was removed to a children's refuge, and then to a physical training camp in Berchtesgaden, where he learned shooting, map reading and other military skills. From his early teens, Kohl showed a talent for leadership. He was head of a ten-boy Hitler Youth troop and later was chosen to be a courier, taking secret documents from Munich and Vienna to safekeeping in Berchtesgaden.

Kohl had been raised in a home where serious Catholicism blended with what Kohl described as a "measured sense of nation, without the danger of being lost in a nationalistic wave. My parents felt connected to their Father-

land," he wrote in a book about his youth, *My Parents' Home.* "They identified with its interests, without denying those of 'the others'; they held the
dates of German history in their heads; they were proud of the cultural
achievements of their people; they loved their heritage, its traditions, its
language, and they used the word 'Fatherland' completely naturally." Kohl's
father, Hans, was a World War I officer who later became a financial admin-
istrator for the Bavarian government. In 1933, the elder Kohl feared that
Hitler would push Germany back into war. Later, Helmut recalled, his father expressed abhorrence of the Nazi racial crimes. After the war, the father made a comment during a family vacation that stayed with Helmut:
"May God have mercy on us Germans if we have to pay penance" for what
the German military did during the war.

War's end found Helmut Kohl on the march, fleeing his Hitler Youth
camp just ahead of advancing American troops. On May 8, 1945, the day of
Germany's unconditional surrender, Kohl and his fellow teens were surrounded by a group of just-liberated Polish slave laborers, who beat the German youths, then turned them over to U.S. forces. The Americans assigned
the Germans to three weeks of farm labor, then dispatched them on a five-
week trek back home to the Rhineland. There, Kohl wasted no time launch-
ing his political career. After a brief stint as a farm trainee, he resumed
school, became active in student politics, and joined a European unification
movement that was soon banned by the French occupation authorities.
France was not yet converted to the notion of a united Europe. Kohl was not
to be dissuaded; he joined the Christian Democratic Union and began the
long climb through the party ranks. Tall, though not yet obese, Kohl was an
imposing figure who would be remembered decades later for his ability to
organize student dances, finagle access to U.S. food packets for his hungry
schoolmates, and finesse his own weakness in math and science by wowing
teachers with his command of history and philosophy.

Kohl's early years in politics—indeed, his entire career—recalls nothing
so much as the ward politics of a big, old American city, a brilliant accu-
mulation of favors and debts by a larger-than-life figure who shrewdly selects his allies, serves the needy and savages all who dare challenge his
rise. From the start, Kohl was, like so many of his generation, allergic to
ideology, almost contemptuous of content, and masterfully efficient at the
mechanics of amassing control. He turned a lackluster speaking style and a
paucity of charisma into an asset, appealing to a hurt nation's desire for
leadership that denied its name. Kohl was bright, even thoughtful, but he
always relished his role as the simple, small-town pol; the world leader who
spoke no foreign language; the stumbling, stubborn guy with the huge appetite; the chancellor intellectuals loved to hate. Kohl's Germany was one of

victims, not criminals, one where the tiny group of frustrated military commanders who finally conspired against Hitler less than a year before the end were honored, no, virtually worshiped, as embodying the true spirit of the German people. Kohl's Germany was a place of simple virtues, hard work and fairness, with a busy, careful people who had no more desire to be a world political player than did the gentle Swedes.

If his predecessors in the chancellery had sought to ease the world's lingering fears of a resurgent Germany, even as they presided over the creation of an economic superpower, Kohl took his country's rehabilitation a step further. Adenauer, the bridge from the Nazi generation to the economic miracle, had devoted himself to sinking German roots into the west, cementing the alliance with the United States. Willy Brandt was the first postwar chancellor who could add a moral element to his leadership, by virtue of biography (his courageous role in choosing exile during the Hitler years and then undertaking dangerous missions into the country to help the resistance) and his sense of political theater (his historic drop to his knees before the memorial to those who perished in the Warsaw ghetto). Kohl had no such sense of the dramatic. Rather, his personality splendidly matched his political goal—a seemingly average man seeking only that most unassuming and unthreatening of goals, normalcy.

Kohl cultivated an image of normalcy even in his personal life. Reporters loved to make fun of the Birkenstock slippers he wore at his desk and the collections of aquariums and elephant figurines that filled his office. But Kohl knew that millions of Germans changed their shoes when they came in from outdoors and millions more kept fish tanks at home. In a country with refreshingly little violent crime, Kohl could begin his weekend retreats to his bungalow in Oggersheim, near his childhood home, by ditching his security detail and wandering into a flower shop. He could and did stop into the neighborhood *Kneipe* (pub) in Oggersheim. Just as he had managed to maintain some degree of normalcy in his own life despite his position, so did he seek to make his country feel at ease with itself, despite the past.

Even before the Wall fell, Kohl had pressed his agenda. In 1984, Kohl, whose older brother Walter was killed while serving in the Wehrmacht in 1944, clasped hands with French President François Mitterrand as they paid respects to German and French World War I dead at a military cemetery at Verdun. Kohl sent a clear message: This chancellor saw no shame in honoring those who had served their country. Then, in 1985, Kohl weathered a public relations disaster and risked antagonizing his most valued allies to perform what he considered a long overdue act of healing. By inviting—and finally blackmailing—President Ronald Reagan to pay his respects at the German World War II military cemetery at Bitburg, where more than thirty Waffen-SS troops were buried, Kohl put the United States on notice that it was time to accept the Germans as equals, time finally to end the postwar probation. When war veterans and Jewish groups in the United States objected to the Bitburg visit, Reagan grew jittery. Kohl did not back off. Rather, he bet the farm: The chancellor called Reagan to say that if the president backed off from the visit, the Kohl government would fall. The chancellor aimed his message both at the wider world and at a domestic audience that he believed was finally ready to embrace its war dead and mourn without shame. German history is not just Auschwitz, Kohl often told his aides. It was left to President Richard von Weizsäcker to present the other side of the equation, to warn his countrymen that "anyone who closes his eyes to the past is blind to the present. . . . All of us, whether guilty or not, whether old or young, must accept the past. We are all affected by its consequences and liable for it."

As bold as Kohl's Bitburg gambit was, only the fall of the Wall freed him to push past the conditions of Germany's Cold War parole. The East German revolution was the signal for Kohl to break out of the "golden handcuffs" West Germany had gamely accepted to prove its postwar loyalty to the western allies. Just days after the Wall opened, without advance notice to Washington or the other western capitals, Kohl announced his ten-point plan for German unity. Those governments were miffed, and Kohl was unapologetic. "That's how the Americans consult us when they announce a policy—after the fact," said Horst Teltschik, Kohl's top foreign policy adviser. No one could ever doubt Kohl's devotion to a Germany that faces west. But sovereignty, he told his aides, was going to mean just that. Kohl's plan lacked an eleventh point that Poles said should have guaranteed their border with Germany. And it lacked an eleventh point that Jews argued should have recalled the Holocaust and pledged Germany to a future of tolerance and openness. Kohl never considered the kind of historical statement that the freely elected East German parliament would issue as its first major act four months later, a moving apology to victims of the Holocaust by a government that had spent four decades denying responsibility. There was no need for any such apology, Kohl aides told me. The chancellor believed Germany was beyond that, both externally and at home.

As the unification process sped along, Kohl promised that the new Germany would act its size, expand its military role to include participation in U.N. peacekeeping forces, and spend billions to stabilize the fragile independence of the east European countries. Kohl also had some demands of the west: He wanted German, the language of what was now Europe's most populous country, to join French and English as official languages of the European Community. He wanted Germany to sit alongside the world's other major powers on the United Nations Security Council. And above all, he wanted an end to condescending lectures from abroad about what Germany should or could do.

In the coming years, Kohl would repeatedly nudge his often-reluctant country toward an independent sense of itself, even as he continued his comforting rhetoric about European unity and the western alliance. In 1991, Kohl and Foreign Minister Hans-Dietrich Genscher virtually forced the European Community to reverse course on the dissolution of Yugoslavia and recognize the new countries of Slovenia and Croatia, without extracting even a paper guarantee of rights for Moslems and other ethnic minorities. Many Europeans would later conclude that German policy emboldened Serbia to charge ahead with its war on Bosnia. Kohl also decided to attend the reburial of Frederick the Great in Potsdam, a midnight ceremony at which politicians praised the Prussian virtues (rigor, discipline, military smarts) that many postwar Germans, east and west, found embarrassing.

Kohl was driven to show the outside world that Germany was not to be feared, but also not to be dismissed. If he chose to be the first western leader to meet with the shunned Austrian president, Kurt Waldheim, as Kohl did, inviting the old Wehrmacht lieutenant to lunch in Munich in 1992, then he alone would make that decision. And if Jewish groups called that gesture a display of "shocking moral insensitivity," then Kohl was confident enough to grab a microphone and tell reporters, "Whom I meet here in Munich, I as chancellor will decide. I do not need any advice on that." As always, Kohl was less interested in making a substantive point than in gaining political advantage. Kohl sought not to absolve Waldheim of participating in "acts of Nazi persecution," as the United States government had accused the former U.N. secretary-general, but rather to appeal to Germany's jittery conservatives, voters who might enjoy seeing their chancellor stand up to those foreigners who monitored the Germans' every utterance to assure against a drift back toward Nazism.

Again and again, Kohl risked the wrath of his foreign allies. The first dangerous moment came only a few weeks after the fall of the Wall, when Kohl refused to guarantee the East German–Polish border, named the Oder-Neisse line after the two rivers that define the frontier. No one ever accused Kohl of wanting to reclaim the Polish lands that had been part of Germany until Europe was carved anew at the end of the Thousand-Year Reich in 1945. But the chancellor was willing to provoke his allies and stonewall the Poles to send a message to those 12 million Germans who traced their heritage to territory taken from Germany at the end of World War II. Week after week, pressure mounted abroad. The Poles went ballistic, the Soviets muttered ominously, and even the Bush administration, which had a policy of supporting the Germans almost no matter what, broke silence to urge Kohl to guarantee the border. The chancellor insisted he could do no such thing. He was sorry, but his hands were tied. Legally, he could not make such a statement. The flap "considerably slowed down the process of German unity," the U.S. ambassador to Germany, Vernon Walters, told me.

At the height of the controversy, Kohl took the unusual step of inviting a small group of foreign correspondents to lunch. The chancellor was in an unusually testy mood that day. He snapped at the waitresses serving lunch because one of them accidentally banged one plate against another. "Not so loud, please!" Kohl shouted across the room. And again two minutes later, when a waitress clearing two glasses clinked them together, "Quieter! It's really terrible." Served last, Kohl waited impatiently for his food, holding his fork in his fist and tapping it against the table. The chancellor opened the discussion with an unsolicited comment on a story in the French paper *Le Monde* that characterized him as having "an appetite for two."

"When you work fifteen or sixteen hours a day, your eating habits get screwed up," Kohl said. And then, he nervously began reading from notes justifying his position. He recounted the legalities of parliamentary decisions about borders. He recited the numbers of West Germans who sent Care packages to Poland. And then he said, "You know also that terrible things were done to Germans by Poland after the war." Kohl insisted Germany would guarantee the border only if Poland dropped its claims to reparations for the 2.5 million Poles subjected to forced labor by the Nazis. He said it would be "criminally negligent" to back down from his refusal to affirm the border.

And then, less than forty-eight hours later, Kohl unconditionally reversed himself. "Mistakes were made on all sides, including by me," the chancellor said after Foreign Minister Genscher threatened to pull down the ruling three-party coalition. The border was set, the Poles could pursue their claims, the world could relax. And the German expellee community—those millions who had lost their homes and fled west after the war—knew their chancellor was on their side, even if the end result wasn't to their liking. As suddenly as the whole controversy had brewed, it vanished. At home, it was explained as simple politics. The chancellor needed conservative votes to win reelection that year; a bit of nationalistic muscle-flexing might help. The particular issue on which Kohl made that stand mattered hardly at all. I didn't realize how true that was until I learned that a decade earlier Kohl had approached a friendly German journalist, Peter Scholl-Latour, and told him that he wanted to do for German-Polish relations what Adenauer had done for German-French reconciliation. Kohl asked the journalist to write him a speech recognizing the postwar German-Polish border.

Scholl-Latour wrote the text and brought it to Kohl, who, in the interim, had spoken to his party advisers, who thought such a declaration might be unpopular among the exile community. So Kohl told the journalist thanks, but no thanks. "That's Kohl to me," Teltschik said. "He doesn't care a whit about the Polish border. He has virtually no interest in the content of political issues. His attitude is, 'Man, how can I win the next election?' "

Kohl was above all a pragmatist. He was no orator; indeed, throughout the unification process, he never once gave the kind of stirring speech, the pitch for the history books, that most politicians would have delivered. But to call Kohl content-free, as some of his aides did, was a bit much. Kohl always sought to justify his childhood decision to love his country. Toward that end, Kohl would even act in ways that defied his vaunted political savvy. In 1993, searching for a successor to President Weizsäcker, Kohl painted himself into a corner. Suffocating at the bottom of the polls in the east, the chancellor promised to pick an easterner for the largely symbolic, but nonetheless crucial, post of president. Kohl chose Steffen Heitmann, an unknown state official in Saxony, whose right-wing credentials and tough talk sounded the right tones for the chancellor's reelection interests.

But within days of the announcement that Heitmann was Kohl's man, the newcomer started inserting foot into mouth with alarming frequency. "Germany can only accept a limited amount of penetration by foreigners," Heitmann said, adding that the country was now "overrun with foreigners." He boasted that he had steered clear of participation in the 1989 revolt against the communist regime. He scolded eastern women for bellyaching about being removed from the workforce and advised them to keep quiet and raise families. And he said it was time for Germany to break the "taboos" of history and put the Holocaust "in its proper place."

After a few months of that kind of talk, Heitmann was eased into political oblivion. And, as he had been countless times in his decade in office, Kohl, too, was pronounced finished. Of course, Kohl could not have known how thoroughly Heitmann would self-destruct. But he did know he was picking a fringy fellow, as he had with Interior Minister Manfred Kanther, a hardliner whose law-and-order rhetoric was calculated to take the wind out of the sails of the far-right Republicans and the neo-Nazi shock troops on their flank. In the years after it became clear that unification would be a task for generations rather than a few years, Kohl took to playing with fire. Public frustration with Germany's direction—its dwindling economic power, its fraying social system, its deepening east-west divide—was spoiling Kohl's dream of Germany returning to equality with its allies. The chancellor was reluctant even to set foot in the five eastern states. He waited for months in 1991 before summoning the courage to face the seething electorate in the east. On that trip, he was greeted in Erfurt by eggs, boos, catcalls, and street theater, including an elaborate funeral for Truth (a reaction to Kohl's "no new taxes" about-face.)

Kohl charged ahead with his push for normalcy. For more than two years, through more than 2,000 violent attacks on foreigners, through murders and bombings, Kohl refused all entreaties, even from close advisers, to make any public gesture of sympathy toward Germany's 6 million foreign residents. Unlike Weizsäcker, Kohl never went to a refugee shelter or a foreign family's home to show solidarity. Kohl rejected his staff's recommendation that he go to the Sachsenhausen concentration camp near Berlin after neo-Nazis burned down the Jewish Barracks there. Instead, Kohl pushed for policies that Franz Schönhuber, the former SS officer who headed the far-right Republican party, said were "precisely what our program called for."

At a celebration of his tenth anniversary in office, in the midst of a torrent of antiforeigner attacks, Kohl's speech included the ritual nod toward the Nazi burden, but with a sharp reminder that those times were long ago. "The horrible acts of Nazi barbarism remain tied to the German name. That remains a shame for our country. Now, we need to listen to each other, to talk with one another, and above all, to believe in the future of our country. But antiforeigner sentiment and traces of anti-Semitism, of course, are not Germany." Despite his public opposition to the idea, Kohl privately believed in setting up an immigration system, aides said. But for political reasons, the chancellor and his party adopted the slogans of their far-right opposition, focusing on foreigners as a destabilizing force in German society.

Kohl knew that polls repeatedly showed two-thirds of Germans eager to draw a thick line separating themselves from the Nazi past. The chancellor believed his country was ready to jettison the timid, atoning, shuffling personality of the West Germany that emerged from postwar American domination. Kohl's attitude toward far-right violence was not a result of any political nationalism unleashed by reunification. Rather, it was a calculated, if shortsighted, reaction designed to keep Kohl in power long enough to show the world and the German people that the Nazi legacy was truly dead and buried. The chancellor longed for a Germany that would be permitted to step down from the dock and be a country that could make mistakes and follow policies—whether brilliant or boneheaded—without echoes of goose steps.

To achieve that, Kohl believed he had to remain in office, possibly for the rest of the century. Kohl saw himself as the last German leader whose views were formed by memories of the war and the U.S.-led reconstruction of a devastated land. He knew he was the last German chancellor who would

feel an emotional bond to the United States, a connection born of eating
from Care packages and chatting up GIs for a stick of gum. He saw the
United States as the only dependable guarantor of peace and stability in
Europe, and he believed that only the American military presence in Germany and western Europe protected Germany against the Sonderweg, the
temptation to break away from its western anchors and go it alone. For all
his pride in Fatherland and the trustworthiness of the new Germany, Kohl
knew his country needed to be tied irrevocably to its western friends, or else
the lures of the east—as economic market, political playground and perhaps even military battlefield—might eventually prove too strong. Kohl
worried that he would be the last chancellor to view European unification as
the crucial barrier against a return to Germany's classic—and ultimately
self-destructive—tendency to seek its fortunes by twisting arms to its east.
That self-image may sound grandiose, but much of it was true. Germany did
lack political figures with a strong sense of national purpose or identity. Being world champion in exports was no longer enough, especially since Germany was in grave danger of losing that title. And German politicians of the
next generation, whatever their political bent, did have a more ambivalent
attitude toward Americans. Most accepted the notion that the U.S. military
presence was critical to maintaining stability in Europe. But that support
for U.S. troops was tempered by considerable skepticism about the degen-
erative effect of American culture on German society and the arrogance and
condescension of the world's only remaining superpower. Kohl squared his
doubts about the United States with his deep respect for the country, its
power, and above all, its generosity of spirit.

Kohl was a man torn between his everlasting belief that there was nothing abnormal about the country that had honored him with a rich life and its
highest post, and his gnawing desire to have his allies abroad share that
trust in Germany. Kohl was also a consummate electoral politician of the
old school, a German Lyndon Johnson, an operator who felt it necessary
every few years to wipe out rivals within his own party. The result was a
"tabula rasa" that would leave his Christian Democrats stripped clean of
attractive figures for decades. This combination of bedrock confidence in
his own sense of nation, hunger for foreign approval, and instinctive political ruthlessness created a chancellor of contradictions. Kohl could threaten
to declare a national state of emergency to combat the influx of foreigners
into the country, then turn around and profess to be stunned that U.S. con-
gressmen and opinion leaders were concerned about Germany's direction.

In 1994, Kohl, no longer able to base a campaign on economic strength
and personal optimism, became a scold. He told Germans they needed a
"new awakening," something to shake them out of their loafing and whining,

something to put them back to work. In his final election campaign, Kohl had three choices, none of them terribly appealing. He could blame his own policies for his country's troubles—a nonstarter. He could blame forces outside Germany—which, to some extent, he did, tracing some problems to the worldwide recession and the onslaught of immigrants. But to his credit, Kohl focused considerable rhetorical attention on basic, structural problems in his own society. "No other country would have responded to its unification—a gift of history—with so much public brooding," Kohl told one audience. "One reason for this, at least here in the west, is our unprecedented prosperity, something that motivated many . . . to react with excessive nervousness or even hysteria to the slightest fluctuations and changes." Kohl believed that by appealing to German insecurities and presenting himself as the only alternative to radical experimentation, he could once more cheat the popularity polls and slide into office. On the occasion of his tenth anniversary in office in 1993, the chancellor's staff gave their boss framed clippings of newspaper articles announcing his political death over the years. Kohl roared with laughter over the gift, clearly relishing the chance to inspire more such news copy.

In October 1994, he cheated political death—barely. Kohl won the narrowest of victories over a hapless Social Democratic opposition. His Christian Democrats limped back into office with barely four in ten votes. Their partners, the Free Democrats, seemed headed for extinction. Kohl had achieved his main goals, neutralizing the extremist parties of the left and the right, but the majority of German voters were ready for someone fresh, if only such a person would appear. Absent any attractive figure, Kohl was still in charge, but his position was so weak, he would have trouble getting anything through parliament. The passing of the generational baton had been postponed; the country seemed headed toward several years of stagnation.

But Kohl, as always, kept normalcy on the agenda. He took personal control over the renovation of the tomblike Neue Wache, the former imperial guardhouse on Unter den Linden, eastern Berlin's main boulevard. Despite widespread protests, the chancellor decided that the monument—which the communists had used to show off their goose-stepping honor guard—should be the country's central war memorial, dedicated to both the perpetrators and the victims of the Holocaust. Overruling his own panel of historians and curators, Kohl chose the centerpiece of the building, a Käthe Kollwitz statue of a grieving woman slumped over her dead son, a Pietà. Built by the Prussians in honor of those who fell in battle against Napoleonic forces, the Neue Wache reopened in 1993 with a new inscription, TO THE VICTIMS OF WAR AND TYRANNY. That confusion of soldiers and civilians, victims and perpetrators, Jews and Christians in a single memorial—as well as the use of a Christian symbol to recall the murder of 6 million Jews—led to considerable protest, but Kohl would not be moved.

For all his apparent confidence in the German people, for all his public certainty that the Nazi yoke could one day be cast off, Kohl was, in the end, not really so certain. A close aide told me that even in that magnificent moment on the field in Dresden in 1989, Kohl was worried sick that the crowd would burst into the forbidden first stanza of the national anthem, the one that begins, "Deutschland, Deutschland, über Alles," rather than the West German alternative lines of "Unity and Law and Freedom." Later, during the wave of antiforeigner violence between 1991 and 1993, Kohl tried to maintain an aloof public image. Behind the scenes, he was so upset by the attacks' impact on Germany's foreign image that he ordered American and British newspaper articles translated and put on his desk each morning. The chancellor was rattled: During those same months, aides said, Kohl often angrily cut off discussions of right-wing violence. He did not want to hear it.

Unification had seemed at first blush a crowning glory, a historic achievement that would resolve the German Question at home and abroad. With the calming overlay of European unity, the Germans could now convince their friends and neighbors that fears of the volatile nation at the center of the continent were unfounded. "In this century, a lot of terrible things happened, things done in the German name," Kohl told me in an interview at the peak of the unification process. "This is an opportunity for the Germans and for me as head of the government to try to make a contribution to redress that balance, to put in order that which has been put in disorder. . . . If we believe that Germany is my Fatherland and Europe my future, then the problem is solved."

Two years later, Kohl could no longer muster that kind of ebullience. He was convinced that if European unification was not completed, if his generation could not etch in stone Germany's commitments to the west, his country would drift back into the danger zone. He had, aides said, completely personalized this stage of German history. He truly believed in the slogan he had originally planned to use in the 1990 campaign, before the revolutions of 1989 altered the electoral calculus. "It's me or chaos," Kohl had planned to say. In a 1993 television interview, Kohl admonished the Germans to stop moping about the hardships of unification and start doing something about it. He reminded them of the sufferings of war, and of what he had seen when he was a young boy. And he warned, in a way that no other western leader had in recent years, that "the old evils" had not vanished for good, that in a very few years, Europe would stand once more before a decision between war and peace. "If we are not successful in binding

German unity and European unity together in the next few years," he said, "we will have failed before history, and the generation of our grandchildren will have to pay bitter penance for that. We need a new framework for living together. All of us in Europe need that, but the Germans need it more. If we don't build a common European roof over the united Germany, we will see—although many don't believe this—that the old evil spirits now on view in Yugoslavia will return to central Europe. We are not immune to nationalism, chauvinism, and hatred of foreigners, to all the evil spirits that have found a home here often enough."

PART II

◄◦►

The Wall
Between
Germans East
and West

AFTER THE WALL came an experiment that could not be permitted to fail. It would be extraordinarily expensive and unexpectedly painful. It would prompt Germans east and west to wonder what really bound them together. The eastern German experience in the years after unification is fascinating on its own: Unlike their impoverished neighbors behind the former Iron Curtain, eastern Germans had all the tangible resources they needed to make the transition from communism to capitalism. A generous government in Bonn saw to that. (And for all their resentments, western Germans swallowed huge tax hikes to pay for the reconstruction of the east.) The easterners' monumental struggle despite all that support demonstrates how deeply the totalitarian system had been suffused into the spirits of many Ossis.

But the eastern Germans' story is essential for another reason, as I discovered when I moved from Bonn to Berlin in 1991: It is a particularly revealing window onto postwar German identity. Separated from their cousins for four decades, the easterners, including the once proud Prussians and Saxons, had been locked out of their country's recovery, denied its wealth. By the end of the nineties, their part of Germany will boast the country's best infrastructure and most advanced technology. Yet eastern Germans continue to see themselves as second-class citizens. Punished twice by this century's sociopathic ideologies, Germany's east bears the wounds of the Cold War without having reaped its benefits—a burden that often seems unfair.

Few in the east would return to the oppression, conformity and environmental ruin of the communist years, but many dream of a day when their western brethren can understand the sacrifices forced upon those who were caught on the wrong side of the Wall. Only then, they say, will it mean the same thing to be German in Dresden as it does in Cologne. Only then will the rest of the world be able to speak dependably about a single Germany.

5

The Ossietzky
School

IN THE MOST hard-line state in the Soviet world, freedom lay in waiting in
the high school Russian class. The revolutions of 1989 had roots tracing to
Germany's Ostpolitik and the Soviet Union's economic crisis, to the arms
race and to the repressive regimes of the East Bloc and their cynical stand
against reform. But the collapse itself began in the most logical yet unex-
pected way: from below. Long before the thousands began their flight to the
west, many months before the millions began their candlelight protest
marches around East German cities, a handful of students at one school in
an East Berlin neighborhood of shade trees and true believers managed to
shake their country's geriatric leaders to the core. The Carl Ossietzky
School was a magnificent structure, a concrete fortress lightened by Art
Nouveau flair, an interior that spoke of serious learning and the importance
of the intricate. In Erich Honecker's workers' paradise, the Ossietzky
School was a palace of privilege. Located in Pankow, the favored neighborhood for many of the communist party's most dedicated servants, the school
always boasted among its students—selected after rigorous screening for
intellectual potential and political pedigree—the children of the powerful,
sons and daughters of Politburo members, government ministers, the military and diplomatic elite and the offspring of some of the most courageous
dissidents.

The story of the Ossietzky School—indeed, the saga of East Germany's
belated, truncated revolution and what followed—is one of history's gifts to

understanding. These were the Germans stripped of western riches, clean of creeping Americanism and postmodern artifice. Their struggle to deal with stress and opportunity, and the evolution of their troubled relations with their western cousins, provide a window onto a society plagued with a chronic case of identity deficit disorder.

At Ossietzky, as in every East German school, the curriculum was mandated by the dictatorial education minister, Margot Honecker, sharp-tongued wife of the country's supreme leader. Just as the Honeckers had worked together since the 1960s to combat the incursion of Western beliefs over their beloved Antifascist Protective Barrier—the Berlin Wall—so did they seek to smash any influence from Mikhail Gorbachev's revolutionary ideas about openness and reform. "If your neighbor put up some new wallpaper, would you feel obliged to do the same?" asked East Germany's chief of ideology, Kurt Hager. German socialism was different, the Honeckers believed. Besieged from both sides, it had to be defended with a vengeance. Born from the trauma of war, this socialism was the sole foundation of its state. Unlike Czechoslovakia, Poland or Hungary, this communist state's calls to patriotic duty or nationalist tradition fell flat. The East German regime could not mix its own home brew of Leninist theory and national identity. East Germany could justify its existence only one way: It was the communist German state, in sharp and eternal opposition to the capitalist German state across the Wall. The stakes, Honecker believed, were too high to permit any other formulation. Even nearly half a century after the war, he would tell interviewers, the forces of fascism were strong enough to require strict controls on information, travel and political dissent. Gorbachev's reform agenda was the greatest threat to Honecker's country since the mass emigration that prompted the erection of the Wall in 1961. Yet as a virtual colony of the Soviet Union, East Germany could not dare build walls against the great bear that still kept 400,000 troops on German soil. Instead, the Honeckers picked their battles.

The foment in the Soviet press particularly frightened the overseers of East German information policy. The Stasi secret police had done a splendid job of suppressing dissent, creating a network of informants that was perhaps the state of the art in the East Bloc's struggle against wayward thinking. The Wall helped, to be sure. Anytime the East Germans determined that someone stepped too far out of line, the offending party could be sold to the west, eliminating the problem and earning hard cash in one simple step. But beginning in 1985, East German teenagers and their teachers discovered that while their government resolutely resisted Gorbachev's *glasnost* policy of openness, they could snatch an illicit glimpse of a changing world in each school's most widely despised classes—the mandatory

Russian language lessons. Soviet newspapers and magazines used in language instruction were increasingly suffused with all manner of forbidden material—political essays, reportage on social problems, frank discussions of corruption and east-west relations.

At Ossietzky, students and teachers devoured every new copy of *Moscow News* and *Literaturnaya Gazeta,* marveling as the certainties of official history faltered and crumbled. Soon, the school's more liberal teachers slacked off on teaching the required version of Stalinism. With the quiet blessing of school director Rainer Forner, Soviet publications—arriving now with articles and entire pages snipped out by East German censors—drifted from language classrooms into history, Marxism-Leninism and other classes, in direct violation of state policy. Then, in 1987, *Sputnik,* the German-language magazine the Soviets had long published to promote goodwill among the subject people of East Germany, began to export Gorbachev's new attitude. This direct proselytizing of *glasnost* alarmed Erich Honecker, who banned the magazine. At Ossietzky, the idea that the Honecker regime was cutting up and banning Soviet newspapers seeded student and faculty cynicism.

The cancellation of the school's subscription to *Sputnik* forced a confrontation. Several students wrote letters to government offices protesting the loss of their favorite magazine. Immediately, the school director got rockets from the government asking why Ossietzky students had sent such letters. Parents—especially the most prominent ones—wanted to know why their children were coming home uttering heresies that could get the entire family in hot water. Parents summoned Forner to meetings and passed word of the student rebellion to the highest levels of the communist party. But Forner, like a rising number of loyal East Germans, was no longer cowed by the ritual discipline of the state or the conformist angst of the *nomenklatura.* He was beyond the reach of letters of reprimand. Indeed, the director soon would allow his pupils to go even further, so far beyond the pale that a single school on a quiet, leafy Berlin street would become the subject of urgent Politburo discussion.

Those were months of rapidly declining public confidence in the communist regime. When the rock group Pink Floyd played an outdoor summer concert on the western side of the Wall in 1987, several thousand partying East Berliners thronged up against their side of the divide, straining to hear each forbidden lyric. When the police tried to push back the crowd, the people chanted Gorbachev's name. In January 1988, several prominent human rights protesters, including Bärbel Bohley, who would go on to play a leading role in the fall 1989 revolution, were arrested when they distributed petitions calling for liberal travel laws and a free press. The old men in

Berlin remained unmoved, but the winds blowing from Moscow were encouraging. In February 1988, Gorbachev told the Soviet Communist party's central committee that every people had the right to "choose freely its social and political system." In East Berlin, the appalled elders of the government reacted by expanding their ban on Soviet heresy: They ordered Soviet films removed from all East German cinemas. And then, May 1989 brought local elections that were crassly and obviously fixed, producing a 98.85 percent margin for officially sanctioned candidates when opposition and abstentions were plainly at all-time highs. Even loyal communists could no longer take seriously the country's farce of a democratic vote. At Ossietzky, students began voicing doubts they dared not express at home.

"The official policy was that we don't need *perestroika* and *glasnost* here," Forner said. "But the students kept asking why. All attempts to keep the country's problems separate from school were failures. We had to make compromises almost daily. I wanted the students to speak openly. But we had to be able to be sure that this discussion never left the inside of the school, because every attempt we made to let students criticize conditions in our country was interpreted as antisocialism. We tried to enforce very strict rules about how far our discussions could go. Students could criticize, but it could never be antisocialist."

But once the criticism began, there was no tempering the flow. In 1988, shortly before the annual military parade that would mark the thirty-ninth anniversary of East Germany's founding, about a dozen Ossietzky students chalked a petition on a classroom blackboard protesting the use of tanks and artillery to celebrate the birthday. Among the students who led the protest was Carsten Krenz, son of Egon Krenz, Honecker's hard-line deputy and eventual successor. Another of the troublemakers was the son of Vera Wollenberger, a prominent human rights activist who had recently been arrested and imprisoned for demonstrating against the government's denial of due process and free speech to dissidents. At party headquarters, word of the petition spread quickly and led inevitably to a crackdown. Officials of the Education Ministry visited Forner and graphically explained his alternatives: Admit he had erred in fostering antisocialist behavior, or watch his career end without a trace.

Forner stood by helplessly as Margot Honecker sent three of her own senior officials into Ossietzky to supervise the school. "They said we were not qualified to lead the school politically," said Annerose Gerecke, the school's deputy director. "The supervisors were here every day from 7 A.M. to 8 P.M. They took Herr Forner by the hand every step of the way. They said he had to be helped. They said we were politically negligent even to listen to opposing views." Gerecke and several other school administrators were required to write and deliver self-criticisms before their colleagues. Forner was ordered to meet with parents individually to apologize for the incident and explain the school's protections against antisocialist activities. Two students were transferred to another school. Four were expelled. And several others, including young Krenz, were reprimanded.

But if the old men of the Politburo thought they had nipped this outburst of dissent in the bud, they were blind to dissatisfaction oozing up throughout the long-repressed society. The state still remained confident in its machinery of repression. East Germany had never produced a Havel or a Walesa. There was no renegade union to fear, no underground press to quash. The country's leading intellectuals—writers such as Christa Wolf or Stefan Heym—occasionally uttered mild criticism of the system, but generally preferred to be co-opted by the status and perks offered to artists in official favor. True rebels were quickly and efficiently neutralized. Some were enlisted to work as Stasi informants, allowing them to maintain their illusion of opposition even as their reports helped the secret police limit dissidents to a state-written script. Others were punished brutally or subtly, in mental hospitals or through complicated campaigns designed to ruin reputations and destabilize fragile minds. Finally, there was the ultimate sanction: removal from the country. Before the Wall finally fell, West Germany bought freedom for 250,000 East Germans and opened the gates for thousands of elderly people, freeing the East of expensive pension obligations. The west's willingness—eagerness, even—to take in troublemakers as their own was seen in Bonn as a humane, liberal policy. But it allowed the Honecker government to prevent the development of the angry circles of professors, journalists, writers, scientists, women and students who corroded totalitarianism elsewhere in the East Bloc in the 1970s and '80s.

East German intellectuals tended to act as the system wanted them to—up to the very end, when many underwent overnight conversions to the capitalist credo. Until the final days of the Honecker regime, Kurt Masur, conductor of the Leipzig Gewandhaus Orchestra and, later, of the New York Philharmonic as well, conformed to the role of good East German intellectual. Masur was, if one accepts his public pronouncements at the time, always willing to do his part for the cause, even if he said he never belonged to the communist party. He was a personal favorite of Honecker's. Masur's travels and recordings were an important source of hard currency for a country swimming in debt. For his support of the system, Masur was rewarded with one of the most expensive and impressive public works projects of the country's forty-year history, the Leipzig Gewandhaus, a marvelous concert hall on the city's main square. Honecker personally approved and supervised the project.

When I first interviewed Masur a month after the Wall opened, Honecker was gone but the country's future was still quite uncertain. Masur was basking in the publicity generated by his courageous role in helping to prevent police violence against citizen demonstrators in the 1989 revolution. But unlike his countrymen who were testing their new freedoms with considerable abandon, the maestro wasn't ready to cut off his benefactors. The party was down, but not yet for the count. "We don't need any alms from the west," Masur said. "All these years, we were able to resist the wonderful temptation of the beautiful fruit and cheese in the [West German] shop windows. We can be a better democracy than the other in the west. All these people on the street who are clamoring for unification have to realize that the SED [the Socialist Unity party, the communists' official name] is an established organization and they are trying to change."

Even as unification grew more likely daily, Masur argued that the communist system was no impediment to artistic excellence. "Look at the house where Schiller was born," Masur said. "No one would move into it today. No one could be moved to write the 'Ode to Joy' living in that house today. But look: Even though they were limited by their surroundings—the tiny houses of that era—people were free to create." Similarly, he said, the people of East Germany faced difficult times and considerable deprivation. But spiritually, they could carve out the freedom to create good works. "As artists, we had privileges," he said, "but we've also helped people. I never lost my head in excesses. I tried always to remain who I am. I wouldn't give much credence to this anger of the people you hear so much about. Of course, people had to live so long without being able to travel, and that was wrong." Masur conceded it was impossible to have a career in the arts without playing along politically. He recalled his own near-rebellion in the 1960s, when he told his handlers at the Culture Ministry he would flee to the west if he didn't get permission to perform there. He got both the visa he wanted and a new job as conductor of the Dresden Philharmonic. He was theirs.

A violinist who played under Masur at Berlin's Comic Opera in the 1960s, Jakob Wirtz, recalled that the conductor had long been a servant of political fashion. The day after Honecker built the Wall in 1961, Wirtz maintains, Masur came into rehearsal wearing—for the first time—a communist party pin on his lapel. "We were all shocked," Wirtz said. "Then he told those of us who lived in the west of the city—and we were probably almost half the orchestra—that we must either move to the east or leave the orchestra. It was the saddest day of my life."

Masur denied wearing the party pin and said the West Berlin musicians at first were allowed to remain in the Comic Opera. "But then they found that half of the orchestra had one lifestyle, with cars and big apartments, and the other half had another lifestyle. This makes problems, so eventually some had to leave. It was unfortunate."

Masur was clearly uncomfortable talking about the politics of East German art when the country was still a police state teetering at the edge of self-dissolution. Blessed with a magisterial voice and majestic blue eyes, Masur could play the dictatorial maestro when he cared to, but he was a gentler man than many of his colleagues in the musical stratosphere, and sitting in a sun-drenched room of his own concert hall, he could afford to display his uncertainties to a foreign visitor. Leaning forward as if in search of approval, Masur described navigating a middle course between confrontation and co-option. He scoffed at East German artists who "didn't realize that the words they used had been used too much to have any power anymore—power, trust, socialism. They lost their meaning." And he recounted how, in the final days of the Honecker regime, he did step forward, along with five other Leipzig luminaries. In Leipzig, Berlin and other cities, police had been using rubber truncheons, water hoses and sticks against the soaring legions of demonstrators. In Leipzig, on Monday, October 9, 1989, there would be no Chinese solution, even if the authorities in Berlin had ordered violence. Masur and five other city leaders took to the radio and the city's public address system to beseech local military commanders not to use force against their own citizens. It was a watershed in the mounting revolt against the government. Although some have argued that Masur and the others switched sides only so they would not go down with their doomed rulers, the outcome of that fall's events was not yet certain in October. Masur and his impromptu committee risked their reputations, even their lives. Perhaps it was the conductor's way of proving to himself that despite decades of doing things the system's way, he could indeed still answer to his conscience. Perhaps he recalled the stained reputations of Herbert von Karajan and Wilhelm Furtwängler, great conductors whose Nazi sympathies tarnished lives of supreme artistry.

"To have power is a very dangerous thing," Masur said. "Who in my profession can overcome vanity so well that he can say Karajan was the greatest conductor? Yes, I wrote a letter to Honecker at his retirement, wishing him health and thanking him for building this concert hall. You know, this man Honecker had dreams as a young man. Sigmund Freud should discover what happened to him. He lost family members in the concentration camps, he resisted Hitler. For many years, he fought for his ideas. Then came Gorbachev and suddenly there was a great politician in the world who stole the show from Honecker in his own country. Some people cannot overcome their selfishness." At the end, Masur could afford to be modest and self-satisfied. "I only tried to stop something bad," he said. "The events in

October required that someone who had a certain influence try to do what must be done—a humanitarian gesture. I was, briefly, a politician against my will."

Masur has spun around himself a useful and moving myth, but the full story is, like much in a repressive society, murky, contradictory, and ultimately, tragically human. Police records made public after the demise of East Germany revealed that the communist authorities quashed criminal charges against Masur after a 1972 car crash in which the conductor apparently fell asleep at the wheel. Three people, including Masur's wife, died in the accident. The communist government went to some lengths to keep the incident quiet, hoping to save their star performer from prosecution and a loss of prestige. After the father of one of the crash victims wrote to then–East German leader Walter Ulbricht to complain that the police refused to investigate the incident, the family was offered a new car. Masur later said the government's decision not to prosecute him was "legally contestable," but that the loss of his wife was deemed punishment enough. Did Masur feel trapped in his country's debt after that? Or did he simply relish remaining at the helm of his country's premier musical organization, bringing light into the milky grit of the Leipzig winter sky? Like so many others, Masur made choices, and like people in any society, he found some paths easier than others. His government was artful at dangling its offers in the most attractive manner. Masur was far from alone in choosing compromise over the painful, heroic way of a Havel or a Walesa.

As late as 1988, a young East German could write an essay called "The Phantom of East German Opposition"—published in West Germany, of course. Those brave few who stood their ground sometimes managed to remain in the country, usually because they criticized only Honecker's execution of communism, not its ideological foundations. Unlike many of the dissidents who filled the prisons and mental wards of other Soviet satellites, East Germans were often like the true believers at Ossietzky, dedicated socialists with no secret hankering for western ways. They wished only that their leaders would show a more human face. To call this an opposition would be overly generous. It was, rather, a dissident faction that the government easily dismissed as intellectual dreamers and religious cranks. In those days, intellectuals on the fringe of the East German polity were not terribly different from many working-class East Germans in their dependence on the state for cradle-to-grave security. Unlike other East Bloc countries, East Germany could for many years rely on a popular consensus that the welfare state compensated at least somewhat for the material deprivations of the Soviet empire. But East German socialism could not live up to its ideology, while West Germany offered its citizens a far greater level of affluence and a much better blend of individual rights and collective well-being.

All Germans wanted their state to provide them with the essentials they or their parents had gone without in those painful postwar years of shame and defeat. Jobs, housing, child care, medical service, funeral benefits—both Germanys delivered state-guaranteed basics. And both were rewarded—at least for a time—with support from large majorities of their populations. Even if a Solidarity had developed in East Germany, it would have drawn precious little support before the late eighties. Popular consensus in the east broke down only when the country's inability and unwillingness to provide a standard of living anywhere near that of the west was revealed to be the result of deliberate policy, a corrupt wizardry manipulated by the old men behind the Politburo curtain. Only after the gerontocracy's corruption and inflexibility were laid bare did the popular craving for jeans, VCRs and V-6 cars take center stage. People wanted the world they saw each night on western television.

Even the few dissidents who stood up to state pressure over the long run remained surprisingly loyal, identifying with their oppressors. The east's most prominent renegade was Wolf Biermann, an enormously popular folksinger who combined the voice of a Theodore Bikel with the potent wit and anger of a Lenny Bruce. In 1964, the East German Culture Ministry banned Biermann from performing publicly. He nonetheless managed to become the best-known performer in the east, thanks to western publishers, record companies and radio stations, which pumped his words and sounds back across the Wall. While Biermann was in the West German city of Cologne for a concert in 1976, the East Berlin government revoked his citizenship. Thirteen years later, Biermann was a mercurial man with a thick black mustache. His voice surprised with softness and shook with anger; his droopy eyes spoke of the exhaustion and exasperation of one who was tired of always being right. He was a committed leftist whose father and nineteen other relatives were murdered in Nazi concentration camps because they were Jews or communists or both. "In East Germany," Biermann once wrote, "no one has as much difficulty as a genuine communist."

In December 1989, when I saw him at his first concert in East Berlin after being allowed back across the Wall, Biermann drew a nostalgic audience of a few hundred. He sang a ballad in which the Politburo appeared as a flock of blackbirds in a dream, finally ready to "forgive us for all the bad things they did to us." But by then, Biermann's political agenda—a separate East Germany in search of socialism without state repression—had been displaced by popular infatuation with the magic of reunification. Two

blocks from the concert hall, East Germans chuckled at the idea of the rebellious singer, now settled into a lumpy middle age, returning to the House
of Young Talent. Biermann scolded his countrymen for their desire to disappear into the very West German society that he found constricting, selfish
and overly competitive, a society that had made him a celebrity, with a life
in Hamburg far more comfortable even than that inside the walls of the
communist party's leafy ghetto at Wandlitz near Berlin. Outside of intellectual circles where people had extensive, illicit contact with western books
and artists, Biermann's criticism of the capitalist world had limited appeal.
The most powerful symbol of those revolutionary weeks was not the West
German flag or the pear-shaped image of Helmut Kohl, but the simple,
bright yellow banana. The rare fruit was suddenly available and affordable.
What had not existed now did. If that was the west, few would even dream of
denying it to themselves.

Whatever the driving force—fruit or philosophy—East Germans had
been distancing themselves from Father State for several years. As sudden
as the revolution of 1989 may have seemed from afar, the East German
economy had been sliding for several years, even if the CIA hadn't noticed.
West German political parties were so fearful of instability that they di-
verted their eyes from the evidence. The Honecker regime was so fossilized
it could no longer adjust to the relatively modest needs of its people. But in
the streets of East Germany, some who wanted to escape drove around with
white ribbons pasted to their cars, as if they were coming from a wedding.
Everyone knew what it really meant.

On a popular East German TV variety show, *A Pot of Color,* a singer with
no record of political troublemaking used the program's live outlet to send a
shock message in early 1989: He spontaneously scrapped the planned song
and launched into a ballad called "We Don't Need Any Lies." The program
was shown live, but the offending song was sliced out of the next day's taped
rebroadcast. On that same broadcast, a comedian performed a sketch with
an opera singer in which each discovers he has been cast on the other's program, even though the comedian can't sing and the singer can't tell jokes.
The comedian delivered the punchline: "We're not the only ones who've
been miscast." And with that, the studio audience of 2,000 jumped to their
feet as one, cheering as they laughed.

Even in communist institutions charged with the sensitive task of creating new generations of followers, a virus of skepticism and downright disbelief seemed to have been loosed into the system. Markus Zimmermann was
a wiry teenager with a dedication and intelligence that propelled him up the
ladder of socialist achievement with record speed. He advanced from the
Young Pioneers through the Free German Youth *(Freie Deutsche Jugend)*

and on to the paramilitary Society for Sports and Technology, winning awards in motor sports, shooting, radio operation and political education. He spent evenings at teas at the German-Soviet Friendship Society, chatting with Soviet soldiers about solidarity with the beleaguered Afghan communists. But even as Zimmermann ascended on a trajectory that would no doubt lead to party membership and a career in the inner circle, he wondered why the topics he was most interested in were considered off-limits. In every group, from the Pioneers to the Rabbit Breeders Club, the political discussions were identical, limited to peace, the next economic plan, and solidarity with the Third World and socialist brethren. Never the Wall. Never freedom to travel. Never the reasons why the communist party held a monopoly on state power.

To discuss those issues, some young people turned to the Lutheran Church, where peace prayers and youth discussion groups blossomed in the late eighties. Church groups became so popular that the Free German Youth resorted to bribery to prop up its attendance figures. The youth group lured young East Germans to its parades and demonstrations by offering tickets to rock concerts or the occasional banana to take home to grateful parents. Zimmermann, still true to the system, tried to breathe life into his FDJ chapter. Armed with articles from West German leftist newspapers to which his father had access at work, Zimmermann sought to open political discussions about topics that actually interested his friends. At school, he submitted a project in which he conducted man-on-the-street interviews about growing disrespect for rigged state elections. His project was confiscated. Zimmermann was nineteen and an enemy of the state.

That happened in 1987. In the following months, Zimmermann came to see his Free German Youth as a latter-day Hitler Youth, an organization that also had uniforms, torchlight parades, a heavy emphasis on peace, and an absolute ban on political pluralism. Life in East Germany seemed ever more contradictory and intolerable. Zimmermann felt lost at home. His eyes turned westward, but he was no dissident. He did not want to begin life again in a new society. He wanted to better his own. Only the events of 1989 saved Zimmermann from retreating into his own private world, unable to do what was required to conform. Zimmermann was quick to join the reformers. In 1990, he became East Berlin's youngest freely elected city councilman and, charged with running youth programs, he hired streetworkers to comb clubs and hangouts for kids like himself, kids who seemed lost and headed for the violent, self-loathing underground of skins, neo-Nazis, and alcoholics. He had ambitious goals and little impact. "We went right from crafts afternoons at the Pioneer group to Rambo videos on the new VCR," Zimmermann told me later. "Once the Stasi was gone, everything we had been forbidden surged forward: sex, violence, drugs, the radical right, hatred of foreigners. We're overwhelmed."

Zimmermann belonged to the obstreperous few, but even if most young East Germans were not prepared to break the rules openly, the government feared its control was slipping away. Beginning in 1985, the Stasi churned out one report after another fretting about growing cynicism among young people. Western music and the ironic attitudes increasingly popular in the U.S.-influenced West German pop culture were corroding the east's ability to steer and curb the excesses of adolescence. In the Politburo, the old men peered out from behind stacks of pessimistic reports and ordered state television to create a youth program. Torchlight parades, crafts classes and evenings with the Soviet military could not cut it against MTV clones, so, in 1986, the government media authority permitted a half-hour monthly youth show called *Klik!*

Which was exactly the sound heard across the country as kids flipped the channel to far-slicker western TV stations, whose production values and frank discussion of sex and politics left East German TV showing its tired old propaganda to an aging, dwindling audience. "Life had become much more conflicted and we tried in our media to present a world free of controversy," Hans Modrow, East Germany's last communist prime minister, told me. "While the government kept comparing itself to the world to our east, the people were looking to the west. Honecker imagined the world as he wanted it to be, and we all looked away from reality."

In 1987, state TV asked Georg Langerbeck, one of its youngest foreign correspondents, to create a two-hour youth broadcast with videos, games, sports, coverage of environmental issues and a modern, western look. But when Langerbeck and colleagues proposed exactly such a show, the party hierarchy immediately knocked it down. Music videos required cash—hard currency that would have to be paid to western companies. And the producers asked for expensive Sony equipment capable of technical feats unknown in the East Bloc. The Politburo said it couldn't afford western tools. But the real reason the new program was vetoed was the proposal that it be broadcast live. The old men were hip enough to know that live meant beyond party control.

Then, in late 1988, Eberhard Aurich, boss of the Free German Youth, met with Honecker to deliver bad news. In one year, membership in the organization had plummeted from 90 percent of young East Germans to less than 75 percent. The Politburo considered the reasons and concluded that blame should be placed not on ideology or the lack of consumer goods or official corruption, but on East German TV. They appropriated a million marks for the very youth show they had rejected a year before.

The program, named *1199* for the postal code of the TV studio, premiered in September 1989. It revolutionized East German television. Broadcasters actually looked into the camera, facing their viewers, instead of staring down at their approved script as eastern newsreaders did. The program was fast-paced and bright. But what made it an instant hit was its honesty in spite of the system. A report on the first program was censored by political officers in the state TV hierarchy because it included street interviews with young East Germans who said that people taking "extended vacations" in Hungary that summer really wanted to leave their country forever. But the next week, the *1199* staff added savvy to their courage: A commentator discussing the border situation in Hungary and Czechoslovakia submitted one text to the higher-ups, then read a completely different script on the live broadcast. He included a direct slap at Honecker. The party leader had announced that no East German should shed a tear for anyone leaving the country. "I shed tears for every one of them," the *1199* commentator said.

Outraged, the TV bosses called meetings and prepared to pull the plug on *1199*. But then came the ratings: Nearly half the young people in the country were watching. The program stayed on. Encouraged, the young reporters pushed on, producing segments on church youth groups, disaffected teenagers, and even corruption in the ruling party. The *1199* staffers had watched a grumpy Gorbachev go through the motions of communist solidarity at the October celebration of East Germany's fortieth birthday. But when they heard Gorbachev say, "If you want democracy, take it and it will be yours," the hopped-up video revolutionaries at *1199* took the Soviet leader at his word. Within a few weeks, *1199* was drawing half of all East Germans, not just the young. Soon, the program was scarfing up as much broadcast time as it could, grabbing hours away from the Russian-language programming that filled East Germany's Second Channel. In October, before Honecker was forced out, *1199* producers taped a discussion between Harry Tisch, leader of the country's monopoly trade union, and a group of young factory workers. Tisch was stymied by several questions, and the moderator asked the aged communist if it would not be best for him to step down if he could not answer the people. The workers quickly picked up the challenge, shouting at Tisch to quit. Back at the studio, executives said they could not possibly allow a member of the Politburo to be treated so rudely on national television. The program's producers brought the question to a staff meeting: The staff of one hundred threatened to quit en masse if the interview was not shown. It was.

By mid-November, when official censors gave up completely and vanished from the studios, *1199* had broadcast twenty special programs and was churning out six hundred minutes of new programming weekly, taking viewers inside the long-secret party leadership ghetto of Wandlitz, entering East German prisons to reveal conditions and cover a hunger strike, even invading Stasi headquarters. While the nation watched slack-jawed, reporter Jan Carpentier, not previously known for deviating from the party line, fearlessly poked his way into the country's most heavily guarded reserves. When Carpentier confronted sputtering Politburo members with video footage of lush displays of fruits and vegetables he found in a Wandlitz shop open only to top party officials, the country reacted in mass street demonstrations, holding hand-drawn banners reading only BETRAYED! In a society accustomed to TV fare limited to Sorbian dance recitals and travelogues on Bratislava, this was *Geraldo*, *60 Minutes* and MTV rolled into one. The program was besieged with 50,000 letters a week. A twenty-four-hour hotline for tips on investigative stories was overloaded.

"Live is live," Langerbeck said. "It is antithetical to control." Kohl's government had done nothing to prepare for this moment in history, but the west's TV channels unwittingly had done crucial spade work in the east. Ossis were, indirectly, part of a democracy, albeit one they could watch only from afar. So when they acquired the tools of that democracy, such as live TV, East Germans, despite their apparent political complacency, knew what to do. In the coming months, *1199* would guide its viewers into the new life, using actors and animation to define new ideas such as "market economy," "career choice" and "credit cards." The program reported on life on both sides of the former Wall, delved into the developing skinhead and neo-Nazi scene, and tried to export its in-your-face style of journalism to the sedate streets of Bonn.

Eventually, like so many eastern institutions, *1199* was swallowed up by the west, becoming an occasional and unremarkable entry in the united German TV schedule. The program lost its sense of purpose. But *1199* had helped lure the genie out of the bottle. Even if the East German revolt was the calmest of all in the East Bloc—even if the hundreds of thousands of ordinary citizens who marched for their government's demise at night then showed up for work on time at six the next morning—still, there was no going back.

Back in the confines of Honecker's Socialist Unity party headquarters, the old men were still trying to paint the accelerating exodus as a capitalist plot. Children were encouraged to inform on suspicious behavior by parents planning unusually long vacations. Schools were ordered to instruct students that it was legally and morally wrong for families to leave the country. A lead story in the national party organ, *Neues Deutschland,* told the bogus tale of an East German vacationing in Budapest who was offered a cigarette by a foreigner and woke up to find himself in Vienna. But the old tricks just weren't working anymore: With such tales, the party managed only to unite the country in cynical laughter.

Ossietzky's 1989 fall term began with student protests so open that the faculty gave up all pretense and joined in. Gerecke, the school's student affairs director, met with other teachers in Ossietzky's communist party cell. "We invited our nonparty colleagues to the meeting and we decided to give our views to two newspapers," she said. The faculty delivered reports on events inside the school, including resistance to the state takeover, to the state youth newspaper, *Junge Welt,* and to the main East Berlin daily. When the papers published articles on the school, the state secretary in the Education Ministry was sacked. But it was too late for easy fixes. Ossietzky's chapter of the Free German Youth collapsed like a burst balloon, with membership dropping in one year from 176 out of 180 eligible students to 10.

Inside the classrooms, more than a few of the school's twenty-eight teachers felt imbued with the courage to ignore the curriculum they had spent decades shoving down the throats of sullen students. Teachers heaved the hated 676-page textbook *History of the Socialist Unity Party,* a compendium of party documents without a single picture, onto the refuse pile. History teachers brought in their own books on Marx and Lenin and taught material permitted in no East German curriculum. They talked about 1848, the Thirty Years War, the French Revolution, World War I, the Weimar Republic and even, in a couple of classes, about Stalinism—the persecution of communists by communists. It was, for students raised on a steady diet of tripe about the ruling party's relentless march toward perfection, a revolution. Fascism was no longer portrayed as something imposed on Germany by capitalists; now teachers discussed the complicity of the previously pure working class. The Nazis were no longer seen as the ancestors only of today's West Germans; instead, teachers revealed that Germans in all parts of the country had supported the Nazis. The main victims of the Holocaust were no longer communist street fighters, but Jews.

In December 1989, Rainer Forner quit the party. The day before he tore up his membership booklet, he sat for four hours before an investigating commission looking into the school's breaches over the past year. "After surviving those hours," Forner said, "I felt I never wanted to subject myself again to these forces. I wanted to feel I could run my own life, based on common sense."

At Ossietzky, even the state takeover of the school's daily life could not halt the disintegration of state control. In mid-1989, to vent student frustration, Forner permitted the creation of a Democracy Wall, inspired by the protests of Chinese dissidents at Tiananmen Square. Students could post articles, leaflets, announcements of any political stripe. Debates raged among hard-core socialists, fans of various West German parties, environmentalists and neo-Nazis. The wall outgrew its designated space and spread across the school's cavernous lobby.

Students didn't know what to believe anymore. "They told us the Holocaust was the most perverse side-effect of capitalism," said Michael Gaffer, a twelfth-year student. "Now we're disillusioned. We realize we don't know very much. We've come to the edge of an abyss."

"We are in twelfth grade now, and we want to start again, from the beginning of history," said Raul Hasert, then a seventeen-year-old student. "Everything we know is so one-sided. They admitted that 1953 [the workers' revolt in East Berlin] happened, but they said it was the Soviet Army coming to help us against counterrevolutionaries. I believed it then. Now I guess it's not true. I want to know about the Cultural Revolution in China, about Stalinism, about what really happened when they built the Wall."

This was the entire text of the official East German high school history book's account of the building of the Berlin Wall: "In the night of August 12–13, 1961, units of the National People's Army, together with the working-class militia, border police and the Volkspolizei [people's police], supported by troops of the Soviet Army, placed the previously open state border of East Germany with West Germany under control and reinforced the protection of the border with West Germany. This operation was outstandingly planned and excellent in its organization. All armed organs fulfilled their task of struggle with high readiness and efficiency, in close mutual cooperation. This action came as a complete surprise to the ruling circles of the United States, West Germany, and other NATO countries. The most aggressive forces of West Germany had already planned a victory parade in Unter den Linden."

A month after the Wall opened, as the collapse of the East German state accelerated, the political pressure on Ossietzky slackened. A few teachers—shaken by the changes, shocked that their colleagues would openly spurn the curriculum and other state rules—mounted a rear-guard action for the party, urging that their fellow teachers be disciplined, downgrading students who uttered heresies in class. But on Democracy Wall and on the front lawn, students were creating a pluralism that knew no bounds. They taped up placards, held debates, argued in the hallways, and blasted each other in the truest democratic forum, bathroom graffiti.

As the old order dissipated over the next few years, there was little to replace it. No new books, no new curriculum, no new rules. Students held assemblies and voted on whether they should be graded at all. Students decided whether and on what they should be tested. Some teachers were forced out because of their leadership roles in communist organizations. In early 1991, Forner, like all communist-era principals, was removed from his position, but because of his school's unusual role, the director was allowed to land gracefully: He got a position as head of a residential school outside of Berlin. Every teacher at Ossietzky had to fill out a form detailing his political activity under the old regime; unless the teacher had a leadership role in the school or the party, the forms were locked away, to be seen by the new authorities only if someone accused the teacher of having been an informant or an ideologue. "I was never in the party," said language teacher Monika Schmidt. "But we all worked for the system and none of us stood up to oppose it. In the end, we were all guilty. We contributed to the system. And now some of us lose our jobs, and some of us stay. And who knows why?"

Ossietzky's student petitioners were rehabilitated, the transferred students returned to their schoolmates. The remaining teachers searched for books and other teaching materials that might be appropriate to the new times. The staff had no time even to consider how they might go about picking the next year's students.

Students were alternately thrilled by the new possibilities and nostalgic for the certainties of the past. "Most of the knowledge I have I will never use," said Monika Newiger, who was sixteen when the Wall fell. "But it is part of my life. I was brought up in this society and I'm still influenced by the views of the old times. OK, now we can get out of this cage we had and really do what we want. But there was no time to think about what happened."

More than a year after East Germany ceased to exist, the new Berlin Wall—the conflict between east and west—was already evident. Schmidt told of attending a seminar on the new literature curriculum being introduced in eastern schools. The instructors were western Germans, the students were eastern teachers. "They tried to teach us how to write a letter," Schmidt said. "They began a lesson on short stories and a western teacher asked us, 'What is a short story? Have you heard of Hemingway?'

"I told her, 'Yes, but our students read him in English.'"

Inside the bathrooms at Ossietzky, the graffiti changed. No more long treatises on environmental corruption and capitalist intentions. Instead, the walls spoke of new tensions and allegiances. A few loyalists defended the withered communist party, now renamed the Party of Democratic Socialism. Several proffered a pox on all political houses, as well as on Nazis and communists everywhere.

FUCK THE TURKS! said the most common graffito. SKINS ARE NOT NAZIS, said another.

THINK ABOUT IT, said a third. DO YOU WANT TO MAKE TURKEY OUT OF GERMANY?

First Train Out

The Wall will remain as long as the conditions that led to its construction remain unchanged. It will still be there in 50 years and also in 100 years. —*Erich Honecker, East Germany's head of state and communist party chief, January 19, 1989*

SEEN FROM THE wrong side of the Berlin Wall, the west, delivered daily on TV, shimmered like a bejeweled, implausible paradise. In the early years after the Wall was built in 1961, even Elke and Ekkehard Hotz, communists loyal and true, watched western broadcasts with the volume low and the set pointed away from the window, so no noisy neighbor could detect the treason within. In the Wall's last years, no subterfuge was necessary. Reality, or at least a few bits of it, was finally being recognized by the East German regime, and if the entire country wanted to watch the West German football matches and the Rudi Carrell variety show and even the capitalist version of the world news, well, three decades of coaxing the kids to inform on Mom and Dad's choice of channels had had no impact whatever on TV habits, so let them have their plug-in drug.

The Hotzes watched it all, the western game shows and the sports, the lush ads and the news reports about West German kids shooting up drugs or chaining themselves to fences to protest their own government. And still, Elke and Ekkehard remained what they had been raised to be. Secure in their identity, the Hotzes were good communists, party members who believed in the system, believed they lived on the moral high ground, even if the folks on the plains below looked like they were having a better time. Even now, after the system had caused them more pain than any couple should have to endure, they still called each other "honorable coworker," and only half in jest. Elke was an army brat, daughter of an officer who never entertained a non-Marxist thought in his life. Or so he said. Actually, everyone in the family well recalled the days when Papi had barred any nonfascist thought from his mind. Papi went from brown to red in the flash of defeat, his daughter said, which was nothing to be ashamed of, since it was what so many men had done in Germany's Soviet Zone.

By the late 1980s, Ekkehard knew things were bad, knew even that the system was punched through with corruption. Elke's father, behind his facade of rectitude, happily accepted a regular supply of western medications, one of the perks of his position as a regimental commander of the National People's Army and deputy liaison to the Soviet forces in Germany. But Ekkehard needed no secondhand proof. He'd had his own run-ins with the state. The Party Control Commission revoked his membership back in the seventies because Ekkehard, then doing his stint in the military, had refused to cut off contact with his ninety-year-old grandmother in West Berlin. Ekkehard was so distressed, he began considering flight to the west, a line of thinking that landed him in jail for two years on suspicion of plotting *Republikflucht*—escape from his home country.

For years afterward, Ekkehard had trouble finding decent work. To protect socialism, officials told him, Ekkehard could only work where there was no danger that his antistate views might infect the other workers. He had trouble getting a visa to take vacations even within the East Bloc. And Elke was forced to pay for her husband's transgressions. Her boss kept needling her to divorce Ekkehard or lose her position. She refused all entreaties and was eventually sacked from her job as a sales clerk. The Hotzes' loyalty was hit again in 1980, when a fire in their house in Oranienburg, less than an hour's drive north of Berlin, melted away almost everything they owned. The fire, the Hotzes believed, was part of the regime's campaign to drive Elke from her husband. It didn't work. Elke quit the party instead.

Seven years later, despite rejection by the party they called their own, despite ostracism by Elke's embarrassed father, the Hotzes were still capable of moral outrage. When a friend described to them how the party rigged 1987 election returns to eliminate public evidence of rising discontent in the crumbling state, the Hotzes registered their protest by withholding their vote in a local election, an act certain to attract the secret police. On the morning after the election, a city official came to the Hotzes' house to discuss how they had voted.

Someone must be confused, Ekkehard said, because we didn't vote.

Yes, you did, the party official said. The voting list showed the Hotzes voting by absentee ballot because they were away on vacation. The Hotzes got the idea, but refused to play along. They met with the mayor and told him they really had not voted. Stasi agents—the all-knowing men of the Ministry for State Security—visited the couple and their workplaces. "Suddenly, I couldn't qualify for any raises or promotions," Elke said. "The vacation house on the Baltic Sea we reserved every summer was no longer open to us. Everywhere we turned, doors would close. You couldn't defend yourself against it."

Elke was transferred from an office job to shift work in a warehouse. Ekkehard was called to the vegetable-fat factory where he worked as a locomotive driver. For three hours, factory party officials yelled at him for not voting, threatened to cut his pay, lectured him on the benefits of socialism. They recounted the difficulties of raising two children without an income and threatened to make the Hotzes' life truly miserable. Hotz refused to recant his decision not to vote. Ekkehard was put on the production line, then his hours were sharply reduced. His family spent the next two years scraping together a living from odd jobs and the kindness of old friends.

And within days after their abstention at the polls, the Hotzes' house burned again. Immediately, Stasi men arrived at the house to inform Ekkehard and Elke that their insurance was insufficient to cover damages from the blaze.

By September 1989, the Hotzes had finally lost faith in the country born the same year as Elke. The first cracks in the Iron Curtain had already appeared. In May, the Hungarians began to dismantle the barbed-wire fence separating communist Hungary from capitalist Austria. By summer, thousands of East Germans vacationing in the East Bloc states of Poland, Hungary and Czechoslovakia were extending stays and leaping fences to gather at West German embassies. From there, they hoped to breach Europe's divide and reach the long-forbidden west by emigrating over the newly opened border. On July 7, Mikhail Gorbachev, eager to roll on with reforms at home and unload the burdens of empire, instructed the Warsaw Pact to jettison the Brezhnev Doctrine: No more would the threat of force from the Soviet Union hang over the countries of the East Bloc. The liberation was implicit, but revolutionary nonetheless: Find your own way, Moscow was saying. Just how quickly and harshly the dominoes would fall, no one could begin to guess.

In Oranienburg, people could not speak or think of anything but the events in Hungary and Czechoslovakia. Everyone seemed to know someone who was packing up or getting on a southbound train to see what developed. There was little discussion about what it all meant, whether their country would survive, whether they would be punished for trying to leave, whether the Stasi would regain its courage and slam the doors shut once more. The air was rushing out of the balloon, and while most people waited silently to see where it would all lead, the adventurous and the angry were ready to start anew.

On September 29, eight days before Gorbachev was to be presented with a gala military parade at East Germany's long-awaited fortieth-anniversary celebration, Ekkehard turned to Elke at breakfast and said, "I just don't want it anymore."

"Do I have to start again from nothing?" Elke asked.

"Yes."

Ekkehard said it, but he wasn't sure he could do it.

For a remarkable number of Germans, east and west alike, the Berlin Wall was not something that happened to other people. Few families lack a dramatic tale of someone who, by luck or cunning, managed to breach the Wall. Even before he began his long diplomatic career, Jürgen Sudhoff had an intimate relationship with the inanimate barrier that split his country. He was in Berlin in the summer of 1961 when the East Germans built their Antifascist Protective Barrier. A law student, Sudhoff rose on the morning of August 13 to hear on the radio that West Berlin had been cut off from the western world by barbed wire and concrete thrown up overnight. He jumped into his car and drove through the still-open Brandenburg Gate to take his maid home to the East Berlin section of Prenzlauer Berg. Sudhoff drove fast. He had no idea whether he would be able to get home to the west. As Sudhoff sped back toward the crossing to the west, Red Army tanks lined up along Unter den Linden, the east's main boulevard.

Sudhoff was passing a Soviet tank when a young man grabbed the door handle of his car, dove into the backseat and said, "Drive on, drive on!" They were among the last to make it across to the west that morning; Sudhoff's stowaway said his thanks and jumped out of the car as soon as he was safely out of the Soviet zone. That sufficed as Sudhoff's Wall story for the next twenty-eight years, until the summer of 1989.

By mid-August, it already had been Sudhoff's most frenetic summer. On August 14, in his capacity as a top official of Bonn's Foreign Ministry, he met with Hungary's foreign minister, Gyula Horn, at the West German Embassy in Budapest. Horn was overwhelmed by the tens of thousands of East Germans filling his city and its makeshift refugee camps, demanding passage to West Germany. Hungary had established its own variety of independence from the Soviet Union and had opened Pandora's box by taking down the barbed-wire fences along its border with Austria in May. But Horn did not want to risk everything on behalf of a few thousand East Germans who smelled escape. "We are not a refugee country," Horn told his West German visitor.

Sudhoff, an elegant, soft-spoken diplomat whose English suits and gleaming eyes described a man who was anything but a bureaucrat, listened at length to his Hungarian colleague. He nodded understandingly, shook his head when Horn raged against the contradictions of the disintegrating Soviet Bloc. Finally, Sudhoff delivered a single sentence of advice and counsel: "Close your eyes and open your borders."

Horn was quiet. He turned toward his German friend and threw his arms up over his head. The gates were lifted. To work out the details, Sudhoff set up a meeting between Horn and Chancellor Kohl at a West German government guesthouse, a session kept so secret that only six people knew of it— a precaution necessary because Horn could not count even on the support of his own Politburo. The East German government, begged by its socialist ally to cooperate, stalled, blustered and finally watched helplessly as the Hungarians waved the ecstatic Germans through.

A few short weeks later, after 50,000 East Germans had used the Hungary Gap to escape to the West, Czechoslovakia, which had a regime far closer to East Berlin's hard line, faced its own German refugee crisis. Sudhoff flew to Prague for an old staple of German diplomacy, a meeting with Wolfgang Vogel, East Germany's merchant of mercy. For years, Vogel had been the lawyer who singlehandedly negotiated the sale of East German troublemakers to the west. It was a seedy trade that both sides tried to keep quiet. But it produced profitable transactions for both Germanys: By buying freedom for the iconoclasts of communist society, the west could strengthen its hold on moral superiority in the tense competition across the Iron Curtain. And by excising its most visible boils, the east could maintain its conformist grip on political and social discourse at home while acquiring the hard currency it desperately needed to stay afloat.

The people trade had been going particularly well in recent months, because East Germany's tiny dissident community had been more vocal than ever before, and the East Berlin government was eager to toss out troublemakers. But by the time Sudhoff and Vogel met to negotiate the return of the East Germans who were stuffed into the West German embassy in Prague, the rules of the game had clearly changed. Hungary had shown what was possible. And back in East Berlin, a group of dissident artists, scientists and intellectuals had founded New Forum, the country's first nationwide opposition group—a direct, open challenge to the Honecker regime. In Leipzig, Pastor Christian Führer's weekly prayer for peace at the St. Nikolai Church, long tolerated by the state as a pressure valve for all manner of malcontents, overflowed onto the streets, giving birth to Monday night demonstrations that would soon attract hundreds of thousands of ordinary people, most of them walking silently around their city, flickering candles in their hands. Despite all that, the Politburo dispatched Vogel to Prague to bring the fleeing East Germans back home. The lawyer was authorized to offer only the promise of greater travel freedom within the next six months. Two hundred East Germans took the deal; the vast majority refused to budge from the overcrowded embassy grounds.

"The people in Prague just laughed at Vogel this time," Sudhoff recalled. "I was afraid they would kick him. I told him, 'Herr Vogel, you are too late.' "

Earlier in that revolutionary summer, Ekkehard Hotz's nineteen-year-old son by his first marriage had struggled for days over whether to report for military duty or skip out the back door through Hungary. With his father's encouragement, he hopped the train to Budapest. Now Ekkehard had more reason than ever to give it all up. In those days, everyone in the east still spoke in code. You never knew who might be listening, and all too often, you knew exactly who was. Everyone had a group, the friends at work or in the neighborhood about whom they were absolutely certain, people they could tell anything. But even among themselves, they spoke the secret tongue, more out of habit than precaution. At work one day, Hotz said, "Elke and I are thinking about renovating the place." In the tortured subtext of a repressive society, that meant fleeing to the west (an apartment under renovation was acceptable reason to travel to visit friends or relatives).

"Ja, Ekkehard, renovate the place and then get out!" one of Ekkehard's buddies said.

On September 29, the Hotzes watched the *Tagesschau,* the west's main TV news broadcast, and saw thousands of East Germans massing inside the gates of the West German embassy in Prague. They decided their time had come; to wait might mean to be left behind. With all those people in Prague, no one knew when the government might close off the escape routes. East Germany was about to mount its mammoth celebration of the country's fortieth birthday—complete with a state visit by Gorbachev himself on October 7—and the politicians would have to act soon. Suddenly, even in the Oranienburg supermarket, people openly gossiped about who was going and which course was right. Go? Stay? No one knew. "Everything was in chaos," Ekkehard said. "We knew they'd have to let the people out of the embassy soon, and we knew we could only stand being out in the cold with the children for a couple of days."

Together with another couple, they decided to go that night. To leave was to give up everything material—home, furniture, clothing—and a good deal of the intangibles they held dear. For all they knew, they might never see their parents again. The Hotzes didn't dare tell the children—Mirko, ten,

Katja, seven, and Philipp, just over one year old—anything other than that they were taking a short vacation. (But Mirko told his father quietly, "I know what you're planning.")

To avoid suspicion, Ekkehard bought round-trip train tickets to Dresden, about halfway to Prague. At 3:30 A.M. on September 30, the Hotzes left home with a single bag, overflowing with diapers and other supplies for the baby. So as not to look like refugees, they took nothing for anyone else. In the morning rush hour, Dresden's cavernous railroad station, a prewar hulk, teemed with East Germans headed south to the Czech border and with police, railway police and Stasi agents, busy combing through the trains, hauling off anyone who looked like he might be fleeing the country. The Hotzes, congratulating themselves for traveling without luggage, rushed off the Berlin-Dresden train, found the bus station and hopped aboard a bus to a small border town. At the checkpoint, they watched as, directly in front of them, a young German woman hauling baggage was taken into custody.

After gathering courage at a local bar, Ekkehard and family began their long march to the west. He approached the East German border guard and asked—in as casual a voice as he could muster—"How many Pilsner Urquells can I bring back from Czechoslovakia?" Crossing the border to buy the East Bloc's best beer was a time-honored East German tradition and a good cover for the Hotzes' odd trip without luggage—if the guard was willing to suspend disbelief in the midst of thousands of people rushing the border in obvious escape attempts.

The officer sent the Hotzes on to a second guard station to ask about the beer there. The second guard smiled and said, "Bring back as much as you want." They were in. Two buses, several hours and three cranky children later, the family arrived in Prague. It was late in the afternoon, the kids were hungry, the parents frightened and lost. After some wandering, they latched onto a column of luggage-laden East Germans and finally reached the embassy at about 6 P.M. The crowd of escaped easterners was already backed up out of the gates of the compound and onto the alleyways around it, packing the streets for three blocks in all directions. Eleven thousand people were crammed into the area, surrounded by hundreds of Czech police in riot gear and hundreds more Czechs, many of them bolstering their socialist brethren with biscuits, blankets and bowls of soup.

Shortly after the Hotzes arrived, they heard voices over a loudspeaker. Hans-Dietrich Genscher, West Germany's foreign minister, stood on the embassy balcony with Sudhoff. They announced that everyone would be taken to the west. Thousands erupted as one. The cheers were deafening, the tears flowed freely. Except among the children. Trained well by their state, many of the children had to be dragged along into the unknown, afraid that their own parents were about to commit the crime of *Republik-flucht*—fleeing their country.

Genscher gave his word, but no one knew when the East Germans would be allowed to leave. The temperature dropped to freezing, part of the crowd started pushing, mothers clamored for the diplomats to let their children inside to warm up. Before midnight, women and children were allowed into the building; there, the Red Cross crowded children onto the few beds and handed out the remaining biscuits. Outside, Ekkehard and a few of his instant buddies warmed themselves with a bottle of vodka handed into the compound by a friendly Czech. Eventually, he got a few moments of sleep lying on a stone.

"I told them we're going to West Germany today, and they cheered. And then I said we're going by train, through East Germany, and there was a dead silence." Sudhoff's decades of quiet, even tough diplomacy had not prepared him for his new role as savior to cold, hungry, fragile East Germans. The hopeful, frightened eyes that peered up at him compelled Sudhoff to say something more, something that could not be twisted in the long, freezing night into a sign that the gray suits from Bonn were going to turn these 11,000 people over to the Stasi.

Sudhoff delivered. He promised the crowd he would go with them on the train. He personally guaranteed their passage to the west. Instead of making yet another deal with Vogel, Sudhoff had waited, knowing that the mounting pressure on the East German regime would soon break even communist boss Erich Honecker's iron resolve. On September 28, the foreign ministers of the Soviet Union and the two Germanys met in New York and cut the deal: West Germany would send trains to fetch the easterners and bring them across Europe's divide. But at Honecker's insistence, the trains would make a face-saving detour through East Germany, as if the travelers had come home and then were "expelled" by an angry government. The East German Foreign Ministry denounced the train passengers as antisocial vermin who had "trampled moral values." Sudhoff savored the idea of thousands of East Germans repeating the 1917 journey of Lenin, as he was transported in a locked railroad car through the German Reich.

To maintain Honecker's pride, the East Germans gathered in Prague would travel sixteen hours without food or water, on trains going six miles an hour, stopping again and again without explanation so East German authorities could clear the tracks and stations ahead of thousands of other easterners eager to jump aboard the only train out. From the East German–Polish border to the heavily fortified West German–East German divide, Sudhoff played cat and mouse with Stasi agents who roamed the train menacing the bewildered, exhausted passengers. As the secret policemen poked their heads into one compartment after another, Sudhoff followed immediately behind, showing his face, repeating his promise that every person on board would reach the final station in the West German town of Hof.

The night the Hotzes waited for word about the trains to freedom was cold and unsettling. Too many bottles of Czech vodka made the rounds. People were shoving and surly. It was hard enough just keeping the kids together. On the train, at least, everyone was searched to be certain there would be no drinking on board. And then the trip itself. Imagine, going back into the place they thought they had left forever. When Elke saw they were being sealed onto trains of the East German Reichsbahn, she suspected—no matter what the West Germans told them—that they were all being sent back to the east for punishment. Then, when she saw the Stasi agents climb aboard, and when the agents collected everyone's identity papers, Elke was certain the great adventure had come to a miserable end. Only later would they learn that the East Germans had confiscated ID documents to bolster their official claim that the refugees were traitors being deported because of their disloyalty.

The train kept moving, if barely. There was an unexplained delay of nearly half a day outside of Dresden. Ahead, well out of sight of anyone on board the train, police were beating a crowd of 3,000 of their own countrymen, people desperate to hitch a ride on the freedom train. Seen from on board, East Germany, home until two days ago, seemed eerily different. Whichever way they looked along the tracks, the Hotzes saw police, army troops and border guards. Only the rail stations were completely, frighteningly deserted. "It was like in a science fiction film," Elke said. "You could only see trees and then just beyond the stations, just Army with riot helmets and incredibly heavy weapons." Ahead of the train, East German forces removed, one by one, hundreds of citizens who had lain down on the tracks, some because they wanted to get on board, others because they were angry that anyone would abandon the only country they had ever called their own.

At about 8 A.M. on October 4, the train arrived at the West German border town of Hof. Ekkehard: "Champagne, craziness, all hell broke loose. Big crowds, everyone hugging everyone else."

Elke: "It was just enormously overwhelming. The people were there with soup and bananas for us. We kept jumping back and forth from one side of the border to the other. There were things for the children—food, drink. An old lady said, 'Come, let's find something for the children.' We had no western money, but someone—a reporter from Swiss radio—gave us fifty Swiss francs and someone else gave us a hundred fifty marks."

The West Germans housed their new citizens—as ethnic Germans and residents of a territory the Bonn government never legally recognized as foreign, all easterners were automatically granted West German passports—in a school gymnasium. But there was so much outside to explore. Elke went to a supermarket to get some things for the children—and to see what it was like. She had been raised in such a strict communist home that she had never even been to an Intershop, the East German stores that sold western goods, but only for western currency. Other than on television, Elke had never seen the blizzard of color, the orgy of choice the average western market offered. Everything was new, clean, just as she had seen on TV. She bought candy. Then Match Box cars for Mirko. Inside the store, a man walked up to Elke and asked if she came from the east. When she nodded, he handed her a 100-mark bill—$65. "He was gone before I could thank him," she said. She could think of only one thing: jeans for the children.

Elke and Ekkehard went to a restaurant near the gym and ordered their first western beers. It was a beautiful day and as they sat on the terrace, Ekkehard asked his wife to go inside and get cigarettes. She went, but she didn't come back. After a while, Ekkehard went to find her and discovered Elke sitting with a bunch of Wessis. The Hotzes spent a couple of hours drinking and laughing, and before they knew it, they had an offer to stay right there in Hof and run the restaurant.

It was all too new. They declined. Anyway, the Hotzes already had a place to go—Bocholt, in the country's extreme west. Ekkehard's son had ended up there; now they sent him a telegram. The next day, they got a response: Wait right there, I'm on my way.

So it was that four days after they had left Oranienburg with nothing but the baby's bottles, the Hotzes climbed into a Volkswagen Golf the son had borrowed from his western boss and drove to a new life. Along the way, they stopped at a rest station and Elke went to the bathroom. After ten minutes, she emerged breathing hard to hold back tears. She had stood over the faucet for what seemed like hours, trying to figure out how to turn on the water. Elke stared and stared, but she could find no handle to turn, no button to press, no pedal to step on. Elke Hotz had met one of those fantasmagorical inventions of the wealthy west, the electric eye, and the eye had won.

In East Germany, Father State always handled everything. Where to go to school, what to study, what kind of work to do, where to live, what to wear—the state took care of those decisions. If forms had to be filled out, the state provided someone to do it. When Elke and Ekkehard reached the west, they found a welcome shot through with the same kind of paternalism to which they were accustomed. The man Ekkehard's son worked for gave the Hotzes two hotel rooms and food for their children. The city of Bocholt enrolled Elke in a computer course. People handed them money and gifts just because they were from the east. Later, the city put them in a refugee home crowded with Poles and other non-Germans. But within three weeks, the city corrected its mistake and gave the Hotzes three rooms of their own elsewhere in town.

Still, it didn't take long before the Hotzes realized that life in Bocholt was going to be very different indeed. Elke tried to get work, but the city labor office wanted proof of her past employment. She explained that she had left the east in haste, taking nothing but the baby's bottle. She had no documents and no way of getting them from the crumbling country she had left behind. "How can I prove where I worked?" she asked one bureaucrat.

"Get the information from your union," the West German said.

"How?" Elke said. "Everything—our five-room apartment and everything in it is all gone, confiscated by the state." The encounter ended in stalemate.

Ekkehard tried to find work driving locomotives for the West German railroad. Sorry, they said, our trains use a different technology, and anyway, we have no proof you did this in the east. "The trains were identical," Ekkehard said. "I knew that because I had trained with Wessis back home, but I couldn't prove my experience."

With their unemployment benefits running out, the Hotzes searched the newspapers for work. They found an ad seeking someone to run a snack shop. The Hotzes agreed to rent the place for $1,200 a month. What they didn't know was that they would have to pay for garbage pickup, heat and electricity on top of that. It never crossed their minds that selling sausages might fail to cover the monthly nut, let alone to make a profit. Within six months, they were $6,000 in debt. They had to shut down.

Luckily, Dresdner Bank was only too happy to lend them the $6,000. The Hotzes had no idea that the very same bank would close their account when they fell two months in arrears. "We had customers, steady customers, but not enough," Elke said. "We had friends, but there were always limits. We were always the Ossi. Always the foreigner. We were never at home."

There were tense moments when Wessis would come in to the shop and complain loudly about lazy Ossis who don't know how to work. Ekkehard: "I told one of these guys, 'When my locomotive didn't work on a Sunday, I had to go in and make it work—somehow. Find me a Wessi who would go to work on a Sunday. Find me one.' " But when he was alone, Ekkehard knew he had not mastered the west. The furniture fiasco had shown him that. He and Elke had ordered beds and couches. But the furniture didn't arrive by the promised date, or even in the following two months. By the time the store delivered the goods, four months after the order was placed, the Hotzes' finances had taken a tumble and the couple could no longer afford what they'd ordered. They refused to accept the furniture and soon found themselves the subject of threatening letters from the store's lawyers. A contract, in the west, was a contract. Ekkehard paid a $350 fine for that lesson.

In mid-1990, the Hotzes got another offer, to run a bar, an ongoing business with a regular clientele. This time, rent included living quarters for the family. This time, they thought they could make it. And they did, for a time. There were no major losses. No gains either. But then the owner sold the place out from under them. The Hotzes had to move. They took on a third place, another snack shop closer to the city center. The owner required them to buy his entire inventory for nearly $30,000. The Hotzes didn't have it, and they weren't about to go back to the friendly bank that bailed them out the first time. So they went to a tax adviser, who arranged other credit for them. "It was amazing," Elke said. "We only had to sign the paper, even though we had nothing."

It was a disaster. The losses mounted so fast, the Hotzes could hardly even count them. By summer of 1991, the Hotzes were in over their heads. They had to bail out. Once again, as they had in the fall of 1989, Elke and Ekkehard looked at each other over breakfast. Once again, they worried about starting over with nothing. Once again, they gathered a few things and woke the children in the middle of the night. They fled at midnight.

The Hotzes came back to Oranienburg just as they had left it—with nothing, except a huge debt, a Fiat Ritmo, Bina (their scraggly black western dog), and a bundle of bitterness and frustration. But the Hotzes did not come back to nothing. In the year and a half since the Wall fell, Oranienburg had changed. The new life was not terribly visible at first glance, although the first renovations were under way and a few new shops had opened on the main street. Around town, the same old people were still in charge. The deputy editor of the local paper that used to print nothing but party-approved blather had been bumped up to the top job. The local employment and housing offices were still run by the same people who ran them before the revolution.

When they returned to Oranienburg, the Hotzes went to the police station to comply with the German law requiring all citizens to inform the authorities of their residence. The head officer was the very same man who had been in charge under the old system. Elke asked how he had managed to keep his job amid the wholesale changes when East Germany ceased to exist. "He laughed and told me that after the revolution, they just exchanged some staff with the police station in the next town and that made people think 'Aha, everything's different now.' "

But there were real differences, too. Youth clubs and day-care centers had closed for lack of funds. Communist school principals had been sacked, old textbooks pulped. But what the Hotzes most appreciated about their return, what made them feel Oranienburg was truly home was what had not changed—the openness, the warmth, the things easterners talked about among themselves. When they first arrived back in town, the Hotzes stayed at the town motel. They were virtually penniless, but they knew the owner, who heard their tale and gave them a special low rate. The Hotzes had made friends during their years in the west, friends they enjoyed being with, friends who even visited them later in Oranienburg. But when they thought back to evenings spent with western friends, they recalled conversations about things—what car the new neighbor had, where their next vacation would be, who had a new coat. In the east, conversation centered on politics, the children, the future.

They had, they realized after their western adventure, little in common with Wessis. Elke and Ekkehard knew they had been—and still were—economic naïfs. But they considered Wessis politically simpleminded, unable to discuss the theories behind the politics of the day. Still, the division was more than an information gap. "The people we knew in the west, well, we had acquaintances, but I don't think they were real friends," Elke said. "Here I can go to people anytime, for help, to talk, whatever. Not in the west. You just don't drop in on someone whenever you want."

They soon found a rundown $280-a-month apartment, owned not by the state, but by a landlord from western Berlin who never showed his face. Even here, the Hotzes had to think about things they never had to before—finding a doctor, paying taxes, choosing insurance. And there was no longer anyone who would fill out forms for you. In some ways, the Hotzes had a leg up on everyone else because of their time in the west. When they moved into the new apartment, Elke knew she had to bring witnesses over to record the conditions so they couldn't be blamed for preexisting damages. But such moments did not relieve the image Elke and Ekkehard had of themselves as second-class citizens in a society they did not, and honestly, probably never would understand. Elke enrolled in a government training course on care for the aged; Ekkehard signed up to learn how to install hot-water heaters.

"That the old system is gone, good," said Ekkehard. "But to declare everything from that time bad—why? We had sports clubs, day care, youth clubs—all closed now. Why does it have to be one or the other? Why not some from each? I admit, we still don't really understand how capitalism works. We went to a very hard school and we finished the course, but it's a completely different mentality."

After four decades in a society where no one moved, Elke and Ekkehard were getting pretty casual about picking up and going. By 1993, it was clear: Oranienburg wasn't working out. There was no work, and the schools and the neighborhood were increasingly infested with the western habits that drove the Hotzes nuts—street crime and right-wing radicals, a dog-eat-dog atmosphere, a quickened pace, the loss of *Menschlichkeit*, the simple kindnesses of one neighbor for another.

So they were off again, this time to a village so small they had to laugh. Rohrlack was a two-hour drive north of Berlin, home to 160 people, 60 of them children. This was *echt* (genuine) East Germany. The Stasi was gone, no longer did little Volkspolizei cars chug over empty cobblestones. But there were no signs of western colonialism either. Cherry, apple and pear trees lined the roads and rose back on fields for as far as you could see. A handful of houses dotted the rutted road. There was not a single sign of commerce, not one incursion by the forces of marketing and full-color advertising. Perfect, the Hotzes thought on first viewing. They did not want to join their former countrymen in the rush to buy, the lust to adapt to western ways. This time, they said, they were settling in for good. The kids would move on after they finished school—nothing to keep them here, the parents conceded—but Elke and Ekkehard had had enough. They had no work, no money, and they needed a place where that would hardly matter. Not that they were destitute. Thanks to generous welfare benefits—unemployment, disability, bonuses for bearing children—they had managed even without jobs to find money for a new color TV and a satellite dish.

But they still sat on tired, standard-issue East German furniture with yellowed varnish and worn terry-cloth upholstery. They wore—with the addition of T-shirts and jeans—the same old brown and beige shoes and polyester pants churned out under socialist five-year plans. There was no one in Rohrlack to compete with, no need to keep up with the Schultzes here. Tucked behind the thick walls of an eighteenth-century farmhouse once home to the pastor of the long-shuttered village church, the Hotzes—there was a fourth child now, a baby named Mareika—were twelve miles from the nearest store of any size, twelve miles from the older kids' school. They were utterly dependent on a rare, unreliable bus, and Ekkehard said that suited him fine.

He had grown frail, his back pain flaring nearly every day now. He moved with the slow shuffle of a man of retirement age. But he still laughed easily, and his aviator glasses and Fu Manchu mustache, his slight build and dancing eyes were reminders that he was only in his mid-forties. "Every day, I see a new animal, maybe a bird I never saw before, or a pheasant, or a certain kind of rabbit," he said. "Of course, it's boring for the kids—they watch a lot of MTV, a lot—but it's what I want. I couldn't be in the city any-more. We needed someplace where things were going to stay the same."

Alas, even Rohrlack was changing, at least to the discerning eyes of its longtime residents. "Build the Wall nine feet high and keep the shitty Wes-sis out," said one of the Hotzes' new neighbors, and Elke and Ekkehard nodded in agreement.

"Then we'll have our children back," Elke said. "Only then will we be rid of these theatrics in our schools—the skinheads, such ignorance. The kids don't know what a concentration camp was, who Hitler really was. You can't tell kids about the camps anymore. They don't want to hear. When we were young, we met people who'd been prisoners in the camps. We knew what Germans had done. Now our kids wear swastikas, they pass around copies of *Mein Kampf,* and they don't understand anything. That's what the Wessis call freedom."

Even in this tiny village, a few local kids were beaten up by drunken neo-Nazis from nearby towns. Kids brought home videos with the most amazing things—sex acts and murders, things the Hotzes had never even contem-plated, let alone seen. But the mom-and-pop grocery on the main street still opened if you knocked on a Sunday or an evening. "Everyone has time for you," Ekkehard said.

"It's like time stopped," Elke added. "They don't know anything here. Some frozen potato puffs came in at the store and the women didn't know what to do with them—after four years of western products. They still use ninety percent GDR products."

In Neuruppin, twelve miles away, the kids' school was still in the grip of the old communists who had run it for years. That pleased the Hotzes no end. The principal was tough, there was no graffiti, and "it's just like old times there," Ekkehard said. "The only thing I don't like is they're forcing the children to go to religion classes now."

There was plenty of time to gripe in Rohrlack, as anywhere in the east. With more than a third of the working-age population out of work, the Hotzes and their neighbors persuaded each other that Germany was on the edge of a precipice, ripe for a repeat of the ugly past. They lamented the lack of po-litical leadership, and longed for the security and certainties of communist days, even as they paged through their *Quelle* merchandise catalogues and flicked through the satellite-delivered channels, spending a while with *Dal-las* on ARD, zapping over to the nude quiz show on RTL, finally staring into the night to the alien beat of MTV.

The economic boom that turned some eastern cities into speculator heaven had left Rohrlack so far behind that land could be bought for as lit-tle as $40 for a quarter-acre. There were rumors about Berlin developers looking over one farm or another as a potential golf course or weekend get-away condo complex, but few projects took even the first step toward reality.

The brick-and-fieldstone church behind the Hotz house was shuttered, its doors caked with spider webs, its floors lined with mounds of bird droppings. The East German government had built a brick wall across the middle of the church, although no one quite remembered why. There were rotting pews, and the ruins of an organ that once pealed songs of joy and mourning. When we opened a side door with the keys the Hotzes found in their farmhouse, Ekkehard realized he was entering a church for only the second time in his life. We walked through the building and found a Bible dedicated to "the rebirth of our Fatherland," dated Easter 1913. Down the road, we found a decrepit World War I memorial (7 men from Rohrlack died in battle; 25 returned to their homes.) Ekkehard grew misty-eyed. He had been through so much, in so many places. He used to know who he was, an East German worker with a particular role in a country with a certain set of rules. Now he was getting by financially, but life seemed empty. Even here, far from the city, where every day was like the last, where he could marvel at the pheasants and storks, the grand variety of birds, the open land-scape—it wasn't enough. He wanted something to do. He wanted to feel like he belonged. It wasn't the money, he insisted. "If I have to eat potato soup twice a day, I'll do it. We just need to have a chance, so I can believe that the children will become something."

By 1994, the Hotzes' adventure in the west seemed like something from the deepest past. They kept in touch with a few friends, but their contacts became rare and empty, obligatory cards at Christmastime. Even after their western sojourn, the Hotzes remained mystified by the health-care system, by the entire bureaucracy. In Rohrlack, folks turned to the Hotzes for advice; here, Elke and Ekkehard were the worldly wise. Alone at night, the couple looked each other in the eyes and laughed at the very idea. They saw themselves as lost lambs in a country gone wild.

Wall-Mart

We are the people. —*Chant at East German demonstrations, October 1989*

We are one people. —*Chant at East German demonstrations, December 1989*

We were the people. —*Chant at East German demonstrations, March 1990*

EVEN THE LIGHT was different on the other side of the Wall. By day, the east was darker, gloomier, muffled under a blanket of gray mist created by the most foul of pollutants, decades of neglect, and a streetscape that seemed to swallow up even the bright neon from advertising signs posted to compete with the west (THE SOVIET RAILROAD: INTERESTING AND PUNCTUAL!). But it was at night that the eeriness of the east emerged. Along the rutted streets, vertical shafts of pale purple fluorescent light glowed from apartment windows, piercing the night, casting an aura of harsh irreality over the land. I noticed this effect dozens of times before I could find the source. I learned that some East Germans believed plants responded well to a nightly dose of ultraviolet rays. These purple tubular lamps were ubiquitous, and virtually unknown in the west. Unlike sputtering Trabi (Trabant) cars—lawn-mower motors inside a Plexiglass shell—or shops that announced their purpose with utilitarian signs such as FOOD and TOBACCO, the purple plant lights would survive unification. Western marketers would do their best to reupholster the east in the searing primary colors of modern advertising, but at dusk, the old communist haze would return, a comforting, if otherworldly, relic of a world gone by.

It was on one of those eerie eastern mornings that I realized just how sharp "the turn" was. (From the start, easterners uncertain about the future of their revolution hedged their bets, calling the events of 1989 *die Wende*, the turn.) After spending the night in East Berlin, I drove back across Checkpoint Charlie to the western side of the city. The first faint glimmering of day was reaching above the horizon when I pulled into the border station, the first car in line. I had made this crossing so often in my short time in Berlin that I knew the drill: Hand over passport, visa and press passes. Get stared at indefinitely, inscrutably. Respond quickly and politely to curt, suspicious questions about where I'd been, whom I'd seen, what I had in the car. Extract no response whatever to attempts at humor or friendliness. Drive slowly and carefully into the west after gate suddenly opens with not a word from the robotic, expressionless guard.

On this morning a few weeks after the opening of the Berlin Wall, the baby-faced guard was just arriving to begin his shift. Bundled against the cold, he put his rubber stamps in order, shuffled a few papers inside his frigid booth, and stepped outside to the gate that blocked my lane. He waved me ahead to his window, leaned over, and switched on fluorescent lights above and beside us. Then, he took a step toward me, put his hands on his belt and said dramatically: "God spoke and there was light." The East German border guard laughed, and with that, eliminated, for one motorist at least, the mystery and power of the repressive state. My friend the guard flipped casually through my passport. He asked me if the Grand Hotel—the communist regime's Japanese-funded, Scandinavian-built hostel for visiting capitalists—wasn't ridiculously expensive (it was). He worried that perhaps I couldn't afford the Grand (I couldn't; the newspaper paid). Reassured that my company was doing right by me, the guard smiled and said, "Ah well, if they're paying, it doesn't matter what the price is." Some easterners caught on very quickly.

The days and months after the revolution of 1989 were a period of public and private euphoria matched in modern times only by the bedlam unleashed at the end of World War II—in the victorious countries, of course. Germans had known no such event with the power to push onto the streets the most private of emotions. Three days before Christmas 1989, I went to the center of Berlin to watch the opening of the Brandenburg Gate, the majestic twelve-columned symbol that sat for twenty-eight years in the middle of a desolate no-man's land formed by the two ribbons of concrete that were the Wall. Tens of thousands of people on both sides of the city waited for the official opening, standing for hours in muddy parkland as they were pelted by a driving, icy rainstorm. I met old people who wistfully recalled the Nazi parades that had passed through the Gate. Charlotte Peer, a Berlin resident since 1939, described the potato fields Germans had planted in the shadow of the Gate in the lean years after the war. I met teenagers who knew little of their city's history but understood this was a moment they ought to witness. After Kohl and the East German prime minister, Hans Modrow, spoke, I rushed to stand beneath the Gate, to touch the columns that had been off-limits for so many years, to step over the line from west to east and back, again and again.

That's when I saw Antje Zirzow. She was dripping wet, strands of black hair plastered against her face. Against her shoulder, she held Ruth, nine months old and bundled so she looked like a bedroll. Zirzow was twenty-five years old and worked in an East Berlin day-care center. She had come this day to see and touch the Gate she had only stared at for all her years. And now she stood crying, holding Ruth close to the stone column, pressing against it, almost caressing it, with her other hand. I asked why she had brought her baby to the Gate on this cold, wet day.

"It's a hell of a year to have been born in," Zirzow said. "Who knows what it will be like when she's older? We knew that what we had would have to end sometime. But it was so quick. I'm so happy and so scared. I've never been to the west. I always wanted to, but I never had the chance. And now that I can, I don't know what to do there. And my baby: What will she do? What will her world be?" She turned away from me, to face the Gate, and again she cried.

Even with such anxieties, those were such heady days that people could, and did, believe that the Germans east and west would reunite into one people even before the two states merged. Within a few months, the Brandenburg Gate would be repainted and the plaza around it converted into an open-air bazaar where chunks of the Wall were hawked alongside Soviet and East German military hats, belts, watches and assorted other debris of an empire gone bad. Architecture suddenly made sense; buildings that had faced only a featureless strip of concrete now looked directly onto offices and apartments on the other side of the city. Berliners rediscovered their neighborhoods, strolling back and forth across the former divide, recalling the city's prewar personality, marveling at the different ways the two sides had developed. Old bus routes were revived, train tracks reconnected.

East Germans tested their newfound freedom to express themselves. One day, crossing by foot from East Berlin to the west through the newly cut Brandenburg Gate checkpoint, I saw an East German border guard stop an easterner and dress him down for entering West Germany through the OUT gate. "Why do you think we cut two holes in the Wall?" the guard shouted. "You come in one way and out the other. You think you can just ignore the signs? Look: IN and OUT. Can you read?"

The easterner looked at the guard and snapped, "There is no more 'in' and no more 'out'. And soon, your job will no longer exist." With that, he walked freely through to the west.

Sometimes it seemed as if all of East Germany went on extended visits to the west between November 9, 1989, when the Wall opened, and July 1, 1990, when West Germany gave the east the Deutsche mark, creating a single economy overnight. In those first months, every visit to a West Berlin store was like peeking into F. A. O. Schwarz in mid-December. The wonderment on the easterners' faces, the way they picked up products and held them gingerly, their intent looks as they listened to the tired spiels of the slicer-dicer demo men—I couldn't stop watching. Schools closed so children could go see the west. A frazzled cashier at Woolworth's, Sabina Welde, went home each day feeling warm inside despite the endless stream of customers: "They are so pleased by how things are wrapped," she said.

I followed Klaus Garz, who sat in traffic for seven hours to bring his wife to see West Berlin, as he spent a day trying to spend every pfennig of the $29.28 in western money he had collected from friends and relatives, and the $65 in welcome money that the West German government distributed to each easterner crossing the border. He ended up with a big bag full of candy, a pink toy telephone, and enough deodorant to mask the odor of an entire village. The excitement of those days was not limited to Berlin. I visited villages along the old German-German border and found people like Horst Haase, a former communist party member who had endured extraordinary isolation because he happened to live in K-10, the restricted zone that stretched back into East Germany for several miles from the border with the west. Police checkpoints guaranteed that even Haase's eastern relatives couldn't visit him because only a select few East Germans were permitted within range of the frontier. "There are many wonderful things now—bananas, all kinds of foods in the stores, no more fences," Haase said. "The most wonderful thing is that now you can speak in a normal tone in a restaurant."

Thousands of easterners arrived in the west daily—for good. Some didn't trust the permanence of their travel freedom. Some were simply so eager to live the western way that they picked up and moved. At first, they were welcomed with open arms. I visited makeshift refugee centers where western Germans dropped by with homemade sausages, boxes of oranges, cases of wine, and bouquets of flowers—anything to show their joy over the end of the division. Western political parties hurried to associate their names with the birth of a new age: The Free Democrats, for example, papered eastern towns with posters showing a rainbow and sunshine under the words IT'S SPRING AND WE ARE SO FREE.

But amid all this heartfelt pleasure and surprise, people took time to consider the past, the difficulties ahead, and the wrongs committed by a government that spied on its own people, suppressed individual initiative, and wantonly poisoned the earth. At a Bonn high school, students and teachers alike tempered their enthusiasm for reunification with warnings that, as Stefanie Busse, a 16-year-old student, put it, "We have to be careful. If they have too much power, the Germans become maniacs. You've seen it in two world wars already."

In the eastern town of Wolfen, where the polyester factory had been shut down after nearly half of its workers were exposed to poisoned water, thousands of people gathered in the main square to cheer a speech by the West German foreign minister, Hans-Dietrich Genscher. But when the flowery rhetoric about the destiny of a united people ended, the citizens of Wolfen had something else on their minds. A clot of fourteen people gathered around me and two other foreign reporters. The East Germans wanted a reality check: Were West Germans really serious about unification? Would members of the communist party be hunted down and prosecuted? And then a storm of questions about the environment. Is the air really so much better in the west? Are the cars cleaner? And finally, a woman who had worked in the polyester plant for twenty-four years, since she was sixteen, took my hand and said, "Let me ask you, does it really smell awful here?"

The pace of change was breathtaking. Just ten weeks after the Wall fell, a single edition of the East Berlin daily *Berliner Zeitung* illustrated the west's reach into the formerly closed society. The newspaper began listing daily levels of sulfur dioxide and other pollutants in the Berlin air. An article described the legalization of joint ventures with western companies. Another news story announced that Philip Morris, the tobacco giant, would use material from East Germany to make its cigarettes. An ad for Gromo Interiors offered curtains and carpets to easterners remodeling their homes. The first signs of unemployment in the east bubbled up as the East Berlin government officially classified 1,029 people not as jobless, but as being "in need of reeducation." A notice asked citizens to help find a missing child. The East German National People's Army tried to shake people back to a former reality, lamely threatening that citizens born in 1972 had one month to register for the draft, or "police measures will be taken." A news article lamented the sudden and precipitous drop in blood donations, noting that those easterners still giving blood were going over to West Berlin hospitals to do so. A front-page story said that in the first month of 1990, East Germans had already made 10 million visits to the west. The adjacent headline revealed that every second tree in the east suffered from disease. An advertisement placed by a West Berlin horse track offered the Saturday racing card, along with betting information. In the classifieds, East German typists, upholsterers and painters offered their services, while others sought to sell their Meissen porcelain, Chippendale chairs, and twenty-year-old Trabant cars. The personal ads included this: "Woman intent on staying here [in the east] looking for man intent on staying here, if possible with children."

And on page 2, in a new feature, a correction box, the newspaper published an extraordinary note to its readers: "On August 2, 1961, we wrote an article accusing Horst Jahnke of helping people to flee the country. We have now learned that the court acquitted him of the charge on November 14, 1961. What we said then was, in other words, incorrect and unfortunately not corrected then. The current editors have distanced ourselves from the practice of prejudging people in the press. We would like Mr. Jahnke and his family to excuse us for this injustice."

For a year after the Wall opened, East Germans experienced one historic event after another. Within days after the Honecker regime fell, the chants at the street demonstrations that would eventually attract more than half the East German population changed from "We are the people" to "We are one people." Unification, which Kohl still considered a ten-year process, was happening without the government's slightest effort. East Germans hurtled through the landmarks: Their first free elections in fifty-eight years. Day X, the July 1, 1990 switch to the West German mark. The first withdrawals of Soviet troops from their East German bases. And finally, on October 3, 1990, East Germany's departure from the roster of nations. With each landmark, the people of the East purged themselves of some part of their past. Day X, when banks handed out freshly printed Deutsche mark notes in exchange for miniature and meaningless east-marks produced an extraordinary display of sidewalk refuse. I started the day intending to talk to East Germans about their monetary merger with the west. But I found myself combing through dumpsters and garbage cans piled high with the refuse of a discarded system. Old ledger books told stories of shops and family finances going back to the thirties. Bars tossed entire supplies of beer glasses because the exclusive contracts with western breweries required them to use glassware emblazoned with the western brand's logo. Sidewalks overflowed with ovens and light fixtures, clunky East Bloc TVs and radios, chairs and tables, plastic shoes and polyester pants.

In place of all that, merchants stocked everything and anything western. The old socialist brotherhood restaurants—cavernous places where grumpy Slavs served brown food if and when they felt like it—closed quickly. The Sofia was transformed into the Spaghetti Company. A Ladbroke's betting parlor opened below the Prague restaurant. Flower boxes blossomed overnight. Satellite dishes sprouted on the balconies of drab, war-pocked apartment buildings. Billboards for Bulgarian appliances and Czech pharmaceuticals seemed to shrink next to new ads for American football (DO BROAD SHOULDERS MAKE YOU WEAK?) and the Rolling Stones (Mick Jagger's trademark lips, a universal language, sufficed).

On that first day of the new economy, in the city of Frankfurt on the Oder, at the East German–Polish border, I watched George Haake stare at a window display of groceries for a very long time. Finally, I asked what he was looking at. "Salad dressing," he said. "I'm trying to remember the last time I saw it." A row of bottles of West German dressing had been placed haphazardly in front of two dusty old cans of Cuban sardines. Inside the store, a man waited in line for an hour to buy a single item, a bottle of Heinz ketchup.

At a Konsum supermarket, a line of seventy people stretched out the door. Crowds gathered around brightly packaged western goods. As everyone around her grabbed cartons of West German milk, Gurdana Samtleben said softly, "Honestly, our milk tasted good, too." But she bought the west stuff, too, at three times the price of eastern milk.

"We're destroying our own economy," said Annette Makulla, who made a point of picking up eastern butter for 70 cents rather than the package from Denmark for $1.55. But she conceded she would probably switch to the western brand sooner or later. "Western butter certainly tastes better. Ours is mostly water when you cook with it." The hunger for anything western was palpable. Radio call-in shows offered advice on banking, driving, taxation, clothing styles—whatever was alien. On a new eastern radio program, *American Dance Tracks*, a listener named Angela from Leipzig called in to ask: "I'd like to know please, what does 'featuring' mean, and what is 'remix'?"

The DJ patiently explained the English terms in the western dialect of Germlish, a hip mix of the two languages. "Featured," he said, "tells you there is a lead singer in the band. The singer is gefeatured."

Given the country's lust to "test the west," the results of the east's first free elections, in March 1990 should have surprised no one. Kohl's Christian Democrats offered quick unification and a swift, easy transition to capitalism. "They have the money and they're ready to send it over," Frank Losansky, an auto mechanic in Wandlitz, told me after casting his ballot. The campaign to elect the government that would close out East German history was an education in western politics. Easterners marveled at the balloon giveaways, fashion shows, beer blasts, free films and other gimmicks western parties used to attract attention. Even the former eastern communist party, now the Party of Democratic Socialism, got into the act, showing the movie *Dirty Dancing* at a campaign party in Frankfurt on the Oder.

East Germany was overrun with western party workers who fled home every night, or at the least, every weekend. While in the east, they stayed among themselves, sealed into their western cars, avoiding eastern food. They imported their campaign literature and were quick to criticize their own Ossi candidates as soon as the token easterners were out of earshot. At the Christian Democratic victory party in Berlin, where Kohl completely overshadowed Lothar de Maizière, the demure viola player who had been elected prime minister, party officials took no chances: They imported West German wine, West German cheese, West German crackers, even West German water.

That euphoria leads to disappointment is no revelation. But the dreams liberated by the fall of the Wall cannot be dismissed merely as the romantic idealization of the long-forbidden West. The end of four decades of division, the end of Yalta, may have come too late for many middle-aged Ossis grown accustomed to the restrictions of dictatorship. But many youths cherished the chance to think anew, or simply to embrace small joys: Christmas lights, VCRs, winter fruit, and children's clothes that didn't unravel after a single wash.

The Wall had been built so well—at places, it was ten-foot-thick concrete reinforced with row upon row of steel rods—that it took vast teams of workers two years to tear it down. In some ways, it would always stand in the minds of those it was built to hem in. But in the first years after the Wall opened, many easterners felt they had been exorcised of one of its most disturbing effects—the nightmares about the Wall that had shaken the sleep of so many.

Jutta Voigt's dream began with narrow alleys and gentle evening light in a city such as Paris, London or West Berlin. A sweet smell to the air, a small café, lobster on the table, a fine wine. She sees Jean-Paul Belmondo and Jean Seberg kissing each other. They smile at her. "Don't they realize that I am illegal here, that my presence is completely forbidden?" She leaves the bar and runs into a communist East German philosopher. "What are you doing here?" she asks. He turns red. "How long have you been outside East Germany?" she insists.

"A year and a half," he replies, turning redder. "It's always the 150 percenters who bail out first," she thinks. And then: "I must get back, must get back, back. I am in the west. How I got here, I do not know. Somewhere there must have been a gap, a hidden door, an entry. Now I must return. I run, stumble, fall, stand again, I am terribly afraid. How will I get back in without a passport, visa, entry and exit permits? They'll want to know how I got out. There they are, in their glass booth, I can see them with their border-guard faces, how they check everything. I had no permission; they'll put me on restriction. I'm afraid. And I wake." Voigt, an East Berlin writer, had this dream about twenty times in the years before the Wall fell. "When I awoke, I was always happy," she said. "I had seen the West and I was lying at home in bed."

Others dreamed, similarly, of mysterious visits to the west that ended with capture or a last-second return to home. It is remarkable how often easterners told of dreams in which the west appeared as a romantic vision of Paris, Rome, or Madrid, rather than any West German scene. Renata Rauch, another writer, always began her REM visits to the west wondering just how she had managed to get there. Her west was a place with no distinct image, just an overwhelming sense of pressure and panic, a dark, empty landscape where she was watched closely. She had to find her grandmother, if only for a few moments. Grandmother had been too ill to visit the east; Renata's family tried to get permission to visit the west, but they were always refused. In the dream, Rauch feels a panicky fear, even though she is vaguely aware that she is at home, asleep. She loses her way, loses track of time, realizes she must return to the east before midnight. But she cannot find the border. She is desperate, alone. "I cannot do it, I cannot do it." She wakes. "My grandmother waited for a very long time. She died in 1980, at the age of ninety-four. I never did see her again."

The Mother of the Revolution never embraced her child. Month after month, year after year, Bärbel Bohley—the woman who, as much as anyone else, defied the East German state to create an organized opposition—seemed defeated, crushed by what she had wrought. Deprived of her dream of an independent East Germany living the mythic Third Way between capitalism and communism, Bohley became the national nudge, always carping at the way things had turned out, always standing before the Germans as a noisy, insistent reminder of what could have been. Her New Forum, the group that organized the silent, candlelight marches that surrounded and eventually strangled the Honecker government, had been the right movement for the moment. It had been at once independent enough and unthreatening enough for half a million East Germans to put their names to petitions for change within socialism. New Forum became a symbol of peaceful revolution without ever adopting a platform or philosophy of its own; it was the perfect outlet for people who knew what they did not want, but did not have the foggiest notion of what should come next. The intellectuals behind New Forum were captives of East Germany's defining myth—the notion that somewhere beneath all the corruption and oppression hid an honest, pure idea, the utopian socialism of their founding fathers, the courageous communists who had opposed fascism. It was a myth powerful enough to imprison even those who knew that their country had soured beyond repair.

In the minds of many, New Forum came and went in a matter of weeks. It was overtaken by the prospect of bananas and Deutsche marks so quickly that the dreamers who created New Forum soon became the German equivalent of Abbie Hoffman and H. Rap Brown—answers in nostalgia trivia games. Except for Bohley. She would not go away. She was altogether unlikely: In a political system that proclaimed itself gender-blind, but reserved its only position of female power for the dictator's wife, Bohley propelled herself to the fore. In a country whose intellectual elite produced few iconoclasts, but instead stretched out in the velvet coffin of official art, Bohley was a painter willing to sacrifice her career to seek personal freedom. And in a society with a history of authoritarianism, Bohley fancied herself a rebel. The tragedy for her as for all the East German intellectual dissidents was that Bohley and New Forum resisted hierarchy so determinedly that their movement quickly became paralyzed by internal debate. In their drive to distance themselves from German authoritarianism, they became so rigid that they cut themselves out of their own revolution.

She has the round, soft face of one who does not yell. Her brown eyes are so invitingly clear and liquid that many people recall them as blue. She seems to have hair, a thin tousle of curls lying in every which direction, only to warm her scalp. But it is her voice that stands out: so gentle, the consonants so effortlessly formed, a river of clicks and lifts creating long German sentences that flow with conviction and shimmer with righteousness. Bohley dressed in black much of the time; she was, after all, a Berlin painter. But whether she sat under a single spotlight in her living room or stood before thousands of demonstrators, she was just the symbol the opposition needed: charismatic yet unthreatening, an honest woman who seemed bright enough to outsmart the old communists, but not clever enough to fool the *Volk*.

Usually, revolutionaries at least pretend to admire and respect the people for whom they fight. Bohley never bothered with pretense. (Once, when I asked her to help clarify the hazy origins of New Forum, she said, "I thought it up," and waited for the next question.) She did what she wanted to; she refused to be controlled. From the early eighties, when she first challenged the regime by publicly opposing the admission of women into the military, she found friends among church workers, intellectuals, scientists and artists on the dangerous fringe of society. In 1983, Bohley and thirty other women dressed in black gathered at Berlin's Alexanderplatz to pronounce themselves unwilling to serve in the military—a direct challenge to a new draft law. Five women were arrested; Bohley managed to slip away. But a year later, Stasi agents nabbed her. They charged Bohley with "treasonable passing of information" for telling a western journalist about women's peace initiatives. Bohley, then thirty-seven, broke with the East German dissident pattern: She refused the government's offer to deport her. If she was to be punished, she said, she wanted to stay in her own country. She would not let the state rob her of the meaning of her actions—a challenge to her fellow East Germans to stand up against the system they loathed.

Bohley and her friends took their inspiration not so much from dissident movements in other East Bloc countries, but from the early German socialists they idolized. In 1988, Bohley and a couple of dozen other people active in church discussion groups decided to unfurl a banner at the annual state demonstration marking the murder in 1919 of Rosa Luxemburg and Karl Liebknecht, founders of the German Communist Party. The church group's unauthorized banner quoted Luxemburg's famous line: "Freedom is always the freedom of those who think differently." The Stasi were neither moved nor amused. The demonstrators were arrested. Although Bohley had organized the protest, she did not take part, heeding a warning not to join the march because of her past legal problems. Still, a week later, she was detained and charged with "treasonable activity."

After the 1988 incident, the Stasi offered Bohley the usual nonchoice: ten years in prison or exile. With such high stakes this time, she caved. She went to West Germany, then to Britain; after a year, she was allowed home. "In Poland and Hungary, people like us went into the opposition," she said. "Here, we just go west. The Poles and the Hungarians felt occupied; we felt guilty. We accepted Soviet occupation as punishment for the war. It took us a long time to discover that people who were persecuted by the Nazis—our leaders—were also very good at persecuting. Those who understood that left. In every corner—the economy, politics, culture—it's as if all the progressive forces emigrated."

Bohley quickly joined with friends who agreed that the nascent dissident movement sheltered by the Lutheran Church needed to break out of its religious cocoon and show its face to the rest of the country. In the summer of 1989, she, biologist Jens Reich and others decided to take advantage of sharply increasing public dissatisfaction with the Honecker regime. New Forum was born just as the first East German tourists were finding their way out via Hungary. Bohley abandoned her painting and turned her studio and small apartment in Berlin's Prenzlauer Berg section into the movement headquarters. Volunteers hand-copied flyers and petitions. Artists and writers sought connections in other cities. Students claimed a corner of Bohley's couch and stayed the night, arguing tactics and theory. A good many of the people who spent that fall in Bohley's apartment later ended up serving in the Bundestag, the Bonn parliament. A good many others, Bohley most prominently, would remain reluctant to join the establishment. They wanted something more than travel visas and seats in parliament. They would never quite articulate what it was, but they missed it all the same.

One New Forum activist who chose the other path was Joachim Gauck, a pastor from Rostock who went on to become custodian of the Stasi archives, a morally and legally demanding position in which he decided who could know what about the millions of informers who oiled East Germany's machinery of repression. "I was a realist, willing to be in coalitions," Gauck said when I asked about his differences with Bohley. "We had to get things done and we didn't have time for hand-wringing. I don't like people who scream and cry, and when they're suffering, they're happy. That's really German. I don't like that." The West German perspective was little kinder. "Bärbel Bohley should get a statue in bronze for what she did," said Burkhardt Dobiey, an official in Bonn's old Ministry for Inter-German Relations. "But her concept of life is not what most people wanted."

In the summer of 1989, Bohley and two friends, sitting in an East Berlin courtyard, dreamily promised one another they would travel together to Italy the next summer. To their own amazement, they did it. On their drive south, they stopped at the Austrian-Italian border. There, high in the Alps, the sky a crystalline blue, the air almost painfully crisp, they pulled off the road. They were beyond what had been, for all their lives, the frontier of possibility. Together, they cried until their eyes hurt. "How," Bohley wondered later, "could anyone have deprived another of this?"

That story would likely surprise many Germans, east and west. Publicly, Bohley never gave the impression that she savored her new freedom. She never made a point of telling TV audiences what she told me on a snowy evening four years after the opening of the Wall: "I love the freedom, the possibility to see pictures and read books I want. I like to drink dry wine instead of sweet, which was all we had here before. The small freedoms—eating Italian cheese or traveling to New York, seeing buildings repaired and flowers in the windows—are not to be underestimated." Instead, she allowed herself to become a symbol of growing unhappiness in the east, the regret that East Germany had not survived in some form, so it could make its own mistakes, create its own identity. "Since 1961, individual identity has fallen away and we were fixated on the west," Bohley said. "Taking to the streets and demonstrating was an attempt to find our own identity. So in only two months, we put holes in the Wall and again people start looking west. And there's nothing you can say against that. That's what's so frustrating. We can't make people believe that it's like 1945 and we have to create a new society. They just look west."

A month after the Wall fell, Bohley watched with horror as the reunification express gathered steam. "Reunification would mean being swallowed up by the west," she argued then. "For forty years, we've lived with this ideology and people are captive to it. To give it up suddenly would be like another rape." The communists were finished; she knew that. But she held out for some kind of humane socialism, even though she conceded total ignorance of economics. Bohley and her friends were prisoners of the very ideology they had risen up against. Raised in a country that drilled into its children their identity as inheritors of the antifascist mantle, they could not make a final break with socialism. It was inextricably linked in their minds with opposition to Nazism. New Forum's thinkers stayed up night after night flailing about, searching for a political structure they could embrace, one that would answer the public clamor for western life without giving up their only positive self-image: their link to the communist heroes who fought Hitler and ended up in concentration camps. It was a hopeless pursuit, and one the vast majority of the public considered superfluous. Within three months of their greatest triumphs, Bohley—and New Forum—were beside the point.

The next years only deepened Bohley's bitterness. She campaigned relentlessly to expose people such as Manfred Stolpe, the former East German church official who became premier of the eastern state of Brandenburg, only to find himself tainted by evidence that he had informed to the Stasi on dissidents working with the church. Stolpe was a hero to many easterners, a rare Ossi in power, a seemingly honest man who had done what he had to in the old days, figuring that if he could stay in good stead with the secret police, he could do some good in his church work. Bohley never bought that idea. Stolpe had compromised on his morals; he had started down the slope and she could not stand to see him excused for that. She denounced him as a dealer who had sold out true dissidents and thus sapped the east of any hope for change. Bohley lost friends as she unbendingly argued that it would be morally wrong and historically destructive to allow those who betrayed their soul mates and relatives to the secret police to hold positions of honor.

On a winter's day outside Bohley's Fehrbelliner Strasse apartment, Vietnamese refugees darted from the entryway of her building across to the supermarket, hawking bootleg cigarettes, scurrying from occasional police patrols. Bohley's was a typical old East Berlin apartment building: A once-grand entryway, left to rot for half a century, was dark and dank, the floor rippling, the stench of urine rising up the stairwell. Outside, graceful stone

adornments had long since fallen to the street. Pollution had withered facades that had survived World War II's bullets. Since the public spaces
were everyone's, they were no one's, and they looked it. But inside each
apartment door, completely different worlds awaited. Bohley had transformed her home into a bohemian lair, dimly glowing by candlelight. Tall
bookcases and racks of paintings soothed the eye. Up a spiral staircase,
Bohley had added a new white Siemens clothes washer in the kitchen since
I'd last seen her. But she still lived without central heating, "like a real
Ossi," she said. On the walls, her own drawings and watercolors presented
controlled abstractions, squared-off shapes that streaked and bolted across
the canvas, but always ended cleanly.

"It took me a long time to realize that the people here were so materialis-
tic, that people were more interested in things than in ideals," she said. "In
the long run, the people in the east were more satisfied than those in the
west. We had low living standards, but there was some justice—everyone
had work, medical care and housing. Of course, freedom is worth something, and now we have that. I don't like this whole East Germany nostalgia
that's rising as a defense against the way the Wessis rule us. But what else
do we have? They destroyed our political culture before it even developed."

Even as she denied it, she slipped into that longing for what was. She recalled the "niche society" in which people retreated into tight circles of
friends, a private world that offered space apart from surveillance and conformism. "The fridge was open for all," she said. "We used each other's
baths." Her stubby red fingers, a vestige of her years working with canvas
and color, wrapped themselves around her shoulders. "When I see the brutality of right-wing radicalism, how fast it blew in here, I wonder what that
old warmth was. And then I think, maybe we're not really far from the Wessis. We thought of ourselves as pacifists, but every youth here learned to
shoot. They all learned to use hand grenades."

Bohley never painted again after the Wall. "I'm a politician now, I guess,
but a politician from below. Painting is a matter of looking, taking time. This
is no time to paint, not for me. I'm trying, all the Germans should be trying,
to come to terms with the past. Before, we were told we were living for the
socialism that would come in fifty years. We can finally live in the present
now. That means we have to try to make things better now." She was forty-
seven years old in 1994 when she finally decided to do what she had refused to do in 1990: run for office. New Forum, which had soaked up more
than 200,000 members in less than six weeks during the fall of 1989, now
had only 2,000 supporters. The last faithful named Bohley as their top candidate for the European Parliament, a largely meaningless debating society
with lovely quarters in the French city of Strasbourg. Bohley never had a

chance; she won only token support. Voters knew who she was, but she was a symbol of the past, a gentle, righteous voice in a time that seemed to call for moral flexibility.

As she continued to search for justice, Bohley watched those around her test the new life, some happily, others not. She saw hopes about the west soar, then crash when the new system seemed uncaring and impersonal. And everywhere she turned, from intellectuals with whom she spent her evenings to neighbors she chatted with in the supermarket, she saw the same depression. "People just pull out of politics," she said. "They just want to be left alone." Bohley could not quite accept that withdrawal. Her revolution was supposed to bring people together to create a society based on honesty and cooperation. She never imagined that people might want only the freedom to have nothing to do with others.

The train drifted by one stilled factory after another. In front of each, and at the entrance to every town, empty, scrawny flagpoles stood sentinel, their white paint peeling, the East German flags long since removed. In a few places, the colors and stripes of corporate logos, the new candidates for the people's allegiance, flew where communist banners once rippled in the wind. On the train home to Berlin from Leipzig one day in 1993, I saw a landscape far from the blooming paradise Kohl repeatedly described in his 1990 campaign.

The train crawled past old women leaning on hoes. Still dressed in their standard-issue blue East German work smocks and flowery Soviet dresses, the women hobbled along in prerevolutionary shoes. A baby blue Trabant, abandoned at trackside, was covered with graffiti that said CANNIBAL CORPSE. A group of children skipping home from school reflected the transition: Some wore the junior version of the worker's jumpsuit, others were in full Wessi, jackets and pants decorated with splotches and swirls of earth tones and pastels, go-go boots and stone-washed jeans, bulky book boxes hanging from their shoulders.

Some changes were dramatic in those first years. New railbeds were being built, and alongside the tracks, the windows of decrepit brick apartment blocks were punctuated by glistening white satellite dishes. Life outside might still look grim, but inside those apartments, the video screen offered the illusion of infinite possibility. On the train, I met Klaus-Dieter Gerlach, a rail engineer and charter member of what politicians in Bonn called the Lost Generation, those middle-aged easterners who would never adjust to western ways and never again find work. Gerlach, forty-six, still had his job with the Reichsbahn, but he had already lost the circle of friends who had been his solace since childhood. "There were ten of us and we did everything together," said the chubby fellow with a puffy face and droopy eyes. "Drinking Thursday nights, with the families on Fridays, Saturdays out with our wives to a show or a concert. We had organized activities, train outings, crafts. There's nothing anymore, not at work, not among friends. And slowly, the circle broke apart. Two are unemployed, three moved to the west to try to use their skills in jobs there. The rest of us, maybe we talk once in a while on the phone, but there's jealousy now. One will say, 'Why do Karl-Heinz and his wife have work, but I don't?' Some earn money and some don't. So you can't go out and be together and have fun if everything in your life is insecure. Our whole experience is worthless now—our educations, our professions, our degrees. I trained as a railroad man and that was a career that was passed on through generations. Now I have no future."

The Ossis lived under a repressive system, but they had a diverse economy that, while corrupt and inefficient, provided an income and at least the patina of meaning to all. Then, after 1990, the easterners watched as that economy was *abgewickelt,* a newly coined word meaning "un-developed" or "dismantled." Factories closed. Hospitals, schools, libraries and child-care facilities were shuttered. The Treuhand, the semipublic agency set up to sell off East German industries and attract western investors, quickly became established in the Ossi view as the main destroyer of the east's economy rather than as architect of the new era.

Bonn politicians heard such complaints and shrugged. Werner Hoyer, a bright young star in the Free Democratic Party and one of the country's most sensitive leaders, dismissed Ossis over the age of fifty. "They will never adjust. That sounds cruel, but it is reality. It is sad, but they are the Lost Generation." Four years after unification, Hoyer said neither his nor any other major party had made any special appeal to eastern voters because "you would indeed run the risk of losing support in the west if you were demonstrably eastern in your orientation."

Most disturbingly, it was not just the older generation that was displaced and depressed. College students, even teenagers, told me of seeing all certainty sucked from their lives. When I asked Axel Senst, a twenty-eight-year-old agriculture student at East Berlin's Humboldt University, whether he could compete with his western counterparts, he said, "I won't ever be able to. Perhaps my child will." Some children watched as every adult role model in their lives was stripped of purpose and dignity: parents unemployed, teachers sacked because they had held positions in the party, favorite TV performers taken off the air because they were politically tainted, politicians discarded because of old Stasi ties.

"People here have no special love for their old identity," said Hinrich Lehmann-Grube, a westerner who moved to Leipzig to become mayor in

1990. "But they lost their identity with unification, and they need something." He spent most of his time as mayor dealing with Ossis and their lost connections. Some tasks were simple, such as teaching secretaries not to blow on each Xerox copy in an attempt to dry it. But others were so complex they seemed destined to remain perplexing for generations. What was he supposed to tell parents who asked what their teenagers should study to have a good shot at a job?

Most Ossis had long since decided not to look back. But some couldn't help growing nostalgic. By 1994, young easterners—some too young to remember the real thing—were flocking to GDR parties at east Berlin's Palace of Tears, the nightclub built out of the old customs station where visiting westerners bid sad farewell to their eastern lovers when the curfew for capitalists fell each midnight in the communist era. Eastern night crawlers paid with old east-marks, wore their old Free German Youth uniforms, and listened to the tinny tunes of socialist rock. The whole scene was somewhat tongue-in-cheek, but only somewhat. The same could be said of Ossi Park, the theme park that developer Frank Georgi planned to build near Berlin on the site of a former East German army base once called Leadership Complex 5000. This was not to be another Euro Disney. Georgi, a concert manager who fled East Germany in 1989 through the back door in Prague, had a bracing smack of realism in mind for his visitors. The whole park would be surrounded by barbed wire and a concrete wall. Instead of parades, visitors would be corraled into state-sponsored mass demonstrations featuring lines of tanks and long placards with slogans ending with exclamation points. Gruff Stasi agents in plainclothes would spy on the tourists and take them away to isolation chambers if they attempted to escape. Visitors would be required to exchange a minimum of hard currency, just as westerners had to in the old days. Georgi promised to ferret out all the fine old East German goods—aluminum utensils, tissue-thin paper, putt-putt-puttering Trabant auto engines. Even the toilet paper would be authentic—the scratchy old "Stalin's Revenge" brand, guaranteed, so said the the old joke, to turn the last asshole red. Although some western investors were interested in the proposal, Georgi himself wondered whether Ossis would want to wallow in their past, even for laughs.

Most Ossis were simply too vulnerable to bear that kind of sarcasm. It was no wonder western con men found ready suckers in the east. Such was the desperation to adapt that when a westerner arrived with a get-rich-quick scheme, many Ossis were only too happy to sign up. Books by Dale Carnegie rocketed to the top of the eastern bestseller lists and stayed there, year after year. Easterners flocked to retraining centers, some sleazy, some perfectly well-meaning.

Gisela Tautz-Wiessner, once a stewardess for the legendary Pan Am, West Berlin's link to the world, traveled around the east revealing the secrets of the new life. With unending patience, she trained hotel workers, corporate managers, restaurant waiters and even the unemployed in the unwritten rules of western behavior. "Smell," she told a room full of eastern German hotel managers, "is a very important point. Everyone has body odor. What can you do about it?"

Silence. Finally, Winfried Mitzlaff, a hotel convention manager, raised his hand. "Wash," he barked.

Tautz-Wiessner, elegant and graceful, put on the most serious face she could muster and looked each student in the eye. "Washing is not enough," she said. "It is important also to use deodorant. Without deodorant, it just will not be enough." She gave it to them straight, whether the topic was body odor, eye contact, small talk or wardrobe. Her recipe was a mix of positive thinking, American sales tactics and traditional central European manners. "Their first reaction is always 'Aha, another one of those *Besserwessis* (know-it-all Westerners) coming to tell us we don't even know how to behave,'" she told me. "But once they see that I'm not going to accuse them of being apes who don't know anything, they're hungry for the advice. And they do need it. Even today, if I'm in a restaurant, I know immediately if the waiter is from the east or the west."

"Our people have to know what western standards are," said Joachim Öhme, manager of the Residence Hotel, which paid Tautz-Wiessner nearly $1,500 for a one-day seminar. "Relations with guests in East Germany were completely different. You didn't have to care for the guest. The waiter chose who to serve and it was a privilege to be seated. Today, we have to get used to the idea that the guest is king."

Students wrote down each instruction as if it were word from on high. Such strange ideas, such arbitrary rules: Stand as if you were being dangled from a string. Smile on the telephone—people can hear the difference. Use your customers' names as often as possible. Manfred Becker, the hotel's chief concierge, interrupted. "I have to say, what is the point of friendliness if you're only going to see the person once for a few seconds? You can't make a friend in a few seconds."

Tautz-Wiessner smiled gently, looked Becker in the eye, and responded, "I would rather be superficially friendly than risk wounding anyone."

Becker was not convinced. "When does it become phoniness?" he demanded.

The instructor assured Becker that a concierge need not worry about appearing to be phony. And she added a tip: "Watch Americans, they're much better at this sort of thing." At such seminars, the two cultures, east and west, clashed constantly, and not always in good humor. At one Tautz-Wiessner session, Ossis and Wessis argued extensively over whether it was necessary to leave messages on phone-answering machines. Easterners said it was impolite to leave a recorded message. Westerners insisted it had to be done. As usual, Wessis had the last word.

Another time, the instructor asked her students for examples of good manners. "Tact," one student offered. "Politeness," said another.

"How about honesty?" Becker, the concierge, said.

Tautz-Wiessner stopped. "I have problems with that," she said. "You can't tell someone they look fat just because it's true."

But all the training in the world could not help millions of easterners who lost their jobs because the Soviet Bloc collapsed. Eastern businesses simply had no more markets. Four years after unification, nearly half of East Germany's 1989 workforce of 9 million was not working. Most eastern businesses and retail outlets were branch or franchise operations of western companies. When the overall German economy sank into recession, western companies did as businesses do everywhere: They cut back not at home, but in the field. Mercedes said it would not build the massive truck plant it had announced with much hoopla for a site south of Berlin. Major German automakers began exporting tens of thousands of jobs.

The Kohl government had been certain that investment would pour into the east once the depth of Bonn's commitment to rebuild the infrastructure became clear. The worldwide recession, and a growing realization that Germany faced difficult structural problems, foiled the government strategy. Some economists and bankers had argued all along that Bonn needed to do more to save jobs in the east, that the east, like West Germany in the fifties, needed extensive state subsidies for its major employers. For decades after the war, the giants of West German industry remained state-supported: Lufthansa, Volkswagen, the entire telecommunications branch, the rails—Bonn had always been comfortable with a level of socialism from which Americans would have recoiled. But no such effort was made in the east, because Kohl didn't think it would be necessary, because the eastern European markets were lost, and because the task of rebuilding the region was already stretching Bonn's budget—and all of Europe's—to the limit.

"The introduction of a market economy is not so much an economic transition as a cultural one," said Kurt Biedenkopf, the western premier of the eastern state of Saxony. After optimistic beginnings in the east's most economically promising and prosperous region, Biedenkopf concluded it would take three to four generations to create the decentralized economy and political mentality necessary for equality between east and west. Eastern states suffering from pathetically small tax bases and overwhelming debt burdens sought to establish basic services taken for granted in the west. By 1995, Saxony expected to spend nearly half its budget on interest payments. Meanwhile, deindustrialization continued apace. Employment in Saxony's soft-coal industry would plummet from 125,000 people in 1989 to 25,000 workers by the mid-nineties.

At street level, the most obvious effect of wholesale job cuts was the removal of women from the workforce. West Germany's success at maintaining low unemployment levels through the postwar era resulted in good measure from a consensus that women should stay home. Women are largely invisible in many professions. The western German system prohibits many mothers from working: There is little part-time work. Shops are forbidden by law from opening in the early morning, the evening or through most of the weekend. Schools operate mornings only, leaving children to be cared for at home at noon or 1 P.M. Exporting that system to the east proved particularly traumatic. In 1989, nine of every ten women in East Germany worked. Women held exactly half the jobs. By 1993, they held fewer than a third of the jobs. Some were pleased to be free to stay home with their children. But many others were embittered by the loss of purpose and income. Germany's long-quiescent feminist movement quickly became dominated by eastern women, who led a failed drive to regain abortion rights. (Abortion had been legal in East Germany, but despite a parliamentary attempt to ease the west's strict antiabortion law, the reunited country's high court rejected a nationwide liberalization.)

Although many eastern women believed they were doing better personally in the reunited country than they had under communism, they seemed nonetheless depressed and lost. Marriages dropped by 65 percent in the east from 1988 to 1992. The birth rate fell like a stone, from 12 per thousand in 1989 to 5.3 per thousand in 1993—lower even than the lows hit during the two world wars. Most sobering of all, the number of eastern women who underwent sterilization soared, in one clinic at Magdeburg jumping from 8 in 1989 to 1,200 in 1991. Some women even complained to authorities that their western bosses had made sterilization a condition of employment.

Women's work in the old East Germany had been far from idyllic. Biedenkopf, the western politician and sometime economics professor, told of the woman he saw each day hanging around near his office at Dresden University, occasionally watering a plant. Finally, Biedenkopf asked the woman what her job was. She stood straight up and announced proudly that "I am responsible for the flowers on the second floor." Communist society created her job to grant her some income and purpose, and to give the state considerable control over the woman. Of course, her job did not survive westernization. It cannot be said that that woman misses her work. But even with support from the west's generous welfare system, she surely misses having her own income and above all, the social contact and daily structure jobs provide. In the old system, she was something. Now, she doesn't know what she is.

8

Survivors

TWO MEN IN their twilight years refuse to act their age. History has stolen too much from them, too many chances, too many people. These are strong and confident men. As their world shifted abruptly from one structure to another, each was left to find his own place, his own kind of freedom in a society run by stingy and jealous men. The men are German, and they have suffered German fates, the strangleholds of authority and bureaucracy, the stupidities of extremism and rigid idealism. Yet, even after Weimar and the Nazis, even after the Stalinists and the Wall, these two, unlike many of those around them, do not long for stability and comfort. They want only the time and opportunity to do it again, their way. And there ends their common ground.

One of the men, Egon Zeidler, is an economist turned grocer, a gruffly gentle man with a walrus smile and a whale of a mouth. If you have a day, he can tell you a tale. Zeidler slipped into communism by accident and bucked the system every step of the way. He went to jail for refusing to conform. Finally, in his later years, he got his wish and the system fell. Only then did his beloved capitalism rear back and deliver a blow that would pin almost anyone to the mat.

The other man, Karl-Eduard von Schnitzler, also bucked a system in his youth. He is an aristocrat who heaved wealth and stature overboard to fight for the ideals of his adolescence. He chucked gold to wave the red banner. His courage led not to sacrifice and deprivation, but to a long life of privilege and prestige in a society ostensibly committed to its eradication. And then he too got socked; his beloved communism crashed and burned, leaving him with nothing.

To be an old German man at the end of the twentieth century is to be victim and victor many times over. In the end, it is to have led a life designed to crush hopes, soil ideals, and instill cynicism. But Zeidler and Schnitzler are men of unimaginable bounce. Or stubbornness. Or discipline. Neither could be smothered. Both showed a resiliency contrary to stereotypes of the Germans as fine technicians who panic in the face of defeat. Both are, pardon the expression, survivors.

> *Schni* (n.): a unit of time in communist East Germany, expressed as the amount of time needed to get out of one's chair, step over to the television set, and turn off the aggressive, insistent voice of Karl-Eduard von Schnitzler.

"Martha"—the familiar snap resonated across the house. "A beer!" The voice would be familiar in any East German household, even five years after Karl-Eduard von Schnitzler vanished from the TV screen. Schnitzler, a nobleman in the ruins of the people's paradise, had the same old regal manner, the same winter tan, the same righteous glare. But he was seventy-five, and the beer he barked for wore a western label. His cigars remained Cuban, but now he had to pay western prices for them. The life Schnitzler built for himself as renegade and revolutionary, as proud traitor to his family tradition, was over. He was on the defensive. He shaved off his trademark goatee. The beard was only a propaganda ploy, anyway, a trick devised by party psychologists to add a measure of wisdom to the aura of the party's chief purveyor of agitprop. For thirty years, he was in charge of molding East Germans' class consciousness and crafting the image of the enemy that justified his country's existence. In his heyday, Schnitzler was a persistent pest, a prickly propagandist whose weekly *Black Channel* program on East German TV was the communists' chief weapon in the losing battle to persuade the citizenry that West Germany was evil incarnate, the successor state to Nazi Germany, an imperialist power bent on eliminating the peace-loving German Democratic Republic.

The latest calendar on the wall of Schnitzler's house in deepest suburban Berlin was tacked up in late 1989, about the time the world he believed in was wrapped up and packed away, for good. For several years after his sudden ouster from the TV studio, Schnitzler mostly stayed inside, the better to avoid the stares and remarks from strangers on the street. And yet this old dog would not die. He slowly crept out of his isolation, returning to his old haunts, making the rounds of the lecture circuit, even the occasional TV appearance. He won new followers, a growing body of embittered Ossis, people who may have laughed along with the rest of the country when Schnitzler was in his prime, but who now saw him as someone with courage and tenacity, someone who still believed in a system that offered, in theory anyway, fairness and security. Schnitzler had little time left; he knew that. Still, he was intent on using his remaining years to launch a comeback, not just for himself, but for his beloved communism. And with the former communists making strong showings around the east, and even winning their way into parliament five years after the Wall fell, Schnitzler could haul out the old rhetoric about inevitable victory and inherent superiority. He would never again be despised by an entire nation, but maybe, just maybe, this propagandist, last of the old school, could unsettle the new rulers and revive nostalgia for a regime gone by.

Every Monday until three weeks after the Berlin Wall opened, Schnitzler presided over *Der schwarze Kanal* (Black Channel), treating his viewers to snippets from West German television, parading before them the ills of western society, defending East Germany's despised border guards as "my godchildren," and denouncing his countrymen for bucking against the communist government's travel ban. While Schnitzler enjoyed almost unheard-of carte blanche to visit the west, he filled his TV commentaries with slicing attacks on East Germans whose "lust for adventure could be more properly satisfied in the building of our socialist fatherland." On TV, Schnitzler was an alligator, a rough-skinned old revolutionary, snapping suddenly at his enemies, then retreating into calm. West Germans found the whole act outrageous. To East Germans—especially those in the Valley of the Clueless, that unfortunate southeastern corner of the country near Dresden where western TV signals could not reach—Schnitzler personified the system's refusal to look up from its doctrine and see how people really lived. When Ossis finally took their pain and frustration to the streets in 1989, Schnitzler was one of the demonstrators' main targets, particularly in Dresden, where TV viewers' only alternative on Monday nights had been Soviet army training films on East Germany's Second Channel. "Turn Off Schnitzler!" the crowds shouted. "Schnitzler to the Muppet Show!"

Schnitzler was born to be revolted against. His family, titled for centuries, was prominent in business and politics in western Germany, mostly in Cologne. A cousin, Georg von Schnitzler, was a director of I.G. Farben, the conglomerate that made Zyklon B, the gas used in Nazi concentration camps to kill millions. That Schnitzler was convicted of war crimes, but was later paroled and died a wealthy man. Another cousin ran the family bank and provided his home to Adolf Hitler for the signing of the secret deal that brought Hitler to power in January 1933. Schnitzler's father was a director of the Reichsbank, and Eduard and his three siblings grew up in luxury and prestige in Berlin's wealthiest suburb, Dahlem, and later in Cologne. While one of his brothers became a Nazi and later killed himself as the regime went up in flames, Eduard and another brother rebelled. They became communists, "traitors to our class," Eduard said with a self-satisfied smile. His elder brother volunteered to join the Soviet Red Army, was imprisoned once he was identified as a member of the Farben Schnitzler family, and later was rehabilitated and elected to the Volkskammer, the East German legislature. Eduard, youngest in the family, got his party card in 1928 and immediately rushed into street battle against the Nazis, who retaliated by beating and detaining their prey. In the early years of the Hitler regime, Schnitzler worked as a courier, commuting to Switzerland with messages and secret plans to save fellow reds from brownshirt persecution.

Drafted into the Wehrmacht, Schnitzler caught grenade bits in his knee in North Africa, served on the eastern front, and finally was deployed to occupied France, where he made contact with the resistance and conspired to divert Nazi gasoline supplies to the underground. Schnitzler's superiors discovered his betrayal of the Reich, had him arrested and tossed him into a Paris prison. A U.S. air raid provided cover for a jailbreak, and Schnitzler disappeared into the resistance, working with a variety of Allied officers. That work positioned Schnitzler for his entrance into the propaganda world, where a turncoat aristocrat was a welcome novelty. Within days after war's end, Schnitzler was on the BBC, broadcasting a German-language antifascist radio program called *German Prisoners of War Speak to the Homeland from London.*

A few weeks later, Allied commanders, desperate for reliable Germans who could run the occupation press, picked Schnitzler to run the Hamburg-based North German Radio. Schnitzler programmed antifascist, prodemocratic news and commentaries. At first, he avoided overt communist propaganda, but he also barred from his station mainstream German politicians whom he considered closet Nazis. That policy—which eventually extended to a ban on Konrad Adenauer, the former Cologne mayor emerging as the Allies' choice to lead the new Germany—got Schnitzler into trouble, and in 1947, after he devoted more and more airtime to the glories of the Soviet Union, his British overseers axed him. The first winds of Cold War were brewing, and Schnitzler took sides: He went to the Soviet Zone, to East Berlin's Berliner Rundfunk.

There, Schnitzler's rhetoric took a sharp turn toward the left. He began preaching Leninist orthodoxy and used his experience in the west to rail against a Bonn government he described as a nest of unrepentant Nazis.

East German party boss Walter Ulbricht took a liking to Schnitzler—the leader was so taken by the idea of a nobleman choosing communism that he forbade Schnitzler to drop the aristocratic "von" from his name—and together they devised *Black Channel,* which would use the voices and images of western TV to counter the public perception that the west was the up-and-coming Germany.

Schnitzler defended the communists' every move. When the truth was indefensible, he denied it. He affected outrage as he contended that no shoot-to-kill order had ever been given to East German guards stationed along the fortified border with the west. He portrayed the east as a country where workers enjoyed extraordinary options and the west as a place of unparalleled deprivation, even as his viewers unwrapped Christmas packages of cured meats, jams, and exquisite chocolates sent to them by their "poor" relations in the west. As the world eastern viewers saw through the prism of western television grew ever more miraculously bright and comfortable, Schnitzler's fossilized style became a joke, an insult to the nation's intelligence. He was a relic, a firebrand whose Monday evening rantings seemed as outdated and outrageous to East Germans as a William Jennings Bryan oration might seem to a nineties couch potato. The whole nation claimed not to watch anymore, but watch they did, even if only to laugh, even if only for the pleasure of switching over to the West German channel midway into Schnitzler's first sentence. The "red Goebbels" still set the tone for East Germany's self-justification.

Even after it was all over, Schnitzler, proud and bullheaded, conceded little error. "The program worked for a long time," he said. "It created a clear class attitude and enemy image. But, like the Wall, it lasted too long. I never said anything I didn't believe at the time. I might have had incorrect information. There's nothing wrong with agitprop; churches have been doing it for two thousand years. What the people want is one thing; what they should have is another. You can easily influence what they want; that is the role of propaganda." Such bravado was silenced on the last Monday in November 1989. The Politburo gave him five minutes of airtime to deliver his valedictory, in which he declared German socialism a success, called himself a "weapon in the class struggle for the defense of my socialist fatherland," and announced he had not a thing to regret.

There would be hardship. After the demise of East Germany, his pension was cut by more than half. Both he and his wife, a Hungarian Jew, lost their incomes when they were fired from East German television. The Schnitzlers still had their comfortable house on the outskirts of town, in a wooded enclave of communist privilege, with a lovely garden and an impressive library. But their Wessi had come to visit, to announce his intention to reclaim his lost property. The Schnitzlers were assured they could stay in the house they had lived in for three decades, but the Wessi was already taking measurements and getting estimates on renovations.

Schnitzler, like the best propagandists, lived secluded enough from the surrounding misery to believe much of what he said. After decades of steeping himself in a black and white view of the world, he could not see the shades of gray introduced into the east by reunification. He was blind to the hefty dose of socialism embedded in the West German system, which offered a rich menu of subsidies and benefits even as it preached the merits of competition and market economics. Schnitzler had hawked conspiracy theories for so long, he almost bought them. Almost. In the grand tradition of manner-born revolutionaries, Schnitzler managed to make it through the run of German communism with traces of his humor and class identity intact. He could argue the advantages of socialism one moment, then refer to the German lower classes as "sheep" the next.

Those same faceless followers made life miserable for Schnitzler after 1989. For many months, Schnitzler was afraid to venture out, even to the food market. "There was such hate against us, hate and insults, telephone terror, at one point it was thirty calls an hour," Schnitzler recalled. He began carrying a heavy cane to defend himself against fellow citizens who shoved him to punctuate their verbal denunciations. The rabidly anticommunist eastern tabloid *Super!* made Schnitzler a particular target, plastering huge, outraged headlines across its front page anytime a western TV channel invited the old man to relive his *Black Channel* days on the air.

The public antagonism died off after a couple of years. He began holding lectures, and the audiences grew larger and more friendly. His book *Red Channel—Poor Germany* appeared and even though it was trashed by critics, east and west alike, the publisher had to go back for repeated printings. Schnitzler's readings became popular gatherings of Ossis searching for a new old identity. The crotchety old propagandist found himself a regular on the chat shows that dominate German prime time. He went on TV for a one-time-only reprise of *Black Channel* in which he accused Chancellor Kohl of lusting after territory stretching to the Black Sea. Schnitzler delivered fiery speeches before vestigial communist parties in Germany, Austria and Belgium. And he claimed that Germany's domestic intelligence agency was tracking him, tapping his phone and sending agents to observe his public appearances. His message was not terribly new: The West was driven by profit and greed alone. The working man was destined to be the victim of a cruel system. The Deutsche mark was the modern substitute for the concentration camp. The demise of eastern universities, intellectual academies and social services was a concerted effort to destroy eastern confidence. Easterners would one day realize all this and rise up against their oppressors.

Like so many intellectuals, east and west, Schnitzler weaved a crazy quilt of pessimism and self-denigration based on his discomfort with being German. "I am not ashamed to be German," he announced one minute, only to say a few seconds later that "it is suicide for anyone to rely on Germans learning democracy. Our much-vaunted pacifism is skin-deep. We are a people who need authority. That is why socialism is our only alternative to imperialism and war."

Schnitzler defied forty years of facts and portrayed the east's poverty and depressing grayness as the legacy of luck rather than mismanagement and corruption. ("We happened to get the more war-ravaged part of Germany. We got the poorer part of Germany. We had to pay billions in reparations to the Soviet Union and Poland.") He was an unrepentant purist who denounced his Party for Democratic Socialism for turning to the right and forsaking its communist roots. The closest Schnitzler came to an apology was to say that "there was, of course, a certain gap between reality and ideal. That's true everywhere. I will say that an incorrect security doctrine arose, and in an un-Marxist fashion, it watched over people's daily lives in a completely improper way. But that was a policy error, not a crime. Brecht said, 'Communism is the easiest politics to explain and the hardest to achieve.' "

Like so many who believed in East Germany's moral superiority, Schnitzler was ultimately puzzled by the transformation of Erich Honecker from antifascist street fighter to architect of a paranoid, oppressive bureaucracy. Schnitzler's explanation was among the more benign. "Honecker's tragedy is that he surrounded himself with the wrong advisers," he said. "I can only wish West German politicians had as good an antifascist biography." Schnitzler's worship of East Germany's founding generation was typical of the country's mythmakers; his version excluded the fact that Ulbricht and several other founding fathers who spent exile years in Moscow were only too willing to provide their Soviet protectors with lists of German communists to be purged of Jews, independent thinkers and those willing to compromise with Social Democrats.

"I still say East Germany was the best that the German people have produced in history—no Reich, no war, no genocide. This larger Germany already has an Africa corps in Somalia, sent ships off to the Gulf War, and set the fires in the Balkans. What I said about the crimes of capitalism was the pure truth. We see that now firsthand. The people realize finally they were bought for a few bananas and some traveling."

Schnitzler relished each venomous phrase as he dispensed it, as if he were testing the script for his next TV commentary. There would be no more *Black Channel,* of course. But the old man would turn out his books and

speeches until the end, pining for the return of a world that never was, re-
tiring each evening to a box of aromatic cigars and the warm, woodsy comfort of a life left largely untouched by the wild winds of the politics outside.

In the honored position above his desk in his dusty, dreary office backstage
from his corner grocery, Egon Zeidler posted a sales photo of a red Pontiac
Trans Sport van. It was his grail. It was the one thing in the office guaranteed to bring a grin to the old man's tired face. That, and the dream he had
held close since boyhood—to travel one day across the ocean on a tramp
freighter. "Not a luxury liner, no use for that," Zeidler said. "I wanted to get
on board, work, get to know the crew, be of some use. I had a cousin who
went on a tramper. I was fascinated and jealous. I looked into it and it would
cost twenty-two hundred dollars. That's seven months of keeping the shop
open. And so it's out of the question. My former bride and I have been together for forty-three years—you might say I've known her a few months already—and what she really wants in life is to keep this place open, even as
it swallows up our savings every month."

The tiny shop, on the ground floor of an apartment building at the corner
of Wetterseestrasse and Eschengraben in the Pankow section of eastern
Berlin, was packed so tightly with goods, it seemed to have been designed
by an autistic child. The grocery store belonged to Egon and Brigitte now,
after unification, just as it had before, even under communism. So determined had they been to keep it out of the state's hands that Egon went to
jail, gave up his life's savings, lost the family house in one of Berlin's best
suburbs, and even divorced Brigitte (on paper, anyway) to save the store
from zealous tax inspectors. The Zeidlers held on, even when it meant living in three small rooms between the crammed storefront and the impossibly stuffed storeroom in the back.

And then, when the inevitable finally happened, and the whole East German house of cards fluttered to the table, Zeidler was ready to roll, a born
capitalist itching to share his economic zest with his fellow eastern shopkeepers, bleary-eyed refugees from state planning and central control. Over
the years, Zeidler's business acumen had won him the attention, wooing,
and finally the spurned rage of East German rulers. Zeidler was still sputtering over their inane interferences in his life, even as a new force stepped
in to make his days miserable. The capitalism that came east in 1990 was
not the level playing field Zeidler had learned and lectured about in the old
days. The big supermarket chains burst into the east at the moment of monetary unity that July. In a matter of weeks, Zeidler's shop was in trouble
again, going down as inexorably as it had under communism. The new era
had more than its share of disillusioning days, and by any reasonable mea-

sure, the corner store was a flop. But that did not stop Egon and Brigitte. If their beloved shop was going to die, the Zeidlers were going to have a blast watching it go.

That was Zeidler's way, always had been. "I'm from the war generation and I learned one thing in the Nazi time: We Germans must absolutely avoid being arrogant and overestimating ourselves. And that goes for me, too." He grew up in Dessau, in what would later be East Germany, and served in the Wehrmacht as a marine. "Oh, the Nazis were very attractive to us as young people. Like the discos today—organized leisure. The Hitler Youth didn't cost anything. And the Nazis themselves, they looked like semigods."

Zeidler's father, a salesman, was a skeptic, and he passed on his views to his son. One day in 1939, when Egon was twelve, he watched a column of scrawny concentration camp prisoners being marched through his city's streets by guards who pounded all but the quickest inmates with rifle butts. "I had no idea what they were, but my father knew," Zeidler said. "All the adults knew, of course. And from that day, I had my image of Nazism. Everything clouded over for me then. To see such terrible treatment of people. They were just bones. I had just had a Bible lesson that said, 'Do unto others and give of your own.' And my father and I talked about that horrible line, *'Deutschland, Deutschland über Alles,'* and I asked, 'What if everyone said that? "England, England über Alles?" ' My father said I took it too concretely, that it only means 'Above All Else, My Fatherland.' I asked my father, 'So why doesn't it say that?' "

The German war machine was not known for its tolerance of such discussions. Young Zeidler knew he would not fit into the Waffen-SS, which was, by that point in the war, drafting boys directly into its ranks. When he turned seventeen, Zeidler talked his draft officer into letting him join the Marines, which had the reputation of being the service least controlled by hard-core Nazis, rather than the SS. But even in the Marines, Zeidler's attitude and his tendency to run off at the mouth provoked trouble. A Nazi political officer complained to Zeidler's captain that Egon was voicing opinions contrary to the good of the Fatherland. The captain told Zeidler to shut his trap; the next time the political officer asked Egon to recite the justification for the Reich's war, Zeidler saluted and said, *"Am deutschen Wesen soll die Welt genesen"* (The world will do it Germany's way).

In late April 1945, Zeidler was stationed on an island between Germany and Denmark. Every morning, he watched brown-uniformed party officials step aboard German planes taking off for Sweden. None ever returned. It was all over; they were fleeing. Zeidler approached his old nemesis, the political officer, and said, "It seems it is no longer such an honor to be a German soldier." For that remark, Zeidler was sent to a court-martial and sentenced to death. Although the Wehrmacht executed some of its own soldiers as late as June 1945, Zeidler was saved by war's end.

After the war, Zeidler enrolled in business school in the west, earned a degree, and in 1950, despite his antipathy toward socialism, moved back to Berlin, to the Soviet Zone, to be with Brigitte. "Love knows no limits," Zeidler said. "I never believed the city could remain divided for four years, let alone forty." He taught at a school of commerce and developed a devoted following among the students. He had a tendency to ramble ("I just need one word and I'm off like a ski jumper"), but young people adored his sarcasm and folk wisdom. Older people were less amused: Zeidler's advocacy of consumer goods ran contrary to Marxist belief in the primacy of production goods. He lost his teaching position, only to regain it after the failed 1953 people's uprising persuaded the communist bosses that some attention needed to be paid to making consumer products.

Beginning in the mid-1950s, Zeidler, who had been teaching business skills and advising large East German industries, was appointed to a state committee on small businesses. He was eventually given the task of organizing the nationalization of the very family-owned businesses he had been working to save. "I couldn't reconcile that with my beliefs," he said. "I refused to do it and I was sent off to the desert." He was sacked. He sold potato peelers from a box on the "Alex," Alexanderplatz, East Berlin's main square. His former students searched him out and together they held symposia on the broad concrete plaza. Zeidler was holding forth on the Alex one day in 1959 when an emissary from the East German Council on Economics approached and invited him to head its light-industry department. Zeidler accepted and became the only member who did not hold a *Parteibuch* (party book).

After a couple of years on the council, he was assigned to a secret project called Object Green. The task was to assemble essential western goods that were simply unavailable in the East Bloc. Object Green, he soon learned, was the communist bosses' retreat at Wandlitz, outside Berlin. To bring Politburo members' houses up to decent standards, Zeidler had to buy chrome, door hinges and assorted kitchen supplies in the west, and then sneak them back east in briefcases. A few months into the project, Zeidler realized that the rush to assemble large stockpiles of western goods had a deeper meaning. The east was building up supplies of building materials and precision equipment because the long-rumored closing of the border was in the works. Zeidler and his wife began talking about committing their country's most grave political crime: *Republikflucht*, fleeing to the west. The birth of their youngest daughter in May 1961 made escape harder—a family leaving with three children would look suspicious. Still, they planned. Zeidler knew construction of a barrier was imminent, but he knew no dates. That summer, Zeidler slowly carried all of his books to West Berlin and transferred his savings to a western bank. But somehow—Zeidler suspected the Stasi had a mole somewhere in his own extended family—the secret police got wind of the Zeidlers' scheme. On August 8, only days before the Wall was thrown up, the couple's identification papers were confiscated and they were restricted to their neighborhood. They were stuck in the east.

Over the next years, "the garbage kept piling up on my soul," Zeidler said. In 1961, he gave a speech at East Berlin's Rotes Rathaus, the City Hall, in which he spelled out the corruption involved in building the Wandlitz retreat. At a conference of party functionaries, he directly criticized Politburo members and revealed details of the secret construction program. Zeidler was immediately fired. He became a nonperson in the eyes of the government. Although he found work as director of a small company that made printing machines, he knew he had permanently broken relations with the regime.

Yet the East German communists, always a bit more open to individual initiative than their Soviet overseers, tolerated Zeidler's dabblings in private business. In the 1960s, he ran the only independent business at East Berlin's Schönefeld Airport, a service that repaired cars for travelers while they were away and picked them up at the airfield when they returned. Time and again, the state threatened to nationalize the business. Each time, Zeidler maneuvered to save it, until finally in 1974, the government came at him with a tax bill for ten years of arrears. Zeidler refused to pay, arguing that the tax was confiscatory. He was fined 500,000 marks and sent to prison for eighteen months. The government nationalized his house in Zeuthen, the same leafy suburb where von Schnitzler lived. The Zeidlers had to move into a small apartment in the inner city. Still, Egon would not conform. He taunted the Stasi agents, interrupting his own phone conversations to bark, "Excuse me, this conversation is going to last a while so you'd better change the tape or it will be embarrassing for you later."

While Zeidler was in prison, Brigitte took over the private grocery in Pankow. After Egon's release in 1976, he joined her—secretly, since he had officially divorced her to keep the taxman at bay. Then in 1985, the tax authorities hit again, socking the Zeidlers for more than the store was worth. The couple continued only by firing their three employees and shrinking the operation to a size they could manage themselves.

In the last years of East Germany, the government finally tired of harassing Zeidler. Official attitudes toward limited private enterprise relaxed a bit. So when the revolts of 1989 came along, Zeidler was satisfied to watch from afar. He told himself he was not the demonstrating type. But inside, he rejoiced. He would finally get the chance to run his business as he had always wanted to, selling products he chose, at prices he set. He had spent so many hours over the years preaching capitalism that his children sped to the border: Two moved west to start their careers and a third found work in western Berlin while living in the east.

Still, just as forty years of life under socialism had altered Zeidler's appearance—his teeth were falling out, he had a pasty complexion and he wore the East German uniform of polyester clothes and flimsy sandals with thick socks—so had it affected his view of the world: Profit had taken on a dirty taint. Zeidler said it would violate his "social conscience" to take too much profit, to add stress to his customers' already tense lives. He raised the prices of sweets to nearly prohibitive levels because he didn't like the idea of children ruining their teeth.

East Berlin boomed in those first months. On October 7, 1989, there were seven hundred small, private businesses registered in East Berlin. Eight months later, the city had received twelve thousand applications for business licenses. Within days after the Wall opened, Zeidler began wheeling and dealing. From his tiny office, where he paced the sticky, worn-through strips of linoleum, Zeidler worked the phone (when it worked), setting up the first contacts with West Berlin wholesalers, persuading them to sell him wares even though he could pay only with virtually worthless east-marks. Even before the two Germanys merged their economies in July 1990, Zeidler's shelves were stocked with 150 western products, including Nesquik hot chocolate, Ghostbusters candies, West Berlin beer, French wine, Dutch ice cream, and the ubiquitous Coke. Eastern goods—blandly marketed, sloppily packed, low in quality—went begging. Profits shot up at first. There were lines out the shop entrance. Everyone wanted to try the western foods, smokes and snacks. People who ordinarily bought no wine popped in and picked up four cases of French burgundy.

But very quickly, Zeidler saw disaster coming. The twin shocks of the demise of state price subsidies and the advent of widespread unemployment had injected the east with the virus of mass depression. Within weeks, the new edginess became evident. For the first time, Zeidler suffered shoplifting. It got so bad, he had to install a video surveillance system. In the first month alone, Zeidler caught three young men with apples, candies and pots of yogurt in their coat pockets. "We always had huge numbers of unemployed people," Zeidler said, "but we also had a guaranteed right to work, so the unemployed were paid to do nothing at work. They had a place to go, a sense of purpose, and an income. Now they have nothing."

People had to eat. They would shop somewhere. But Zeidler could see his customers' loyalties shifting. In the summer of 1990, he predicted he would close before year's end, as western supermarket chains took over state-run stores, slashed prices and drove corner grocers to their graves. He was right. Dozens of Aunt Emma shops, as Germans call mom-and-pop operations, did succumb to the western chains' dumping practices. Unlike in other countries, Ossi entrepreneurs like Zeidler could not fight back by extending hours and stressing convenience; federal law forbid any store from opening in the early mornings, evenings, Saturday afternoons, Sundays or holidays. "We fought and survived forty years of socialism," he said in 1992. "We will not survive three years of market economics."

But Zeidler did continue, largely by pumping his remaining savings and his small government pension into the store to balance the books. At an average subsidy of $320 each month, the Zeidlers were rapidly eating through their retirement nut. Truth was, the shop no longer had a prayer of making money. A year after unification, turnover at the shop had plummeted by 80 percent from 1989 levels. The average purchase per customer slipped from 12 marks ($8) to 3 marks ($2) in one year; clearly, shoppers were stopping into Zeidler's only to pick up something they had forgotten to get at the supermarket or at one of the western Berlin discount warehouse markets they traveled to in an attempt to economize. The shop's rent skyrocketed from 400 east-marks (worth less than $20) to 2,000 Deutsche marks ($1,300) in less than a year. Utility costs leaped to western levels. But eastern incomes remained at about one-third of western salaries through the first two years of unity.

"We have a responsibility to the old people who can't walk to the supermarket," Brigitte said.

"We are not Caritas" (the main German charity), Egon replied.

The cowbell attached to the door jingled only once every few minutes. A little girl buys a candy bar. A boy asks for a Coke. An old woman selects a jar of sausages in water and one potato.

"I always thought I understood business," Egon once said. "But imagine the pain and absurdity of realizing at the end of every month that we have to put money into the store. I know a lot about economics, but I don't know why it is that a video camera that costs three hundred dollars in a store in Schleswig-Holstein (in the west) costs four hundred forty dollars from a wholesaler in the east." Wholesalers told Zeidler and other eastern merchants that it cost more to haul goods to the east from western plants. But in fact many western suppliers were taking advantage of both the eastern hunger for anything western and the lack of serious competition in the new region.

Even after unification, the old East German system seemed to haunt the

Zeidlers. For many years, the family had owned four acres of forestland south of Berlin, a cherished homestead that the family had managed to keep away from the sharp fangs of the state. But a few weeks after East Germany slipped into oblivion, the Zeidlers went for a Christmas walk on their property, only to find that half of the land had been cleared of its hundred-year-old Douglas fir trees. The state forestry enterprise, in its final days, had simply taken the wood. The state forester admitted the felling had been done without a permit and in violation of a ban on cutting of privately held forests. But the state forestry company had been dissolved and the state government, which was responsible for the surrounding land, was nearly bankrupt. "Once again, we are dispossessed," Zeidler said. "That is the reality of East Germany." The crowning blow came a year later, when Zeidler's daughter received a letter from the state forest management office ordering her to reforest the land.

Zeidler's long-held trust in the free market dissolved over the years. He came to believe that eastern businesses should be given some protection against competition from the powerful west. He clamored for price controls, low-interest credits, training for shopowners. On a more practical level, Zeidler worked on a couple of schemes. He looked into turning the shop's back room into a snack bar. His children told him he was out of his mind to invest in a new business at age sixty-five. "What else should I do?" Zeidler shouted. "Sit in a saloon and twiddle my thumbs?"

And Zeidler became unofficial adviser to hundreds of would-be businesspeople in Pankow, satisfying work that unfortunately brought in barely any income. "My colleagues knew as much about economics as a blind person knows about the color scheme," he said. In his section of Berlin alone, seven hundred small shops failed in the first year of unification.

Despite his proficiency at complaining, Zeidler managed to find reasons for hope. He bought a computer and taught himself western tax codes. In 1992, eastern products made a comeback. The fascination with things western had run its course, and eastern pride became if not chic, then at least a satisfying defense mechanism. Zeidler proudly showed off cases of Berliner Pilsener beer ("The Beer from Here!" the labels said), jars of sauerkraut from Thuringia and red cabbage from Leipzig. "The customers say, 'Thank God, once again cabbage that tastes like ours.' The western German cabbage is tasteless. We have our own prune jam again; the western is too creamy and tastes like wallpaper glue. Ours is spiced with cinnamon."

But stocking and eating your own horseradish and blackberry jam was no substitute for making a profit. Another western chain supermarket was being built within walking distance, the fourth in the immediate neighborhood. By the end of 1993, Zeidler's was the last mom-and-pop shop left in the Pankow area. He gave up his last two storerooms in back; at the new western prices, they remained unrented.

Zeidler, like so many of his neighbors, turned his wrath on Kohl and the Bonn government. "Those famous words from our chancellor—'It won't be worse for anyone,' Ha! It is worse for millions. This is a robber society, and the lies from them are not so different from the lies we always heard. But you won't hear most people saying this. We haven't learned to be critical yet. The psyche of our people hasn't caught up to the new system. Everyone's concentrating on his own navel. Our neighbors don't exist for us anymore. Everyone's buying locks and cutting themselves off from the other."

The old man grew heavier by the year. His hearing faded, he was losing his hair. The savings could only support the store for another few years, if that long. And yet Egon and Brigitte went out and bought themselves a new Subaru minivan, four-wheel drive, enough room to sleep in. They drove up to the Baltic coast, parked near the beach, and imagined they were masters of their own seaside castle. "You know, I think all the time about how hard it's been, all these years, and now again." Egon ripped open a new pack of Camels and sucked on one for a long moment. "We had weeks when I bought a pig's head and made five or six meals out of it. And now, a new system, and such unfair rules. And then I slap myself on the cheek"—and he did just that—"and I say, 'You asshole! This is a once-in-a-thousand-years moment. We've had the luck to live in a time when freedom came and our grandchildren might even live in a world of peace, a world without weapons.'

"I am no victim. I reject the word. I am a man whose fate was handed out just as any other. My gut gets fatter and fatter. If I compare myself to someone starving in Bangladesh, I am no victim. But my generation was laid on the cross again and again. I did lose chances. And there are things in my mind that I don't even know are there much of the time. This business of being German is always there, somewhere. Somewhere in my head, I still think if we Germans aren't going to be a great military power, then we should at least be a great economic power. And then comes that national pride that someone—I don't know who—can awaken. And I ask you, what is the next step? Kicking the next guy. That's how it starts. But I have my grandchildren. Thomas is sixteen, he is a mensch. He is neither Ossi nor Wessi. He feels no connection to Germany or to the west. He has no patriotism to anyone. He is a person, just a person."

9

Carpetbaggers
and Scallywags

Unity was better when we were divided. —A character in the Distel cabaret in eastern Berlin, 1991

We were the perfect relatives: You could always invite us. We would never come. —Another Distel character, 1992

RENTING A GLEAMING black Audi for my visit to Rangsdorf was probably not the brightest of notions. Sailing past long-abandoned border stations on the outskirts of western Berlin, zipping by graffiti-covered guard towers and bullet-riddled warning signs, I reached the cornfields and pig farms of southern Brandenburg in less than an hour. Rangsdorf was once a weekend getaway for Berlin's well-to-do, a stately village of large homes with red-tiled roofs, manicured rose bushes and tall maple trees. Until the start of World War II, commuter trains ran every twenty minutes between Rangs-dorf and Berlin, carrying tired city dwellers to the fresh air and pristine lakes of the countryside. Nazi generals and admirals made Rangsdorf one of their favorite retreats. The communists, too, reserved the town's finest houses for privileged party insiders. After the fall of the Wall, Rangsdorf's collection of pocket-sized summer cottages and neglected but regal man-sions was invaded by western developers hungry to recreate a weekend playland. The people of Rangsdorf were accustomed to large-scale inva-sions: their town was home to two Soviet Army garrisons and one of the oc-cupying force's most important helicopter bases. But despite the endless rumbling of Soviet jeeps through the village and the incessant beating of chopper blades overhead, the invasion that most rattled Rangsdorf in the first years after reunification was the surge of BMWs, Mercedes and Audis that signaled the return of the owners.

It wasn't until the early 1970s that East Germany went on a nationalizing binge designed virtually to eliminate private ownership of real estate. Until the Berlin Wall went up, some West Berliners had kept weekend properties in the East, either for their own use or for some minimal rental income. But after the Wall was built, East Germany declared all western-owned houses abandoned. (Despite that bit of legal bravado, East Germany continued until the seventies to pay lip service to the rule of law, regularly making minuscule deposits into East Berlin escrow accounts in the names of West German landlords.)

By the mid-1980s, the East German regime was backing off from communist dogma about all property belonging to the people. Especially in towns like Rangsdorf, where housing consisted predominantly of single-family homes rather than Stalinist apartment blocks, authorities began offering citizens the chance to buy the houses they lived in. The experience of ownership, communism aside, inspired many East Germans to begin renovations the state had postponed for decades. It was a happy development for everyone involved, improving the housing stock, relieving some of the misery and stagnancy in the countryside, easing the administrative burden on the central government.

That is, until the Mercedes and the Audis began rolling into town. The procession began the first weekend after the Wall opened. Throughout West Germany, families had passed on from generation to generation pained and proud recollections of homesteads, estates, farms and weekend getaways left behind, emotional stories of lost lands and confiscated castles. That collective memory fed the deep ambivalence toward what many in the west dubbed the "so-called German Democratic Republic."

Now, suddenly, a visit to the old homestead was as easy as getting in the car and taking a Sunday drive in the country. A very long drive in the country. The east's narrow, rutted, tree-lined lanes—beautiful reminders of what driving was like in the era before highways—were immediately transformed into a traffic mess worthy of the Hamptons or Cape Cod on a summer Sunday. The first confrontations between Wessis and Ossis were traffic altercations, inevitable clashes between Beemers and Trabis, between polished, strong metal and pollution-pocked, soft plastic. After a few weekends of sharing the roads, no one in Germany had the slightest doubt which society was going to be in charge of the coming merger.

But the drama on the highways paled next to the angst that seared life in villages such as Rangsdorf. Eighty percent and more of the properties there were formerly—or still, depending on how you looked at it—owned by westerners. So, even a year after the Wall fell, when I drove my Hertz Audi into Rangsdorf, I knew Wessis were unloved. But I did not expect to see old women stop chatting in their front yards to scurry back into the house and draw the curtains. I was startled when one man grabbed a garden hoe and held it menacingly at his hip. And when I stopped at the lakeside boathouse to ask for directions, I was speechless when the clerk greeted me not with "Good day," but with a snarled "Grundstück" (Property). The woman at the boathouse, like virtually everyone else in town, had seen Wessis in Audis clutching old photographs, yellowed maps, fraying property records, barely legible letters and all manner of evidence that one or another house in town was theirs, and they would like it back now, thank you. Everyone in town had heard about the angry West Berlin woman who dropped onto the boathouse office counter a picture of her mother posing before a Rangsdorf house, then demanded to know where Taunus Strasse was. Told there was no such street, the woman stormed off, only to return after a short time, waving a Nazi-era map of the town in one hand and the communist version in the other. Taunus Strasse's name had been changed to Goethe Strasse. "You can't hide my house from me anymore," the woman shouted. "I'm going to get it right now."

To East Germans who had papers saying they owned their houses, and to Ossis whose rental leases guaranteed their occupancy "for life," the arrival of the western owners rocked the foundation of their lives. "I'm seventy-nine," said Edith Meyer, who had lived in her house—which she thought she owned—for twenty years. "What else can happen to me? The heir of the Wessi owner—he's the stepgrandson—came with a woman and a young son and introduced himself. They said they want the house back, but I can stay until I die. He won't put any money into it, but I can stay. Of course, they don't want our houses, they would just tear them down. They only want the land underneath, so they can get money for it. It's so crass. They just appear. It could have been done decently."

As I pulled up to the corner across from Rainer and Andrea Friedrich's house, I saw Rainer jog into the house. Then, people peeked at me from behind the curtains. Finally, both Friedrichs emerged as I approached their gate on foot. They looked like relatives awaiting bad news about loved ones at a crash site. Their anxiety as I stepped toward them was matched only by their smiles of relief when I told them who I was. "Our Wessis haven't come in yet," Rainer said.

"But we've seen them a couple of times," Andrea added. "They arrive in their Mercedes, park right in front, sit in the car and take pictures. If I look through the window, they take off. Where have they been for thirty years? We saved this house."

"They could at least look us in the eye." Rainer shook his head. "We're all Germans. Look, this house is my life. Nobody forced these people to leave. And I obviously didn't choose to be born in this country. Well, let me say this: I will do everything in my power to protect my property. This house would have gone to seed without us. We saved this house."

Whose property was it? Rainer Friedrich was born in this house. He knew no other. He insulated the cellar and installed new windows. He painted, caulked, raked and mowed. He considered the sixty-year-old, two-story house, and all the apple trees and rose beds, the vegetable garden and the tree swing—all of it—his. But he had no title. In 1990, when East Germany ceased to exist, the Friedrichs were still negotiating to buy the house under the communist system, which would allow them to own the building while the state retained the land beneath it. Until their ownership was complete, however, the Friedrichs continued to pay rent of $47 a month (the rent was quadrupled in early 1991.) But the end of the country meant the end of the purchase process. Everything was frozen. The Friedrichs stayed in their house, waiting for a court ruling that could come anytime in the next decade or two.

The West Germans claiming the house had left it in 1960, shortly before the Wall was built. Under the reunification treaty between the two Germanys, property claims—and there would be 2 million of them—were to be handled according to the principle "Return before compensation." That meant West Germans and others whose property was nationalized by the communists could have it back, as long as they planned actually to live in it again. If they only wanted the old place back as an investment property, they could be paid off in cash. There were protections for old folks, and longtime tenants had to be given reasonable time to quit the property, but the law was severe enough, cruelly so in the eyes of most easterners. Not that people in the west were terribly happy with it either: Many western investors held back from building factories or opening shops in the east because of uncertainties created by the property claim law. Who would build a plant on land that might belong to westerners whose property was taken by the communists, or to Jews whose property was seized by the Nazis?

The property claim dispute soon developed into a huge industry that supported hundreds of lawyers (including some easterners) and promised to keep the courts busy for decades. The city of Leipzig, for example, had 60 lawyers in 1989. By 1994, there were more than 500, more than half of them westerners, most slogging away on claims. In the small eastern town of

Quedlinburg, home to 30,000 people, 31,000 property claims were registered by 1993, freezing investment and development. Only a few months after unification, some members of the Kohl government admitted that the
policy of returning property rather than handing the former owners a check
was an economic mistake. But it would be some years before the west realized what a huge psychological error the policy had been, how much damage it had done to whatever goodwill might have existed between east and
west. Even a series of shocking suicides did little to shake western complacency. In 1992, Detlef Dalk, a town council member in the east, hanged
himself and left a letter to Kohl describing his despair over the previous
owner's effort to regain control of Dalk's house. Psychiatrists in the east reported ten times the usual level of suicides in the first years after unity, not
solely as a reaction to property claims, but as a reflection of deep disorientation in many eastern lives. The west's blindness toward that damage was
not so much intentional as a result of a genuine and precipitous slackening
of interest in the east after the initial euphoria. Unification quickly metamorphized from joy to burden for many westerners. Their taxes jumped repeatedly. And everything the Ossis did seemed to rub the sheen off the
image (and self-image) West Germans had worked so hard to polish since
the war. Western resentment expressed itself variously as lack of interest,
rejection, and an arrogance so overbearing it threatened to keep east and
west apart for generations.

Bonn is as pretty and quiet as a capital can be. It is a college town with a
large population of retired diplomats and bureaucrats. Always considered
West Germany's provisional capital, it never developed the trappings of an
important city: No grand public buildings, no tourist attractions, no important symbols of the nation's past or present, none of the tensions and street
confrontations of a country's focal point. The city's first national-class museums, a fine showcase for traveling art exhibits and a gallery devoted to
West Germany's postwar history, did not open until several years after reunification, long after parliament voted to return the reunited country's seat
of government to Berlin. Even after unity, Bonn remained a distinctly western place. Less than an hour's drive from Holland and Belgium, it was a
jumping-off spot rather than a destination. With no airport of its own and
only difficult connections by train, Bonn offered German politicians relative seclusion. Only on the rarest of occasions did Bonn leaders face public
opinion directly. Protests were infrequent. And easterners were virtually invisible. Only a handful lived in Bonn after reunification. Few national institutions bothered hiring Ossis—hardly any could be found in the news
bureaus, lobbying groups, embassies, parliamentary offices and ministries

around town. And surprisingly few of Bonn's ruling elite—even among those who were working on unity issues—could be bothered to travel to the other side of their own country.

"They are total strangers to me," Angelika Volle, a prominent researcher at the German Society for Foreign Affairs, told me one day in 1991 at one of Bonn's little Italian restaurants where ministers and their deputies went to see who was eating lunch with whom. "I don't know any east Germans. I know more Hungarians and Poles. The east Germans don't know anything of Europe. They've never traveled. They've never been confronted with being German and taking responsibility for the past. We had all these painful discussions during our student days. What did our parents do in the Third Reich? What did we do to the Jews? The east Germans haven't begun to deal with any of this. My friends are British, French and American. I speak their languages. The east Germans don't. They may turn out to be good Europeans, or they may be nationalists. I'm not proud of being German. I am German. That's what my passport says. But in the west, you find more and more Germans questioning those feelings. I don't think people in the east are thinking about it. OK, I was born in the west with a silver spoon in my mouth, and I am willing to pay for their integration into this country. I'm even willing to pay higher taxes for it. But even I wouldn't take a holiday in eastern Germany."

Volle's attitudes were not unusual. Theo Sommer, the wise and witty publisher of the opinion weekly *Die Zeit*, told me that easterners threatened to dilute west German democracy because they are "xenophobic, condescending and isolated. Europe means nothing to them." Sommer dismissed the vaunted openness and friendliness of eastern society as the "solidarity of the air-raid shelter." He moodily concluded that the last, best hope of resolving the east-west split was intermarriage.

Two years after the fall of the Wall, a senior official of the Federal Press Office and a director of Bavarian television proudly said they had not yet been to the east. Neither had any great desire to go. Rüdiger Löwe, the TV executive, even had relatives in the east. "We exchanged letters and sent Christmas parcels to them every year, just like everyone else," he said. "But I feel no connection to them."

"We have nothing in common with them, except our dark past," said Eleonore Linsmayer, the press officer and later a German ambassador in central Asia. "The easterners remind us of what we worked so hard for so long to live down." She told a story of rising resentment among westerners. Her nephew, twenty-six, and son of an ambassador, was beginning the process of seeking a foreign service job. Even before completing an application, the young man believed the system was rigged in favor of Ossis: The

Foreign Ministry's long-standing requirement that applicants be fluent in either English or French had been replaced by a rule allowing any United Nations language, including Russian, the foreign language most widely studied in the east. That adjustment in the hiring rules was enough to outrage an entire class of westerners seeking to represent their country abroad.

Nor was western disdain for the east limited to those accustomed to holding power. At the Nonnenwerth School, a small private high school south of Bonn, western teenagers told me about their school's annual trip, a popular event that combines learning with travel. In 1991, nearly sixty students signed up to visit Rome or Paris; only eight expressed interest in an eastern German adventure. Although some students seemed genuinely thrilled by unification—one said he got excited every night when he saw the weather map on TV without a border line drawn through the middle of Germany—most seemed bored by or dismissive of their eastern brethren. "We're two extremely different types of people," said Cornelia Kuss. "We think so differently. We learned to make decisions all our lives. They have to decide for the first time, 'what am I going to do in school, after school, for a career?' "

I asked if the students could envision marrying an easterner. "Why not?" Kuss said. "I marry a person, not a country."

Another student, Renata Niffgen, couldn't bring herself that far. "We live so close to them," she said, "but it's a tremendous distance between us."

Whether they wanted to or not, many western Germans could not avoid contact with the east. In the years after the Wall tumbled, western businesspeople, educators, lawyers, police, politicians and academics crossed the old border to make money, spread the gospel of competition and capitalism, retrain workers, and bridge the gap created by decades of separation. Some came with goodwill; others did not. Some came of their own sense of obligation or adventure; others had to be lured with cash, cars, cellular phones and free air tickets to avoid the dreaded overnight in the east. The Bonn government instituted its own shuttle flights to Berlin so civil servants could get to the east for breakfast, put in a full day, and be home in time for the evening news. Every night at the tiny departure lounges at the Leipzig and Dresden airports, hundreds of western businessmen lugging briefcases in one hand and satellite phone cases in the other overwhelmed the bar and filled every inch of floor space, waiting for inevitably delayed escape flights to heated rooms and strong water pressure, to less polluted air and more edible food, to a place where people spoke "proper German," to the west. The scene at the eastern airports was a cacophony of carpetbaggers shouting into portable phones, haggling about land deals and contracts, rustling charts and blueprints, snapping and poking at beleaguered Ossi airline and auto-rental employees.

In Bonn, many of the 10,000 government workers assigned to the east called their hardship pay bonuses *Schmutzgeld,* dirty money, or a *Buschzulage,* a bonus for toiling in the jungle. In 1993, the entire government of the eastern state of Saxony-Anhalt was forced out of office when the public discovered that the premier, Werner Münch, and three other ministers—all western Germans imported to show Ossis how to run a state government—had paid themselves more than $525,000 in bonuses. In nearly every industry, I met westerners who had considered work in the east and turned it down—either because of the distance they felt from easterners or because of the inconvenience of being away from their families (few Wessis would consider subjecting their children to eastern air and schools).

Imported westerners were needed to teach easterners how to run shops, market products, manage staff, keep books, use computers, or deal with customers. But sometimes westerners were brought in simply to be westerners, to set examples of initiative, hard work and individual achievement—concepts many westerners believed were unknown in the east. Sometimes, just being western was not enough. At the Buchenwald concentration camp, where East Germany had built a monumental memorial that managed to portray the Holocaust as a campaign against communism, the eastern director of the memorial was quickly ousted because of his membership in the communist party. But his western replacement lasted only fourteen days. It turned out he had been a member of the West German Communist party. Another Wessi historian was quickly ushered into the job.

Most westerners who worked in the east did so only on visits that combined a quick deal with the requisite gawking. (By 1993, 62 percent of western Germans had spent less than a week in the east, according to a poll by the weekly newsmagazine *Der Spiegel.* The same survey found that more than 70 percent of Ossis had made extended visits to the west.) In 1991, I joined a busload of western German journalists on a trip to Chemnitz and listened as they spent the entire ride pointing out the windows and laughing uproariously at the backwardness of the Ossis. As their eastern bus driver pointed out notable sights around town, the western reporters repeatedly cackled over the Ossi's pride in unimpressive municipal buildings, puny sports facilities or what the driver called "the highest autobahn bridge in the five new states." The single eastern reporter on the bus sat silently in the back, his lips white with anger. He watched his western colleagues point at a wrecked Trabant and guffaw when a Bonn reporter said, "Poor thing—must have met a BMW and lost!" Another reporter, for the highly respected *Frankfurter Allgemeine Zeitung,* regaled his pals with the tale of the Ossi who tries to get prompt service in a newly refurbished eastern restaurant. The waiter tells his customer that change will come only slowly in the east: "You've waited forty years, you can wait a little longer for your dinner."

Even years later, many westerners could not restrain themselves from having fun at the expense of the Ossis. In 1993, I watched two western Berlin lawyers dining at the east side's best restaurant, the splendidly renovated Borchardt. One lawyer summoned the waiter and asked, "Doesn't your chef understand how beef is to be cooked? This is a delicate piece of meat. Where is he from anyway, Saxony?" The lawyer turned to his friend and added: "Who do these people think they are? Asking for another ten percent wage increase when they still work like Russians. This is a developing country and they think they can just walk into the modern age."

Language, presumably the Germans' great advantage over other East Bloc countries trying to adopt western ways, was often used to divide east from west. Wessis who successfully argued for repeal of the east's right-turn-on-red law routinely dubbed the move the "socialist right turn." On a visit to the Quelle mail-order company's headquarters in Nuremberg, I talked to western managers about the hundreds of eastern workers they bused in every morning, many of them from towns more than three hours away. "We had to get our managers used to the Saxon language," said Quelle's personnel director, Günther Haase, one of innumerable western slaps against the thick dialect spoken in the south of eastern Germany. Haase repeatedly referred to his western employees as "German workers," while calling his Ossi workers "these people."

Before he died in 1992, Willy Brandt, the former West German chancellor, told me that he and others in the Bonn leadership had made two major errors in their assumption that unification would be a relatively quick process. First, the west failed to realize how deeply easterners had been changed by living through three generations of dictatorship. Easterners "never experienced personal responsibility." The second mistake was a failure to see how well younger west Germans had heeded the dictum to face west. Wessis in their twenties and thirties simply did not see easterners as their own kind. Sometimes the message emerged in crass demonstrations, such as a march by several hundred university students in the western city of Wiesbaden. Students chanted "We're hungry, hungry, hungry . . ." to the tune of the Libby's ad jingle, demanding that the state government pump more money into their student meals rather than use the funds to build student cafeterias in the east. Sometimes the message was more fashionably clothed, as when Birgit Breuel, chief of the Treuhand, the agency in charge of selling off eastern industry, told me that her job was "to clean up forty years of history. The people here will never love us. The people didn't really finish the revolution. They expect us to finish it for them."

Western Germans were often arrogant, using Ossis for what they wanted and discarding them when they were no longer needed. Western sports authorities were ecstatic about their unique chance to take advantage of the successful, if corrupt, East German Olympic training system, bringing dozens of eastern athletes to the 1992 Games in Barcelona. But eastern coaches were not invited, ostensibly because the team could not afford to bring them. Cost concerns did not prevent Olympic organizers from importing two cooks for the western German equestrian team.

The Kohl government spent $600,000 on a cartoon film that was supposed to explain market economics to Ossis. The ad agency that made the movie—a western firm, of course—portrayed the Ossi as a cute, slightly dim dog that barks happily when Ludwig Erhard, architect of the 1950s West German economic miracle, throws it a one-mark coin. Eastern reaction to the film was fierce enough to prompt the government to lock it away, never to be used. Advertisers seemed especially prone to colonial condescension. Ads seeking to introduce western products to Ossis often included that extra touch that went just beyond the pale: A radio spot for Pampers patiently explained what disposable diapers are ("Then you just throw them away!"), and then added a language lesson. Since the diapers are marketed with the English words "Boys" and "Girls" on the boxes, no problem in the west, special ads for Ossis included pronunciation lessons. "Not Geerls, Girls!" the chipper announcer said.

Sometimes the east-west gap seemed good-humored. Both Ossis and Wessis wrote jokebooks about each other. A westerner: "We used to have a Doberman, but then we got ourselves an Ossi—it's much braver, and it's satisfied with less." Or, from an Ossi: Ossi and Wessi stand together on an eastern beach. The Wessi says, "Oh look, there's the lifeguard who saved my life this morning." "I know," the Ossi replies, "he already gave me his apologies." The ultimate Ossi-Wessi crack was the one attributed to former Foreign Minister Hans-Dietrich Genscher. An Ossi tells a Wessi, "We are one people." The Wessi replies, "So are we!"

Behind the jokes was a gap that widened dangerously with the years. In 1991, a majority of Germans on both sides told *Der Spiegel* that German unity mostly meant "joy that the division was overcome." By 1993, the Wall in the Head, as Germans came to call their differences, was growing, according to 64 percent of westerners and 74 percent of easterners. Ossi and Wessi couldn't agree on much. Why was the east deindustrialized? Because western Germans let the factories die, said two-thirds of Ossis. No, because of decades of mismanagement by the communists, said an equal number of Wessis.

Ossis' stiffest complaints often stemmed from western policies that were reasonable by almost any standard. The Kohl government and western industrialists agreed to boost eastern salaries to western levels in less than a decade. But even that schedule left some Ossis in Berlin sharing offices with Wessis who made twice their salary while working two hours less per week.

Despite such inequalities, many westerners chastised Ossis for being ungrateful. But some in the west realized the depth of the gulf between the two peoples. Wolfgang Bernhardt, an industrialist who went east to help privatize the communist trade organization, urged fellow Wessis to consider that western Germans were now as alien to Ossis "as the United States was to us in the first years after 1945."

Western Germans often drew analogies between 1990 in the east and 1945 in the west. Finance Minister Theo Waigel called unification a "zero hour" in which an entire country starts over, working together to build a new society. The trope was well meant, but wrong. In 1945, western Germans were all in the same boat, picking over a ruined landscape, confronted with the reality of crimes beyond imagination. Everyone was hungry, nearly everyone displaced or disoriented. What the Nazis hadn't destroyed, the Allied armies had. Brick by brick, potato by potato, West Germans were forced—with massive American aid—to rebuild their own country, creating their *Wirtschaftswunder,* the economic miracle of the 1950s and '60s. In 1990, East Germany, though corrupt and totalitarian, was a functioning society with its own traditions and institutions. The collapse of the Soviet Union meant the loss of its primary markets, and the fall of the Wall opened the east to a rainbow of variety it had been forbidden. But this was no zero hour; it was much more complicated than that. The east did not enjoy the sense of shared purpose and equal suffering that had made the west's task so clear after the war. In eastern Germany after unification, some people continued the work they had done before, some entire professions no longer existed (doping specialists for Olympic athletes, Marxism-Leninism professors, political officers in the military and police, censors), and some people realized they would never work again. In such a varied society, the concept of the clean slate could not have universal appeal.

Nor did West Germans ever have as fresh a start as they often describe in retrospect. As Wolfgang Benz of Berlin's Technical University and other scholars have shown, postwar West German democracy could not have been created without the expertise and connections of more than 8 million Nazi party members, many of whom remained in prominent positions after the war. Yet, despite Bonn's failure to continue the denazification program begun by the U.S. occupying forces—or more likely, because of that failure—Wessis in charge of reunification launched a rigorous drive to exorcise communist party members from positions of power in the east.

Of all the western policies that sparked eastern rage, the expulsion of party members from university faculties, government offices, and other public positions was the most divisive. Many easterners were thrilled to see their former oppressors tossed onto the street. People like the Hotzes complained incessantly that the same communist bureaucrats and local informants who had made their lives miserable over the years still held powerful positions, while good noncommunists couldn't find jobs. The decisions to try nineteen-year-old East German border guards for shooting at their escaping countrymen, while the big bosses were let off and Honecker was permitted to join his family in the sun in Chile, enraged many Ossis. But other easterners were equally angered by the dismissal of good scientists, philosophers, and high school and elementary school principals simply because they carried party cards. Michael Brie, a distinguished philosopher, was fired from Humboldt University in eastern Berlin because he volunteered that he had given the Stasi the names of antiapartheid activists in the Third World who might be useful in the campaign against the South African government.

"I had only Nazi teachers when I was in school," said Margarita Mathiopoulos, a western German who was brought in to teach political science at Humboldt. "Why can't we allow the Ossis to clean their own house? They fired the only female law school dean in Germany, at Humboldt, because she was in the party. But why couldn't her own colleagues have made that judgment? The eastern professors here are humiliated that they cannot renew their own institutions as their colleagues in Poland, Hungary and the Czech Republic can. Why must the best eastern academics go to the United States to speak?"

Heinrich Bortfeldt, an eastern historian, lost his job when east Berlin's Academy of Social Sciences, where nearly all the scholars were party members, collapsed. Bortfeldt had joined the party only at age twenty-seven, after much soul-searching. His parents repeatedly warned him never to join. They had seen too much pain from the kind of political certainty that infects those who wave a banner of any color. But Heinrich eventually rejected his parents' entreaties: "I said, 'Oh please, we are a new generation, we'll do it better.' To be honest, no one forced me into the party. I was a true believer."

Bortfeldt knew the system was repressive and petty. He had seen his parents' anguish when the communist government forced them to give up his grandparents' farm so it could be collectivized. As a young teacher, Bortfeldt was required to teach that Russia was the glorious future of communism, even though he knew the Soviet garrison in his town was filthy and decrepit. In school, when a teacher got young Heinrich to admit he watched

West German television, he was required to perform community service in penance for his transgression.

Yet he was grateful he had been given the chance to be the first person in his family to study at university. He admired many of his country's leaders. He found inspiration in Honecker's survival of a decade in concentration camp. He found egalitarianism in the presence of Jews such as Politburo member Hermann Axen in the upper reaches of the East German regime. And he was proud that several elder members of the communist government had fought on the right side in the Spanish Civil War. In 1988, after considerable hesitation, the government allowed Bortfeldt to take a three-month study trip to the United States, his primary field of research. But when Bortfeldt returned brimming with questions and observations he wanted to share with his colleagues—questions about obvious discrepancies between life in America and the marginal existence of his fellow East Germans—the academy gave him twenty minutes to speak and warned him against making any comments that could be interpreted as soft on capitalism.

When the revolution began, Bortfeldt could not summon the courage to break with his party. Only some months later could he reconcile his admiration for the party with revelations of corruption and venality deeper than anything he had imagined. By then, his political views had become irrelevant to the outside world; employers would see only one thing—his party membership. Every eastern public employee and job applicant was required to fill out an extensive form detailing all contacts with the Stasi or the communist party, along with details of any schooling or business travel outside of East Germany.

For the first time in his life, at age forty-one, Bortfeldt found himself applying for jobs. He spent a happy year in the United States, pleased to find that American academia was open to an English-speaking eastern German and that American society loved nothing more than a repentant ex-communist. Back home, things were much grimmer. Humboldt's history faculty rejected him; by the end of 1993, the postunity department had hired thirteen historians—twelve westerners and a sixty-three-year-old easterner. By 1994, Bortfeldt had cobbled together a living, teaching police recruits in the eastern state of Brandenburg, writing occasionally for western journals, and leading a seminar at western Berlin's Free University. There, the director of the North American Studies Institute informed Bortfeldt that he was "overqualified" for a staff position. It was increasingly clear to Bortfeldt that he would never regain a place on the faculty of a German university. He was a charter member of the Lost Generation—just like his father, who was drafted into the Wehrmacht and wounded in Russia, and then returned to a country that had washed its hands of everything for which he had fought.

Bortfeldt was, in one view, the classic *Mitläufer*, one who runs with the crowd, a nice-enough man who made the wrong choice and paid the consequences in the new society. But he was also one of the many easterners who used the party as much as the party used them, who played along in order to do the work he wanted to, but never crossed the line to toil for the Stasi or spy on his fellow citizens. The Bortfeldts were the brains of eastern Germany. In many cases, they were cast aside, denied the chance to reform their own institutions. That sense of disenfranchisement was by no means limited to intellectuals. In one case after another, western Germans stripped easterners of the small things that, added together, had been their identity.

One of the smallest, yet most revealing examples of this phenomenon was the altering of street names. East Germany had used street names as part of a comically simplistic propaganda campaign. Across the country, streets were named for revolutionary heroes such as Abraham Lincoln, Julius and Ethel Rosenberg, Karl Marx, Che Guevara, and a long list of communists great and slight. My favorite intersection was in East Berlin, at Ho Chi Minh Alley and Indira Gandhi Boulevard. Western authorities (as well as many eastern citizens) were eager to jettison the silliest names. Kohl was so annoyed by the street signs that he "would like to jump out of his car and rip the signs down himself," said his chief personal aide, Eduard Ackermann. Few people shed tears for the loss of Leninallee or Avenue of the Cosmonauts. But did a Potsdam street named for a Russian spaceman have to be rechristened in honor of the American astronaut Neil Armstrong? Many easterners resented that the decisions, especially in Berlin, were made largely by westerners, and they especially resented the removal of names of worthy people who just happened to be communists. Berlin's Senate proved truly vindictive: It ordered the renaming not only of Bruno Baum Street, named for a Jewish communist who died at Auschwitz, but also of Pushkin Street, on the grounds that the writer was Russian rather than German. When Berlin Jews protested against the removal of Baum's name, a spokesman for the city's Christian Democratic Union justified the change by noting that Baum had worn a red triangle at Auschwitz (for communist prisoners) rather than the yellow triangle sewn onto the uniforms of Jewish inmates. Easterners protested that while western authorities seemed anxious to wipe away any vestige of communist rule, they were none too eager to cleanse western street names of Nazi influence. Efforts by descendants of prominent Jews to have their family names restored to streets whose names were Aryanized by the Nazi government in the 1930s were largely futile.

Numerous streets in western Berlin are named after prominent Nazis, such as Werner Voss, a World War I pilot who painted a swastika—a symbol of German racism even before the Nazis—on his own fighter plane, and Karl von Einem, a Prussian war minister who went on to run for office as a Nazi candidate. Many more western streets carry uncontroversial names given them by the Nazis to replace names of Jewish Germans.

One of the most inspiring and exciting walks available in Berlin is a stroll along the former death strip, the swath of green that runs through the center of the city where the Wall once stood. In the new neighborhood emerging where the east's City Center and the west's Kreuzberg sections were once divided by concrete, it is now possible to walk back and forth between east and west, comparing architecture, faces, the physical evidence of history. On one such walk, I noticed new street signs on the eastern side. They were posted on every corner. What could the old names have been, I wondered. I followed several streets until I found leftover eastern signs—a bit smaller, with the immediately identifiable, old-fashioned eastern lettering. The street names had not been changed; only the typeface was new. In a city so strapped for money that it was closing kindergartens, even the telltale eastern typeface had to be eradicated. The message was clear and painful: Nothing, not even your street signs, must remain of the old system.

Unaccustomed to standing up for what they believed in, many easterners reacted to the imposition of western ways not with protest, but with a depressed retreat into the solace of their apartments, their families and their beers. On one occasion when Ossis banded together in a grass-roots effort to save one of their own institutions, they were handed their heads on a platter. The fight for DT-64, the radio station that had come closest to an antiestablishment, renegade voice in the communist east, caught western Germany's media leadership off guard. The unification treaty included a provision to shut down eastern radio stations and replace them with new branches of the broadcast voices controlled by the Bonn government. But as DT-64's date with silence grew near, the eastern station's fans revolted. Western broadcasters proposed to replace DT-64 and its Ossi staff with a youth station called Rockradio B—run by Wessis. DT-64's loyal listeners in seventy-three cities collected 300,000 signatures on petitions, staged hunger strikes, and mounted demonstrations and twenty-four-hour vigils. It was by far the most popular, angry and honest shout of resistance to be heard in the five years after the Wall fell. It was also resolutely ignored. Western broadcasters called DT-64 a relic of communist rule. It would not fit in with the design for eastern broadcasting created in Bonn. In the two broadcast authorities created in the east, ten of the top eleven managers in 1993 were westerners. At the headquarters of Germany's main public network, ARD, staffers referred to the two eastern stations, MDR and ORB, as "occupation agencies." By eliminating DT-64 and other eastern holdovers, the Wessis hoped to cut off the flow of nostalgic recollection that threatened to turn into eastern, and possibly antiwestern, pride. DT-64 was not revolutionary; it was a rock radio station whose DJs occasionally grumbled about society's elders and leaders. But by the time of its demise in 1992, DT-64 had been transformed into a rallying point, a symbol of Ossis' lost identity, and, in the end, a sign of their helplessness and second-class status.

Most of the west's major publications and broadcast outlets avoided targeting the eastern audience. The governing theory assumed that Ossis would, sooner or later, adopt the reading and viewing habits of their western cousins. In reality, that shift would come much later, if ever. After an initial fascination with the variety, color and openness of western publications, Ossis overwhelmingly decided to save their money and time. The only western voices to succeed in the east were TV listings, celebrity mags, sleazy porn sheets and the lowest-common-denominator shows of private cable channels—mostly dubbed versions of Hollywood cops-and-robbers shows and cheap remakes of American 'reality' programs about firemen and rescue workers.

But one newspaper sought—over the outraged protests of the Kohl government and the western media establishment—to nourish a separate eastern identity. *Super!* was a purely western invention, a loud, crass, cynical creation of the Bavarian press magnate Hubert Burda and Australia's amoral purveyor of tabloid titillation, Rupert Murdoch. Despite Murdoch's attempts to buy mainstream status in the United States, his true love remained the splashy tab—huge headlines, big breasts, pure outrage. (SHUT THE WINDOWS, CLOSE THE DOORS! THE MURDERER IS AMONG US! read one headline. OSSIS MUCH HEALTHIER THAN WESSIS! cried another.) *Super!* sought to summon eastern resentment against the west and reward it with a daily paper that would stand by the beleaguered Ossi no matter what tricks Kohl & Company could devise. In Murdoch's vision, *Super!* could be the prototype for a chain of papers stretching across the former East Bloc.

At first, the formula seemed to work. Ossis grabbed the paper's daily "Orgasm Report" on the sexual experiments of newly liberated eastern women. Brimming with optimism, brashly indignant over the myriad slights committed by rich invaders from the west, *Super!* was advocacy journalism gone over the top. Readers loved it when *Super!* gloated over Wessis who got their comeuppance. The classic example was the headline BOASTFUL WESSI BEATEN TO DEATH WITH BEER BOTTLE—ALL OF BERNAU REJOICES, the heartwarming tale of a poor westerner who went east to rip off the Ossis but did not survive the adventure. *Super!* could be counted on to unmask ex-communists still living high on the hog. And *Super!* pampered its readers with all kinds of services—job fairs, an Anger Hotline, help cutting through the western bureaucracy, and a staff inspector who fought for lower rents. *Super!* made an enemy for life of Helmut Kohl when it cheered SPLAT, SPLAT, A DIRECT HIT! on its front page after protesters slammed the chancellor with eggs on one of his rare visits to the east. But in time, the cynicism of the project became clear. The top staff was almost entirely imported from the west. The paper's political editor, Michael Schwilk, was typical, a Bavarian family man who would no sooner bring his family east than he would invite a serial killer to spend Christmas with the kids. Schwilk, like many *Super!* editors, commuted across the country each weekend. "I live in a small village," he told me. "The school bus arrives each morning and takes the children. They sing a song and say a prayer. When I tell people back home what it's like here, they look at me like I'm from the moon."

Schwilk's attitude toward easterners was actually more generous than that of many Wessis—he believed his eastern colleagues to be equally capable, if insufficiently trained. But Schwilk also voiced stereotypical western views of the Ossis: "They want everything right away—the house, car, the trip to Jamaica. After the war, people in the west didn't get everything for years. My father didn't get his first car until the sixties, not one year after the war." In the end, Schwilk and his fellow editors had too simplistic a view of the east. They thought a black-white, us-them view of the world would be enough. For about 400,000 readers, it was. But by the time the publishers pulled the plug in late 1992, when *Super!* was losing millions every week, the idea of feisty separatism as a salve for the east's problems had run its course. Some Ossis were well enough adjusted that they considered reading the western papers. And many others had grown so disaffected that they saw no salvation in either assimilation or separatism.

Other, less cynical news organizations tried valiantly to bridge the gap between east and west. In Berlin, the *Wochenpost,* an old eastern weekly, was transformed into the country's freshest, most probing journal, as editor Matthias Greffreth, a Wessi, crafted a staff that was equal parts Ossi holdovers, Wessi imports, and young Ossis carrying minimal communist-era baggage. Although the weekly made little headway in the west, where few seemed interested in reading about the psychological and economic traumas of unity, the *Wochenpost,* at least for a time, was a rare specimen, an attempt to merge two cultures without destroying either. It never caught on with the public; the paper never made money.

Another adventurous editor, Monika Zimmermann, tried to bring western and eastern journalists together at a daily newspaper, *Neue Zeit,* also in Berlin. Zimmermann retained the extremely short articles and simple writing style of the old communist papers, but pushed her eastern writers to take stands and grow comfortable with giving readers their own interpretations of events.

"The easterners have a deep inferiority complex," said Zimmermann, a Wessi who had covered East Berlin for the *Frankfurter Allgemeine Zeitung,* which owned *Neue Zeit.* "They take no joy in decision-making. Their self-confidence is nearly nonexistent. We try to give them the courage of their opinions. They don't like bylines, so we created a 'pride page' where they could write longer pieces and put their name to them. It takes a great deal of patience and a selflessness that does not come easily to us in the west. Sometimes it is so hard: Every letter they get from the west, they consider very important and they sit there reading the whole thing. Of course, I know most of it is junk mail, form letters. But they can't tell which is which." *Neue Zeit's* staff seemed to survive the transition in good spirits, but the paper never won many readers. In July 1994, the western owners pulled the plug.

Left to themselves to determine a new identity, many easterners seemed frozen in place. Asked to describe themselves by a pollster in 1993, 54 percent said "East German" while 45 percent said "German." "The western media are filled with Ossis portrayed as criminals and lazy people," said Hans Modrow, the last communist prime minister and later a member of the Bundestag. "There is some truth to that, but it has to be restricted to the people who were responsible for what happened. Now, it is obvious that nothing is to remain of our culture. And we did have a different culture: I lived in an apartment house with forty families, workers and retirees, different ages and incomes. That doesn't happen in the west. My brother lived in the west; his life is defined by his job. Mine was defined by culture, art, literature, things outside my work." Modrow's plaint rang true to so many Ossis that the ex-communists, far from fading out of existence as many in Bonn had predicted, strengthened in the 1994 elections. "Yesterday's Crooks, Today's Hope" was the Party for Democratic Socialism slogan in some 1994 local campaigns, and even if Ossis were only registering a protest vote, their willingness to dance with the one who brought them was revealing.

The turn back to the former communists came in part because Ossis in Bonn had failed to win any influence there. New Forum and the other groups that had led the 1989 revolt produced a few people who went on to play some role in the reunited country, but mostly as editorialists, talk show regulars and street activists. The political figures chosen by the major German parties to serve as "Alibi Ossis," or tokens, were sentenced to careers in which their own colleagues ignored them or treated them like stupid children.

The ranks of eastern politicians were regularly thinned by revelations that one or another character had been a Stasi informer in the old days. At least two eastern politicians committed suicide after such reports; many others vanished in disrepute. One, East Germany's only democratically elected prime minister, Lothar de Maizière, maintained to the end that Ossis need only overcome their "group thinking" and they would find themselves on a par with their western colleagues. But in the halls of the Bundestag in Bonn, it was plain that no matter how they behaved, Ossis would be treated like aliens in need of reeducation. Kohl's top-ranking eastern minister, Angela Merkel, was a bright Ossi who had refused to cave in to the system. Despite her avid interest in politics (when she was eight, she secretly followed Bonn's Bundestag so closely that she knew every minister's name), Merkel chose a career in physics. The hard sciences were an oasis from political conformity; physics faculties were among the few that admitted students who were not party members. Daughter of a western pastor who returned to the east in 1954 out of a sense of obligation to his congregation, Merkel broke into politics in the fall of 1989, joining one of the smaller revolutionary groups. But she was one of the first East German activists to advocate quick unity with the west, and she swiftly moved up to become press spokesman for the last East German government and then minister for women's and youth affairs in Kohl's cabinet.

A shy, timid-voiced figure with a happy, chubby face and ragged, bowl-cut hair, Merkel simultaneously became Kohl's favored Ossi and a standing joke among Bonn politicians. She looked and sounded east—violating Bonn's behavior standards by eschewing makeup, biting her nails to the quick, dressing casually, and refusing to hide behind her staff. But her positions so rigidly tracked the chancellor's every word that, even to her eastern colleagues, Merkel seemed to have checked her free will at the Bonn city limits. "Ah, here comes the chancellor's little puppy dog," a fellow Christian Democrat said when he saw Merkel enter a press conference. Merkel preached the Kohl line even when other Ossi politicians broke with the western party. Far from decrying the loss of child-care services, jobs for women, and the eastern tradition of giving mothers a day off each month to handle housework, Merkel welcomed their demise. "I'm not sure it's so necessary that children go to day care," she said. "Women are expected now to return to KKK—*Kinder, Kirche, Küche* (children, church, kitchen)," the nineteenth-century German formula for a successful female life. Merkel did not wholly adopt that weary model, but neither did she pine for the socialist system that so many in the east seemed to miss. She preferred Kohl's notion that women's obligation was to family, though they might also work if they mastered the logistics themselves. Merkel's submissive approach to politics was interpreted as loyalty by Kohl, who took her to Washington to meet President Bush and then promoted her to the figurehead post of deputy chairman of his party. But elsewhere in Bonn, and especially in the east, Merkel became the prime example of the Ossi politician who went to Bonn and never looked back.

"In the east, we had only one behavior: Don't stand out," Merkel told me. "Now this has to be adjusted. In the west, you have to be self-confident, a little aggressive. You must always smile." But Merkel had none of these western characteristics. (An Ossi student at Humboldt University, Mark Scheffler, once sought to persuade me that easterners' low self-esteem was a positive attribute: "To be self-confident as a German is already a bad thing," he said. "We were raised to be shy, cautious and indirect, and the world should be grateful for such Germans.") Merkel was, as one of Kohl's top aides said, "slight, not accepted, a person with no views of her own."

"I am accepted," Merkel insisted, proving her detractors' point like the exhausted child who stamps his feet and shouts, "I'm not tired."

The sad fact was, "We have no social contact whatsoever with the Wessis in parliament," said Bundestag member Vera Wollenberger, an easterner in the Alliance '90 party, a coalition that grew out of the 1989 revolt. "We are tokens. The Bonn crowd wants nothing to do with us. When we speak in committee, they go get coffee. They see us as a group, not as individual members."

The first years of a new society: Carpetbaggers and scallywags rush into the new land to make money and take advantage of a bewildered, disoriented people. One group sees itself as second-class citizens and another poses as the righteous teacher. Gaps of language, culture and expectations seem minimal at first, but turn out to be yawning gulfs that would take generations to bridge. Disaffected young people have a world of opportunity on paper, but feel limited and unwanted in reality. There are suggestions that quotas might force equality. Newcomers are held to standards far higher than those the established society set for itself. One group earns lower wages and is the butt of the nation's jokes, while the other group lectures them to "do as we did, pull yourself up by your bootstraps." Newcomers are called to give up their past. In American history, the process was called Reconstruction and it was introduced with much fanfare as a process that would be radical, swift and efficient. It was an expensive, haphazard, half-hearted and ultimately corrupt concept, and the result was a psychological, social, economic and political gulf that would remain for more than a century. Even 130 years later, few can foresee a time when racial divisions will be anything but America's open wound.

Eastern Germans have one great advantage over American blacks: Their skin does not mark them as different. They can pass. But their road will nonetheless be hard. In German reconstruction, the west, like the American north, fell into self-doubt and crisis even after it defeated its archenemy. Western Germans have failed to give easterners—or let them take for themselves—the sense of opportunity and control that would make them feel part of the dominant culture. Instead, the west has sought to mollify Ossis with make-work programs, token positions of semiauthority, and bland promises of a better tomorrow.

"Look," said Wolfgang Gibowski, Kohl's top political aide, "we call it unification, but in fact the east acceded to our system and they don't know much about it. Their thinking is not inspired. Even if they are sitting in the Bundestag, there are only a very few of them who really understand the western system. These people cannot deal and think in western categories. We are westernizing the east. This is not a merger. We are doing with the Ossis what you did with us after World War II. The situation is again one following a war, this time a cold one. We, with the Allies, beat the east. But you had the power and the arguments of battlefield victors. We don't have that advantage because the eastern Germans think of themselves as equals. We aren't even allowed to call this reeducation. We can only offer information and they can say, 'No, we have our own identity.' This is a question of generations. Finally, in our lifetimes, the categories of east and west will disappear. But it will be a long, painful process of growing together."

PART
III

❧

The Wall
Between
Germans and
Others

AS FAR APART from one another as eastern and western Germans drifted during their decades of separation, a still wider gulf divides Germans from the foreigners who live among them. East Germany's official propaganda boasted of the communists' brotherhood with the Third World, and thousands of African and Asian workers had been imported over the years to perform grueling tasks that Germans were unwilling to accept. In West Germany, millions of *Gastarbeiter* (guest workers)—Turks, Yugoslavs and Italians eager to clean kitchens, mine coal or collect refuse in exchange for generous German wages—arrived for short stints and stayed for the rest of their lives. But the foreigners in Germany's postwar population remained rigidly separate from the natives. In the East, they were housed in ramshackle dormitories hidden behind industrial complexes. In the West, they gathered in urban ghettos, speaking their own languages, attending largely separate schools, making few inroads into the mainstream.

The fall of the Berlin Wall and the influx of immigrants unleashed by the revolutions of 1989 forced Germans east and west to consider anew their relationship with those who were not like themselves. Once again, Germans were confronted with a question that had plagued them since medieval times: Who is a German?

Who can become a German citizen? What defines Germanness—blood or place of birth? And with 16 million eastern Germans seeking to climb out of second-class citizenship, what is to be done with 6 million "foreigners," many of whom have never lived anywhere but Germany?

In a society battered by change, simple answers seemed appealing, particularly to those whose lives were most shaken by the new competition for jobs and status. But simple answers have a dismal track record in Germany, and so the country was thrown once more into a period of painful self-analysis and self-doubt. The exasperating requirement of Germans that they be one way because their parents were another hung over each decision—how to treat foreigners, whether to accept refugees, what to do about immigration. It all seemed a harsh testing of the soul.

And it seemed especially harsh because just when many Germans felt they ought to be celebrating a new identity and a new nation, they were sent hurtling back to the most painful time of all. With more than a million refugees pouring into the country and thousands of neo-Nazis lighting the night with Molotov cocktails aimed at anyone with dark skin, Germany was being forced to reopen questions many had considered solved, or at least calmed—questions of who belongs, and who does not. And so the talk once more was of Germans and Jews, two peoples trapped in an eternal relationship, burdened by a history that could not be undone.

10

Germans and Jews

Do you celebrate Christmas like we all do? Is Germany your home? Are you German? —TV talk show host Alfred Biolek's first three questions to his guest, a German-born Jewish dental student who has lived nowhere but Germany (February 1992)

You are a German citizen of the Jewish faith. Your homeland is Israel. Is that correct? —Karlheinz Schmidt, chairman of the Rostock City Council's Interior Committee, questioning Ignatz Bubis, chairman of the Central Council of Jews in Germany

In other words, you want to know what I'm doing here. You see a Jew as something alien. The fact that Germany's Jewish community no longer exists is linked to questions like that. —Bubis, in reply (November 1992)

You are really Jewish? That is very good. Really. I admire members of the Mosaic faith. —A young assistant to Chancellor Kohl, to the author at a cocktail party in Bonn, 1991

Ju-de, Ju-de, Ju-de (Jew, Jew, Jew) —A chant frequently heard from German soccer fans, directed at a player who commits a foul

THE GREAT JEWISH neighborhoods of German cities lie behind iron gates and concrete walls. They are often among the city's prettiest, most leafy quarters. They draw few visitors, but much attention. They are cemeteries, and their every corner, their every occupant, their every stone, is lovingly, fastidiously recorded in academic works, in fine, heavy coffee-table photo books, in slide shows and museum exhibits. The Jews of Germany, but for a tiny vestigial community now being overwhelmed by Russian Jewish immigrants, are dead. The Jews of Germany live above all on television.

There they are the walking skeletons of the infamous concentration camp newsreels, each clip so familiar that even the casual viewer might believe he could identify individual near-corpses as they hang from the shoulders of American and British soldiers. The Jews of Germany, as seen on television, are faded, off-speed snippets of Einstein and Freud, Kurt Weill and Otto Klemperer, usually lugging suitcases, departing. Or they are nameless victims shuffling through the streets toward a rail depot. Or they are dead, in mounds, awaiting burial by bulldozer.

Sometimes TV presents fictional Jews of Germany, thin figures with sad, deep eyes, kinky hair, hooknoses, and dramatic roles of infinite goodness. They tend to have a lot of silent scenes, moments in which the script calls for them to blink with a knowing sorrow. Sometimes, German TV Jews are more confrontational, more discomfiting. In 1993, state-funded ZDF television showed a soap-operatic series called "If Angels Travel," about a group of German tourists visiting Israel. Coproduced with Israeli state TV, the program featured an episode in which two elderly German women break away from their travel group and happen upon two German-speaking Israeli women. The Israelis invite the Germans to coffee and cake. Their polite chatter soon gives way to the discovery that the older of the Israeli women spent part of the war in the concentration camp at Theresienstadt. There is a long, painful silence. Then a few hesitant attempts to revive the conversation.

"Those were such bad times," one of the Germans says.

The Israeli folds her arms across her chest, refuses to engage in banter, decides to let the Germans squirm.

"We didn't know, of course," a German woman says. "We were teachers in a school."

More silence, then, hurriedly, a few pleasantries and the Germans rise to leave. On her way out, one of the Germans offers to leave her home address "in case you might be able to come visit, return to see your homeland."

"No," the older Israeli woman says. "I won't be going there." The Germans scurry away, the story moves on to a brighter subplot.

The very next night, also on state-supported TV, the sequel to the controversial and masterful epic film *Heimat* (Homeland) included a scene in which a German filmmaker, Reinhard Dörr, travels to Venice and meets a German Jewish photographer, Esther Goldbaum. As their relationship develops, Dörr decides to write a screenplay of Goldbaum's life. In exchange for her telling him about her family's experience during the Third Reich, he agrees to pose as a model for her camera.

Goldbaum poses him in awkward, twisted positions, on all fours, pressed up against a wall, against windows. She smokes obsessively as she snaps close-ups of his flabby body. As he repeats, "I want to know your entire life," she orders him to strip. She pries open his mouth and shoots directly into it, then kisses him as if it were her last act on earth.

We next see the two, German and Jew, in bed. He says: "When you were nine, your mother was killed at Dachau. You were with your aunt in Switzerland and you asked her every morning when your mother was going to come to get you. In the end, your mother was only a single photo, a piece of paper. And that's how you began to make pictures." Dörr talks about Goldbaum's parents, a German Nazi and a German Jew, and about how she loved them all the same.

"You are counterfeiting me," Goldbaum accuses. "That's kitsch, exaggeration. I am me, me, me."

"It's a story," says Dörr.

"But it is much too romantic, much too German."

"But a beautiful story," says Dörr, and he gets up to leave. "Your story is now my story." The line is wonderful in German, because the words for "story" and "history" are the same.

In Germany today, Jews are history. They are forced down the Germans' throats like bitter medicine: Hardly a week passes without a TV documentary on one or another aspect of the Holocaust; publishers never tire of recording the cultural legacy of German Jews. Jews are embraced as a tragic loss. At a Berlin museum opening of an exhibit wholly unrelated to Jews, I heard a curator launch into a long, emotional speech about what might have been, if only . . . The pictures that might have been painted, the plays and books that might have been written. Another day, I listened to two bankers talking about the innovation missing from German corporations, and the contribution German Jews could have made.

Jews in Germany are spoken of with the heavy, somber tones of a funeral director. Politicians troop off to annual memorials of Kristallnacht. In one city after another, the ruins of synagogues have inspired reconstruction plans, attempts to recreate the symbols of Jewish life down to the last detail, but without the remotest prospect of a revived Jewish community. "Sometimes," said Julius Schöps, a German Jew who runs an institute of Jewish history at Potsdam University, "I ask myself whether perhaps Jews are remembered only because they are no longer here."

In 1992, a Berlin museum mounted an extraordinary exhibition, a once-in-a-lifetime collection of thousands of precious prayer books, illuminated manuscripts, artworks and other artifacts of Jewish life, gathered over five years from more than three hundred sources from Manhattan to Morocco. If "Patterns of Jewish Life" had appeared anywhere else in the world, the exhibit would have been hailed as a curatorial masterwork, a dazzling chronicle of Jewish life from antiquity through the centuries. But the show was created by Germans, in Berlin, in the Gropius-Bau, a building still pocked with bullet holes from the final hours of World War II, a museum a stone's throw from the underground remains of Gestapo torture cells. The curators set out expressly to counter the usual German concept of Jews—as victims. The show was designed to bring alive the richness of Jewish religious, artistic and cultural tradition, the diversity that Nazi Germany set out to exterminate. But by stopping short of the present, by presenting Jewish life without Jews, the exhibition opened itself to criticism that it was instead fulfilling Hitler's dream of a museum of Judaica that would recall a dead religion, a wiped-out people. The exhibit elicited sarcastic attacks such as one from Michael Wolfssohn, an Israeli-born Jew who teaches at the German national military college in Munich. "How can Germans prove good convictions?" he asked. "Above all, through intensive engagement with Jews. But careful: Not with living Jews. There you could put your foot in it, burn yourself on hot iron, or get your fingers caught. No, busying yourself with dead Jews is less dangerous. So, lots of dead Jews: Yes. Living Jews: Problematic."

The exhibit's curators, like Germans on the whole, grew exasperated by the criticism from all sides. They had sought only to do good, to lead the Germans out of ignorance about Judaism, to smash stereotypes. Instead, they were pummeled for leaving out the living Jews, just as they were attacked for slighting the Holocaust, relegating the horrors of this century to a single room in the vast exhibition. The curators had fallen victim to the postwar German dilemma—when the subject is Jews, Germans can do no right. So many people are constantly on the lookout for evidence of wrongdoing. Sociologists and journalists are forever taking Germany's anti-Semitic pulse, producing surveys that show a hard, seemingly permanent anti-Jewish core of about one in every four Germans. To be sure, in the years after unification, attacks on Jewish cemeteries and synagogues did shoot up along with assaults on foreigners. But the first and most puzzling phenomenon a Jew in Germany is likely to experience is what appears to be precisely the opposite of the historic problem: philo-Semitism. In the ever-burgeoning mountain of literature examining the roots of the Holocaust, a popular theory says that the Germans were so easily led into the state religion of anti-Semitism under Hitler in good measure because Germans and Jews shared rather similar interests and values. They were neither "other" nor "brother," but something uncomfortably in between. If that was true before 1933, when there were 600,000 Jews in Germany (about 1 percent of the population), it could no longer be argued with a straight face in the

1990s, when there were perhaps 40,000 Jews—few of them of German descent—in a country of 80 million people. And yet with each passing decade, the strange subculture of philo-Semites grows, especially among the well-educated. They honor the crimes of the past not with indifference, but with a pained devotion to the history of the Jews, and even to the religion and its modern practitioners.

There are Germans who "collect" Jews like an overexcited hostess adds potential party guests to her card file. There are Germans who study Jewish history and religion as a form of reparation. There are Germans who have built careers out of mourning the loss of the Jews. Other than Americans, Germans are Israel's most frequent visitors. There is a curious phenomenon among some intellectual Germans, who, when they meet a Jew, apologize. Hemming and hawing follows, accompanied usually by a sheepish shuffling of feet, perhaps a cough, a mumbled reference to "those terrible times," or a sentence fragment such as "Of course, people my age are not personally guilty, but. . . ." Jewish foreigners who spend time in Germany are often confronted with these confessional moments, and few have the slightest idea how to react. I know I didn't.

German attempts to repair the wounds of history can be so awkward and self-deprecating as to evoke pathos. Many German cities and towns have established Christian-Jewish Cooperation Societies, consisting almost entirely of Christian Germans who gather to chat about the past and research the Jewish histories of their communities. A handful of Jewish speakers travel the circuit of these clubs, delivering dinner addresses and making themselves available for awkward conversation. Such events almost always include a ritual appeal for Jews who might lend some credibility to the organization's purpose. An officer of the Evangelical Church in the Rhineland gave a speech in 1990 that stated the Germans' predicament with shocking plainness. Speaking on the topic "The Renewal of Relations between Christians and Jews," Peter Beier bemoaned the lack of "Jewish conversation partners in our local communities. I am absolutely convinced that our effort would bring concrete results if Jewish conversation partners were available in our communities. We killed them all." With that, Beier moved on to another topic.

German Jews who work in universities, institutes, museums and the news media often joke about how easy it is to win government grants for any project related to Nazi oppression of Jews or Jewish life before the 1930s. More Yiddish movies are shown on German TV than anywhere else in the world, including Israel. German volunteers work for Jewish relief organizations in Israel and the United States. If in 1936 the Nazi party issued warning cards to Christians who committed the crime of being treated by a

Jewish physician, by the 1990s, I could meet in a Berlin doctor's waiting room patients who said they had chosen this internist because "Jews make very good doctors."

There are famous cases of children of SS men and Nazi leaders who convert to Judaism, devote themselves to Jewish-Christian reconciliation, or otherwise dedicate their lives to atoning for their parents' crimes. But there are many more Germans with no particular family background to be ashamed of who throw themselves into things Jewish. Since 1986, Katherine Ziebura has worked for a Berlin city office that invites German Jews living around the world to visit their birthplace. The program is one of many throughout Germany designed to acquaint those who fled from Nazi oppression with the country that has developed in the decades since. Ziebura finds names of potential visitors by placing ads in newspapers in New York, Toronto, Jerusalem and cities in South Africa, Australia, South America and Europe. She has come to love the work, to enjoy the old-style, refined German that many of the returning Jews still speak, to relish the moments of discovery when a former Berliner figures out exactly where his family's house stood. ("They don't feel like Germans anymore," she said of her visitors. "But a lot of them do feel like Berliners.") Ziebura's office is filled with old maps of the city, Nazi-vintage prints featuring Adolf Hitler Square and Hermann Göring Street.

Her work has changed the way Ziebura views herself, her family, even old Germans she sees on the street. "I'm glad I didn't have to live then. I don't know how I would have behaved. I hope I would have had civil courage. But I can only hope. Of course, I have no personal guilt, but I have a terribly great responsibility for what we have taken on. When I look at old people now, I wonder, Were they? Weren't they? This common expression, 'I didn't know anything about it,' that simply cannot be true. My parents, well, my father was already dead when I started this work, so I don't know. My mother—she died last year, she was eighty-four. She had very dark hair and a long nose and always had problems because of how she looked. She stayed to herself because of it. I had an uncle who died at Dachau because he had been engaged to a Jew, I don't know the whole story. I can only be happy my parents were not convinced Nazis. But the pain was there, and remained until and after death. There's been a very sharp breach of trust between the generations, and it will last for generations."

Some Germans seek out Jews to make amends. Or they confront their elders about what they did back then. A small number even marry Jews. The German actor Armin Mueller-Stahl, who played a Jewish grandfather in Barry Levinson's *Avalon* and a Hungarian-American who turns out to have been a Nazi war criminal in Costa-Gavras' *Music Box*, stunned me when I met him by claiming, "I am a Jew." I had asked Mueller-Stahl, who was known for refusing to play bad Germans in Hollywood movies, if he was in danger of being typecast not as a Nazi, but as a Jew.

"Since *Avalon*, I am a Jew in America," the actor said. "When I got the role, I had terrible fear. How can I as a German in America play a Jew? I can't describe how hard it was. But now—I just had two other offers to play Jews. I cannot refuse. I am a Jew." My jaw must have dropped. "No, really, I give you my word. I may really be a Jew; my family history is very unclear. All my friends are Jews. I feel like a Jew."

In fact, Mueller-Stahl knows his relatives are not Jews, even if there is murky talk about an ancestor who may or may not have been Jewish. But postwar Germans, and especially intellectuals, have adopted Jews as a symbol of righteousness, honesty and purity, a symbol in perfect opposition to the obscenities of the Nazi era. It is a convenient and honestly intended myth, offering the aura of confrontation with the past, as well as the hope of absolution. But the image of the pure Jew is so rigidly held that it is destined to disappoint, leading the most well-intentioned Germans back toward intolerance. When the editor of a leading German newspaper returned from his first visit to Israel, he told friends he had been shocked to see prisons in the Jewish state. "I never imagined that Jews could be criminals," he said quite seriously.

The German artistic establishment is fully prepared to land with all its might on anyone who dares sully that image of Jewish perfection. Consider the movie *Europa, Europa*. The 1991 release tells the story of Salomon Perel, a Jewish boy who survived the Holocaust by enlisting in the Nazi Army and attending an elite Hitler Youth academy—all the while keeping his pants on to prevent the Germans from noticing that he was circumcised. Sally Perel saved himself with deceit, brass, and adolescent overconfidence, as well as considerable luck. The movie was an unusual hit in America, running for nearly a year in New York and Los Angeles, winning rave reviews and mentions on dozens of Top Ten lists. But *Europa, Europa* was DOA in Germany. Movie houses refused to screen it, and audiences stayed away from the few cinemas that did. Critics bashed it: *Die Welt* called the movie "voyeuristic, speculative and sex-obsessed." Another newspaper called the story line "unbelievable." But Sally Perel's story was true, and Perel was alive to testify to the film's accuracy.

So when the German film industry group that nominates movies for the Best Foreign Film Oscar rejected *Europa, Europa* because its subject was "embarrassing," the movie's producer, Artur Brauner, went ballistic. Brauner, an elderly German Jew who had made a steady, varied stream of movies in a career stretching back to 1946, accused the industry of blackballing his movie because it showed a less-than-perfect vision of a Jew. "The board says the film doesn't show Jews as good people and doesn't show good Germans either," Brauner told me. "All I hear from people in the German film business is 'Ach, Herr Brauner, the Holocaust again. There has to be an end to all this.' They hate this subject, they really hate it, and now, with unification, they think they can just put an end to all this and start over."

The magazine *Der Spiegel* agreed, writing that *Europa, Europa* broke the stereotype of Jews as "serious, noble and terribly pained" and "violated a German taboo" by featuring a Jewish character who is "cynical and opportunistic." Under attack, the Export Union, the board that nominates films to the Academy, retreated to a curious defense. They claimed that *Europa, Europa* was not a German movie because its director, Agnieszka Holland, is Polish and because some of the film's funding came from France. (In June 1933, the Nazi Propaganda Ministry decreed, "A film will be recognized as a German film if it is produced in Germany by German citizens of German descent.") Brauner countered that the movie was produced by a German, made in the German language, with a German cast, and was even certified by the German government as a German production. The film board would not back down, so the movie was ineligible for Best Foreign Film. But U.S. members of the Academy—coaxed along by the movie's American distributor, Orion Classics—expressed their disgust with the Germans by nominating *Europa, Europa* for best screenplay. Facing American competition, it lost.

Only after the Oscar controversy erupted in the United States did *Europa, Europa* win substantial publicity in Germany, and only then did the German media discover that Perel was alive and well and living in Israel. Invited onto a TV talk show, he told his story. Interviewer Roger Willemson wasn't buying it. "How can it be?" he insisted. "How could you have passed as an Aryan? You look so much like the stereotypical Jew."

The *Europa, Europa* flap was the kind of dispute about things Jewish that exposes deep discomfort with a subject many Germans find unfairly burdensome. When Benjamin Navon was Israel's ambassador in Bonn in the 1980s and '90s, one of his jobs was to honor Germans who were "righteous gentiles" during the Nazi period—that is, people who helped save Jews. But time and again, Navon told me, Germans who had acted courageously half a century earlier were reluctant to admit to their acts now. They were afraid their friends and neighbors would somehow hold it against them.

Behind the relatively small number of Germans who declare themselves anti-Semitic lies a larger pool of latent anti-Semites. In a *Spiegel* poll, 64 percent of those surveyed said Germans "don't trust themselves to express their true opinions about Jews," and 41 percent added that "the topic of

Jews is somehow unpleasant to me." Poll figures only hint at the deep ignorance many Germans suffer about Jews. In a 1992 *Spiegel* survey, only 23
percent of Germans said it is wrong to speak of Jewish guilt for the death of
Jesus, 39 percent said the Jews were partly or wholly guilty, while the rest
did not know. When my wife taught a course on American legal practice at
Bonn University, she presented her students with a case that happened to
involve a rabbi. Then, Jody had to explain to the students—law students
and American studies majors who had traveled widely—what a rabbi was.

Some Germans have a vestigial memory of the Jews who lived among
them. I once attended a premiere at the Cologne Film Festival of the David
Mamet movie *Homicide,* in which a Chicago detective works on a case involving a Jewish family whose members speak Yiddish when they don't
want the cop to understand them. As the Yiddish dialogue washed over the
packed theater, nearly everyone around me began whispering to seatmates,
checking to make certain both that they caught the meaning (German and
Yiddish are so similar that Germans can easily understand the Jewish dialect) and that the language they were hearing was indeed Yiddish.

Edward Serotta, an American photojournalist who lived in Berlin while
working on a book about Germans and Jews, often visited German classrooms at the request of teachers who wanted their students to meet a Jew.
Ed started by asking who in the room had ever met a Jew. Rarely had anyone. Then he engaged the class in a little exercise: "Let's talk about the differences between Germans and Jews. It's 1940. What would you do? Would
you exterminate Jews?"

The students look down. "I don't know," is the most frequent response,
along with "I hope I wouldn't."

Serotta listens, waits, then nods. "OK. For you, National Socialism is an
ethical question. Not for a Jew. I would be dead, or in the best case, in
flight." Serotta's stark method grew in part out of frustration with the German school circuit, an experience I and many other Jews, German and foreign, shared. Placed on display in German schools, Jews meet a wall of
nervous silence. Sometimes this is only adolescent awkwardness; sometimes it is broken by an angry outburst against the teacher who has imposed
this embarrassing hour, this impossible confrontation, upon innocent children. But always, the silence is born of ignorance. Germans, growing up in
a country without any significant Jewish presence, do not know where to begin. Stereotypes flourish, even among the brightest. When a German Jewish
scientist who lived most of his life in New York returned to Berlin in 1992,
he found that even bright colleagues were capable of saying, "Ah, you are
Jewish. But you speak German so well!"

Even an abundance of goodwill is insufficient to save Germans from the ceaseless beating of the past against the present. One day in 1992, I received a call at my Berlin office from a Hamburg city official who wanted to talk off the record. We had never spoken before; the official said he was calling because "your newspaper represents certain important interests in your country." The man was reaching out for help. He had no idea what his city could do to halt the escalation of a bitter, violent controversy between a real estate developer and Jewish protesters from several countries. The dispute focused on a site in Hamburg where the developer, Buell & Liedtke, planned a $200 million shopping center, including a department store, movie theater and café. But before bulldozers could begin preparing for construction, Orthodox Jews from Israel, Belgium, Britain and the United States announced their intention to stop the project.

The site had been a Jewish cemetery for more than three hundred years before the Nazis destroyed it and built two air-raid shelters in the sacred ground. When a department store was built over part of the cemetery in the 1950s, no Jews objected. In fact, it was the German Jewish community that sold the land to the department store chain in 1953. That was back when most Jews would have nothing to do with Germany.

Now, activist Jews from outside Germany were fixing for a battle. A judge refused to block the development, so the Jews decided on a course of civil disobedience. They imported from Belgium and Britain a few dozen young students and old men, dressed in black coats and scraggly beards, and they blocked the bulldozers. The city had to decide whether and how to enforce the developer's right to use his land. My caller wanted to know how Hamburg could avoid a PR nightmare, how the city could act without sparking comparisons to the Nazis. He recited a long list of steps the city had taken over the years in search of reconciliation with the Jews: rebuilding the city's main synagogue, supporting artists and historical exhibits, teaching the young about a community that was no more. All those efforts were about to be overwhelmed by a single incident. Eleven U.S. senators had signed a letter imploring the chancellor to intervene, but Kohl had brushed them off, calling the affair a local matter over which he had no influence. I told the man I wasn't in the PR consulting business, but I agreed that any violent confrontation with the Jewish protesters likely would submerge Hamburg under a deluge of the worst kind of publicity. The developer had said he was willing to sell the property, but the city said it could not afford the $30 million price tag, and the federal government would not enter the fray.

A few days later, the worst possible scenario unfolded. After an appeals court rejected the Jewish groups' arguments, protesters broke through police lines to occupy the sacred site. With TV cameras recording their every lunge and pull, Hamburg police dragged demonstrators away from the property and into paddy wagons. "These are pictures that stir terrible memories—German policemen taking away Jews," began the anchorman on Germany's main TV channel that night. The German media, which had ignored the controversy for weeks, awoke, and their TV pictures instantly flashed around the world. A classic clash between property law and God's law had run squarely into an even more sensitive conflict: German against Jew. My caller had seen it coming, but had been powerless to halt the confrontation. To be sure, the Jewish activists took advantage of German sensitivity about their image in the outside world. But it is also true that the Germans—as they had for forty years—had proceeded as they could not have were there still a significant Jewish community in the country. The dispute was eventually resolved quietly when the developer examined the exact location of the historic cemetery and altered his building plans, moving the garage from underground to rooftop and arranging for Jerusalem's chief rabbi to supervise the limited digging necessary before the shopping center's foundation could be poured. Of course, those concessions could have been made a couple of years earlier, without the violence, but that would have required sensitivity that comes only with personal experience, and if one thing is missing from relations between Germans and Jews, it is experience with one another.

There were many such confrontations with the past after unification, in part because East Germany had never dealt with its Jewish legacy except to deny responsibility and blame the west for the Holocaust. When the Kaiser supermarket chain built a store on the grounds of the Ravensbrück concentration camp north of Berlin in 1991, the company at first tried to weather the inevitable storm of protest. "There is no law against bad taste," said a spokesman for the Brandenburg state government. But despite a promarket demonstration by local residents (HONOR THE DEAD, BUT DO SOMETHING FOR THE LIVING, their banners said), the company was forced to back off. It donated the nearly completed store to the state government to use as a cultural center.

Some awkward moments stemmed from ignorance, and some from latent or overt anti-Semitism. In 1992, the German Interior Ministry repeatedly denied to me the existence of a form its border officials used to categorize people applying for residency in Germany. The form, used in several German states, required officials to note the shape of the applicant's nose. A German nose was described as "normal;" a variety of codes were given for "abnormal" nose shapes found in other parts of the world. When an official finally conceded the existence of the form, he called it "routine."

•   •   •

For most of the five years he spent trying to save his career, Wolfgang Lob, a minister in the German Evangelical Church, wanted to believe he was the victim only of a mistake—not a vestige of official anti-Semitism. Following church rules, Lob let his superiors know when he planned to marry. He got a quick answer: The moment he wed, Lob would be fired, even defrocked. Lob's intended was Yael Wilf, who is Jewish, and Evangelical Church rules forbade any minister to marry a non-Christian. Lob appealed the decision, citing a 1980 church decree that admitted complicity in the terror of the Third Reich, sought reconciliation with Judaism, and promised to halt efforts to convert Jews. But church elders proved unwilling to tolerate Jewish spouses of pastors. Lob and another minister were fired for marrying Jews. A third minister, Irmela Orland, was banned from leading a parish after her Jewish husband refused the church's request that he be baptized.

Church officials insisted that their rule, far from being a relic of anti-Semitism, had the opposite intent. The idea was to prevent a repeat of the Nazi era, when thirty-five Evangelical ministers whose wives were Jewish were sacked. Several of those pastors committed suicide. The postwar church decided it would spare its ministers that pain by forbidding intermarriages. There was a certain logic to the rule, however thoughtless and cruel it seemed to those whose love ran smack into the edict. But Lob never understood why the church clung so tenaciously to the rule. As his doomed appeal made its way through the church hierarchy, Lob was stunned to find his mailbox and phone-answering machine filled with accusations that he was fouling his own nest. In the end, Lob lost not only his job, but his ordination. Lob and Wilf moved to Holland. "Once again," he said after five years of fruitless argument with the church he still wished to serve as minister, "the German church has proven itself a mirror of German society."

Even the best-intentioned Germans often grow up without meeting a Jew. So when toy witches appeared in shop windows in the Rhineland with crudely shaped yellow stars pinned to their chests, the young shopkeeper could and did plead innocent to any anti-Semitic design. Similar innocence likely was behind the comments of a sportscaster on the Tele 5 channel, who while covering the U.S. Open described the New York crowd's enthusiasm for tennis player Aaron Krickstein by saying that "he is the clear favorite because he has a very Jewish name and this city has a large population of Jews."

But just as the yellow stars come from somewhere, so do the frequent references to Jewish power that pop up in politics, the press and everyday conversation. (In a 1992 survey by Der Spiegel, 36 percent of Germans agreed that "Jews have too much influence in the world.") When I interviewed a couple about the stress of living one flight above eastern Berlin's hottest nightclub scene, Hans Joachim Huntscha said his only hope of shutting out the all-night noise rested with the city's Jewish community, whose offices were just down the block. "The Jewish community has not yet weighed in with their great influence," Huntscha said.

In an otherwise admirable speech to the Bundestag early in 1989, former federal minister Erhard Eppler said American opposition to German unification came primarily from "influential groups." No one in the chamber needed to ask whom they might be. That same year, Kohl's spokesman, Hans Klein, used the term "international Jewry" in a speech. Several years later, *Der Spiegel* described eastern politician Gregor Gysi, the only prominent Jew in German elective politics, as a "hooknosed operator."

Euphemisms abound for the power supposedly wielded by American Jews in Congress, the news media, and Hollywood. References to "East Coast newspapers," "East Coast urban special interests," "enemies of Germany," or "people who emphasize the dark side of German history" became so routine after unification that in 1993, a Free Democratic party staffer wrote a memo urging party officials to refrain from public use of such code words for Jewish influence. The staffer, an American named Bret Haan, said most party leaders grew sharply defensive after the memo, but one took him aside and said, "You're absolutely right."

Some Germans dispense with euphemism and say exactly what is on their minds. When Manfred Stolpe, premier of the state of Brandenburg, visited the editorial offices of the *New York Times* in 1993, editors posed tough questions about Stolpe's undercover work on behalf of the Stasi while he was a ranking church official under communist rule. The next day, a reporter for the *Berliner Zeitung* wrote an article explaining that the *Times* was hard on Stolpe "because of the Jewish religious affiliation of many on the executive level and among the editors." (Another Berlin paper, the *Tagesspiegel*, later took the *Berliner Zeitung* to task, wondering how exactly the "executive level's Jewish religious affiliation appears; perhaps it smells or tastes like a pastrami sandwich or a portion of gefilte fish. . . .")

Distasteful comments sometimes stem from a willful denial of facts. Asked in 1992 how many Germans had known about the extermination of Jews during the Nazi years, 58 percent said either "very few" or "a minority." Only 16 percent replied "the majority." Although most Germans grow up without meeting a Jew, *Stern* magazine found that 50 percent of Germans estimated the country's Jewish population at more than 500,000, a tenfold exaggeration of the actual figure.

Even experienced politicians often assume that German Jews' first allegiance is to Israel. Franz-Dieter Schlagkamp, mayor of a small town in the Mosel Valley, wrote to Ignatz Bubis, head of Germany's Jewish community, that "I pray to God that I never have a Jewish fellow citizen." The mayor, who addressed Bubis as "the top Jew," said he could not imagine the peace of his little village of vineyards being shattered by Jews and "their irritating barbs." The village rallied around its mayor, testifying to his humanity toward foreigners. The big-city press professed shock, but Bubis merely shrugged his shoulders. He got such letters every day, not necessarily from mayors, but not from the radical fringe either.

Bubis' rise to prominence was a brilliant accident of timing. As neo-Nazis stepped up their campaign of violence, forcing the country to confront its relationship with foreigners and others who did not fit in, leadership of the Jewish community changed hands for the first time since the end of World War II. The death in 1992 of Heinz Galinski, the seventy-nine-year-old Auschwitz survivor who ruled the community with an iron fist, brought about a shift of generations and temperament. Galinski was a righteous, angry figure, forever shaking and shouting on TV to remind Germans of their obligations to Jews. But for all his rage on behalf of the 6 million who perished, Galinski was in the end a comfortable figure for the Bonn government, which could count on Galinski's support as long as it showered the official Jewish community with financial aid and Galinski himself with the trappings of power (bulletproof limo, bodyguards, ready access to the chancellor).

Ignatz Bubis would not be bought off so easily. Where Galinski welcomed police bodyguards as a sign of his stature, Bubis tolerated them as a symbol of government insecurity about its image abroad. "The state is afraid," Bubis said. "If something happened to me in this office—God save us, what would the foreigners say?" A wealthy real estate developer from Frankfurt, Bubis, fifteen years Galinski's junior, used his boundless energy and media savvy to broaden German Jewry's agenda, to reach out to Jews long alienated from the official community, and to confront publicly the kind of official anti-Semitism Galinski had been willing to suffer quietly. Bubis would not limit himself to seeking better care for Jewish cemeteries; when few German politicians would face the reality of antiforeigner violence, Bubis challenged Germans to examine their laws and their attitudes toward the "other," whether Jewish citizen, Turkish guest worker or Gypsy refugee.

Bubis differed from his predecessor not only in style and intellect, but in his ability to grasp the change in the nature of German anti-Semitism. The antiforeign and anti-Jewish attacks of the early nineties were not the anti-Semitism in spite of Auschwitz that had so angered Galinski, but a new anti-Semitism because of Auschwitz—a calculated and purposeful shattering of postwar Germany's greatest taboo by extremists and young people who felt marginalized in the reunited country. The ringleaders of the far right, ever in search of a powerful weapon against the establishment, knew—sometimes instinctively, sometimes through careful study—that anti-Semitism had been an effective rallying point in a weak Germany between the world wars. The Nazis used anti-Semitism masterfully to restore a sense of stability and security in a time of turmoil. Now, with the country's stabilizing forces seemingly sputtering amid the turmoil of unification, the far right would offer the same old elixir—a turn against the other. Bubis saw the strategy for what it was and confronted reasonable Germans with the reality the Bonn government refused to accept—that while the neo-Nazis themselves remained a fringe movement, portions of their ugly message were seeping into normal, acceptable discourse. Large majorities of Germans were eager to move on: 62 percent told *Der Spiegel* that "46 years after war's end, we shouldn't talk so much anymore about the persecution of the Jews, but rather draw a line under the past."

The impact of antiforeigner and anti-Semitic violence was immediate. In Berlin, members of the Jewish Culture Association received so many threats that they asked the organization to send its newsletters and other correspondence in unmarked envelopes, without the Jewish star that was part of the group's logo. Wherever he went, Bubis carried folded hate letters he had received at home. For the first time in his life, such letters were being signed, and the signatures were those of respected citizens, lawyers, businesspeople, members of mainstream political parties. Once when I met with Bubis, he had three letters in his jacket pocket. One was a standard-issue rant from an eighty-six-year-old German man who signed his name and said the Jews were responsible for everything bad. The second was from a member of the governing board of the Free Democratic Party—in which Bubis was active. The board member commiserated with Bubis over the police's lax enforcement of laws against hate crimes. "In your homeland, police would never act so weakly," the letter said.

Bubis responded, "No, that happens in Frankfurt all the time."

The third letter was from another fellow Free Democratic leader, offering Bubis 150 tickets to a sports benefit against antiforeigner violence. "For your countrymen," the letter said, meaning Jews.

The tendency to negate the citizenship of German Jews even has a legal foundation: In an unusual 1991 ruling, the High Administrative Court of Berlin ordered a Jewish couple from Latvia deported, ruling that even though the couple's ancestors had lived in Germany, the couple was Jewish, and under German citizenship law, a person can be German or Jewish, but not both.

Bubis' people, whatever they were called, were not even half of 1 percent of the German population, but the violence against foreigners, together with Bubis' energy and good humor, gave the Jewish leader an extraordinary opportunity to voice his message of tolerance. Jews were the canary in the mine; if anti-Semitism was on the rise, perhaps Germany had changed less than its leaders had always contended. What Bubis had to say was not comfortable, but he said it in a heartfelt, almost gentle manner that appealed to many Germans.

"Forty percent of Germans have never seen or heard a Jew," Bubis told me. "The hate has always been there, but the atmosphere in the country has changed, and now, for the first time since the war, it is acceptable to express these sentiments openly." Surveys tracking attitudes over time supported Bubis: The Allensbach Institute regularly asks Germans if "we should help the Jews in every way we can because they have suffered greatly." In 1960, 46 percent of Germans agreed; by 1987, that figure had dropped to 26 percent. More recently, the proportion of young eastern German men agreeing that "the Jews are Germany's misfortune," a standard Nazi propaganda phrase, jumped from 19 percent to 29 percent from 1990 to 1992, according to a study by the Technical University in Berlin.

The media couldn't get enough of Bubis—he was presentable, rational, emotional, patriotic and critical, all at once. THE MAN OF THE HOUR, said *Die Woche*. GERMANY'S CONSCIENCE, said the *Wochenpost*. "I HAVE NO FEAR," headlined a *Stern* interview. On TV, his voice would catch as he testified to his love for country, then again as he detailed his dilemma: If the hate continued to mount, he would have to consider leaving Germany. There was even a brief flurry of interest in Bubis as president, but that idea petered out quickly when polls showed that four in ten Germans would not accept a Jew as head of state.

Before political groups, unions, business conventions and anyone else who would have him, Bubis hammered home his message: "Germany is the only country where you hear talk of Germans and Jews. You would never hear anyone say 'Americans and Jews' in America. We Jews in Germany still live in our own ghettos. Even the official government term for us, 'Jewish fellow citizens,' excludes us. Why aren't we simply 'citizens'? For the great majority of Germans, a Jew is a foreigner, a stranger. My citizenship is in the papers every day. But the polls show that to 57 percent of Germans, I am not a German citizen."

Reunification, Bubis argued, eroded some of Germany's democracy. It bared the country's racial definition of citizenship. The influx of asylum-seekers in the years after the Wall fell led the government to rescind its liberal guarantee of asylum to all political refugees, a decision that only fed the xenophobia of the radical right. Whenever Turks were killed or foreigners' houses bombed, Bubis was besieged by reporters: Was it time for Jews to leave? Bubis' very presence became a barometer of the political condition. There was, of course, no such simple equation. Living in Germany had never been an easy decision for a Jew after the war; Jews in Israel, America and elsewhere could not fathom why any Jew would stay in the country of the Holocaust. The few thousand who did stay, most of them Polish and other Eastern European Jews who had nowhere else to go at war's end, have always been an unusually fluid community, living in Germany for a few years, then in the United States, Britain or Israel, then perhaps returning again, sometimes for business reasons, sometimes to satisfy a yearning for German language and culture.

Bubis' reasons were as typical as any, a combination of accident and affinity for a place that, despite it all, was home. His family fled from German Silesia in the face of Nazi terror. They went to Poland, but that was no escape. His mother died at home; his father, a brother and a sister were murdered by the Nazis. Ignatz survived in slave-labor camps, making munitions until the Soviet Red Army liberated him in 1945. After the war, he wanted to emigrate to America or Palestine, but after bouncing around displaced-persons camps for some months, he ended up in Berlin and soon got started in business. Jewelry dealing led to gold trading, then to real estate development; he married a French Jew and they lived in Frankfurt, where they became very wealthy. That prominence made Bubis a target of West Germany's leftist youth in the 1960s; students occupied his properties and denounced him as a "Jewish speculator." Bubis would not be cowed. He confronted and debated the students, just as he did in 1985, when he led protesters onto a Frankfurt theater stage to halt a performance of a Rainer Werner Fassbinder play in which a character based on Bubis was called a "rich Jew" who "drinks our blood."

Bubis does not look the part of a street fighter; he is overweight, short, jowly, jovial. But also tough: When soccer fans sitting behind Bubis at a Frankfurt stadium heard a referee's call they didn't like, they began chanting "Jew to Auschwitz!" Bubis jumped in: "Do you know any Jews? No? Well, let me introduce myself: I am one. Do you have something against me?" The fans were silenced, for the moment anyway.

Bubis decided decades ago that if he were going to stay in Germany, he would have to stand up for himself. When the Fassbinder play was running, Bubis gave himself a choice: Fight back, or emigrate. Despite his business success and patriotism, Bubis and his wife actually considered emigration at several points. In the early fifties, they planned to move to Paris, but in the end decided it would be too difficult to start life over yet again in a new culture. Other times, the United States was the lure. By day, the move seemed rational. But at night, Bubis realized he was most comfortable in Germany. He was a German Jew, even if he knew his country had not and likely would not ever see him as anything but an outsider. In the curious formulation that Hitler forced on the official Jewish community—and which the community retains to this day—Bubis and his wife are called "Jews in Germany."

"Many in my generation have a hard time seeing themselves as Germans," Bubis said. "Until 1933, there was such a thing as German Jewry. That was murdered. After I came back to Germany in 1945, I, too, felt like a Jew in Germany. This was not my homeland. My hometown of Breslau [now part of Poland] seemed foreign to me." Only several years later, after he finally admitted to himself that he was staying, did Bubis begin to redevelop a relationship with Germany. And only twenty years later, sometime in the sixties, did he decide that "I once again felt like a German Jew, as a German citizen of Jewish faith."

That self-definition remained rare among Jews of Bubis' age. Younger Jews, many of whom have known no other home, show a greater willingness to identify with Germany. But even that limited sense of belonging was easily and quickly shattered by attacks on Jewish cemeteries and concentration camp memorials. Bubis' twenty-nine-year-old daughter, born in Frankfurt, studied in Paris for two years and then decided to move back to Germany. It was, she told her parents, where she belonged. But then came the years of violence. Bubis' own child had to tell her father that she was one of those German Jews who was "sitting on packed luggage," watching, waiting to see if it would be safe to stay.

"I love this culture," said Bubis the father. "But there is so much violence, and the Germans are too quick to come up with all kinds of excuses—the economic situation, the social situation. If this continues, I may become the problem. I have also loved women I never got. Germany has no tradition of democracy; it does not flow in our blood. We are trainees in democracy. There is the danger that we will decide to try something else."

Bubis' public message was directed at Germans, but his first priority remained an audience equally suspicious and perhaps even more resistant to change—Jews. This subculture was so small that some children of Jews in Berlin and Frankfurt were sent abroad for college largely to improve their chance of finding a Jewish mate. The few thousand long-term members of the community were mostly elderly, and even their children often had only the most tentative ties to Germany. They lived, for the most part, among themselves, in exile at home. Often, they seemed utterly without outside support. Israel has long opposed the existence of a Jewish community in Germany, combining the argument that all Jews should live in Israel with a special plea for Jews to avoid the land that spawned the Holocaust. Alphons Silbermann, an eighty-five-year-old sociologist in Cologne who studies his fellow Jews in Germany, describes a double isolation, one imposed by other Germans, the other by Jews in the rest of the world. "The remaining minority is viewed with a certain disdain by Jews outside Germany, as a group of traitors, opportunists, even adventurous fools who are not afraid to live among their murderers," he said.

A siege mentality developed over the years. Even in Berlin and Frankfurt, the two largest Jewish communities, everyone seemed to know everyone else. When I visited the main Frankfurt synagogue's Rosh Hashana (New Year's) services one October, I was surprised to see how blithely members of the congregation accepted the rigorous security measures executed by uniformed and plainclothes police in front of the temple. A van full of police stood parked across from the building, while detectives intercepted all comers on the temple's front steps, halting anyone with long hair, informal dress or swarthy looks for a closer inspection. "Your papers, please," the police said, as all eyes turned toward the potential terrorist. In the end, no one was taken away, no one prevented from worshiping, but one young man had to wait until police could confirm his identity with headquarters, and another had to prove his Judaism by finding an elder of the congregation to vouch for him.

Inside the restored temple, under a towering dome decorated with an abstract design of Stars of David, the crowd of nearly 2,000 was suddenly exuberant, hugging and kissing friends and acquaintances, exchanging holiday wishes, trading the latest business gossip in a mélange of German, Hebrew and an occasional bit of French. There were perhaps 100 teenagers and children, many of them richly tanned, and they danced and played in the courtyard while their parents prayed. The teens flirted with one another; they had clearly known each other for many years. Some had paired off, and simple math made it clear that others would not have that option, not here anyway. Whom would they find? Would they be lost to the Jewish community? Would they have to leave Frankfurt, even leave Germany?

Older women used the High Holy Day as a chance to show off their furs. Clusters of friends gathered to figure out the identity of a new face or two. The scene could just as well have been played out on Long Island or in Shaker Heights—until services ended. Then, even before they reached the police officers who patrolled back and forth across the synagogue's entryway, men swiped the yarmulkes off their heads, laughs and shouts were squelched, and Frankfurt's Jews disappeared silently into the German night, the clip-clop of their heels echoing across the city streets.

Jews growing up in Germany come to consider abnormality normal. The law exempts them from the military service mandatory for all other German males (Jews need not even perform the alternative service required of Germans who have conscientious objections to Army duty.) The exclusion was intended to spare Jews from having to wear the uniform of their persecutors. But the effect is to cement the separation of Jews from other Germans, even as the policy exposes a vein of self-loathing—why should Jews, some of whom serve on German police forces, be spared service in a democratic military designed to have nothing in common with the Nazi Wehrmacht? The same kind of self-doubt emerges in government efforts to assure the security of Jewish worship and culture. The sight of police carrying submachine guns on twenty-four-hour patrol outside Jewish synagogues and institutions, as well as searches of Jews on their way to worship, is intended to discourage terrorism. But—especially considering the light security surrounding the most prominent German politicians—the protection also sends a message that Jews are not safe, that somehow, Germany remains a forbidding and frightening place for Jews to live.

The fall of the Wall brought not only a rise in violent nationalism, but also a dramatic change in the composition of the Jewish population. German Jews became a minority within their own community, as immigrants from the former Soviet Union arrived by the thousands. By 1994, only 10 percent of the Jews in Germany were of German descent. The arrival of at least 10,000 Soviet Jews in the first two years after the Wall opened presented the Interior Ministry with a dreaded dilemma: The government had always favored the reestablishment of a viable Jewish community, but politicians feared that accepting large numbers of Soviet Jews would anger Israel, and the German public was in an uproar about the uncontrolled influx of foreigners into the country. (A remarkable 91 percent of Germans told pollsters that Soviet Jews got better treatment from Bonn than any other group of foreigners—a patently false statement.)

No one in Bonn wanted to touch this issue. But there was no choice. In 1990, the government halted all legal immigration of Soviet Jews, arguing that the numbers were simply too high to be handled decently. The policy did not hold: the state of Lower Saxony rejected the federal position. It considered any Soviet Jew of German descent to be German, just as the law granted automatic citizenship to ethnic Germans living anywhere in the world. In Bonn, politicians proposed quotas, which the Jewish community promptly rejected.

Meanwhile, the refugees kept coming. In East Berlin, Annetta Kahane—a Jew who was in charge of refugee issues for the reform government that served during the interim between the communists and the westerners—tried to find beds for arriving Soviet Jews. But when she called a West

Berlin official in charge of refugee camps, he replied, "Frau Kahane, five hundred Jews! Isn't that a bit much? I mean, I already have a hundred of them on my desk. Terrible." Kahane reminded her colleague that Berlin had been home to 175,000 Jews half a century before. The western bureaucrat was unmoved. Kahane had to find housing in the east.

The problem did not subside. In 1991, Germany threatened to deport about three hundred Soviet Jews who had emigrated to Israel but then sought refuge in Germany when the Gulf War broke out. Reaction to the threat forced Bonn to back down; the Jews stayed. Then, in 1992, Jews in the former Soviet Union filed more than 25,000 applications to move to Germany. German diplomats delayed, freezing action on the applications. This time, they were lucky; some of the Jews did decide to stay home. But others slipped into Germany, fleeing a deteriorating situation back in Moscow and St. Petersburg, where nationalists harassed Jews, threatened their children and scrawled swastikas on their apartment doors.

"You have two weeks to leave the country, you dirty Jews," said an unsigned letter found by one St. Petersburg family at their apartment doorway. When I met Eduard, a fifty-four-year-old machinist, and his wife, a secretary, they were living among a thousand other Soviet Jews in a rundown apartment complex on Berlin's eastern edge. Eduard's grandparents had left Germany for the Ukraine a hundred years before. Now the grandson was back, determined to create a new life in Germany. "Certainly we have some fear," he said. "But there was fascism and there is the German people, and I believe there is a difference. Life will show."

Soviet Jews arrived knowing little about their religion. They might stay for many years, or perhaps they will move on, to Israel, back to Russia, to another refuge. But whoever constitutes the Jewish population of Germany, the community will remain small, far smaller than the enduring issue of Germans and Jews. That relationship remains a living confrontation: It remains illegal for Germans to own a copy of *Mein Kampf* or to make anti-Semitic remarks, even to a friend. As long as those taboos remain, it will be clear that no scar tissue has grown over the wounds of this century. Tensions between Germans and Jews remain, and both groups need those tensions. Both have come to define themselves by the other's anger and pain. The cycle of victimization and self-assertion in which Germany is caught continues, in part because of Jews' constant reminders of the Nazi period and the Holocaust. In the secular world of American Jewry and in the ritual of observant Jews around the world, Jewish identity is increasingly defined by the two unifying events in accessible Jewish memory—the Holocaust and the creation of the Israeli state. Jews need the Holocaust. But so do Germans, much as they may deny it, because virtually everything modern Ger-

many takes pride in—its democracy, its European identity, its western orientation—stems from its rejection of Nazi extremism. Germany, too, defines
itself by the Holocaust, and Germans, in their insecurity, often look toward
Jews and other foreigners for acceptance and approval of their differences
from their parents and grandparents.

Every society is a tapestry of contradictions, every country a mystery
molded from history and culture. For half a century, Jews have watched the
Germans and wondered—can they change, have they changed? It is impossible for a Jew—German or not—to live in Germany without being reminded of what the parents and grandparents of those living today did or
allowed. It is impossible to ignore the heartfelt confrontation with the past
that many Germans have chosen. No other society in history has taken its
misdeeds, its most shameful chapter, and willingly, voluntarily incorpo-
rated its memory into its daily life—its TV programs, its laws, its education
system. And yet it is also impossible to ignore the anti-Semitism with and
without Jews that infects all levels of society, sometimes venally, sometimes
out of pathetic ignorance. In the coming years, Germany will be forced to
define itself; its 6 million foreign residents will demand that. The answer
will require a long, difficult struggle, and it will determine not only the
country's relationship with the "other," but also its ability to transcend the
past. The story of Germans and Jews is not over. Until the Germans decide
who they are, both peoples will live with uncomfortable reminders. The city
of Berlin has for some years planned to build a Jewish Museum, designed
by an American Jew, Daniel Libeskind. Again and again, the museum was
delayed, by financial concerns, by political considerations. Libeskind,
dispirited, eventually left the country. But the centerpiece of the museum
was already completed before construction began in 1994. The design was
intended to symbolize the absence of Jewish life: The core of the building
will be a long, hollow space.

11

A German
Pendulum:
Father and Son

THEY LIVED ON a perfectly straight street lined with scrawny young pine trees and nearly identical stucco houses, a rare strip of American-style suburbia in Germany. Theirs was a well-to-do neighborhood, silent but for the songs of robins on a cool spring day. The Althans house faced the world with the same white lace curtains that marked every other house on the street. In the secluded backyard, where Günter and Ingrid relaxed during afternoon hours hoarded from life's obligations, they lovingly created a cocoon of color, a flourish of flowers and blooming trees, a haven from the harshness of daily routine. At work, there were the usual political battles and personal jealousies that stole attention from the blind and deaf children to whom Günter and Ingrid devoted their professional lives. The country was shaken by economic distress and social disorder. Every day, Günter Althans learned on the news about another crime against foreigners, another attack by right-wing extremists. And each time he heard of a fire-bombing or a murder, Günter's thoughts turned immediately to his middle child, his oldest son Ewald, who grew up in this house and became a Nazi.

With each new report of charred houses and cornered refugees, Günter reminded himself that his son was never violent physically, that Ewald repeatedly assured his dad that he deplored such attacks, that surely the thinking behind these assaults was too primitive for his own flesh and blood. And then the father questioned himself: "Of course, thinking can be violent. And my son does believe things that are dangerous." And all those anguished years raced through the father's mind, a thousand times and again—his son's ties to incorrigible, unrepentant Nazis; the police knocking at the Althans door at six in the morning, search warrants in hand; the constant arguments; the ineluctable sense that he was losing his boy. And finally, the day in 1986 when Günter Althans turned to his twenty-year-old son and delivered an edict: "I ordered him out of the house, so I could honestly say that he was no longer legally registered here, so the police would stop coming here to find him."

When he was thirteen, Bela Ewald Althans invented his own political party. He called it the Blues. Ewald—he preferred his middle name because it sounded more German—had always been a child who concocted fantasies about power and justice. He had, his parents always said, lots of ideas. Ewald's teachers branded him an individualist, which meant that he would not do as he was told. The teachers grew ever less tolerant of Ewald's ways, and Ewald grew ever less interested in what the classroom had to offer. He searched for something else. At first, he thought he would follow his father's path as a committed leftist, someone who fought for justice for the weakest elements of society. Like his father, Ewald was inspired by the Nazi genocide to work toward a different Germany, one in which Jews and others who did not fit the Aryan stereotype could be comfortable. Growing up in a home where both parents had devoted their professional lives to educating the handicapped, Ewald knew the power of a commitment to others.

But Ewald's path turned. Perhaps the seed had been planted back when he was one and a half, when his parents split up. Ewald would stay with his father, who remarried when the boy was three. His mother drifted off, losing contact with her ex-husband and her children. Perhaps the roots of Ewald's attraction to the fringes lay a generation or more removed, in hazy family stories about Nazi grandparents, of relatives who went along to get along, and others who did more. Or perhaps the search for roots is foolhardy. Perhaps Ewald's embrace of extremism was an adolescent rebellion that froze in place, held steady by the money, emotional support and camaraderie of old men who were experts at pumping restless young souls full of importance and power. Whatever the reasons, the pressure that bore down on Günter Althans as he sat in his pristine backyard, smoking small Dutch cigars called Schimmelpennincks, was relentless. His son the Nazi. His son who kept a portrait of Adolf Hitler on the wall over his desk. In the Munich office where Ewald Althans recruited young toughs to his ideology of hate, he stockpiled reports purporting to show that the Holocaust never happened. He ran a $400,000 annual operation with the ultimate dream of destroying German democracy and launching the country into another paroxysm of nationalistic rage and racial cleansing. Günter's son was the subject of magazine cover stories, TV documentaries, and a film called *Profession: Neo-Nazi.*

Before he turned twenty-five, Ewald Althans had been convicted of several crimes, was under surveillance by Germany's domestic intelligence agency, and was a leader of the international radical right. Germany's new Nazi movement was tiny and splintered, but intelligence officers and politicians across the country agreed that the far right had potential to blossom— if it could find a charismatic leader of reasonable intelligence. Ewald Althans had been bred—almost like something out of *The Boys from Brazil*—to be exactly that. He was blond, blue-eyed, six feet four, lean, with close-cropped hair, gestures carefully copied from old films of Hitler and Goebbels, and a rhetorical style that could bring audiences to their feet. Althans claimed to be able to summon several thousand angry young men to a demonstration on short notice. He clearly had the ability to import all manner of illegal Holocaust-denial literature into Germany. He was chief German sponsor of the British historian turned Holocaust denier David Irving, one of the celebrities of the international denier circuit, a genuinely respected intellectual who forsook a career as a mainstream historian to join the French academic Robert Faurisson and the Boston engineer Fred Leuchter in lecturing to motley audiences of pimply skinheads, conspiracy-minded misfits and old Nazis. Althans relished the camaraderie of the international "revisionist" scene. He thought it lent him respectability. He thought it proved he was a leader of his country, or at least of one of its important movements.

The young Althans had turned his life story into a faint carbon of Hitler's path toward fanaticism: a tale of repeated rejection by the establishment, beginning with a school that dismissed him because he attended radical demonstrations, a father who threw him out because of his political views, government agents who prevented him from finding work, and police who ended his dreams of a career playing the trumpet by bashing in his teeth.

The father tried, as any good father would, to find what was right about his boy. "In many areas, Bela [Günter still called his son by his first name, even if Ewald had rejected it] has been confirmed in his judgment of the situation," the father said. "Many years ago, Bela said wait and watch what will happen when 200,000 Russian Germans a year come to Germany and the economy declines. Look at Germany—strikes, demonstrations, economic crisis. There's nothing left for the people to feel joyful about. Doesn't our country have the same right as any other to control its borders? Does our past prevent us from having the same reasonable laws as other countries?"

Sometimes the father tried another tack: "Lots of what Bela says is just

provocation. I wouldn't take it too seriously. We can't expect the same outlook from our children as we had. Bela feels proud to be a German. I would
never agree with that, even if I can still be glad I grew up here." Günter
blamed himself and his ready acceptance of the left's ideas about child-
rearing—tolerance for all excesses, an avoidance of discipline—for his
son's extremism. "I don't really believe Bela's anti-Semitism. What he says
has little connection to what I think he actually believes. At twenty-eight,
you can still be very immature."

But neither he nor his guest bought that line. Günter Althans sighed,
drank his coffee and stared out over the flower beds.

Günter spent his childhood in the Third Reich, then lived under the Soviet
occupation, and finally survived four years in the communist German Democratic Republic before he fled west. In an orderly, comfortable life, he has
made time to think about political philosophy. He is a teacher because he
wants to be. He teaches handicapped children because he believes he has a
duty to help them find a place in society. And Althans is a disciplined man,
harsh on himself. He is formal and proud of it. He chastises younger colleagues who dare to address him as *du*.

For many months, Althans avoided talking about his son. I had called
him a few times to ask if we could sit down to discuss Ewald, and the father
had never said no, never said yes. He was torn: He wanted to defend himself
against his son's reputation, but he also wanted to defend his son. And some
part of him just wanted to retreat into his lush backyard, far from the shadows of history. And so we played phone tag for the better part of a year. I
called, Althans agreed to an interview. He called back, saying he wanted
more time to think about it.

Another time, six months later, I called and Althans said, "I immediately
end this conversation." I asked if we could talk at a later date. "Yes," he
replied, "some other time." Finally, a couple of months later, Althans responded cordially to a letter I had written him explaining my intentions.
"You have written me a very polite letter," he said. "I have two hours for
you." In the end, Althans was more generous with his time. He was a kind
and thoughtful host who opened his home and his heart to a foreign
stranger.

He believes in being rigidly honest, and so does not shy from the uncomfortable facts about his own family. His father, Ewald, was a convinced communist, and his mother a strong supporter of the National Socialists. Their
political split was deep—deep enough to make a lasting impression on all
six of their children. The mother was, in Günter's words, "always loyal to the
Führer, as was expected of a good German woman." At home, when Günter

was a boy serving in the Hitler Youth, "I truly believed everything the Führer said. At home, we all did. My father was not at home; he went from unemployment to the draft and on to a POW camp. So he had a very different experience of the Third Reich."

After the war, Günter, like many young Germans, confronted his parents with the horrifying discrepancy between history as it had been told within the family and history as it actually happened. Like so many parents who struggled to raise children amid the terror and conformity of the Nazi era, the Althanses did their best to screen Günter from the truth. Günter could not squeeze anything out of his father before the embittered man died in 1949 of injuries he received while serving in the Wehrmacht in eastern Poland and Russia. Günter's mother swore to her son that she never knew what was really going on during the war—nothing about the Jews, nothing about the death camps.

"You have to believe your parents," Günter would say many years later, and he did. But in the first years after the war, Günter found out what had happened. He learned about the camps and the deportations, the tortures and brutalities. By then, Günter's hometown of Halle was in the eastern, Soviet Zone, and like it or not, the new country being built around him was a communist one, a place—if you believed the propaganda, and Günter did—of justice, equality and ramrod resistance to any fascist instincts that might have survived the defeat of the Nazis. "We were the unburdened generation," said Günter, who was born in 1934. "We experienced the war, but we didn't take part in it. We were the people chosen to build the Soviet Zone. We really thought we were creating the New Germany." Günter signed up for the Free German Youth, the paramilitary force the communists set up as the successor to the Hitler Youth. He rose quickly to a leading position in his school's troop. He joined the German-Soviet Friendship Society. And later, as he continued training to be a teacher, he enlisted in Service for Germany, a uniformed unit that was the precursor of the East German National People's Army. Again, he rose easily, riding his intelligence and dedication to the post of lieutenant, winning responsibility for his unit's lodging, clothing and equipment. "I did it all with joy and conviction," Günter said. "I was true to the party line. I joined with our agitprop people and did not question the positions we were taught. If I do something, I do it thoroughly."

Already in those early days, the communists were efficient at maintaining support among their chosen party elite. Althans' unit, in contrast to the general public in those early postwar years of deprivation, had nothing to complain about. For the first time in his life, Althans had long, ironed pants. His commanders regularly distributed shirts, chocolates and other delicacies. "I had no idea then of what we now know," Günter said, "that these were the goods stolen from the Care packages that people in the west were sending east. They told us the chocolates and orange juice came from Cuba."

Despite his affection for the reds' ideas, Günter soon found himself the subject of suspicion. His regular visits to the west piqued the curiosity of East Germany's new secret police. Then came the state's interest in Günter's aunt—as a schoolteacher, she had been a Nazi party member, a near-obligation then and quite the burden to carry now. Günter's father got a tip from a friendly Soviet officer that the state was moving to arrest the aunt; forewarned, she fled to the west. Young Günter's faith was shaken. The final rattle came at a political conference where the bosses handed out slips of paper on which the young cadre renewed their commitments to serve their party. Althans had agreed to stay in the service for another two years, but when he got his sign-up sheet, it said he had re-upped for five years.

Günter Althans, nineteen, would not be lied to. "I was very angry," he said. "I am a fanatic about the truth." On June 6, 1953, he dressed in his uniform with its row of medals. That got him through the first checkpoint, thirty miles outside of Berlin, where easterners were asked why they were entering the capital city. Then, he headed west on the S-Bahn, the elevated train that stretched across both parts of the divided city. As the train approached the border between East and West Berlin, western passengers surrounded Althans and the handful of other easterners, shielding them from East German security police. Althans was in the west. His military career was over. He was one of the million East Germans who would ditch communism and vote with their feet before the Berlin Wall was erected in 1961. Günter would not see his mother again for twenty-three years. The communist regime branded him a deserter and forbade him to enter its territory until the early 1980s, when Günter managed to win permission to travel east as chairman of a group that worked on assisting the blind. Once, he tried to break away from a business visit to Leipzig to see his mother in nearby Halle, but someone informed on him. Günter was caught and detained for a day. His whole family was together for the last time in May 1949, for his father's funeral. His mother was permitted to cross to the west only when she turned sixty, in 1987. She died three years later. "What the Nazi Reich did to us can only be understood in the families that were torn apart," Günter said.

Althans went to school, joined the Evangelical Church and spent a year helping Palestinian refugees in Lebanon. He was disillusioned when he found that the Lebanese were using foreign church workers as a propaganda tool against Israel, a notion that horrified Althans. "I had a deep sympathy for Jews after the Third Reich, and I could not accept the idea that we were used to build up support for the Palestinians against the Jews," he said. Alienated, Althans returned to Germany. For more than twenty years, Althans and his second wife, Ingrid, have taught blind and deaf students in Hanover. He was involved for a while in Social Democratic politics, but eventually concentrated his political activities in teachers' organizations. His days as an active leftist in East Germany had dried up his enthusiasm for party politics. Instead, Althans worked with a commission that prevented the East and West German Braille systems from growing apart during the decades of division. Over the years, Althans' politics moved toward the center; he was tired of stridency and extremes of any kind. He became a moderate, a man whose political religion above all was democracy.

Günter had three children, two by his first wife, one with Ingrid. Two were politically liberal and socially tolerant, like their father. The youngest boy, Florian, still lived at home while finishing his duty with the Bundeswehr and waiting to begin studies to become an architect or veterinarian. Florian played serious cello, palled around with his parents, and shined with a warmth and informality his father never achieved. The middle child, named for his grandfather Ewald, was also bright, musical, and personable, a tall, lanky figure with sparkling eyes and a genial, hale manner.

Bela Ewald Althans was, by consensus of his teachers, his parents and himself, a fresh and rebellious child. He threw tantrums. He was bright, but had little interest in school—except for lessons about the Holocaust. One of his aunts had married a Jew, and Ewald was taken with the man. The boy decided he wanted "to do something for the Jews." He joined one of the many antifascist youth groups run by leftists in West Germany. There were meetings and marches, even trips to concentration camps.

At thirteen, Ewald was at the dawn of his political awareness. He had gone through a long-haired rebellion phase by then; it was the seventies, after all. He had traveled to Israel, in his father's footsteps, with Action Reconciliation, a German group devoted to good works for Jews and other victims of Nazi aggression. "I was searching for something," he said. "I started out very anti-Hitler, and then I started reading history of the Third Reich. It was just too much for me to hear that Jews had to make bread from wood, or that lampshades were made from Jewish skin." Ewald gravitated toward the antifascists as a way of belonging to something, wearing a uniform, perhaps getting involved in a street fight or two.

And then he switched sides. The turnabout came in part from within; Ewald said he grew increasingly frustrated by the antifascist group leaders' attempts to make young members feel guilty about being German. But

Ewald was also pushed: An old Nazi in Hanover happened upon Ewald as he browsed at a flea market display of old Nazi paraphernalia (which is illegal in Germany). Next thing he knew, Ewald was invited to a meeting at Dachau of an organization of artists, teachers and others still loyal to Nazism. Ewald heard lectures on the burden of guilt. He had his first exposure to the underground Holocaust-denial movement. And he met kindly old men and women who offered rousing tales of racial glory and political prowess.

"It's easy to change when you are fourteen," Althans told me. "National Socialism is attractive to a German. It's smiling faces, work, and lots of attention, from the police and the world media. It's black riding boots and uniforms. It's fun. I was always open to other opinions, and I was the only youth at this meeting." In those months of transition, Althans grew more loyal to the far right as he learned just how strong the taboo against Nazism was. In school, and in confrontations with his mates in the antifascist movement, Althans found that Nazi views were anything but welcome. "That was all we as young fourteen-year-olds needed to know," he said. "That we were not allowed to talk meant that we had to be right."

Two old Nazis, ranking officials of the Third Reich, made Ewald their project. They sent him home with assigned readings—*Mein Kampf,* Alfred Rosenberg's anti-Semitic tracts, piles of Nazi speeches. Beginning when Ewald was seventeen, Willi Krämer, Rudolf Hess' chief of staff and an adviser to propaganda chief Joseph Goebbels, tutored Althans in public speaking and fascist ideology for about six years, until Krämer died at ninety-three. But the man who introduced Althans to the international neo-Nazi underground was Otto Remer, head of the radical right Freedom Party and a Nazi Wehrmacht major general who played an important role in breaking up the July 20, 1944 plot to assassinate Hitler. Remer, who went on after the war to create a neo-Nazi party that West Germany later banned, found jobs for Althans, helped him set up his own neo-Nazi cell, taught him how to run and fund a political organization, and made him a star in the worldwide constellation of Holocaust revisionists, fascist gangs, and anti-Semitic activists. Krämer and Remer taught Ewald French and English, had him memorize long passages of Hitler and Goebbels speeches, persuaded him he had the potential to lead his nation. It was not hard to see what attracted the old Nazis to Althans. He shared his father's long nose and narrow features, but Ewald was taller and lighter, an old brownshirt's dream of what the leader of the next movement should look like. The cloning process took a decade, and the work began slowly. Althans was still in school for the first few years, sharing classrooms with Turkish youths at the Bismarck

Gymnasium in Hanover, facing off against foreigners as he mouthed the fascist slogans his elderly friends taught him.

In 1984, Althans heard Michael Kühnen speak at a meeting of old Nazis in Hanover. Kühnen was the charismatic neo-Nazi whom West German intelligence officers had long feared would emerge from the country's splintered and fractious far right. He was lean, hard, a good public speaker. Where other young toughs had failed, he seemed to be uniting the fringy Nazi scene. Althans was one of about a dozen young Nazi leaders who declared themselves protégés of Kühnen. Althans joined Kühnen's Free German Workers' Party—mostly a bunch of skinheads—and later, Ewald created his own German Youth Education Enterprise. That opened him to the same kind of surveillance and legal attention Kühnen faced. Kühnen's every move was watched by several police agencies. There were house searches, arrests, informants, bans, jail terms. Althans enjoyed the chase, even if—perhaps especially if—the police's interest in him horrified his parents. Ewald claimed that after government agents went to three hotels where he had applied for work as a cook, he was turned down for jobs he would otherwise have gotten. In 1985, he was arrested and fined $275 for insulting democracy. The next year, he was convicted of wearing a Nazi uniform. And later, he was fined $6,000 for shouting *"Sieg Heil"* in public. In one year, Althans said, police raided his home or office sixty-three times, confiscating thousands of books and videotapes.

Then, in 1991, Kühnen died of AIDS. Many of the most prominent figures in the neo-Nazi scene had been rumored to be homosexuals; Kühnen openly admitted that he was. Althans denied any sexual relationship with Kühnen or any other homosexual. "What people do in their private lives is their own business," he said. "Politically, I have no problem with whatever it is they may do." In 1993, *Der Spiegel* reported that Althans frequented gay bars in Munich using the pseudonym Bernd Adelmann. Althans denied it.

With Kühnen gone, Althans was on his own. He moved to Munich and opened a storefront office, ostensibly for his public relations firm, but actually as headquarters for his political-organizing efforts. Over the years, Althans would develop a reputation as the "yuppie Nazi," the media-savvy, café-society fascist who dressed in black jeans and boots just like trendy college kids. Althans equipped himself with fax, cellular phones and modern graphics. He even handed out business cards. Althans was equally at ease at a gay bar in Hamburg, a chic restaurant in Munich's university quarter, a beer hall in the old city, or a grungy gathering of junior Nazis in a remote eastern village. "I have gay friends, I have black friends," he said. "They know I'm racist, but that doesn't mean I don't like them. If I see two Vietnamese fighting five skinheads, I fight for the Vietnamese. If anything is unjust, I'm against it." Despite a charming sympathy for the underdog, Althans' concept of justice was confused at best. After all, this was the same young man who saw Germany's tiny Jewish minority as a threat sufficient to justify wholesale deportation, if not worse.

Althans' appeal to both the disillusioned toughs of the skinhead scene and the more intellectual strains of Germany's extremist subculture was no accident. The old Nazis had turned over the care and molding of Althans to one of the world's most successful fascists, Ernst Zündel, a German émigré who moved to Toronto in 1958 to avoid the German draft. Like Althans, Zündel was a graphic artist who made a careful study of the finer points of propaganda. Zündel was a somewhat comical character, a roly-poly figure who wore funny hats, kept a mock concentration camp prison uniform in his office, carried ridiculous signs (THE HOLOCAUST IS PURE HATE) and emulated Hitler, his hero, by painting oils with all the subtlety of a paint-by-numbers kit. Althans avoided Zündel's excesses even as he absorbed what his new mentor could teach him about playing the press, taking advantage of his own legal troubles, and organizing followers whose passions for drink and thuggery hardly helped in the reach toward respectability. Althans "has the world at his feet—the right age, the right looks, the right stature," Zündel said. "He looks like a noble Teuton. If he keeps healthy, he and his generation can change Germany's fate."

Zündel became Althans' primary funding source. The two were funded by a steady stream of contributions from Americans, Canadians, Germans and others. Together, Zündel and Althans annually distributed millions of nationalist and Holocaust denial tracts, as well as tens of thousands of video cassettes, which they considered the most effective weapons in their arsenal—a strategy copied from Ayatollah Khomeini's long struggle to gain power in Iran. Zündel and Althans met regularly with nationalist extremists from South Africa, Croatia, Sweden, Italy, Spain, Canada and the United States.

From the Nazis, Althans learned the value of projecting supreme self-confidence and wild arrogance. "It is my task to lead and take care of others," he would say in public, without a smile. Privately, he told me that some people are born to be Führer types and others must grow into the role. He was not yet there, but he thought he was on the way. Althans' early appeal was based on tired old Nazi cries for *Lebensraum* (living space), national pride, and a firm hand ruling the land. Then, after German unification, the far right got a gift—the wave of refugee immigration that dovetailed with a worsening economy and rising social turmoil to create a new audience for the fascist message. "A radical idea only appeals to young people when they have nothing more to lose," Althans said. He readily conceded that many of his followers were "half-wits," but said he needed the young thugs to win attention to his nascent movement.

The heart of his politics remained the Holocaust. "Only Auschwitz stands between me and respectability," Althans told me. "I won't be held guilty for things I did not do." And then, as he often did while discussing the extermination of the Jews, Althans laughed. It was often hard to tell just how seriously he took his own views. He was shameless in his condemnation of Jews and his denial that the Nazis sought to wipe out European Jewry. "I know there was no Holocaust," Althans said. "The films we've all seen ad nauseam were made by the Allies, directed by Alfred Hitchcock in Hollywood. I'll talk to any Auschwitz survivor. I've been to all the camps, I've seen all the so-called ovens. But Zyklon B was an explosive. Study it and you will see—it could not have been used to exterminate." He could go on in this vein for hours; he often did. His mind brimmed with details of pseudoscience and the historical distortions of his fellow ideologues.

Althans studied Judaism just enough to know the basics of the religion, its holidays and forms of worship. He called himself a Zionist who opposes Israel, a juvenile bit of sophistry that allowed him to outrage Jews and amuse Germany's intellectual far right with misstatements and distortions like this passage from a speech: "I'm a Zionist, of course. Jews should go to Israel. That's what I want; that's what Hitler wanted—the Jews out of Europe. The Jews got their own state from Hitler. But they forgot to say thank you. Israel has a lot of laws I really like, such as they don't let foreigners work in jobs that are reserved for Jews. Non-Jews can't marry Jews. They have the Nuremberg Laws in Israel."

As much as he sometimes dressed up his opinions in hopes of winning mainstream support, Althans was equally capable of diatribes worthy of Louis Farrakhan. "Jews run the movie industry, even in Germany," Althans said. "The names at the end of films look like the Tel Aviv phone book. Jews were installed in all the key positions after the war by the Allies. I know the Jews. I like a lot about the Jew. He's the best conversation partner because he argues well. But we don't want the Jew in our country. We don't need to kill them, just throw them out of the country. We want a Germany for the Germans, not a Federal Republic of Germany for the Jews."

Whatever his father might want to believe about Ewald Althans, any trace of moderation in his views was quickly overtaken by his worship of Adolf Hitler. "He is absolutely a hero," Althans said. "He opened the door to building a supercivilization, really a paradise on earth. Hitler and Gandhi are the decisive models for me. I am living evidence that the time of Hitler is still to come. I am a normal man. I am nice. I am friendly. I am a totally normal man with two feet on the ground and in spite of that, I am a National Socialist. I am twenty-five and I am sitting talking to the *Washington Post*. Of course, I am an extremist. I am a dictator. But this is no democracy. This is an authoritarian society. In time, it will come to me."

It never won him support from mainstream Germans, but Althans repeatedly sought to portray himself as a victim of state repression. For years, he was in and out of court fighting over his violations of Germany's strict taboo against the display of Nazi symbols or possession of Nazi literature. "I am placed on trial for being a National Socialist, and nothing else. I am threatened with prison for putting a picture of Adolf Hitler on my window. I am forced to pay a nine-thousand-mark fine for saying '*Sieg Heil*.' I am the Jew—ostracized, persecuted, watched by the security police in my own country." Althans' trials were an example of the failure of Germany's attempt to outlaw extremism simply by banning it: Althans has been tried repeatedly and punished occasionally for committing acts many Americans would be shocked to learn are illegal in a western democracy. For example, he spent ten days in a youth jail for insulting President Weizsäcker by saying that the German government was unjust.

It is illegal in Germany to deny the Holocaust, a law that gave police many chances to go after Althans. Yet prosecutors most often ended up chasing people like film director Winfried Bonengel, who made the 1994 film *Profession: Neo-Nazi*. The movie, paid for in part with $220,000 in public arts funds, focused on Althans, presenting him at almost heroic angles, using camera position and lighting to imbue the young Nazi with power, height and a glistening aura well beyond reality. The documentary was virtually banned in Germany after critics, Jewish groups and prosecutors declared that it glorified Althans by letting him drown in his own rhetoric of hate rather than specifically denouncing him in an omniscient narration. The problem was solved "German-style," said one TV reporter. "The film, not the Nazi, is arrested." Copies of the movie were seized by prosecutors; a judge declared it unconstitutional because it let Althans insult the dead by denying the Holocaust.

In the film, Althans helps organize a Canadian appearance by Irving, the Holocaust denier. Before the speech, Althans stands off at a distance, watching a pack of news cameras and a cluster of protesting Jews. Althans laughs for the crew making his documentary: "This is my future," Althans says, chuckling. "Cameras before my nose and Jews at my heels."

The courts finally tired of Althans' antics. The young neo-Nazi began 1995 in prison, this time an eighteen-month sentence for spreading racial hatred by distributing thousands of videos arguing that the Holocaust never happened. Politicians cheered the judges' move finally to get tough on Althans and other leading extremists. But Althans' supporters welcomed the sentence, too: It was, they said, a chance for their leader to follow in Hitler's footsteps by polishing his martyr status behind bars.

Sometimes Ewald Althans struck me as raving mad. Sometimes he seemed clear and dangerous. Althans was still quite young, but if there were to be any considerable growth in the neo-Nazi fringe, it would come from someone who had money, international support, charisma and intelligence. Some police sources estimated Althans' following at close to 40,000, others at a tenth of that figure. "What we all fear is a Führer type, someone who can fuse all these various groups," a government investigator told me.

It was impossible for Günter Althans to fear his son. Even after the police came knocking before dawn. Even after the anti-Semitic tirades and the outright denial of history. And yet after fifteen years of this, the father was finally wearing down. This was not a passing phase in a troubled adolescence. His son was a Nazi, as Günter's mother had been.

Günter continued to see his boy when he could. They even argued politics—not that anyone's mind was going to be changed. "As Bela went off in this direction, I thought, 'How long can this go on?' " Günter said. "And he still hasn't found the right way." As Ewald's notoriety grew, others in the Althans family began to feel barbs and, worse, silences. Florian's fellow army conscripts made comments, and Günter and Ingrid's friends at work told them what others said behind their backs.

"They believe what they want," Günter said. "We are who we are. Bela is our son and he chooses his friends and associates himself. When he is in Hanover and he brings someone here, it's not my business if they are left or right. I will not discuss with anyone whether concentration camps existed, because I know they did and I know millions were killed. One day, someone came here and said Hitler did not live. These are young people, you know. They have to be reclaimed by democracy."

Easy words. Perhaps impossible deeds. Günter lectured his son about responsibility and the past; he implored Bela Ewald to claim German history because there was no other choice. To repress it, to wish it away, would only allow it to fester and become an even greater burden. Ewald replied to his father by claiming to be a scapegoat himself. The swastika, the son told the father, was his Jewish star. Günter could only shake his head.

In the front room off the Althans' foyer, an almost life-size portrait of their son Florian is affixed to the wall. There is no picture of Bela Ewald.

12

Fire and Ash

THE SMELL OF an extinguished fire lingered for days and weeks, piercing the nostrils, searing a path to the throat. At Sachsenhausen concentration camp, only black ash remained of a just-opened exhibit on Nazi persecution of the Jews. The exhibit was a work of reconciliation by German curators from both west and east, historians and researchers who felt liberated by the chance finally to tell the story straight, without the overlay of communist ideology. In Rostock, only black ash remained of the apartments of people who, out of ignorance, trust, or simply the rawest of hopes, believed they could start anew in, of all places, Germany. They were Vietnamese and Gypsy refugees, already disoriented and frightened by the abrupt move to a Stalinist suburb near the Baltic Sea coast. The apartments they had filled with cots and scavenged clothing lay gutted by flames. Hallways where children played became tunnels of melted paint and curled metal. On the sidewalks outside, the sound of people going about their business was a crunch-crunch of fire-baked grit being ground into the pavement.

Once again, Germans took to the streets, rising in protest against a situation they could no longer tolerate. But these were very different times from my first days in Germany. Those were bold and powerful nights, whole families venturing out onto normally barren streets to stare down the state and take back their lives. There was a strange order to those marches and demonstrations, an eerie peace to that revolution of 1989. There were occasional outbursts and even assaults on the secret police, but on most nights, the East Germans circled their cities silently, holding candles and singing as one. Perhaps only fear held everyone together, but it seemed at the time to be something stronger: a common cause, a sense that each step in defiance of what was would bring them closer to something better. There were rowdies, too, in those marches, first bursts of nationalism, young toughs with shaved heads waving imperial flags, and singing "Deutschland, Deutschland über Alles." But they were confined to the fringes and no one paid them much mind. History was being written, and no one wanted to look too far back.

Then came the great changes, the new life, with all its thrills and, on the morning after, all its hardships. Those families who had dared to step out of the cocoons they had built against the darkness of public life retreated once more, trying to make sense of the west and its strange ways. And then, jobs vanished by the hundreds of thousands. The flourishing landscape that Helmut Kohl promised—"No one will be worse off" in the reunited Germany—seemed a cynical joke. Lost jobs meant far more than idle workers. Without a place to go each day, many men and women lost the structure of their lives. Families crumbled. Children saw their parents wander through life even more bewildered than they were: How does a bank account work? How do you fill out tax forms? Whom do you turn to for career advice? Who will take care of the children after school? Where do you go now that the clinic is closed?

Debts and doubts mounted. There was, so many said, nothing to believe in anymore. Youth clubs were shut down. All those western politicians—Kohl and the rest who had promised a rush of western investment—they didn't come east anymore. But they did send in the foreigners. Refugees from the war in Yugoslavia, Gypsies, Africans, Kurds, they all came by the thousands. They were housed in old East German army barracks and in apartment blocks where the communists used to put up "guest workers" from North Korea, Cuba and Mozambique.

Before long, the fires were raging. September 1991, Hoyerswerda, a grim town in Germany's southeast corner: a gang of skinheads, coaxed on by local residents, attacked a shelter for 150 foreigners with clubs, stones and Molotov cocktails. A crowd of townspeople stood by. Some applauded. Some joined in the attack. For four nights, the assault continued. Finally, police came and took the foreigners away while townspeople cheered, peppering the retreating vehicles with stones.

The attacks continued throughout that fall, 1,500 assaults in 1991, as many in the west as in the east, though the politicians only talked about those in the east. It was an unfortunate, probably inevitable outgrowth of unification, the politicians and the newspapers said, wayward eastern kids trying to get attention. As the months went on, the assaults faded from the screen. The government said there was a lull in the violence, but the numbers don't show it. No, the lull was in the press, which stopped reporting the attacks, and in the politicians, who stopped feeling obliged to do something about them.

Then came Rostock, August 1992. By now, 70 percent of the refugees on the move from eastern Europe were stopping in the first western country they reached—Germany. Again, skinheads started the assault, gathering outside a suburban apartment tower housing 200 Gypsies and 150 Vietnamese. The skins chanted "Foreigners out!" and threw rocks. For three nights, the crowds grew. Local residents joined in, most just watching, some actually picking up stones and hurling them through their neighbors' windows. By the third night, hundreds of people stood outside the eleven-story building. Beyond them, more than 200 policemen watched from a grassy hill. This night, the skins had Molotov cocktails. They burned the building. Firemen arrived, but the crowd attacked the firemen, and the police did nothing to protect them. The stone-throwers aimed some of their missiles at the police, and every time a rock hit a police officer, some in the crowd applauded. As the flames worked their way up the building, Vietnamese residents fought through the smoke to the roof, finally climbing over fences to the safety of a neighboring rooftop. No one helped. Months later, a government investigative commission asked the police why they had stood by. There had been no order to move in, the officers said.

A few days after the attack, Lothar Kupfer, interior minister of the state of Mecklenburg-Pomerania, which includes Rostock, said there was a good explanation for the attack on the foreigners: "When 200 asylum seekers have to live together [with Germans] in a very tight space, this unleashes aggression in the German neighbors." Actually, foreigners made up barely 1 percent of the eastern population. The overwhelming majority of refugees settled in western Germany. The violence mounted in both parts of the country: 7,121 crimes by right-wing extremists in 1992; another 8,109 in 1993. The violence occurred almost entirely at night and on weekends, a sign that the people who threw the stones and firebombs were not bums, but workers or students. The attacks arose not from the dregs of society, but often from the mainstream, from those families who had the most to lose as Germany went through the trauma of change.

A couple of weeks after the Rostock attack, I went back to the charred apartment building decorated with a giant sunflower mosaic, now a splotch of dirtied yellow against a murky gray sky. The neighborhood of Lichtenhagen seemed pleasant enough, with large grassy areas, playgrounds and a touch of sea air wafting in from the Baltic coast a few miles up the road. But the foreigners' shelter, two entryways of a long apartment block, was scarred black, dripping with the residue of rage. New graffiti on the breeze-way walls read like a debate: Next to a wall full of swastikas, a slogan, HE WHO IS SILENT IS ALSO GUILTY.

"It's quieter now and we're all much happier," Sven Heiden told me. Sven was sixteen and lived just down the block from the fires. He was no neo-Nazi, not political in the least, just a neighborhood kid who said he liked school, liked living here—except for the Gypsies and the Vietnamese. On those August nights, Sven watched the attacks and the fire with relief. Finally, he thought, we'll be rid of these people. "There were no real refugees here. Just Gypsies who want to do better for themselves. It looked awful here, garbage on the street. They stole from stores, threatened the shopkeepers. Their little kids begged. I was in the supermarket and they begged from me. They'd walk five across on the sidewalk and I had to step off into the gutter to get by them. At school, the kids all say, 'Foreigners out!' I don't know. If they fit in, they're OK, but these Gypsies! They threw cats off the roofs. They ate cats, roasted them right here. They shat on the ground. I had to go to the dentist and I saw their shit on the ground."

A group of workingmen stood around a snack stand eating lunch. I asked what they thought of the firebombing. They'd just been talking about it, about how nice and quiet things were in Lichtenhagen now—after the attack. "You have to understand," said Hans Widera, a fifty-six-year-old mechanic, "these Gypsies went into our supermarket and pissed on the shelves. They pissed on the food. Germans can't be expected to solve the world's problems, right? These people eat cats and seagulls. Now the whole world says Germans are against foreigners. Nonsense. We always had the Vietnamese work-ers here and they're no problem. They live OK. We're foreigner-friendly, always have been. But now they bring in these Romanians and Gypsies and give them money and apartments. We have enough unemployment here. Un-derstand, I don't like using violence against them. It is quiet here now, and I appreciate that, but you can't achieve anything with violence."

"Yes, you can," said Franz Tamaz, a thirty-year-old construction worker who made a daily commute to Hamburg, three hours away in the west. "It's more peaceful around here now. Our women aren't being threatened on the streets anymore. I'm not saying I'd join the attacks, but they got the niggers out. We can't take every nigger in Africa because they're hungry."

From Rostock, I drove half an hour east, to a tiny, leafy village called Hinrichshagen, home to only 100 people, most of them farmers or factory workers in surrounding towns. It was the kind of place where bent, elderly farm hands still dragged carts full of sugar beets by hand over rutted roads. After the fire in Rostock, the government removed all the foreigners from the city's high-rises and sent them here, to a former barracks of the National People's Army. Nine hundred refugees, nearly all of them Gypsies, crammed into the long-empty Army quarters, divided from their German neighbors by a tall fence, supervised from a makeshift police station in a portable trailer. The Gypsies were free to come and go, and since the government gave them a cash allowance of about 400 marks ($300) a month rather than providing food, the refugees had to walk the quarter-mile into town to Hinrichshagen's only shop, the one-room Mini Markt.

Charles Lane of *Newsweek* and I stopped at the Mini Markt on our way out of town. As we approached the shop, we saw a dozen Gypsies standing outside the doorway, waiting in line behind a chain. A hunchbacked German man guarding the chain noticed us from twenty yards away. He yelled to us past the Gypsies, "Would you like to come in?" He opened the chain and ushered us past the refugees and into the shop. Inside, the cashier moved us ahead of her Gypsy customer, whom she had just berated for changing his mind about a purchase.

"Is that all for you, gentlemen?" she asked.

Lane, a recent arrival in Germany, responded in halting but clear German. The woman erupted: "For once, I'd like to hear unbroken German." She slammed the change down on the table, muttering about stupid foreigners.

"We're a small town," said the shop manager, Herr Dreher. "We don't know what to do. These people are dirty, they steal, they attack the women. They go over people's fences and steal their rabbits and chickens. We're overrun. I had to put a fence around my house for the first time ever. I don't support what they did in Rostock, but of course, I understand why they did it. The authorities do nothing. And something must be done. I tell you, soon we're going to need these neo-Nazis here in Hinrichshagen."

In the six weeks after Rostock, there were more than seven hundred attacks against foreigners across Germany.

Foreign reporters in Germany learned a new hobby in the years after unification. We collected neo-Nazis. "Have you tried Frank Hübner yet?" an eastern German colleague asked one day on the phone. Hübner turned out to be head of the Deutsche Alternative, a neo-Nazi group in the eastern city of Cottbus. He led demonstrations and held weekly pep talks, where his beery harangues about foreigners and Jews indoctrinated his young charges in the usual mix of hate, historical distortion and Holocaust denial. Like most neo-Nazi leaders, Hübner was much in demand by the German and foreign press. When I got in touch with him, he wanted $325 for an interview. "Security fee," he called it. I turned him down, but many others paid.

For a fee, neo-Nazis would do just about anything. Ask the German and American TV crews who handed out 50-mark notes to kids willing to pose doing the Hitler salute. Ask the skins who agreed to have swastikas tattooed on their fingers.

Like all hobbies, this business of collecting neo-Nazis distorted the scene. Many Germans were outraged that the press paid the radicals any mind. Kids are kids, said people in the government, teachers, our friends in Bonn and Berlin. You have youth gangs, every country does. They'll grow out of it. "They have no ideology," said an aide to Kohl. "That's the crucial difference. The Nazis had an ideology—that's frightening. These kids are a social problem, not a political one. They have no organization, no leader."

Christian Worch, leader of one of the largest neo-Nazi groups, didn't look the part. Moonfaced, with moist, soft hands and manicured fingernails, he was exceedingly polite, independently wealthy, and, according to Germany's domestic intelligence agency, extremely dangerous. Worch, thirty-six, led the National List, based in Hamburg. He could summon 2,000 to 3,000 extremists to a demonstration. He was one of the few neo-Nazis who could bridge the jealousies and competitions that splintered the organized far right. I had to keep reminding myself that the pudgy, soft-spoken fellow who greeted me with a sweet smile and an adolescent's curiosity about me and my work was also a street tough who had been arrested more than forty times and spent four years in prison on a variety of convictions including demonstrating without a permit, publishing a banned Nazi magazine, and appearing in public with a placard saying NO JEWS WERE KILLED IN AUSCHWITZ.

Worch grew up in a family with a long tradition of Nazism. His grandfather was a *Korpsbruder,* a member of one of the private, nationalist militias that helped undermine the Weimar Republic. His great-uncle was a founder of the Steel Helmets, a precursor of the Nazi SA. His father served as a field physician in the Waffen-SS. When Christian was fourteen, several of his classmates tried to interest him in Marxism. The teenager didn't like what he heard and went home to read *Mein Kampf.* "I was looking for something opposed to Marxism and I automatically, naturally gravitated to National Socialism," Worch told me one day over lunch. He had a chef's salad; German food is too heavy, he said. A teetotaler, he drank mineral water.

By his late teens, Worch had established himself as one of the rowdy street fighters who populate Germany's political extremes. Then Worch shifted gears, becoming another protégé of neo-Nazi leader Michael Kühnen, the charismatic organizer who died of AIDS in 1990, leaving the far right in disarray. After reunification, Worch rallied other groups in a campaign to draw eastern German skins and neo-Nazis into the west's organized scene. It wasn't easy. Worch even found himself buying a Breathalyzer machine so he could toss the most flagrant drunks out of his demos. "The people are enraged now," Worch said. "They no longer trust the solutions of politicians. In times of economic trouble, Germans turn to their traditional anti-Semitism and hatred of foreigners. Today, there is no great basis for anti-Semitism in Germany because there are so few Jews. A dead person is no longer an enemy, so that's counterproductive. The problem now is that there are too many foreigners coming to Germany and our biological substance—our gene pool—is being diluted. Our German virtue depends on our regaining control over this. Hate today is directed against foreigners, and the hate is turning to violence because people have not yet learned to fight without violence."

Worch of course denied any connection to the attacks on foreigners, but he enthusiastically supported the aims of the violence, which, he said, was achieving its goals, thanks to the Bonn government. "Where there have been attacks, the foreigners are removed, and we have foreigner-free cities. We could have gotten the foreigners out of Rostock with leaflets and personal argument, but it would have taken longer. This wave of violence helps us, builds sympathy for us, especially if the government cracks down on us. Look, when hate grows inside us, we throw stones at shelters for asylum-seekers. We don't know who's sleeping in there, whether it's men, women or children. Sometimes there are helpless people in there and I find that unfortunate. I don't like fighting people who can't defend themselves. But that's how we are: We Germans incline to extremes. If we get angry, we act. Your people, the Americans, hit on an enemy and then immediately come to help them with first aid." Worch giggled.

"These foreigner-free cities do not solve the problem, except locally. But it shows the people the power of the right. Soon, the violence will die off. And then we are next: People have long avoided joining the organized right because they didn't want to be in a minority. Germans don't like to stick out from the crowd." Worch laughed. "Then we will be able to say, 'Join the majority.' As it is now, only young people come to our rallies. Others are afraid there will be fights. But as our numbers grow, so will the feeling of security, and then we'll see people in jackets and ties, not just in camouflage and black leather jackets."

In the new Nazi state of his dreams, Worch would not be Führer. "We don't have the right strong man yet," he said. "I don't have the charisma for it. Could you imagine Dr. Goebbels as chancellor? No. It's something metaphysical. Kühnen had it. I could be maybe police minister or propaganda minister." He switched from German to fractured English. "But I don't want to be minister for foreign affairs. My English isn't good enough."

• • •

I spent the months after Rostock trying to figure out what the Kohl government really thought of the violence that was hacking away at Germany's carefully manicured postwar image. The chancellor was taking a beating at home and abroad—news reports, human rights organizations, even friendly governments were getting impatient. To be sure, Kohl issued one statement after another condemning the attacks as "a shame for our nation." But he turned down invitations to lead marches of solidarity with foreigners. He rejected staff suggestions that he do as other leading German politicians had done and pay a visit—publicized or not—to a refugee shelter. And whenever he condemned the right-wing violence, Kohl made sure to drop in a line saying it was just as bad as left-wing terrorism of the 1970s, which is to say the attacks on foreigners were neither unique nor a sign of deeper problems.

"It's hard to say why we seemed so hesitant," Peter Hartmann, Kohl's top national security adviser, told me a year after Rostock. "It had to do with our justice system. What one expected from us and what one should expect is that the state react sharply and clearly against this violence. Unfortunately, in the past ten to fifteen years, there's been a definite laxness in our treatment of violent criminals. These lessons have now been learned. But I don't exclude that the problem will return as social stresses develop."

As the violence continued, even the opposition party, the Social Democrats, grew silent. In a cynical sop to mounting public hysteria over foreigners, they dropped their longtime insistence that Germany keep its liberal asylum law, a generous blanket offer of asylum to anyone fleeing oppression. That symbol of Germany's postwar decision to accept responsibility for what happened under Nazi rule was finally torn out of the constitution in 1993. Only a few figures, such as Weizsäcker, dared to admonish the Germans to recognize the importance of making outsiders comfortable in Germany.

In Bonn, I went to see Wolfgang Gibowski, one of the handful of advisers who met with Kohl each morning to discuss the issues of the day. I asked why Kohl had not made any gesture of sympathy for the refugees or any open display of his determination to stop the attacks. "It's not the chancellor's style to react symbolically, even though I would like him to do more of that," Gibowski said. "From your perspective, this is the major issue. From the perspective of the German chancellor, it's one of five key issues. He has spoken out about these radicals: These are poor, uneducated idiots, just intelligent enough to realize they can damage Germany's image. You will never be able to control eighty million people."

I asked why Kohl had not gone to Sachsenhausen after the firebombing of the Jewish Barracks, where Nazis stored Jewish prisoners until they could be transported to death camps. "Oh, we wanted the chancellor to visit Sachsenhausen," Gibowski said. "It was merely a scheduling problem."

Why had Kohl declined an invitation to lead a march of solidarity with foreigners living in Germany? "It's a security problem," Gibowski said. "You can't expect the chancellor to march in Berlin with a million people."

Why didn't Kohl speak out more prominently on the foreigner issue? Gibowski consulted his computer printouts. "Our numbers now show that seventy-seven percent of Germans believe immigration is the number-one problem facing the country. The next election in Germany will be decided right of center. That is what is defining policy right now."

Kohl's aides always told me how proud they were to work for a leader who shied from the symbolic, who tried to persuade the electorate with reason instead of emotion. It was a nice image, a chancellor so cognizant of history that he would limit his palette of colors to the most rational tones. But this was the same chancellor who in 1985 put enormous pressure on Ronald Reagan to visit Bitburg. Clearly, Kohl knew how to send a message, and this time, his target audience was neither Christian Worch nor Ewald Althans, nor even the crowd that gathered to applaud stone-throwers in Rostock. What worried the chancellor was the small but politically crucial slice of German society on the right flank of Kohl's Christian Democratic Union, the voters who told pollsters they longed for *Ordnung*—order—and craved the stability and security they saw seeping out of daily life. That segment of the public was not a bunch of thugs, but a slice of the nation's heart, including a growing portion of the intellectual community.

Kohl's aim throughout the worst neo-Nazi violence was to find a middle course, a way to condemn the attacks without pushing mainstream right-wingers into the far-right Republican party. The Reps had shown occasional strength in local elections since the mid-1980s, and Kohl feared the foreigner issue might catapult them into parliament in Bonn. The Reps were a motley bunch, led by the former SS officer and TV personality Franz Schönhuber, a beery old gent who proclaimed his philo-Semitism ("I even married a Jew!") even as he denounced Jews as an "occupation power in Germany." Despite the weakness of the party leadership, which was forever stumbling over internal disputes, the Reps' campaign slogan, "The Boat Is Full," was a populist success. (An indication of the potential appeal of the far right is the source of the Republicans' voters: The party drew equally from all points along the political spectrum, siphoning votes from the leftist Social Democrats as often as from Kohl's conservative Christian Democrats.) So Kohl picked a tough law-and-order interior minister, campaigned to keep out refugees, met with Waldheim, and angrily chastised American Jewish leaders who dared to criticize him for doing so.

Unlike Kohl, some in Bonn favored a swift, firm crackdown on neo-Nazis, to make a bright public show that violence against foreigners and Jews would not be tolerated. The chancellor's own commissioner for foreigners, Liselotte Funcke, was so fed up with the government's mixed message that she quit in 1991. A year later, her successor, Cornelia Schmalz-Jacobsen, expressed similar frustration, saying, "We politicians have to ask ourselves to what extent we have ourselves contributed to the distortion of truth and polarization in our land." But even people offended by Kohl's rhetorical tactics joined in calling for a halt in the flow of refugees. Nearly always, this argument led to the same warning: If the refugee stream were not capped, the very stability of the country would be shaken and could shatter. Why did so many intelligent people issue such warnings? What were they really saying? Was it a cry for help: "Save us from ourselves?" Was the far right correct about the fragility and artificiality of German democracy? At first, western sociologists and political scientists, politicians and journalists blamed the rise of the far right on the easterners—how they had no experience in dealing with foreigners, how they felt besieged by Wessis, how their insecurities dominated their lives. Somehow, the fact that most antiforeigner attacks took place in the west was beside the point. Explanations for violence in the west often minimized the facts: "It's just copycat attacks. There's been so much of this on TV, you know."

But when the violence persisted, German pessimism arose from the dark. Ernst Uhrlau, chief of the Hamburg agency that tracks extremists, concluded morosely that "only the rightist extremist parties are saying what the silent majority is thinking now. Neo-Nazi violence is the tip of a social protest movement, a battle for resources between east and west. There's a whole new character to the neo-Nazi scene. It's ever more structured, they're ever more willing to act."

Almost overnight, society shifted from denial to hopelessness. Self-doubt permeated the press and academia. Nazi shadows couldn't be far behind. In the Munich daily, the *Süddeutsche Zeitung*, reporter Marianne Heuwagen asked, "What is it in our national character that leads us not to greet our neighbors, or to call the Gestapo and inform on someone, or to attack foreigners or tell the children not to play with Gypsies?"

One political scientist, Claus Leggewie, called the new Nazism "a kind of localized ethnic cleansing. Our children are rejecting the adult version of history. They do not want to live with the blame and the guilt anymore." Leggewie predicted that the far right slowly would leach into the mainstream of German politics. "There is a rising nationalist fervor, a *fin-de-siècle*, last days, apocalyptic mood. There's more fear on the streets, less communication between people. We'll see a purity campaign—Germany for the Germans. That could lead to demands for 'border corrections'—Poland, Czechoslovakia. We never developed a healthy patriotism after the war, and what patriotism we do have depends entirely on our economic power. As our economic situation deteriorates, we are left with no reason to exist. And in a classic repetition of German history, we force our opinion leaders to the extremes."

A year after Leggewie spelled out his apocalyptic vision in 1993, the idea of the far right piling up electoral victories seemed far-fetched. In the 1994 national election, parties of the far right won less than 3 percent of the vote. But Leggewie was certainly right about the ability of a relative handful of extremists to challenge what had previously considered itself a stable society. By breaking taboos and reviving the reality of the "other" as scapegoat, neo-Nazis scratched the veneer of postwar West German normalcy. And then came all those people—immigrants, refugees, hundreds of thousands of them. From Romania and ex-Yugoslavia, Bulgaria and Poland, they wanted their piece of the Mercedes star, the neon symbol of success that rotates atop the tallest building in nearly every big eastern Europe city.

They came even as the Germans, led by their chancellor, insisted that "Germany is not an immigration country"—even though it was the second-greatest immigration country in the world, behind only the United States. The neo-Nazi fringe, once shoved neatly into a corner, moved to the center of national discussion. "In modern German history," the German historian Golo Mann once wrote, "periods of sensible adaptation alternate with periods of explosion. . . . What has characterized the German nature for a hundred years is its lack of form, its unreliability." These were not normal times in Germany. This was a moment of great and ambitious experiment, as a rich nation generously tried to absorb 16 million people traumatized by three generations of dictatorship and deprivation. A people who expected a fresh, clean start after the fall of the Wall learned that this was something altogether different: This was a testing time.

Marzahn was Berlin's lesson in designing inhumanity. At the eastern edge of the metropolis, for as far as you could see, apartment towers stood one behind another in lockstep procession. Wind swept through concrete tunnels, howling around empty courtyards. Broad boulevards that looked majestic in the Central Committee's Five-Year Plan quickly degenerated into wretched urban scars that would not fade. Marzahn, Erich Honecker's socialist paradise, was the shame of the postcommunist city. Ask the residents where they were from and they answered in the same sullen, defeated way American ghetto kids say "The projects."

After unification, Marzahn quickly developed into headquarters for

Berlin's skins and neo-Nazis. In a couple of empty rooms in a low-slung concrete building next to a high-rise, the skins gathered as the sun drops. They called their club Wurzel—Roots. They took over rooms once used by the Free German Youth, the communist group that specialized in torchlight parades and ideological conformity. Skins came to drink, smoke and listen to the strung-out shouts of German head-banger bands whose bass line had long ago burst the speakers on the clubhouse boom box. The kids wore green bomber jackets and jeans, heavy black boots and lots of tattoos on their fingers, arms and necks. They drank from tall cans of cheap Schultheiss beer.

Mike Ruback was a professional boxer in East Germany. After the Wall fell, he celebrated by having a swastika tattooed over his nipple. Not long after that, Ruback killed a Romanian man in Berlin's main rail station and served eighteen months in prison. He remained unrepentant. His story was he was taking a leak and the Romanian propositioned him. At Roots, Mike became the self-appointed disciplinarian. He whistled his comrades to silence and pointed a long, threatening finger at those who failed to comply.

"The Turks are coming to attack us next weekend, I heard it," said Müller, a pouting, nineteen-year-old skin. "What are we going to do about it?"

"We'll get drunk," Mike yelled from his corner chair, tipped precariously on its back legs.

"Totally normal," Müller said. And he slapped himself on the forehead. On Müller's left hand, the top of each finger was tattooed with a letter. H-A-S-S—HATE. "The foreigners get everything—jobs, food, money from the government, whatever they want, because the stupid Germans feel guilty. Who are we to feel guilty? We didn't do anything. My parents didn't do anything. Fuckin' Nazis."

At the other end of the room, Lars rolled cigarettes, picked his nose, and then, hamming it up for my benefit, drove his front teeth through a beer can. Lars, in trouble even under the communist regime for drawing swastikas and shouting fascist slogans in school, was nineteen and something of a celebrity around Marzahn for his great achievement in life: He threw a Mozambican man off the streetcar because he was black. "The foreigners are filthy," he said. "They come here and rob people and women can't even walk on the streets anymore. Before the Wall fell, it was safe here. Now they take away our jobs and let in all the foreigners. We're not fuckin' stupid here. We're going to fight back."

Over at the corner of the big table in the main room, Michael Wieczorek sat slumped in a chair, his leather jacket hunched up over his neck. Wieczorek looked like hell—four days of beard; unwashed, unkempt hair; filthy fingernails; tobacco stains on his fingers. Only when he tried to bring the skins to order did it become obvious that Wieczorek was not one of them. He was the guy who created Roots. He was the scruffy, ballsy social worker from the west who managed to persuade the city to put up $175,000 for the clubhouse and a program of street fairs and travel—including a journey to the Sahara Desert—for Marzahn's skins. "We're trying with small steps to bring them together with each other," Wieczorek told me. "Maybe raise their tolerance, strengthen their identity as youths with needs, not just as radical rightists. I want them to be proud of their identity as skins, but help them to change their definition of skins, away from hate and racism. I want to provoke them and change them, not as their leader, but by working with their heads."

Wieczorek left it to Mike to be house disciplinarian. When things got too rowdy, Mike stood and shouted, "Hey!" That sufficed to calm things. Then Wieczorek could get on with the two items on his agenda: How would the skins celebrate April 20, Hitler's birthday? And were the skins prepared for the Children's Festival they were planning for neighborhood kids? Conversation drifted aimlessly from plans for costumes, races and carnival games to chatter about the weapons the skins might need for protection on Hitler's birthday—a traditional day of battle between left-wing and right-wing youths.

"Foreign residents of the neighborhood called me and said they'd like to come along to the street fair, but they are enormously afraid to be around you," the social worker said. "I told them there'll be no alcohol and this is a festival for all the kids."

"Whoever comes, comes," Lars replied. "We can't do anything about it."

"And one more thing," Wieczorek said. "We want music that you like, but we have to think about having music that reaches out in the direction of what others would like to hear." That bit met with nothing but groans and snorts, so Wieczorek moved on to an even tougher topic. He told the skins he would have a hard time justifying the use of public money to support the clubhouse if it was used for a celebration of Hitler's birthday. He proposed closing Roots that day.

The skins protested that they needed to be there to protect their clubhouse against assault by a gang of Turkish kids who frequently rumbled against skinheads. "We have to defend our place," said Andreas, a sixteen-year-old who was in training to be a butcher. "We'll be the only boys in town that day. Everyone else is going to demos to celebrate Hitler in Dresden and Leipzig."

After appealing to the skins to stay home and avoid confrontation rather than seek it out, Wieczorek put the birthday question to a vote. Five hands favored staying open to defend Roots against attack. Only two sided with the social worker. The rest of the skins didn't bother to vote. "OK," Wieczorek said, "I'll tell the bulls [police] we're going to be open."

The girls in the room—dressed nearly identically, they call themselves "Renees"—stayed silent through the meeting. One, a former leader in the communist Young Pioneers who now sported a black crew cut and long blond bangs, had become little more than a sex slave. She rolled cigarettes for the guys, and Müller boasted that he had trained her to respond to his bark of "Shirt!" by pulling off her top and pressing her breasts against his face.

Wieczorek, a leftist, spent every day and every evening at Roots, swallowing his political views, silently accepting the skins' hateful slogans, only occasionally offering a quiet retort. He ignored all the antics and focused on his goal—to boost the skins' confidence in hopes not that they would abandon their persona, but that they would cast off some of their anger and self-loathing, their armor against the turmoil that hit Marzahn after the Wall opened. "They're searching for explanation," the social worker said. "Their authorities are gone—the authorities of yesterday are the swine of today, the communist teachers, the people who had good government jobs, their parents who told them how good the old system was. We can't turn the skins around a hundred eighty degrees, but I think we can minimize their readiness to use violence."

It was slow work, but there were occasional payoffs. Wieczorek fostered a friendship between Lars, the guy who tossed the Mozambican off the streetcar, and a Japanese photographer who covered his trial. Working with the court, the social worker persuaded Lars to pay the Mozambican man $350 a month in compensation. Wieczorek gently pushed the skins to work with local children. He forced them to accept at least minimal responsibility by requiring them to help organize group trips. He bought plants so they could grow their own garden. He let them do with Roots as they wished.

To which they responded by trashing the place. But then they came back, fixed it up, brought their friends. All went well for a few months. The kids came to trust Wieczorek, even got excited about that trip to the Sahara. "Michael is a totally trustworthy partner for us," said Müller, the nineteen-year-old tough. "The people who count are the ones who really want to help us. Those others just closed all the youth clubs and bars, and that's when the crime really shot up. Crime will keep rising as long as they take everything from us."

All of which sounded very nice, except that a few months later, Roots burned to the ground. It's not clear who did it, maybe one of the Turkish gangs, maybe some disgruntled skins themselves, maybe neighborhood folks who couldn't stand the idea of coddling these hoodlums. Roots wasn't

going to be around for very long anyway; city planners had targeted it for de-
molition because the building had "no purpose," a designation the new
western government applied to many of the now-shuttered day-care centers,
kindergartens and youth clubs.

So after countless hours of Wieczorek's efforts, after several hundred
thousand marks of taxpayers' money, Mike and Müller and Lars and the
gang were out on their own again, making trouble, throwing their arms up in
the Hitler salute, painting swastikas, pressing the buttons they knew would
most upset the distant powers who had ripped the certainties out of their
lives.

A couple of skins from Roots got jobs and seemed to straighten out. But
most stayed in the one place where they felt they belonged—the scene. I
saw some Roots kids sometime later at a Nazi rally in Dresden, the Saxon
city where six of the ten high school student leaders elected in 1991 were
avowed neo-Nazis. A thousand kids, most of them thirteen to seventeen, the
rest only a bit older, milled around under a railroad overpass. Outnumbered
by police, they killed a couple of hours before the older western Germans
who organized the demonstration told them to line up and march. The kids
were punks, pathetic adolescents playing tough. Eight guys gathered
around in an excited circle. At the center, a ninth-grader showed off his new
switchblade. A seventeen-year-old boy with a comic attempt at a Hitler
mustache strutted about thrusting a stiff arm into the air like a Peter Sellers
character. The march organizers tried to stop their legions from drinking,
but it was hopeless. The whole bunch of them were reeling.

A nineteen-year-old named Michael wore an SS insignia on his army
jacket. I asked him why. "Americans have uniforms, Brits have uniforms,
Russians have uniforms. Why can't we? The SS made Germany clean—
clean of Jews, Russians, the enemies of Germany. We don't want any World
War III. We just want a clean Germany. Every German gets work. Foreigners out." Michael was a good boy under the communist system. He did his
time in the Free German Youth, parroted the Marxist slogans his teachers
loved to hear. But underneath, he said, he had always wanted to be a Nazi.
"Don't write any lies," he warned me. "I'm not for gassing or concentration
camps. That was wrong. All we want is a clean Germany, Germany the way
it was before, with our land back. And no foreigners."

And off they went, marching around the city while police helicopters
buzzed overhead and police snipers held the high ground and police dogs
bucked and barked on street corners. As the boy Nazis trudged along,
laughing and playfully shoving one another, local folks stood alongside the
parade route, most silent, some applauding. An old woman smiled and
waved as the parade went by. "Oh, they're nothing to be afraid of," she said.

"They want to wear uniforms and feel important. You know, Hitler did very good things. He built the roads. He taught the children how to behave, how to keep a house. They had elegant uniforms and things ran so well. They got the youth off the streets. And we had work."

A lone man shouted, "Go home. Shame on you."

In the eastern German town of Fürstenwalde, in an apartment complex once used to house guest workers from Third World communist states, 250 Gypsies and Romanians lived in nightly fear of attack. After dark, the men kept vigil outside, patrolling the sidewalk while their wives sat inside with the children. The refugees hung sheets of dark, heavy cloth from their window frames, a crude attempt to catch the Molotov cocktails that threatened to shatter their one remaining treasure, their families. Sleep came only with exhaustion.

A few German social workers, volunteers from Berlin, joined in the vigil. They were angry at their countrymen who refused to stand with the foreigners. The young people from Berlin did this regularly, giving up evenings to help foreigners and weekends to march in proforeigner demonstrations. A major march had been called for a Saturday about a month after the Rostock attack. In Berlin, a city of more than 3 million people, 5,000 showed their sympathy with the refugees. Back during the Persian Gulf War, more than 150,000 people gathered in remote Bonn to protest against American aggression against Iraq.

Back in Bonn, Gibowski, Kohl's political adviser, said the government was worried about the growing reservoir of protest voters, people who, for the first time in their lives, were ready to listen to the extreme right's arguments. By fall 1992, *Der Spiegel* found that 96 percent of Germans believed the country needed to solve its "foreigner problem." Germans blamed foreigners for everything under the sun: Crowding Germans out of housing (said 74 percent of Germans), increasing German joblessness (60 percent), creating danger on the streets (59 percent). In western Berlin, a study of high-school-age students found 21 percent agreeing with the Nazi slogan "*Juden raus* (Jews out)—to the gas chambers."

"Our little paradise is threatened," Gibowski said. "For all those years, the Red Army protected us from asylum-seekers and other foreigners who wanted to share our wealth. Now, we're on our own. We face hard times. We will have to change our ideas about immigration, find some regularized way of letting in some people and keeping others out. But right now, these poll numbers make it impossible for the government to do anything but try to stop the flood of asylum-seekers. I know, someone has to tell the truth to the people. But that's not how the system works right now."

Some months later, Kohl won his feverish campaign to erase the asylum guarantee. The flow of foreigners did ebb. Refugees were stopped at the border and sent home, and Germany's eastern neighbors—Poland, Hungary, the Czech Republic—were forced to deal with foreigners heading toward Germany. Hysteria over foreigners seemed to subside. The most frightening poll figures settled down to more reasonable levels. The government announced a crackdown on the far right, and a few small neo-Nazi groups were legally banned (though most reopened for business under new names).

After I moved back to Washington, I heard little about the young Nazis and their brutal attacks on foreigners. German newspapers rarely mentioned such violence. Perhaps, I thought, the attacks were over. Perhaps it had been an ugly spasm, a reaction to the trauma of unification and little more. But then, on a return visit to Germany, I looked at police reports and brief items on the news tickers. A weekend's round of violence: Gravestones smashed at a memorial to victims of Nazi death camps. Swastikas painted on the gateway to a cemetery for slave laborers who died at the Dachau concentration camp near Munich. A firebomb at the former Ravensbrück concentration camp near Berlin. A pack of one hundred neo-Nazis assaulting a foreigners' shelter with rocks and Molotov cocktails in Greifswald.

Where the smell of ash has not yet faded, embers smolder.

13

Ausländer

"What are you? Where are you from? Not from the castle, not from the village. You are nothing. But unfortunately, you are something, a foreigner..." —A local, speaking to K. in Franz Kafka's The Castle

What is a German anyway? Do Germans have special blood or something? —Dietmar Pagel, principal, Hector Peterson School, Berlin

TURKS ARE THE invisible men of Germany. Their neighborhoods are ghettos, crowded urban streets teeming with stocky women in modest wraps and stubbly men in shiny brown suits. The Turks' birth rate far exceeds that of the German population, and what were once Turkish apartment blocks have now spread to become sprawling Turkish quarters of the big German cities. Here, travel agencies organize the constant traffic back and forth between the two homelands; grocers import the olives and cheeses and spices of the old country; vendors hawk doner kabobs, the tangy meat sandwiches whose name is the only Turkish term most Germans ever learn. About half of the 2 million German Turks were born in Germany, yet only a few thousand have made it through the onerous process of acquiring German citizenship. The rest live largely among themselves, working for Germans by day, building cars, cleaning streets, washing dishes, hauling freight, then retreating by night into communities most Germans never see. And everywhere, within the Turkish sections and for many blocks around them, they live surrounded by the ubiquitous graffiti: TÜRKEN RAUS! (TURKS OUT!)

The struggle between Germany and its 6 million foreigners—8 percent of the population—peaked in ugly and emotional ways during the years after the Wall fell. Many people rushed to cloak themselves in the comfortable costumes assigned to the main roles in the conflict: proud nationalist, angry neo-Nazi, disturbed democrat, anguished liberal, fearful foreigner. Turks were murdered because they were Turks. Gypsies were deported because they were Gypsies. Germans were criticized solely because they were Germans, doing exactly what other countries did. The German press competed to find the most frightening and formidable analogies for the country's predicament: Was it Weimar once more? Was it 1933? I knew Germans who spontaneously apologized when we met at a party or on the street, as if they bore personal responsibility for a youth gang's attack on a Turk, as if that attack were somehow an assault on me. I needed to break out of these ritual responses, and the best way to do that was to ask the simplest of questions.

I visited the Hector Peterson School, a forbidding block of stone hidden in a courtyard off one of Berlin's busy avenues. I picked Peterson because of its students: about evenly divided between Turks and Germans. The Turks were mostly third-generation residents of Germany. Many had never been to Turkey. Few were fluent in Turkish; in the language of the country whose passport they carried, most knew only street slang. In Germany, they lived in largely Turkish neighborhoods and, as children, had played mostly with other Turks. For most, high school was their first chance to make German friends. Their teachers were almost all Germans; the seven Turks on the Peterson School's faculty were paid lower wages than their German colleagues and were barred from becoming civil servants, so they could never win tenure or become administrators. The principal and his staff wanted to show me banners classes had made to pronounce their opposition to racism. They wanted me to watch the Turkish holiday festival they had prepared. They displayed hundreds of signatures students had collected on petitions calling for a change in Germany's blood-based citizenship law. I may have seemed impatient that day. I arrived at the Peterson School with but one question: I wanted the students to tell me who they were.

A group of Turkish teenagers sat down on the concrete steps outside the classroom building. I asked my question. They fell silent. A couple of girls stared at their feet; two boys looked off into the distance. A German boy who was eavesdropping started to answer for the Turks, but I cut him off and repeated the question. The girls began to giggle. Finally, one girl quietly offered, "I'm a Turk, and proud of it."

The dam broke. "No, a German Turk," said another girl.

"I don't know," said Sevda Maras, who was fifteen and had never lived anywhere but in Berlin. "We were born here. We speak better German than Turkish. I'm integrated, assimilated here. Why can't I have a German passport? Germany is only where it is because of foreigners. The Germans won't do their own dirty work. We clean their toilets and build their houses and roads. And then they don't want to see us. But I wouldn't want to be just a German. I'm Turkish, too."

"We live in Turkish culture," said Nilgun Polat, seventeen. "The language, religion, the way we eat, what we do—Turkish. Our kids will be Turkish, too."

"But we can't live in Turkey," Sevda replied. "No way. We've adjusted here. The Turks look at us and see a foreigner. Really, we don't belong anywhere."

Ahmet Gencary was the school's student president, popular among Turks and Germans alike. He had been more optimistic than some of his Turkish friends about finding a place in German society—until recently. He was seventeen, and thought a lot about his future. Like most kids in Germany, he was looking around for apprenticeships, the key to getting started with a good company. But his mailbox filled with nothing but rejection letters. The reason, he was certain, was simply that he was a Turk. "We have real German friends here at school," he said. "They would do things for us, and we for them. But I know what happens next: After they go into jobs, they're among themselves. Their characters will change. They'll be manipulated against us. They'll forget us."

"We're completely cut out in this country," said Ergun Bontana, a seventeen-year-old boy who wore a New York Yankees baseball cap and the baggy clothes that German kids saw Americans wearing on music videos and TV sitcoms. "We have no connection to the government. All of those Germans who go out on the street with candles to show solidarity for the foreigners—what good is that? Where are they the rest of the time? Nothing changes. It's like it was ten years ago and forty years ago. Germans get priority for jobs. Germans get the apprenticeships. We're only allowed a few places in the university. Face it—we're foreigners, and that's all we'll ever be to them."

Ergun's tirade reminded me of Germany's persistent struggle over what to call foreigners. The accepted term for Turks has changed every generation, much as the term for American blacks shifts with remarkable regularity. In both cases, language reflects a society's squirming over the identity crisis of an unassimilated minority. The government refers to Turks—who make up about one-third of Germany's foreign residents—as *Ausländer*, foreigners. The Nazis called their foreign labor force "alien workers." From the 1950s to the 1970s, when Germany invited Turks to do the unpleasant work of a booming economy, foreigners were called "guest workers," the theory being that when their work was completed, they would go home. (Guest workers were once welcomed, even embraced: In 1964, when the 1-millionth guest arrived, the man, a carpenter from Portugal, was greeted by officials who overwhelmed the poor guy with flowers, trinkets and even a free motorcycle.)

But the Turks spoiled the Germans' plan. They stayed. In the 1970s, when Bonn changed policies and tried to bribe Turks and other foreign workers to leave, the vocabulary changed once more. No longer welcome guests, Turks became "foreigners" again. Later still, when it became apparent that a third generation of Turks was growing up in Germany, and that these young people had no desire to move to a country that was no longer their only home, official Germany saw the need for a smoother formulation: "foreign fellow citizens." Which sounded nicer, but posed a distinct problem: The foreigners were not and in most cases could not become citizens of their new home. Since the 1930s, then, the names Germans have used for outsiders have stressed their foreignness.

Outside of government, all this word play was less trying, less subtle. In the media, even after a neo-Nazi firebombing in the western town of Mölln killed ten-year-old Yeliz Arslan, the German-born, German-schooled girl was referred to only as "a Turk born in Germany." On the streets, Turks fared no better: They were Turks, or *Kanaker* (a derogatory term for Turks and other dark-skinned foreigners), or *Scheisstürken* (shit Turks), or just plain "niggers." (Turks are the butt of most German ethnic jokes, both in corner saloons and in polite company. The cracks are not even tailored to fit Turkish idiosyncrasies. For the most part, jokes aimed at the Turks are just old lines about Jews with the target's name switched.)

"Don't we speak all too easily of 'the Turks'?" President Weizsäcker asked at a 1993 memorial service for five Turkish children burned to death in their home in Solingen. From a distance, Weizsäcker's elegant sweep of white hair blended into the white crescents on the Turkish flags draped over the five tiny coffins. And yet, on closer inspection, the president, a German, seemed out of place on the grandstand crowded with Turkish family members and dignitaries. Weizsäcker knew his appearance was late; his words, a weak, human attempt to dam a torrent of grief. And so he addressed not only Turks but the German people. "Are we perhaps trying to say who should stay foreign? Would it not be more honest and more humane to say 'German citizens of Turkish origin'? They live according to the rules of the German state, but without being able to influence them like other citizens. Must it always remain so?" Outside the courtyard of the mosque where Weizsäcker spoke, thousands of Turks jammed the narrow streets, praying for their children in the undulating chants of Islam. Even here, standing in a steady rain among their own, clinging to one another in a moment of despair, many grieving Turks wore stickers on their jackets saying IN GERMANY FOR 30 YEARS.

Over those three decades, Germany exerted precious little effort to integrate the Turks or ease their transition from a Moslem society into the affluent West. Although laws restricting Turkish ownership of German land were relaxed, Turks still faced quotas in universities and laws guaranteeing native Germans first priority for jobs. Turkish is by far Germany's second-most-spoken language, yet someone trying to send a package from a German post office finds forms in German, French and English, but not Turkish. Berlin's 10,000 deaf residents were served with subtitles for TV newscasts, but the city's 150,000 Turks argued unsuccessfully for Turkish programming on Berlin's broadcast channels.

Visit London, Paris or Amsterdam, flick on the TV, and despite the antiforeigner backlash that infects almost all European countries, a casual evening of channel surfing reveals minorities—West Indians in Britain, North Africans in France, Indonesians in Holland—in prominent positions, reading the evening news, appearing in advertising, acting in dramatic roles. Spend a similar evening in a hotel room in Berlin or Frankfurt and you will see no such people. Instead, in a bit of crass tokenism, ZDF television offers Cherno Jabotey, a breakfast-program moderator whose on-air persona is that of the class clown, a jovial fellow who wears unlaced sneakers and shoulder-length hair, signals to the audience that he is a source of amusement, not a voice of authority. When I asked a ZDF executive when Germany would see a Turk reading the headlines on the evening newscasts, he said, "Not in our lifetime." It took Germany's Federal Commission for Foreigners twenty years to hire its first foreign employee, a Turk hired in 1992.

"To have a chance in German society, a Turk has to get famous in entertainment or sports, or start his own business within the Turkish community," said Faruk Sen, director of Essen University's Center for Turkish Studies. "Unfortunately, most of us are not good in entertainment or sports." When ARD television, the main government-supported channel, staged a discussion program on Turks in Germany, they invited journalists from Germany, Israel, Britain and France. No Turks were asked to join the conversation. When Sen complained, he was told the producers did not know of any Turkish journalists. In Frankfurt alone, eight Turkish newspapers with a combined circulation of 270,000 have a staff of 130 Turkish reporters and editors.

"Even if I had a German passport, my hair, my face do not change," said Kadir Ercan. I spent a day at Ercan's storefront, a city-supported agency where he helps Berlin Turks find apartments, get squared away with the Foreigners Office, and fight their way through the maze of German bureaucracy. Ercan arrived in Germany in the late 1970s, intending, like many smart Turkish youths, to remain just long enough to earn a master's degree. He stayed because life was better in Germany, and because he met people, sank roots, felt—at least in his Turkish community—at home. He thought things would change. They didn't. "I pay taxes, too," Ercan said. "I want to be able to help decide about schools and government, but I have no right to vote. They brought us here to work, and now we must live together, but they don't want to see us anymore. The laws may change someday, but what I can't see changing is the way people speak to us. We are always reminded: You are a Turk."

Bahman Nirumand, an Iranian novelist, concluded that "after all the long years I have spent in Germany, I have not yet met a single foreigner who could say without ifs or buts that he felt at home in Germany." Routine discrimination against foreigners is not limited to those who, like the Turks, came from alien cultures. A Bonn correspondent for the weekly *Die Zeit*, Werner Perger, worked as a reporter in Germany for more than thirty years, but was not permitted to attend Bonn news conferences sponsored by the German Press Association. Perger is Austrian, and the association, like many German organizations, required members to hold a German passport. Still, Turks were the most frequent victims of Germany's citizenship-by-blood. Ahi Sema Issever was sixteen when she applied to spend a year in the United States on an exchange program run by the German parliament. Ahi was born in Germany and had never lived anywhere else. She spoke perfect German and ranked first in her class at the Albert Schweitzer School in the western town of Marl. But her application was rejected because, as a Turk under German law, Ahi could not be "a representative of Germany" abroad.

The fall of the Wall and the expansion of the European Community only exacerbated the Turks' woes. Like blacks in Miami who lost jobs, social standing and public sympathy after the Cuban influx of the 1960s, Turks found themselves bumped from second-class to third-class status virtually overnight. Resources once dedicated to Turks were shifted to help eastern Germans adjust to their new country. The growing integration of western Europe will force Germany to grant local voting and employment rights to any Spaniard, Dane or Italian who moves to Germany, while Turks continue to pay taxes and hold their tongues. Foreigners paid 57 billion marks in taxes and social security payments in 1991, but they received only 16 billion marks in benefits.

Over the years, Kohl developed three handy mantras that he recited automatically whenever the issue of foreigners arose: "Germany is not an immigration country" was his blanket explanation for the second-class status of foreign residents. If Germany was not an immigration country, it needed no immigration quotas, no changes in its citizenship law, no antidiscrimination laws, no effort to integrate foreigners. Kohl's standard response to news of violence against foreigners was "Germany is and will remain a foreigner-friendly country." No matter the pace or tenacity of the attacks, the German people were foreigner-friendly, so no far-reaching discussion was necessary. Finally, Kohl dismissed any talk of integrating Germany's Turks by saying that "these people come from a different high culture, with completely different religious and traditional conditions." Taken together, the three comments cordoned off any criticism of German policy. Kohl saw the Germans as a tolerant but homogeneous people, so different from outsiders that it would be foolhardy to expect the two to mix.

Such rhetoric drove second- and third-generation German Turks crazy. They tried to prove their worth, trumpeting their knowledge of Goethe, attesting to their loyalty to the German Basic Law, noting the common roots of Islam and Christianity—to no avail. Many thousands of Germans were willing to enlist in campaigns with names such as "Foreigners Need Friends," or to join candlelight protests against the burning of Turkish children. Schools required students to spend a few hours talking about foreigners; some teachers even took kids on field trips to meet a foreigner. But as Barbara John, Berlin's commissioner for foreigners, told me, "Once you reach the point of saying we're going to take a week and do a project on foreigners, you've already lost." Despite all the public displays of sympathy, there was no push to change citizenship laws or legalize immigration. There was no talk of requiring business, industry or government to integrate foreigners rather than tolerating them as an alien workforce temporarily residing in Germany. A few lonely voices—politicians, activists and business leaders who recognized that Germany's birth rate, the world's lowest, creates a demand for immigration—called for a new approach. But Kohl offered no initiative, even though labor studies concluded that the country would need 20 million immigrants by 2030 to keep its workforce level in the face of declining native population.

Somehow, German Turks found themselves lumped together with foreign refugees as outsiders. Many Turks, Iranians and other long-term residents who look darker than most Germans concluded that the antagonism they faced stemmed as much from racism as from xenophobia. Third-generation Turkish men often complained of their invisibility, the unspoken barriers they faced, the anger and jealousy they ran up against if they dared to befriend German women—the same kinds of discrimination, subtle and open, that many American blacks describe. To be sure, Germany tolerates an overt racism shocking to anyone from a multiracial country: At nearly all levels of society, it is acceptable behavior to speak of "niggers," referring to

American blacks, German Turks, Africans, or other dark-skinned peoples. Oversized cardboard cutouts of African "savages," complete with bones inserted through their noses, stand outside many German bakeries and candy shops to advertise "Nigger Kisses," a popular ice-cream novelty. A state secretary (a top-level sub-Cabinet official) in the Economics Ministry in Bonn once explained to me that Washington Mayor Marion Barry's political career would actually be helped by his conviction on drug charges because "your niggers love drugs, so they'll keep on voting for him." A senior Defense Ministry official in Bonn said German troops were more efficient and better-trained than American soldiers because "we don't have to deal with the blacks and the Hispanics, who simply don't have the basic intelligence to win a battle."

Such attitudes are by no means limited to private conversation. Prime-time television often is a showcase for equally striking views. The *Rudi Carrell Show,* for many years the country's top-rated TV variety program, sought at the height of the antiforeigner violence to show its viewers some of the essential work foreigners do in Germany. Carrell, a Dutch native, took his viewers to a Hamburg restaurant, where he not only found foreigners toiling in the kitchen but an Ethiopian woman who actually ran the place.

"Where do you come from?" the jovial host asked, speaking in slow, clear German so the black woman would understand.

"Germany," the woman replied.

Carrell laughed at the misunderstanding. "But where were you born?" he asked.

"Ethiopia, but I moved to Germany when I was three months old," she said in perfect colloquial German.

Undaunted, Carrell chuckled and said, "Still, you speak German well!"

The woman had had quite enough. "So do you," she said bitterly.

Carrell proceeded with the interview, referring to the restaurateur throughout as an "Ethiopianette."

Many Germans, of course, get on perfectly well with foreigners, fight for foreigners' rights, even marry foreigners (these are almost always cases of German men wedding foreign women.) Weizsäcker even extended a hand to the hated asylum-seekers, visiting their camps, defying his party's line on antiforeigner violence. The murders of Turks in Mölln, Solingen and elsewhere "are not isolated, unrelated crimes," he said. "They result from a climate generated by right-wing extremism. The perpetrators may be acting alone, but they do not appear from nowhere. Extreme right-wing violence . . . is a unique kind of anarchic terrorism which picks on defenseless victims in order to undermine the democratic state." If there was to be any new approach toward foreigners in the nineties, it would grow out of fear, not any idealistic striving for assimilation or tolerance. The German word for it is *Überfremdungsängste,* fear of foreign infiltration. The far right played heavily on this theme; the Republicans party filled its publications with drawings of swarthy, dark foreigners taking German homes, jobs and lives. "Soon, every German will have to take an asylum-seeker into his home," read a poster the Republicans used in state elections. "Whole sections of our cities are being turned into nigger neighborhoods," Christian Käs, the Republicans' chairman in the state of Baden-Württemberg, told me.

But this was not the exclusive turf of extremists; mainstream academics, politicians and clergymen played similar games. As far back as 1981, the federal commissioner for foreigners, Heinz Kühn, said, "If the foreign population rises above the 10 percent mark, any people will become rebellious." A decade later, when the proportion of asylum-seekers and other foreigners jumped to 15 percent in big cities such as Berlin and Frankfurt, that forecast came true. But antiforeigner violence was not a case of spontaneous combustion. Politicians and other opinion-makers lit the fuse. Respected newspapers featured prominent reports on the horrors of street vending, focusing on foreign, and most often black, vendors selling jewelry and clothing on city streets. Local politicians, eager to dramatize the difficulty of housing and policing thousands of new arrivals, made a show of putting asylum-seekers in cargo containers, sports halls, school yards and main city squares—policies that piqued local outrage and satisfied the media clamor for graphic displays of the burden of foreign infiltration. In 1994, the weekly magazine *Focus* ran a cover story on crime committed by foreigners, concluding with a reminder to readers of a Thomas Hobbes quotation about the "natural right of a people to protect themselves," a virtual call for vigilante justice. Newspapers ran series on crime by foreigners, stoking fear with statistics purporting to show that foreigners committed a disproportionate share of crimes.

In 1993, when Kohl was desperately casting about for a way to regain political support from his party's disaffected right flank, he picked Steffen Heitmann, the politically incorrect justice minister of Saxony, as his candidate for president. Heitmann promptly outraged the establishment with statements such as "Germany can only accept a limited amount of penetration by foreigners" and "Germans have a right to protect their identity." Heitmann was dropped, but not before he had made his point: He stated baldly the attitudes that mainstream Christian Democrats were loath to express in any but elliptical terms. The party's ex-manager, Defense Minister Volker Rühe, wrote a memo encouraging candidates to use the "foreigner issue" in their campaigns. The Christian Democratic platform called not for integration of foreigners, but for efforts to help foreigners "preserve their

cultural uniqueness" to "keep open the possibility of returning to and rein-
tegrating into the homeland." Christian Democrats promised voters they
would deliver "the solution to the foreigner problem," a chilling formulation
that conjured up the specter of closed borders, stricter laws and deportations.

In 1992, Social Democratic Party chairman Björn Engholm accused his
opponents of scapegoating foreigners. The Social Democrats papered city
streets with posters showing a frightened black child staring through a
cracked windowpane. But the campaign failed to spread sympathy for foreigners, and soon enough, the socialists came around to the Christian Democrats' line. The opposition party surrendered its decades-old defense of
the asylum law and Engholm called the arrival of a million foreigners in the
years since the Wall fell a "basic threat to German democracy." Kohl,
meanwhile, would not be outflanked on the right. In 1992, he startled the
world by declaring that Germany was on the brink of a "national state of
emergency" because of the influx of foreigners.

In 1993, the parliament finally took the vote Kohl's party had sought for
fifteen years. The capital was paralyzed by a few hundred violent leftists
and anarchists whose antics prompted the government to deploy helicopters, boats and an astonishing display of police force to sneak legislators
safely into the Bundestag. The question that morning was whether to revoke
the constitutional guarantee of asylum, a symbol chosen in 1949 as a guilt-
ridden nation's proud response to Nazism. "This week, we will learn
whether we will have a tolerant, open society or a closed country," TV commentator Fritz Pleitgen had said on the eve of the vote. It wasn't even close.
The borders were tightened by a vote of 521 to 132. Neighboring countries
were coaxed into accepting responsibility for stopping migrants headed for
Germany. The new law's impact was immediate: In 1993, 26 percent fewer
asylum-seekers entered Germany as had in the previous year. The United
Nations High Commissioner for Refugees denounced the new law because
it made Germany the only western country that automatically sent asylum-
seekers home without checking individual claims. But there was no going
back. The Christian Democrats pronounced the foreigner problem "solved."

The asylum vote moved the "foreigner problem" off the front burner. But
the underlying schizophrenia remained: Despite Kohl's mantra, Germany
was and always had been an immigration country. French, Polish, Czech
and Hungarian surnames are liberally sprinkled throughout German phone
books, classrooms and employment rolls. In 1848, the German National As-
sembly held a lengthy and angry debate over the definition of citizenship.
Some legislators were more than a century ahead of their times. The very
concept of a German "leads to a variety of misunderstandings," said one

legislator, Fritsch. "Here in Germany there are not only purely German residents, but also many peoples of other tongues." Another member, Jordan, argued that "anyone who lives in Germany is German even if they are not German by birth and language." The 1848 constitution was never enacted, and the argument about who is a German has gone on ever since.

For centuries until the first unification in 1871, the German states and principalities remained apart because they were a mishmash of peoples from all corners of Europe, people who shared certain traditions and a common literary language, but lacked a singular sense of national identity. Germany was not a nation, but a culture. It defined itself through its language, thinking, music, theater. Only late in its history, when the rise of the nation state all around them made it imperative to organize central Europe into a more competitive structure, did Germans invent the *Volk*, the racially united people who were the German nation. This Germany was not a political community so much as a Fatherland of blood brothers. And even then, immigrants flocked to Germany. In 1925, there were 1.5 million refugees in Germany, including ethnic Germans fleeing lands the country had been forced to give up at the end of World War I, political asylum-seekers from Russia, the so-called *Ostjuden*, or Jews from eastern Europe, and refugees from throughout the continent. Berlin in the twenties was Europe's most intriguing city, a peaceful blend of people from dozens of countries. After World War II, about 8 million refugees fleeing Soviet occupation and hunger ended up in Germany. Between 1950 and 1992, nearly 3 million more ethnic Germans returned to their ancestral home.

The artificial nature of the racially defined nation has led to no end of tragedy and mania in the past century. Unlike the national pride that the English and the French boast of, the German concept of nationhood stems from an identity crisis: It is a nation defined by a negative, through rejection of the foreign. With no colonial tradition, no history of absorbing others into its lore and manners, Germany resorted to blood as its unifier. Germany's citizenship law, which dates to 1913, defines a German as someone born to a German. The result is that a third-generation German Turk—fluent in the German language, conversant in German culture, knowledgeable in German history—carries a Turkish passport, while a farmer from the Volga River valley whose ancestors left Germany three hundred years ago can arrive at Frankfurt Airport knowing not one word of German, having no connection to German culture but for a page from an old family Bible, and be granted a passport on demand.

Actually, most "ethnic Germans" arrive with no such paper proof of their heritage. To check their claims, the German government uses the country's most exhaustive source of genealogical information, the racial records compiled by the Nazis, kept in working order in an underground fortress in Berlin. The largest customer by far of the Berlin Documents Center, custody of which was finally handed over from the United States government to the Germans in 1995, was the Bonn government, checking on the family trees of ethnic Germans returning to the Fatherland. The Nazis considered the Volga Germans—those who took up Catherine the Great's challenge to farm the rich soil of Russia—to be, in the words of the racial laws of the time, "biologically eligible" for Germanization. Nazi citizenship rules tested applicants' political reliability, command of the German language, religious background, and "whether they guard their Germanness."

"Only members of the Volk may be citizens," said the Nazi party platform on citizenship in 1920. "Only those with German blood are members of the Volk, without regard to confession. No Jew can be a member of the Volk."

Today's rules—including a fifty-nine-page questionnaire designed to prove German ethnicity—include no political or religious requirements, but otherwise are similarly onerous. The government says the determining factor in the decision about who is a German is not blood, but whether the applicant belongs to a "persecuted group." Ethnic Germans are granted immediate citizenship only because Germany wants to "alleviate what in most cases are extremely difficult living conditions for these people." But somehow, when other foreigners claim a right to live in Germany because they too fled from difficult living conditions, this is seen not as a valid claim on citizenship. Rather, it is sufficient cause to turn the refugee around and send him home.

For most of the postwar period, the very idea of deporting foreigners, no matter how justifiable the expulsion, was an intolerable reminder of everything West Germany sought to live down. Authorities often looked the other way or stretched out already-slow bureaucratic procedures to avoid the most painful experience a German democrat could imagine: doing something the Nazis had done—in this case, deport people. But these were new times, and with a million unwanted, illegal foreigners crammed into abandoned military bases and school gymnasiums, yet another taboo was destined to fall.

The foreigner problem was, in the minds of most reasonable Germans, an asylum problem, and the most visible, most numerous asylum-seekers were the Gypsies. And so, in 1992, the government made a deal with Romania, from where most of the Gypsies had fled. Germany would pay Romania $21 million in "return and reintegration aid" and the Romanians would take back tens of thousands of Gypsies. The new policy outraged leaders of Germany's longstanding Gypsy community. International human rights organizations were appalled that the country that had murdered half a million Gypsies only fifty years earlier was now prepared to ship thousands more back to a place where their homes were routinely burned to the ground. But in Germany, there was no outcry. Gypsies were, nearly everyone agreed, a special case.

In 1721, Emperor Charles VI, fed up with the Gypsies, ordered all of them living on German territory to be killed. He spiced up his order with an offer of cash to anyone willing to execute his command. More than two centuries later, even though Gypsies had lived in stable communities in Germany for more than five hundred years, the Nazis selected them for eradication. They were, in the official racial classification, "Oriental-West Asian bastard mixtures," unsuited for life in the Reich. Gypsies are dark-skinned people who speak a strange, undocumented language. They are descendants of a northern Indian tribe that wandered to Europe in the tenth century, later became enslaved in Romania and gradually dispersed throughout the continent. Gypsies were Europe's ironworkers and jewelers, horse traders and musicians. In most countries, they were hated from the start, banned from respected professions, restricted to certain areas.

For as long as history has been written, tales of the Gypsy life have ranged from the odd to the impossible. Where there are Gypsies, there are stories of thieving and baby-napping, private flimflammery and public fornication. Those Gypsies who survived the Holocaust and either stayed in or returned to Germany were mostly Sinti, families with centuries-old roots in Germany. They speak a German-influenced dialect. They numbered about 60,000 and while they continued to face discrimination, many were fairly successful in small businesses. But after the revolutions of 1989, hundreds of thousands of Gypsies, most of them Romany—the poorer, larger Gypsy group centered in eastern Europe and the Balkans—fled home in search of opportunity and tranquility. (There are many names for Gypsies, most of them derogatory. The English word "Gypsy" derives from the misperception that the people came from Egypt. The German word *Zigeuner* comes from a Byzantine term meaning "untouchable.")

Between 1990 and 1993, when about 200,000 Gypsies arrived in Germany seeking refuge from pogroms in Romania and civil war in Yugoslavia, the face of German city streets changed noticeably. Gypsy beggars—mostly young mothers clutching babies in filthy clothing—lined the sidewalks. On rural roads, Gypsy men built bonfires, grilled meats, and sharpened knives, while their wives used waste water to rinse clothing. Odd as these practices were, measured against the order of German village life, the Gypsies' strangeness was quickly magnified by local tale-tellers: There were Gypsies who barbecued the neighbor's dog, defecated in public playgrounds, and stashed receipts from street begging into the trunk of a gleaming new Mercedes. The beggars and thieves were anything but representative of the hundreds of thousands of Gypsies, but in a country where the occasional drunk in the main railroad stations is usually the only sign of homelessness, Gypsy beggars who grabbed good spots in front of tony shops on Berlin's Kurfürstendamm or Frankfurt's Zeil made a powerful impression.

Old stereotypes blossomed anew. "You must understand," implored an aide to Kohl. "We cannot tolerate such an influx. These people do not, cannot, fit in. The way they live—cooking outdoors, even going to the bathroom outdoors. We know we have a perception problem with tolerance of foreigners, although the great majority of Germans are very much foreigner-friendly. But the Gypsies present another problem entirely."

In a country where Jews were treated with kid gloves, it was open season on Gypsies. Police confirmed there was no evidence that Gypsies were responsible for a disproportionate share of crimes. But that didn't stop even the most respected politicians from describing Gypsies as dangerous sub-humans. "We cannot accept these people because there is not the slightest acceptance of these people by the German population," Herbert Schnoor, the interior minister in the state of North Rhine-Westphalia, told me. "They cannot be integrated." But if the German population felt the same way about Jews, you wouldn't say they can't be accepted, would you? Schnoor glared at me and said, "Don't be clever."

EVERYONE HATES THE GYPSIES, read a headline in the weekly *Der Spiegel*. The *Hamburger Morgenpost*, an ordinarily reasonable daily, said in 1992 that "one cannot deny—Roma are a serious plague, and this is not a racist remark." That same year, Germany was the only nation among forty-three to vote against a United Nations resolution on the protection of Roma. The German delegate justified his vote by saying, "The Roma do not constitute a minority in Germany. They should not be the subject of positive discrimination. Germany wishes to retain its right to expel Romany refugees."

"Prejudice against Roma is normal," judges wrote in a 1992 deportation ruling by the Federal Office for the Recognition of Foreign Refugees. "Violence against them is understandable." An administrative court in Heidelberg in 1993 threw out a lawsuit filed by a Gypsy group against a newspaper that said Gypsies were unable and unwilling to use toilets and showers. The court opinion said: "It is common knowledge that Gypsies in fact do indeed lack hygienic awareness and do not use toilets or showers; in order to claim the opposite, the burden of proof lies with the [Gypsy group]."

The established Gypsy community watched the ballooning anti-Gypsy fervor with horror. They had seen this before. In 1950, when surviving Gypsies asked the West German government for reparations like those given to

Jewish survivors, the justice minister in the state of Baden-Württemberg rejected the claim. "We have concluded," the ministry said, "that these people were overwhelmingly oppressed and imprisoned not for racist reasons, but because of their asocial and criminal attitudes."

Until the 1970s, West Germany's training manual for police officers said that "Gypsies have neither secure place of residence nor fixed employment. Gypsies are especially known for these characteristics: an unfixed life of wandering and a marked avoidance of work." Only in 1982, after repeated protests by German Gypsies, did Kohl recognize the "countless victims of violence and racial phobia" among the Sinti and Roma during Nazi rule.

Germany's condemnation of the Gypsies was unique in western Europe. Since World War II, Gypsies have returned to and have been successfully assimilated into many countries from which they were deported. Franz Hamburger, a German sociologist, has detailed how Dutch authorities introduced Gypsy families to western ways and built their confidence to such a level that they feel secure in the Netherlands. But in Germany, the focus placed on making anti-Semitism taboo somehow liberated antiforeigner and anti-Gypsy feelings.

The scene was a posh Berlin restaurant at Savigny Platz, a hangout for actors, writers, and people who think themselves quite important. The trendiest of the trendy, dolled up in black-on-black, eyes hidden behind sharp-edged designer frames, lingered over champagne and salads of deer and radicchio. A heavy-set woman and her six-year-old daughter—Gypsies—stepped into the dining room and moved slowly from table to table. The girl held out a worn piece of cardboard. In capital letters, in broken German, it said: HELP! WE ARE HUNGRY! WE LOSE OUR HOME! WE COME TO GERMANY NEED FOOD NEED MONEY! PLEASE HELP!

At most tables, the mother and daughter were ignored. Two Germans reached into their pockets and, eyes averted, handed over some pfennigs. Just then, the bartender noticed the beggars and rushed over to them with a broom. *"Raus, raus!"* (Out, out!) he said sternly. He waved his broom at the woman's filthy skirt. She moved slowly toward the exit, her hand still reaching out toward a customer, until she and her child were shooed out the door. One hour later, they would return.

For many Romanian Gypsies, even dirty looks and open abuse were a considerable improvement over the lives they had known back home, where at least twenty-five Roma villages were burned to the ground by anti-Gypsy mobs in the first years after the regime of communist leader Nicolae Ceaușescu was overthrown. Despite the well-documented pattern of repression of Gypsies in Romania by vigilante groups and police alike, hardly any Roma were granted asylum in Germany. The line in Bonn was that while some Gypsies indeed had a difficult time in Romania, the government in Bucharest was not discriminatory, and anyway, as a German Foreign Ministry statement said, Gypsies are "not popular due to their alien traditions and customs." The Bonn government insisted its deportation policy was not intended to single out Gypsies, but was only a first step toward deporting all asylum-seekers whose claims were deemed without merit. Germany did eventually sign repatriation treaties with all its eastern neighbors, but the Romanian accord came first and was accompanied by government pronouncements that the foreigner problem had been solved.

For many months after the treaty was signed, I asked various government agencies if I could observe a deportation. German authorities were usually polite and cooperative with reporters. But this time, I hit a wall. Official policy was that there was nothing wrong or shameful about the deportations. But no one wanted reports on the departing Gypsies to appear in foreign newspapers. So I set out on my own.

In the shadows beneath a highway overpass in central Berlin, six low-slung buildings sat surrounded by chain-link fence topped with strands of barbed wire. This was the Teilestrasse camp for asylum-seekers. Most of the residents were Gypsies. They could come and go as they wished. The tall fences were there only for their own protection against angry Germans. Children played in the long, dark hallways of the dormitories while their parents hiked to local shops, trying to stretch the government dole of about $250 a month (up to $700 per family). Many of the Gypsy women dressed in their finest for visits to town. They put on delicate, wide-brimmed hats and elegant, high-heeled shoes. They wore gold rings and silver bracelets. Inside the camp, one woman explained, they knew they were poor. Outside, she hoped, "I can at least look like a decent person." While the government prepared deportation papers on them, the refugees lived here and waited. They were prohibited from working. They had only the basics, cots and blankets from the Red Cross, the clothing on their backs, perhaps an old TV or radio scavenged from local trash piles.

Ion Nicolescu, his wife and their three children shared a single room, where they had lived since fleeing Bucharest a year earlier. Nicolescu, forty-four, had his own small moving business in Romania. During Ceau-şescu's rule, Gypsies were second-class citizens, but they were guaranteed work and were protected against the nationalist urges of their Romanian neighbors. After the fall of communism, Nicolescu's moving van was stolen, he lost his customers, and he watched as nationalist gangs attacked Gypsy settlements and villages, burning houses and forcing families to leave. "I saw people beaten, with my own eyes," he said. "I saw villages burning. I didn't want it for my children. There was no more work for any of us. In communism, it wasn't this bad. We had our work, we had our peace. We didn't have much to do with the Romanians, but it was OK. The way it is now, I couldn't stay. We needed to eat. In Romania, there's no bread, no meat. I had to get my family out."

The Nicolescus gathered their children, Lina, Fabian and Mercu, and traveled by train to Poland. From there, with help from a people-smuggler, they walked over the open border to Germany. They found the border police and asked for political asylum. The German bureaucrats took nearly two years to process the paperwork, but the asylum request was denied. Nicolescu knew this was coming. He also knew he could not go back. He presented his case evenly. He had had many months to think about his reasons for remaining in Germany. "I want to live like anyone else, in one place, with work and food and other people. I know what's going on here. We are not stupid. The Germans say we are dirty. But let us live like the Germans and we'll be as clean as anyone. One stove for thirty people—how can you keep that clean?"

Nicolescu, humiliated by his idleness for the past year, did occasional odd jobs for Berlin's Gypsy organization. Most of the time, he could do little but hang around the camp, watching his children, waiting. "I don't like this either," he said. "I'd love to work. Living like this, it's like slavery. I have to depend on them for everything. The Germans say we are homeless wanderers. My family lived in the same village in Romania for five hundred years. Now I go into a store here and the Germans say, 'Raus, raus—Out, out, foreigner.' My children have the same problems. That's what Roma have to deal with, now, before and forever."

When I mentioned the German deportation treaty, Nicolescu leaped from the edge of his bed and ushered me away from his three children. He began to wave his arms. His eyes watered, his lips tightened. He shouted his answer: "I'd rather kill myself and my family than go back. I can't vanish into the clouds. Here killed, there killed. If there was a connection to God, I'd use it right now." Some time later, the government came for him. Deportation. But Nicolescu and his family had vanished underground. He would not go back.

"I'd rather be burned in Germany with a full stomach than beaten in Romania hungry," said Paul Schuster, a Romanian Gypsy writer I met in a back corner room of a majestic mansion overlooking the crystalline water of Berlin's Wannsee. He and other Gypsy intellectuals had come to Berlin to stage a Gypsy cultural festival, to prove themselves to their German neighbors. In the library of this literary institute, I met a novelist whose work had been translated into twenty-three languages; a linguist who had devoted decades to a single project, the reconstruction of the Roma alphabet lost a millennium ago; and a musician who studied the influence of centuries-old folk songs on modern jazz.

The novelist was Mateo Maximoff, a French Gypsy who spent close to four years in a Nazi concentration camp and devoted many years afterward to translating portions of the Bible into Roma. He was a round, fleshy man with long ears and a twinkle in his eyes. He was frail and moved slowly, but when he spoke, I heard the rage of a man who believed he had to speak for others too powerless to speak for themselves. In the late 1960s, Maximoff applied to the German government for reparations for the time he was imprisoned. After a fourteen-year court battle, Maximoff was awarded a pension of $570 a month.

"We will protect ourselves this time," he told me, waving his gold-capped cane. "My people must finally live as they wish. I'm old now, but my next book will be a science fiction piece, takes place in the year 2900. By then, there'll be no countries left, no peoples—just one country and one people, the Romany. All roads lead to Rome, you know. After what they've done to my people, the rest of the world should live in fear of that day. But don't worry, we're not so terrible. We'll even let the Germans into our country."

14

"How Ugly Are We Really?"

We need friends more than others do. —Helmut Kohl, June 1993

A NASTY NIGHT in Bonn. The narrow streets had long since emptied, the bureaucrats were tucked safely into bed, barricaded behind the shutters that roll down over their windows. Windswept rain splattered over the occasional passing car. Inside the Chancellery, only a few lights remained on. Helmut Kohl's advisers sat around a low, glass coffee table, trying to decide how to persuade their boss that something finally had to be done. Germany was being beaten about the head. Every day of that fall of 1992, another neo-Nazi attack, another call from foreign investors wondering whether it was safe to do business in Germany, another exasperated remark from a foreign visitor, another hysterical headline in the British tabloids, another video dissolve from neo-Nazis to Hitler's henchmen on American TV. *Bild*, the country's most popular newspaper, printed a list of ten ways "the world can punish us," including boycotts against German products, arts performers and sports teams.

It was all so unfair, Kohl's men agreed. There was nothing the federal government could do. If young thugs wanted to firebomb a home for asylum-seekers, there was no way to stop it. You can't patrol every shelter in the country every minute of the day and night. The great bulk of the Germans would never for a moment contemplate such terror, but no one abroad wanted to hear that. It was just Nazis this and Nazis that. Foreign newspapers clamored for "symbolic action." They wanted the chancellor to hug Gypsy babies, comfort a Turkish father, march against the violence of the far right. My God, how naive, how presumptuous the foreign press could be. Especially the Americans and the Brits. They think they're still the occupying force, one Kohl aide said. This chancellor knows just how far he can go without alienating conservative voters. Hugging refugees who were taxing the resources of so many German towns and states would not wash. Period.

But something had to be done. It had simply gone too far. Two men in the room wanted Kohl to join with President Weizsäcker and sponsor a mass demonstration in Berlin to put all of society on record in opposition to neo-Nazi violence. The chancellor listened and immediately refused. As he had said before: "You know, I know what kind of public scenes can be staged. I am a specialist—more than anyone else in Germany. I know what the real public opinion is, what happens when I arrive unannounced somewhere in the new [eastern] states, as opposed to what happens when someone has assembled the portable protest groups—likely paying them for their time. And I know exactly what images are then sent around the world." Kohl was afraid anarchists would disrupt any demonstration the government staged. And Kohl—who feared and loathed Berlin the way Americans fear and loathe New York—was especially loath to join any event in the country's once and future capital. There were just too many crazies there, too many factions, too much potential for disaster.

The idea made no headway that chilly, wet night. But in the weeks that followed, Kohl himself began searching for something, some step the government could take to show the world that Germany was not sinking under a new extremist wave. The chancellor started out each day livid about the impact of the violence: Although he knew only a smattering of English, Kohl ordered his staff to put on his desk each day's articles about Germany from the *Washington Post* and the *New York Times*. Bad news was epidemic that fall: If the arson attack on the Jewish Barracks at Sachsenhausen wasn't bad enough, then came the embarrassingly frank words of Foreign Minister Klaus Kinkel. While Kohl sat home in Bonn, Kinkel took it upon himself to go to Sachsenhausen to lay a wreath. But then, asked why he—the foreign minister—had come, Kinkel said, "It's above all a question of how this looks abroad, and that's why I am here as foreign minister."

The criticism from abroad continued unabated. The effect was incalculable: The Goethe Institute reported sharp drops in the number of students taking German lessons at its schools around the world. Tourism was down. Even the Bush administration, which aggressively supported just about anything the reunited Germans might say or do, was worried. At a Washington social event, the president approached the German ambassador and asked, "What's going on over there?"

In October, the half-dozen men who joined Kohl for his early morning meeting began to push hard for a proforeigner demonstration. Weizsäcker, always ready to use his presidency as a bully pulpit, was already on board. It would be televised, with hundreds of thousands of church members and party activists bused in from around the country. There would be celebrities, religious and business leaders. It couldn't lose. Kohl still resisted: Why Berlin? he asked. Too much potential for disaster. Slowly, as the days went by and neo-Nazis shouted *"Sieg Heil"* and "Germany for the Germans" as they attacked more Jewish sites and destroyed more cemeteries and burned more foreigners' homes, Kohl backed down. He would attend, but he would not speak. He would stand to the side of the stage, not on it. Let Weizsäcker do the talking.

Planners worked feverishly to stage an event on November 8 that would send a worldwide message of openness and tolerance. There was discord within Kohl's ruling coalition: Bavaria's conservative premier, Max Streibl, expressed the resentment on the right, denouncing the Berlin event as "a funeral march for a helpless democracy." The planners were determined to send a completely different message. They commissioned a colorful logo perfect for television. They built a pristine white stage and placed it directly in front of an enormous platform for TV cameras. They organized a press center well stocked with food and information. It was the kind of stage-managing that was routine in American politics, but unknown in Germany, where politicians proudly rejected "the politics of symbolism." Political parties lured hundreds of thousands of members onto buses for the Sunday in Berlin. The day was perfect for a demonstration, sunny and cool, and the crowd was full of families. This was the silent majority Kohl had referred to so many times; these were the Germans who were offended by any suggestion that their country might have a latent brown streak, a Nazi strain that had never been eradicated.

There were skeptics in the crowd, people like Joachim Schanz, an architect who stood along the sidelines because he considered the government and the marchers responsible for the violence against foreigners: "First, they encourage the violence by talking about a 'foreigner problem,' then they march here to make Germany look good around the world. It's all a show for the foreign press." Onstage, twelve artists from twelve countries entertained the crowd. A few blocks away, Weizsäcker led a march into the huge plaza across from the Palace of the Republic, once home to East Germany's parliament, now shuttered, a politically incorrect, asbestos-ridden symbol of a country that was no more. But from the start of the march, it was clear that trouble lay ahead. Weizsäcker was taunted and tormented by rowdy *Autonomen,* the mischievous anarchists who delight in disrupting German political events, sometimes playfully, but usually with frightening malice. The president wanted so much to believe in the goodness of the cause that he eschewed all but the smallest security detail, and all along the march route, Germans approached Weizsäcker to thank him for being there.

Kohl had no such illusions. He stayed far from the march. When he arrived at the demonstration site, he gingerly stepped out of his car and into a ring of sixty-four riot police wearing metal helmets and white plastic teargas masks that looked like futuristic muzzles. As the chancellor was ushered into an area tucked off to the side of the stage, far from the masses, out of shot for cameras trained on the speaker's podium, the crowd caught sight of him and began chanting "Hypocrite, hypocrite." It was downhill from there. As the TV cameras turned to note Kohl's arrival, frantic aides ran over to the police and shouted at them to remove their riot gear and replace their helmets with less threatening black berets. They did, but the PR gesture quickly proved futile. As the speeches began, protesters, who had managed to elude security forces and claim nearly all the choice spots at the front of the stage, pulled out trumpets, whistles and projectiles and brought the whole grand show to an embarrassing, humiliating halt. They pelted Weizsäcker with eggs, tomatoes, paint bombs, catcalls and angry chants. Riot police stormed the stage to protect the president with plastic shields, umbrellas and their armored bodies. Weizsäcker gamely tried to read his text, but after a few moments, the sound system was cut off, and all of Germany was left watching a silent screen with a picture of their president peeking from behind a thick line of riot helmets, wiping egg from his eye.

Kohl vanished quickly. Only Ignatz Bubis, leader of the tiny Jewish community, ran up on the stage, grabbed the revived microphone and said, "I am ashamed of what has happened here. We are not in 1938, but in 1992." The disruption continued for half an hour. A sea of people, probably 300,000 or more, watched in bewilderment.

As Kohl had predicted, the demonstration was a disaster. Designed to boost Germany's image abroad, it achieved exactly the opposite, portraying the country as helpless in the face of extremist violence. Kohl's critics blasted him for caring more about foreign opinion than about the victims of violence and the stability of German democracy. "Questions like 'How do we look abroad?' or 'How does this effect investments?' are important, but I can't stand hearing them anymore," said Cornelia Schmalz-Jacobsen, the government's commissioner for foreigners.

But in a country that had measured itself for forty years by the foreign view of its progress, such questions would not fade. Long after the postwar occupation had ended, foreign governments—and especially the Americans, British and French—remained paternal monitors of German politics and morality. And the Germans, trapped in the eternal middle in the geography of Europe, in the struggle between the superpowers, and in their country's historic divided loyalty between east and west, continued to act like an overgrown foster child, still dependent on its parents, still reluctant to go out on its own.

One night, at home in Berlin, I was in one of those midnight fogs, staring into the TV screen, knowing I should go to bed, but not quite able to summon the strength to lift myself from the couch. On the main state TV channel was another interminable talk show, an eclectic mix of writers and entertainers, politicians and people who seem to exist solely to be sardonic. But suddenly, the talk show broke through like high beams piercing the night: "Tonight," the genial host announced, "How Ugly Are We Really?" And there they were, a nightclub singer, a filmmaker and—could it be?— the Foreign Minister, sitting around, talking about just how awful the Germans are, and especially about just how awful the rest of the world thinks they are. Foreign Minister Kinkel, beer in hand, lamented that "the farther we go away, the more problems we see, especially where people live who experienced the terrible events."

Could this happen anywhere else? Is any other country so deeply needy of acceptance from abroad? Germany, to its everlasting joy and frustration, is not just another European country. It is a complex and fascinating culture, trapped in a cycle of pessimism, paranoia and pride. Gordon Craig, the Stanford historian who is the foremost American interpreter of Germany, concluded that Germans "enjoy it when foreigners worry about them," even now, long after the stigma of World War II has dissipated. Cees Nooteboom, a Dutch writer who is his country's leading commentator on Germany, was always astonished to find that Germans who attended his readings were forever asking, "Don't you think we Germans are dangerous?"

Some Germans crave approval from abroad. "The Germans in the past four decades have learned to judge ourselves exclusively by what appears in Anglo-Saxon newspapers," said Johannes Gross, publisher of the business magazine *Kapital*. That exaggerated dependence on outside judgments led inevitably to resentment of foreign reporters and diplomats. Every nuance of foreign reporting on Germany was examined, in government offices, in frequent newspaper reports on "How We Are Seen Abroad," in conversation in boardrooms and corner bars alike. The government commissioned surveys to monitor how Germany stacked up against other countries in the minds of Americans.

"The headline is, 'You like us,' " an aide to Kohl said when I asked how one such poll had turned out. In fact, surveys have long shown that Americans place Germany a healthy third on the most-favorite-nation hit parade, after Canada and Great Britain. In the United States, perhaps because one

in four Americans are of German descent, Germans never have been portrayed as inherently evil, the way the Japanese were during the war.

Sometimes it seemed Germans wanted to believe the worst about their
image. In a country that tends to overdramatize its troubles, no one raised
an eyebrow when the tourism authority included this question in its survey
of potential foreign visitors: "Suppose you want to vacation in a country
from which you consistently hear reports of torture, repression, disappearance of people and slave trading of young women and children. What would
you do?" Well, if you put it that way, 87 percent of those surveyed replied,
maybe we'll just stay home.

Of course, there were vicious and unfair attacks on Germany, especially
at the height of the neo-Nazi violence. Margaret Thatcher convened a
roundtable of experts on Germany in 1990, and five prominent academics
concluded that Germans suffer from "anxiety, aggression, arrogance, lack
of consideration, smugness, an inferiority complex and sentimentality."
Aside from that, Germans were just peachy. Shortly after that brainstorming
session, Thatcher's trade minister, Nicholas Ridley, was forced out of office
for accusing the Germans of plotting to take over Europe, calling them "uppity," and arguing that ceding some of Britain's sovereignty to a German-
dominated European Community was tantamount to "giving it to Adolf
Hitler." The British tabloids were quick to haul out swastikas, paint Hitler
mustaches on Kohl, and use every imaginable Nazi stereotype in cartoons
and reporting on antiforeigner attacks. In Japan, media reports so frightened readers that companies held seminars for executives planning trips to
Germany; instructors recommended dressing as conservatively as possible
so as not to be mistaken for Vietnamese refugees.

In the United States, newspaper coverage of neo-Nazism was, according
to the conservative *Frankfurter Allgemeine Zeitung,* "fair and straightfor-
ward," but the TV images were disastrous. The networks used archival
footage of Hitler and Goebbels mixed with video of skinheads hurling Molotov cocktails. Swastikas dominated the homescreen. The low point came
when ABC's New York station ran a five-part series dubbed "The New Wall
of Hate."

Since World War II, Germany has fought hard to replace war-movie
stereotypes with modern images of a democratic and open land. The government, political parties and their foundations reach out to American
opinion leaders, offering all-expenses-paid trips for journalists, religious
groups, politicians, academics and students. German government and industry generously ply the U.S. market with freebies and enticements, spon-
soring museum shows, TV programs and arts performances, all with the aim
of rebuilding the soiled reputation. And still, the Germany of Hitler and

Hollywood does not die. Half a century after war's end, America's popular image of Germans remains a curious mixture of old and new: monocles, murder and mindless conformity, but also success, efficiency and cleanliness. American reporters in Germany sent home an image of a loyal ally that was a bit shaky in the confidence department, but overall was a dependable democracy recreated in our image.

By the time my colleagues and I arrived in the late 1980s, Germany was changing from a quiet, mostly diplomatic story into a news bonanza—a political, social and economic headline-churning machine. The German government wasn't accustomed to so much attention from the American press, and when the antiforeigner violence kicked in, the counterattack on what Bonn perceived as negative press was swift and unprecedented. "The usual critics," wrote the *Frankfurter Allgemeine Zeitung's* New York correspondent, Jörg von Uthmann, "are incapable of perceiving the Germany of today from a different angle than that of the Nazi era. Like the Jews have to live with anti-Semitism, we will have to live with the [Elie] Wiesels and Rosenthals." Throughout the Bonn government, the hated trio of A. M. Rosenthal and William Safire of the *New York Times* and Richard Cohen of the *Washington Post* were pilloried as a Jewish cabal determined to ruin Germany's image. *Der Spiegel,* intent on clueing its readers into Rosenthal's religious heritage—as if his last name were not enough—referred to him as "Abraham Rosenthal," a name the columnist uses neither in print nor in person. Uthmann was the same reporter who wrote a column accusing me of "never missing an opportunity to recall the crimes of the Nazis." When I asked Uthmann why he said that, he replied, "I am convinced that too much history distorts the view of the present."

The reappearance of old ghosts so spooked German officialdom that policy-makers began to view nearly everything related to the neo-Nazi problem according to how it would play in the foreign press. A long-planned effort to improve young Germans' understanding of the Nazi era by distributing a comic book that told the story of Hitler's rise to power was scratched at the last minute because authorities feared foreigners would be offended by the use of such a frivolous medium.

Government officials started calling me and other reporters to complain that American news coverage was slanted and slanderous. The Federal Press Office, which before the antiforeigner violence had more or less ignored American reporters (and we them), suddenly began peppering us with advice and criticism. After the *International Herald Tribune* published a story I wrote about the economic impact of the neo-Nazi attacks under the headline NOW, 'WHO WILL BUY FROM THE UGLY GERMANS?' I got an angry call from the Foreign Ministry.

"This is anti-German propaganda and nothing less," the livid official said. After offering the usual reporter's defense that I don't write the headlines, I told the fellow the original source of the "Ugly Germans" line—a headline in the German weekly *Die Zeit*. Had the ministry complained to *Die Zeit* about their headline?

"Of course not," my caller explained. "There are certain things that are only acceptable within the family. A German reads that and puts it in perspective. People in your country can't understand this."

The chief of the foreign department at the Federal Press Office, Henning Wegener, was the assigned keeper for American reporters. When other U.S. reporters and I wrote about the German-Romanian treaty that paved the way for the deportation of Gypsy refugees, Wegener called several of us to complain. "You must know that by using words such as 'deportation,' you are causing great sadness," he said. "This is not an expulsion. There is no racial tinge to this. It is a legally settled procedure between two countries. It is, of course, a great relief to our problem. These words 'mass deportation' have terrible, disturbing historical connotations." There was the faintest of pauses. "We have a task force that has met to discuss the proper English translation for the German word *Abschiebung* and we prefer that you use the term 'readmission' or 'retransfer.' "

I grabbed my German-English dictionary and read Wegener the translation for *Abschiebung*. It was "deportation."

"But the *Washington Post* would never use the word 'deportation' to describe a policy of the U.S. government," he said.

"On the contrary, we use it all the time in stories about Haitian refugees," I said. We argued, to no avail. Wegener could not accept that words Germans avoid because of their historical resonance might be perfectly good words in another language, another culture. And I could not accept his idea that because my articles appeared in the *Post*, I had "a special responsibility to consider the effect your reporting has on the State Department and the policy community."

A few days later, a reader in Paris faxed me some documents that provided some context for Wegener's anger. At the beginning of the deportation of Jews from France in 1942, the German chief of the general staff issued a secret order to all officers involved in the operation: They were to cease using the term "deportation" "because this term from the czarist era is still associated with being shipped to Siberia." Instead, the Nazis ordered that the removal of Jews from France be referred to as "sending away for forced labor."

Wegener became my constant correspondent, my fax machine's best friend. When I wrote about efforts to blame Germany's foreign residents for the rise in crime after unification, I cited government statistics to show that foreigners did not commit a disproportionate number of crimes. Wegener faxed over a slew of other statistics and clippings indicating that foreigners were indeed a major crime problem. When I wrote about the debate over citizenship, Wegener took particular offense, sending me a thirty-one-page fax in which he defended the 1913 citizenship law by saying it was no different from Israel's Law of Return—"as alike as one egg and another"— and therefore was beyond reproach. It was wrong to write that German citizenship is based on blood, Wegener insisted. "American readers won't understand that. You should say instead that Germany's citizenship law is similar to that of Israel."

After I wrote a few articles about Gypsy refugees, the chief spokesman for the Foreign Ministry, Hanns Schumacher, sent me copies of ministry cables describing how Gypsies deported back to Romania returned home with new VCRs, TVs, washing machines, refrigerators and other signs of affluence. The government not only monitored my articles but also warned bureaucrats against cooperating with me. On several occasions when I was interviewing government officials, I saw on their desks memos from the press office describing me as "a reporter who is very critical of Germany. . . . Take particular care," the memo said. The government also sought to find out more about me and other reporters they considered problematic. After a British colleague, Robin Gedye of the *Daily Telegraph,* wrote some tough pieces, he found himself cut off from the usual stream of invitations to government social events where reporters in Bonn often met useful officials. A junior staffer from the Federal Press Office once approached my colleague from *Newsweek,* Charles Lane, at a cocktail party and told him that "Fisher's reporting causes us great concern. He's very critical. Is he a Jewish American?" Lane confirmed that I was, and the official replied, "Ah yes," as if that explained everything.

The most mysterious moment came at the end of 1992, when a freelance reporter in Berlin, Margitta Fahr, was summoned to a lengthy interrogation by the Staatsschutz, the security police. Fahr, who had spent four years investigating the neo-Nazi scene, had tried to fax to a fellow reporter a piece of far-right propaganda that included an SS insignia. She misdialed, sending the sheet with the SS symbol to a stranger's fax machine. It is illegal in Germany to possess or distribute Nazi symbols. Fahr immediately realized her error and tried to send an apology to the number she had misdialed. But the fax machine had been turned off. The recipient of the fax called the police, and Fahr was called in.

Staatsschutz agents questioned her for several hours, threatened to prosecute her for distributing Nazi material, and finally, at the end of the session, they brought up a new topic: Marc Fisher. Did Fahr know me? (She did not; we knew of each other's work, but had never met.) Was I in Germany with family? What had she heard about me, my hobbies, interests, hangouts? Who were my friends? Fahr couldn't—and wouldn't—help them. After I learned about the interrogation, I called several government agencies, but never found anyone who could explain why the Staatsschutz was interested in me. The best I could get from anyone came from an official of the Office for the Protection of the Constitution, Germany's domestic intelligence agency, who surmised that the Berlin officers on Fahr's case had read some of my reporting on neo-Nazis and gone off on their own, trying to draw connections between reporters and their sources.

Tension between German officials and foreign reporters peaked in 1993 at a conference held by Bertelsmann, the giant media conglomerate. When Kohl's chief of staff, Friedrich Bohl, defended the chancellor's failure to place himself visibly on the side of the country's foreign population, the assembled reporters let out two years' worth of frustration, pummeling Bohl with sharp, angry questions. Bohl, a fair, reasonable sort stuck with the unenviable task of defending the chancellor's stubborn ways, was alternately conciliatory and antagonistic. As questions hit him from all sides—Why didn't the chancellor go to Rostock, or Mölln, or any of the other sites of major antiforeigner attacks? Why hadn't the government shut down the largest neo-Nazi groups?—Bohl stepped back from the podium, shortened his sentences, and finally lashed out at the Americans.

"I don't see that the chancellor should change anything," he said. "He went to Berlin. He cannot go to every atrocity in Germany. It is not his job. It is not his job and I would oppose his presence." And then, calming, Bohl appealed to us: "We are a young democracy. We make mistakes. We shouldn't have to confirm our democracy. I was born in 1945. I don't have that experience. We have to trust each other. We spent forty-five years building a relationship. We must have trust."

Bertelsmann's chairman, Mark Wössner, came to the rescue of his cornered guest. "You Americans overvalue the importance of symbolism. You have a society addicted to symbolism. Kohl is a hundred percent trustworthy on this. You have to accept that."

The hurt pride Bohl displayed at our meeting emerged in other ways in that tense time. Germans once remarkably solicitous of foreign reporters began to voice their displeasure about press coverage to their friends at the U.S. Embassy in Bonn. And some diplomats were so eager to keep the Germans happy that they took it upon themselves to pressure American reporters to "get on the team." On one occasion in 1993, U.S. diplomats showed up at my office to complain that my articles and those of my colleagues were making the Germans nervous, and that surely I recognized the dangers that could create. "It's important that we not undermine their confidence," one diplomat said.

At the peak of the neo-Nazi attacks, the U.S. ambassador, Robert Kimmitt, a bright veteran of the National Security Council, invited the press corps in for only the second (and last) briefing in his two-year tenure. The session began with a twenty-five-minute tongue-lashing reminding us of the "special responsibilities all of us face. Every day, I read and especially see on television stories in which the facts are not as accurate as you'd like them to be." Kimmitt proceeded to recite the same litany of statistics German officials used to dramatize the country's plight—the 500,000 asylumseekers, 250,000 refugees from the Balkan civil war, and 150,000 ethnic Germans who had entered Germany since the fall of the Wall. "I'm not being an apologist for the Germans," the ambassador said. "But a decided minority is getting a decided majority of the coverage. . . . You should be out there trying to encourage the good guys to do better." Kimmitt admitted that the German government believed American press coverage was causing them political and economic problems in the United States, but he insisted no one had put him up to this dressing down of the press corps.

No one needed to. "We were determined to see only the pleasant side of the Germans," says the narrator of *Here Is Germany,* a 1945 U.S. Army propaganda film made to explain to American soldiers how the Allied occupation of Germany had failed after World War I and why it would succeed now. "This time, we shall remain, for 10 years, for 20 years, until Karl Schmidt [the movie's nasty German John Doe] learns a new way." Half a century later, hundreds of thousands of U.S. troops remain in Germany, but the Cold War quickly scotched any idea of imposing a rigorous, punitive occupation on the defeated Germans. Instead, the U.S. approach to Germany since the war has been a typically American mix of generosity, naïveté, short memories, and fear of offending a friend. After reunification, CIA analysts predicted that by 2000, Germany would try to break out of its postwar role as America's stepchild, reestablishing a German sphere of influence in central and eastern Europe and antagonizing its western European allies. But the Bush and Clinton administrations preferred to view the Germans much as the American public did, as a patriotic and trustworthy people who had a troubled past, but all in all, were a lot like us.

While I was in Germany, the gap between the official U.S. view of Bonn and the perspective I heard from American and other diplomats who actually lived in the country was dramatic. From Germany, the country's structural economic problems, the deep social and psychological divide between east and west, and the continuing struggle to deal with the past—now exacerbated by the legacy of communism—seemed imposing hurdles. But back in Washington, the official line was that the Germans were handling everything wonderfully. Within three or four years, we were told by folks at the State Department, the White House and the think tanks, we would see a new economic miracle and a level of political stability and social accord unmatched in Europe. When I came home to Washington, I was invited to speak to a number of audiences—students, lobbyists and the inside-the-Beltway professionals who call themselves the "policy community." These are people who work at institutes that are largely holding pens for political appointees whose party is out of office or whose reputations have flagged for one reason or another. These audiences were polite and friendly—until I began to spell out my view of a Germany that faced an extended, painful transition to a period of less affluence, economic restraint and powerful pressures from abroad (immigration, unrest and possibly war to the east). Suddenly, I faced frowns, grimaces and finally, gentle reminders that I ought to keep such comments out of the public arena.

"I agree with most of what you've said," one Germanist said after my talk. "But these are not the kinds of things we should be saying about the Germans in public. They need to be encouraged or else their pessimism takes over. You really have to be careful what you say about them or it could be very damaging." After which the very same man joined his colleagues in expressing—privately, of course—his own deep-felt fears of Germany. By dint of my position as a former *Post* correspondent sojourning in the politicoacademic back halls of Washington, I was privy to the background buzz that lurked behind the boosterish public attitude toward Germany. In private, one person after another spoke of NATO as a tool for keeping Germany down, wondered how to prevent the renationalization of German defense policy, and warned against permitting a kind of German hegemony in central and eastern Europe. After four years of being accused by the Bonn government of an anti-German animus, I was astonished to find that most of the American government officials, academics and other folks who think about Germany were far more skeptical about the country than I had ever been. Of course, the notion that public boosterism would spare the Germans from suspecting that their American friends harbored critical thoughts was paternalistic and condescending. It was also wrong: German diplomats knew quite well what U.S. politicians and policy experts really thought. Some were amused by the assumption that open criticism might push the Germans off the deep end. Others found the whole game offensive.

But I did not understand the true depth of German sensitivity toward their image abroad—and the consequent American jitters about offending the Germans—until I unknowingly caused a miniature international tiff upon my return to Washington. Before leaving Berlin, I called a scholar at the American Institute for Contemporary German Studies, Manfred Stassen, and asked whether the institute, a Washington satellite of Johns Hopkins University, might have extra office space I could use to write this book. I sought no money, only a desk, a phone and use of a computer. Stassen was immediately receptive. Within days, he and the Institute's director, Robert Gerald Livingston, gave me the green light to come aboard as journalist in residence. When I arrived in Washington a few months later, Livingston told me that because of a shortage of office space, I would have to spend the fall term down the street at Hopkins' Foreign Policy Institute, then switch over to the German Studies Institute at year's end. No problem, I said.

Nor was it. Everyone was perfectly pleasant and gracious. I never would have known anything was amiss if a source in Germany had not tipped me off to the paper war that had been raging for months over where to put me. From the moment the German Studies Institute agreed to give me office space, some of its staff and trustees protested angrily. Thomas Hughes, former president of the Carnegie Endowment for International Peace, urged the Institute to put as much distance as it could between itself and me, saying it should not "reward" me for writing "critical" articles about Germany. My reporting had upset the Bonn government, he believed, and Bonn might decide to punish the Institute for consorting with me. The Institute depended fairly heavily on the German government for guest speakers, cooperation, and occasional financial support. Hughes and other trustees believed my presence could "do damage to the Institute's reputation in government circles in Bonn," according to an internal memo.

Upset by the discord among his trustees, Livingston decided "to ascertain the official attitude" in Bonn. He contacted Henning Wegener, my Federal Press Office "keeper," and asked whether the government would object if the Institute helped me out. To the contrary, Wegener "strongly recommended that the Institute take Fisher" and said he considered me "sensitive and open." Livingston pursued the matter up the chain of command in Bonn, seeking out several other senior aides to Kohl, all of whom endorsed the idea of my residency. But the Institute's trustees were not mollified. Hughes argued that "influential Germans" were so upset by my reporting— and by what he called the *Post*'s "thirty years of dislike" of Germany—that they would not understand the Institute's decision to house me. What trustees called "the Fisher affair" dragged on for months; because of the possible taint I might bring to the Institute, an elegant compromise was worked out—unbeknownst to me—whereby I was invited down the street to the Foreign Policy Institute to buy time. Livingston tried to persuade his trustees that they were overreacting: Fisher's "name will soon be forgotten in Germany, probably already is," he wrote. Then, during the fall of 1993, both my supporters and detractors apparently closely observed my speaking appearances and other activities. Even the German Embassy got involved; their staffers attended my speeches and reported on what they heard. The Institute waited to see if contacts with me would freeze German government support. It did not. Finally, in December, a high-ranking official at the German Embassy in Washington told Institute officials he was "astonished and pleased" at the "positive attitude toward Germany" that I had displayed at a speaking appearance. Within days, I was invited to take an office at the Institute.

That the Institute's trustees—Americans with a particular interest in Germany, either through business, studies or family connections—would be so nervous that they continued to walk on eggshells even after senior German officials offered assurances is a remarkable illustration of the fragility of the German-American relationship. That an American institution would find it advisable to run a low-level personnel decision past German government officials at the highest level is even more stunning. And yet this case is not out of line with daily relations between Germans and Americans. Beneath public statements of trust and friendship, private fears and outright antagonism are pervasive. Both sides know there are darker, deeper levels to the relationship—and that knowledge leads to all manner of subterfuge and backbiting.

In the mid-1980s, as American Jewish survivors of the Holocaust raised money and planned what would become the Holocaust Memorial Museum in Washington, the German government—fearful that the museum would poison the country's image in the United States—approached museum organizers and offered to contribute several million dollars if a section on postwar German democracy were added to the exhibition. Miles Lerman, chairman of international relations for the U.S. Holocaust Memorial Council, told me the offer was immediately rejected. When my article about the offer appeared on the front page of the *Post,* the Kohl government denied that any offer had been made. Wolfgang Pordzik, longtime director of the Washington office of the Konrad Adenauer Foundation, the political education affiliate of Kohl's party, denied that his organization had approached the Bush administration to suggest that U.S. high schools add the study of postwar German democracy to their Holocaust history courses.

The night after the article appeared, Pordzik called me at home in Berlin and protested that he had no objection to the museum and would never have lobbied the Americans to teach postwar German history. "The story of Germany after 1945 is a story we Germans have to tell," he said. "Your story is

very destructive. I have devoted my entire career to German-Jewish reconciliation. And this is very damaging. My German friends already suspect
me of being more Jewish than I should be." Pordzik said he knew nothing
about any offer to museum organizers. "I've always told Germans who are
worried about the museum that they are overreacting: 'Don't get overdefen-
sive.' "

But the next day, a senior official in the Kohl government told me that
Pordzik himself was one of three Germans who conveyed the original offer
to the Holocaust Memorial Council. "It was done in a way they could deny
it," the official said. "Some people here really didn't know about the offer.
Some didn't want to know. But Pordzik made the offer personally."

German reaction to the museum was overwhelmingly hostile. The *Frankfurter Allgemeine* called the construction of Holocaust museums in the
United States a "ritual invocation of a small slice of history that would lead
to new prejudices." The same newspaper's Günther Gillessen wrote a
scathing attack on the Washington museum, culminating in the statement
that "some visitors cannot bear it, keel over or bail out—that's how in-
tensely the tools of modern media psychology are employed." The only
problem with Gillessen's dramatic picture is that it was an utter fabrication:
His article appeared more than a month before the museum opened its
doors in April 1993. Other German commentators said the Holocaust Museum "relentlessly documents only the bad side of the Germans" and re-
gretted that no one, not even President Clinton, could "exert any influence
over the powerful Jewish organizers." A few dissenters wondered why the
museum had to be in Washington rather than, as the *Frankfurter Rundschau*
said, "where it actually belonged—in Berlin or Dachau." But the dominant
view was that of Hubertus von Morr, a speechwriter for Kohl, who told me
the Chancellery was "very much opposed to the Holocaust Museum. We
cannot understand why America wants its young people to go to that museum and come out saying, 'My God, how can we be allies with that den of
devils?' "

Even if Germans feared that decades of PR work in America would be
undermined by the Holocaust Museum, the clumsy attempt to buy their way
into the project and the open mocking of such museums—"Hell as Theme
Park" was *Der Spiegel*'s term for the Los Angeles Holocaust museum—were
at least counterproductive. As Leon Wieseltier noted in the *New Republic*,
"There is something comic about the Germans asking the Jews to help them
with the image of what the Germans did to the Jews." Whether the issue is
neo-Nazis, Holocaust remembrance, or even something less emotion-laden,
German dependence on foreign opinion has sentenced the country to a
chronic case of the Chicken Little syndrome.

For centuries, foreign countries have controlled Germany's fate. Since the Thirty Years War, foreigners have been in league to prevent German unification. Fear of Germany has driven the schemes of world diplomacy in every era, and today is no different. Even in a theoretically united western Europe, where countries are more interdependent than ever before, suspicion of the Germans is a powerful engine of policy. And if the Germans became more sensitive, even somewhat paranoid, in the postwar period, didn't they have good reason? They were under the thumb of their occupiers. They were hostage to the whims of the superpowers. They remade themselves in the American image, then resented themselves for having become "too American."

The Germans were and remain an insular people. Given their druthers, they'd just as soon be like the Swiss, an unthreatening people satisfied to be ignored or admired. But then along comes some foreigner who calls them Nazis, and the past bursts into the present. Once more, the desire to be liked, to be one of the guys, to be accepted, to be permitted to move on, comes to the fore. "The more the foreign media reports on the violence in Germany, the more we feel we'll never be liked," a banker friend once told me. "We behave like a child. If a child is not liked, he does something bad."

In 1994, the Bulgarian-American artist Christo, after nearly two decades of lobbying and begging, finally persuaded German legislators to allow him to wrap the Reichstag, Berlin's ambivalent symbol of glory and tragedy, in a shimmering silver drop cloth. Christo prefers not to interpret his works, leaving them deliciously ambiguous. So he never answered the insistent questions of legislators who eventually decided to let him wrap the building: Was he wrapping the Reichstag to repress its past, or to reveal it? In a culture of extremes, many Germans felt they had to know. What would the Christo event mean? What would the foreigners say? Every event becomes a nerve-wracking test: Will *Schindler's List* be a success in Germany, and what will the world say about how we react? Can an exhibition of pictures by Hitler's personal photographer be shown in Berlin? What will the foreigners think?

Perhaps some foreigners see Germans as many Germans cannot yet see themselves—as a people who know what they do not want to be, but haven't yet figured out what they are. Distance informs and liberates. By hanging onto every commentary, every news article, every utterance of a Washington pundit or a British prime minister, the Germans act like a child weeping as she plucks the last petals from a daisy. "He loves me, he loves me not." We understand the fragility and simplicity of her emotions. And we know that children grow up. Do nations?

PART
IV

—◄○►—

The Wall
Between
Germans
and the Past

IN A SMALL eastern German village along the banks of the Elbe River, I happened upon a charming little church, shuttered and neglected. As I wandered around the church grounds, Undine Schmidt emerged from her house with a welcoming smile and an invitation to coffee and cake. Over the years, I would have many a meal at the Schmidts' house. We went shopping together, played at the local swimming hole, strolled through what remained of Hohenwarthe's village center. But what was most remarkable about our first meeting was the silence after our chitchat sputtered to a halt. Undine let a few moments go by, drew a deep breath, and then volunteered a chronicle of her family's generations in Hohenwarthe, complete with a cataloging of her ancestor's political leanings and wartime losses. Only when she was finished, only when she had bared her history, did she look up, smile again, and ask, "Should we have that coffee?"

My wife and I spent many mornings in Bonn with a bright, warm, funny woman who opened her heart to us as she tutored us in German. When Sabine Ebel revealed to us many months later that her father had been a Nazi general, her throat tightened, she cast her eyes down, and her face burned with embarrassment. She unloaded the fact out of the blue, and then she could not figure out what else to say, just as her father had refused to discuss his past with her. I wanted then to embrace Sabine, somehow to prove to her that she was not her father. There was no question of blame. Yet, to ignore the deep imprint her family history had made upon Sabine would be wrong. She knew that.

Later, government officials would reprimand me for "forever bringing history" into my news articles. But could one fairly keep history at bay? Richard von Weizsäcker, Germany's president until 1994 and a man who defended his father in the Nazi war crimes trials, saw his job in the years after unification as that of a thinking man's scold, "Germans don't want to be hindered by the past anymore," he told me. "My main task is to remind my western German compatriots that we must take on our history and work through it."

The stories that conclude this book tell of Germans who have chosen to deal directly with the baggage of a society laden with secrets and taboos. These are Germans who have had greatly differing experiences, even though they share similar backgrounds. The fall of one Wall has helped them to discover other, more abstract walls—and to scale them.

15

◄O►

Lost and Found

In 1968, 1984 happened to Gabriele Püschel. From the moment she fell in love with a man from the wrong side of the Berlin Wall, her life turned into a war of attrition against East Germany's totalitarian system. She never had a chance. She became a pawn in an east-west espionage tangle. She found herself wondering whether her own lover was a spy. She risked her life in an escape from East Germany so far-fetched even the West Germans found it hard to believe. And she lost her son. The East German government took her boy away as part of a secret policy of forced adoptions, a cruel, vengeful practice in which hundreds, perhaps thousands, of children were stolen from parents whose only crime was that they had gone west or opposed the government. And then, even after communism failed, even after her country ceased to exist, Gabriele's war dragged on. Currencies changed, politicians came and went, but those whose lives fell victim to the utopian passions and repressive arrogance of the communist system knew no peace.

Well before the Wall was built in 1961, Gabriele bounced up against the strictures of the socialist system. She was a bright teenager, a good student who wanted to attend university. But the government reserved higher education for the offspring of the worker-heroes at the center of the Moscow-imposed ideology. Gabriele's parents were a barber and a seamstress, hardly intellectual pursuits, but university slots were dispensed primarily to families of lower "social status," farmers and miners, for example. Gabriele had to settle for night school.

In 1964, while she studied Romance languages by night and worked days as a translator at the Cuban embassy in East Berlin, Gabriele met Nikolas Kapogiannis, a Greek national who was studying engineering in West Berlin. Nikos came through the Wall as a tourist and the two began an east-west relationship, a logistically difficult but fairly common occurrence in those days. Theirs was a Cinderella existence—one-day visitor's passes to the east expired at midnight, and Nikos had to leap up from romantic dinners and bolt from slow walks and serious talks to race back to his side of the Wall. After a glorious and exhausting few months together, the couple craved some semblance of normalcy. They applied for permission to marry. In early 1965, the request was denied, no reason stated. Nikos and Gabriele, then twenty-one, kept applying—unsuccessfully—for a marriage license. No reason was ever given.

"In the west, you always want a reason," Gabriele, a tiny, hyperactive woman with fingernails bitten to the quick, said many years later. "In East Germany, the reason was that the man says no. The reason was the communist party." Later, Gabriele found out that the Stasi had grown suspicious of her both because she had so many contacts with foreigners through her embassy post, and because she had challenged the state by continuing her education after being denied entrance to university.

In October 1966, Nikos and Gabriele, who managed to see each other three or four times a week, had a son. Through bribes and connections, Nikos arranged a religious marriage at an East Berlin Russian Orthodox church serving Soviet soldiers. The marriage was invalid in the eyes of the state, but a blessed event to the couple and the groom's parents back in Greece. Nikos and Gabriele believed their legal problems would soon be solved. "When you're young," she said, "nothing seems forever except love. Nobody believed the Wall would last. It was a time that would end."

But as little Aristoteles began to roll over and then crawl, mother and father became more desperate to live as a family. They traveled to Bulgaria to scope out the possibility of escaping from the socialist bloc into neighboring Greece, but it was the time of the junta in Greece and the border, never a friendly place, seemed forbidding. Like so many other East Germans, Gabriele and her friends dreamt of a dramatic leap to the west, but the reality of shootings along the Wall, exploding mines in the waters dividing the two Germanys, and electrified fencing along mountainous parts of the border was thoroughly discouraging.

Late in 1967, Nikos' visits suddenly became less frequent. When he did cross over, he would explain that East German border guards were giving him trouble. He assured Gabriele there was no problem in the marriage; on the contrary, he had been talking to important people in the west who might be able to get them out. One day, he brought someone he called his stepsister to see Gabriele. The woman asked lots of questions but volunteered little. Years later, Gabriele would learn from government documents that the "stepsister" was a CIA agent.

Desperate to unite his family, Nikos had gotten embroiled in the never-ending duel between eastern and western intelligence agencies in Berlin. The East German Stasi, seeing the Greek student cross the border several times a week, knowing how painfully Nikos wanted to be together with his family, put the screws on him. He could keep visiting his wife and baby, the agents said—if he agreed to feed them information about Gabriele, her friends and her contacts at the university and the Cuban Embassy.

Nikos went to the U.S. Mission in West Berlin for help. The Americans, eager for an inside look at the Stasi, told Nikos to cooperate with the East Germans and report back to them. Nikos still came east, but less frequently. Gabriele was getting scared. Her husband was slowly slipping away and she found herself under increasingly tight surveillance. She had begun hanging out at the university with the folksinger Wolf Biermann and the scientist and political essayist Robert Havemann, prominent young East Berlin dissidents who shared her frustration with the contradiction between the ideals of socialism and the reality of the Wall. Twice in the summer of 1968, Gabriele was taken to a Stasi office for interrogations. The second time, agents took her identity card, making it impossible for her to travel outside East Berlin.

By then, Nikos had stopped coming altogether. Through friends, Gabriele searched for him, but learned nothing. She would not learn the full story for five years. Nikos, it turned out, had done as the Americans asked, but the Stasi either caught wind of his U.S. connection or decided they didn't need him any longer. Barred from his usual way into East Berlin, Nikos tried a more circuitous route. He was caught, arrested, charged with spying for the CIA, and sentenced to eight years in prison. He served five.

Gabriele was twenty-four years old and in deep trouble. During one of her interrogations, a Stasi officer showed her a protocol, signed by Nikos, detailing her contacts with known dissidents. All at once, she feared for Nikos and suspected that he was working against her, either for the Stasi or in some desperate attempt to get Aristoteles out of the east, with or without her. Stripped of her identity card, subject of an imprisoned spy's protocol, target of nearly constant surveillance, Gabriele felt the weight of the system bearing down on her. "It was like they had put me in prison but they still wanted to see who I associated with," she said. Her apartment was repeatedly searched. Her neighbors were asked about her friends. People who knew how the Stasi worked told Gabriele she would be taken prisoner in a matter of days.

She had to get out. She had no idea how to do it, but figured the best shot was from Bulgaria, whose borders with Greece and Turkey were less tightly guarded than the western boundaries of the frontline communist countries. Gabriele decided she would have to flee without little Aristoteles, then two and a half. "Taking him was impossible. I didn't know where or how I would go. You just act to save yourself, all on instinct. He was safe with my parents and I would get him later, once I was secure in the west. But right then, I was in panic. I just had to get out."

Gabriele asked to borrow a close friend's identity card, without which she had no prayer of leaving the city, let alone the country. The friend was reluctant; helping someone flee was punishable by ten years in prison. "I'll say I stole the card from you," Gabriele told her friend. "Wait two weeks and report it stolen." The friend agreed. On August 20, 1968, Gabriele asked local police for a visa to Bulgaria. Since the photo on her friend's ID card looked nothing like Gabriele, she told the police the visa was for the friend, who was tied up at work.

The next day, Gabriele went to work at the Cuban Embassy, where a driver told her that Soviet tanks had rolled into Czechoslovakia overnight, crushing the Prague Spring rebellion. Borders were sealed; Gabriele's route to Bulgaria was closed off. A few days later, she went to the police to pick up the visa, but her application was denied. No reason was stated. But the police said the visa might be granted if Gabriele's friend planned to travel by air. Without saying so directly—they couldn't since East Germany had not informed its people of the Prague invasion—the police were diverting all travel around (or over) Czechoslovakia.

Gabriele could not afford a flight, but booked a seat anyway, got the visa and then canceled the flight reservation, hoping somehow to use the air visa for rail transit through Poland, the Soviet Union and Rumania, the circuitous passage necessary to reach Bulgaria without going through Czechoslovakia. She left Aristoteles with her parents, telling them only that she was going on a one-week vacation. In honest ignorance, they could answer the inevitable Stasi questions about Gabriele's disappearance without lying.

Gabriele switched her own photo for her friend's on the identity card, went to the train station and asked for a ticket to Warsaw. But your visa is for Bulgaria, the clerk said.

Yes, Gabriele said, but the police told me this is how I must go. She counted on the fact that the clerk, like virtually everyone else in the country, secretly listened to western radio, knew about the Czech invasion and knew that the police could very well have sent a traveler on such a circuitous route. "Luckily, Germans are still like this," Gabriele said. "If you say the police said something, it cannot be questioned."

The same ruse got Gabriele past border guards and the East German consul in Warsaw. Within a couple of days, she found herself locked inside a Soviet railcar, its windows shuttered against the officially denied medieval poverty of Bessarabia, joining hundreds of communist functionaries and the occasional tourist on a long detour that no one mentioned and everyone understood.

The beginning of September brought Gabriele to Sofia, Bulgaria's capital. She hadn't the slightest idea what to do. She spent a month in a student hostel, wandering the city by day. She sent a postcard to a friend, telling him to contact her parents, assure them she was all right and urge them not to report her as missing. Riding Sofia's trams, spending afternoons at the main library, she searched for contacts. One day, she met a Senegalese fire-eater, a performer in a traveling circus. He invited her to see the circus in a town near the Turkish border. She said she would, but knew she wouldn't.

The next day, Gabriele summoned the courage to make her move. She walked past police guards and into a parking lot where truckers who made the long haul from West Germany to Iran were overnighting. On the pretense of hitching a ride to see the Senegalese circus, Gabriele, who had studied Farsi and was fascinated by Iranian literature, befriended some Iranian truckers. They were happy for the company and took her along. As they neared the border, Gabriele made her pitch for a ride beyond the circus and on to Turkey. She found Farsi words she had no idea she knew and spun a tale of a lost boyfriend in Iran, of a lifelong love for a country beyond her reach. One trucker turned her down, but another bit.

Worried sick about getting caught, the driver insisted on waiting until daytime, when border checks were lighter. More than fifty miles before the border, the driver pulled over and instructed Gabriele to crawl under the truck. He showed her how to suspend herself from two pieces of the undercarriage, gripping metal with her hands and ankles while the rest of her body swung freely over the spinning axle. It was October 5, and after some harrowing moments at the border, where she heard guards chatting, watched their feet in the cold fluorescent light, and listened to the deafening roar of cicadas, Gabriele was across. The trucker finished his prayers to Allah, broke out a bottle of Johnny Walker, and collapsed into sobs of relief.

In Istanbul, West German authorities found Gabriele's story hard to swallow. After all her travail, Gabriele insisted on going to Iran, where she wanted to study and earn enough money to retrieve her son. The West Germans said she could go to only one place—West Germany. Gabriele appealed to a Turkish police agent, who pumped her for information and invited her to a series of meals. He was the first person Gabriele told about the boy she had left behind. He said he might be able to get Aristoteles out, but it would take several months. In the meantime, they agreed, Gabriele would fulfill her dream and go to Iran. After several months of adventures in Teheran and Afghanistan, where she saved money working as a translator for German engineers at Radio Kabul, she returned to her Turkish friend. He told her he had arranged for her son to be taken out of East Germany through a contact in Amsterdam. With her new West German passport, she traveled to Holland, met the Dutchman and discovered she would have to wait again. She moved to Frankfurt, West Germany, and got a typing job.

Aside from a postcard she had sent from Istanbul to East Berlin informing a friend she was safely out of the East Bloc, Gabriele had told no one where she was. Yet one night in Frankfurt, her phone rang. It was a Herr Hofmann. "You know me," he said. "I was your interrogator in Berlin."

"He called me Puschi," Gabriele recalled. "It was a nickname only my very closest friends knew. He said, 'You've been very clever, but don't think you can keep going. We are on to you.' "

It was July 1969. In a matter of weeks, Gabriele would find out just how serious the East German government was. That summer, almost a year after she had left her son first with his grandparents and then with her friends, Gabriele had given up on the Turk's mysterious ways and was busy trying to arrange for her friend Gisela Dreyer to take Aristoteles to visit her elderly grandmother in West Germany. The boy would then simply fail to return from the visit. But Dreyer couldn't get permission to make the trip.

Gabriele also set up a uniquely Berlin meeting. On September 18, Dreyer brought Aristoteles to his side of the Wall while his mother climbed a wooden staircase on the western side. Mother and son waved at one another from a distance of about a hundred feet. Dreyer took a picture. It would be the last time Gabriele saw her son as a child.

A few days later, East Berlin police knocked on Dreyer's door. They had orders to take the boy to a state children's home, where, the officers assured Dreyer, she could visit Aristoteles. Over in the West, meanwhile, authorities told Gabriele to file for family unification, a cumbersome but sometimes successful process by which the two estranged states sought to handle the thousands of separated families, cross-border marriages and other human casualties of Germany's division.

Gabriele moved to West Berlin to pursue her case, but she had nothing to go on beyond the news that Aristoteles had been taken. Some months later, a friend in the east wrote in a letter that she had seen Aristoteles in a Catholic orphanage. Gabriele wrote to the Katharinenstift Children's Home, and wrote again and again, but received no response until 1972. The orphanage notified her then that Aristoteles had been there in the fall of 1969, but was later taken to live with other parents. That was the last trace. Gabriele's boy was gone.

In November 1969, less than six weeks after Aristoteles arrived at the Catholic orphanage, Klaus and Petra Voss, loyal communists who were, respectively, editor of a Marxist-Leninist publishing house and a teacher of socialist ideology, came to visit. The Vosses, unable to have a child of their own, had long wanted to adopt. A party friend had told them that a nice little boy had just arrived at the orphanage. (At the family's request, I use pseudonyms for the Vosses.)

"I saw him and he said, 'Are you my *Papi?*' " Klaus Voss recalled. "And I said, 'Well, OK.' He looked so friendly. It was decided right then that we would take him home." On November 6, the Vosses became Aristoteles' foster parents. They knew about the boy's past, knew his mother had gone to the west, knew she had not given up her parental rights. The Vosses got the communist party to assist them in adopting the boy. The couple also accepted the many parcels Gabriele sent to Aristoteles throughout the 1970s in care of the East Berlin district youth office, never knowing if the gifts would reach her son. Even as they dressed the boy in clothes Gabriele had sent, the Vosses asked the youth office to change the child's name so his natural mother could not find him. The government did not object.

A couple of years later, when it came time for an adoption proceeding, the East Germans stuck to regulations and ordered a court hearing. Eva Krebs, a supervisor in the East Berlin youth office, asked the court to strip Gabriele of her rights and award the boy to the Vosses. "The mother left the German Democratic Republic without observing police registration requirements," Krebs wrote. "For the security of the child, it was necessary to arrange care of the child."

The East Berlin court asked a West Berlin judge to forward a handful of questions to Gabriele as part of the adoption proceedings. Gabriele answered as clearly as she could. She remained the boy's mother and never had the slightest intention of giving him up. She was fully capable of caring for the boy and would produce any evidence they wished to that effect. She had sought since 1969 by every possible legal means to unify her family. "I want my son to come to me and I will pay all his costs," she wrote.

On May 11, 1972, the East Berlin court ruled in a sentence of classic socialist construction: "The accused's [Gabriele] permission for the adoption of the child Aristoteles Püschel is replaced." The edict was signed, "With socialist greetings . . ."

"Replaced." Gabriele's authority over her own child had been replaced by that of the government. The East German government took little Aristoteles, changed his name to Anton, and gave him to the Vosses. For the next fifteen years, Gabriele lived the hell of every parent's worst fantasies. At first, she followed the West German government's advice, keeping her efforts on behalf of her son quiet and official. In 1972, she could take the silence no longer and went public, telling her story to *Der Spiegel* and to anyone else who would listen. She appealed to the United Nations, to American presidents, to reporters around the world.

In 1973, Nikos was amnestied from prison. Soon thereafter, Gabriele received a one-paragraph letter from the West German domestic intelligence agency, informing her she was suspected of spying for East Germany. After his release, Nikos—knowing nothing of Gabriele's escape and suspecting that she might be working for the Stasi—had told his story to the West Germans, who wondered whether East Germany might be using Aristoteles to pressure Gabriele.

Investigators soon cleared Gabriele. She met Nikos once more, but they were captives of their mutual suspicions. "He was not sure if I was the traitor and I was not sure if he was the traitor," she said. "Without this system, maybe I would be happy with Nikos today. But the system destroyed our confidence in each other. You can get over a relationship with a man or a woman. But a child is forever." The couple divorced.

Tormented by the knowledge that her child lived less than a mile away but—because of the Wall—completely out of reach, Gabriele conducted an increasingly desperate, painfully public search, banging on the doors of both Germanys, to no avail. But Gabriele's publicity campaign rattled the Stasi and the East German state. In 1976, after Gabriele's biggest publicity splash in the western press, the communist propaganda machine struck back. An editorial in the communist party daily, *Neues Deutschland,* called her "the lies machine." On the east's antiwestern TV show, *Black Channel,* Eduard von Schnitzler spent an entire broadcast attacking her. Gabriele's PR campaign elicited more than indignant denunciations. The East German Education Ministry, run by Margot Honecker, issued a memo that same year ordering that forced adoptions be halted. "I was clearly getting on their nerves," Gabriele said. "If the West German government had pushed then, something could have broken. By then, my child had been with the adoptive parents only three or four years. It would have been easy to reverse it."

But the case—and relations between the two German states—were too complex to allow such direct intercession. While Gabriele tried to reveal one of East Germany's most perfidious practices, West German leaders pressed to smooth relations with the communist state. With the Social Democratic government of Willy Brandt pushing to complete the first treaty with East Germany, Gabriele's plight fell on deaf ears. A high-ranking Social Democratic official, Egon Francke, stated in the West German parliament that there had been no forced adoptions in the east. Years later, Francke was asked how he could have denied a practice that was clearly wrong, clearly ongoing. He claimed he did not remember anything about the topic.

Gabriele never gave up looking, but she also tried to create another life. She pursued an academic career as an Orientalist. In 1971, when she was twenty-seven, she remarried, changed her name to Yonan, and, a few years later, had another son, David, who would fulfill his mother's dreams by becoming a professional musician.

Throughout those long, empty years, Gabriele didn't know it, but there was one person who could have helped—and tried to, if halfheartedly. In 1976, West Berliner Ilse Böhme read a newspaper story about Gabriele accompanied by a photo of Aristoteles as a toddler. Böhme recognized the child. He was Anton, adopted child of her East German brother, Klaus Voss. On her next trip across the Wall to visit Klaus, Böhme told the Vosses about the poor woman in the west who was Anton's real mother. Voss sent his sister away, told the Stasi about the visit, and arranged for Böhme to be banned from the east for nine years.

Böhme did nothing further. But in August 1987, when Anton was twenty-one and as disgusted with the communist system as his long-lost mother had been, a friend of Anton's who escaped to the west showed up at Böhme's house and asked for 20,000 marks (about $13,000) to arrange her nephew's flight west. Böhme wouldn't pay. But she did look up Gabriele's maiden name in the West Berlin phone book and found her parents, who had migrated west after their retirement, as elderly easterners were encouraged to do (so the strapped East German government wouldn't have to pay their pensions). Böhme called and asked the Püschels if they had a daughter whose son lived in the east. Gabriele's parents met Böhme, who agreed to cross the Wall and tell Anton that his mother was alive and still searching for him.

"I knew if he was my son, he would know that his was a stupid country and he would want to leave," Gabriele said.

Anton's fragmented memories of his first years were sometimes so sharp, so vivid, that the Stasi agents assigned to keep watch on the boy warned fellow agents to be careful of the boy's powers of recollection. Even as a toddler, Anton would ask his parents about a wooden dog, which, when pressed, would drop a piece of chocolate. You must have dreamt it, his parents would say. (What Anton remembered, Gabriele would say later, was her mother's wooden chicken, a musical toy that dispensed chocolate eggs.) Anton would ask his parents about an "Aunt Gisela" whom he could picture in his mind. Again, they would tell the boy his imagination was in overdrive. (Anton was remembering Gabriele's trusted friend Gisela Dreyer, known to young Aristoteles as "Aunt Gisela.") And Anton remembered a woman with long, straight hair, hair that somehow summoned his deepest emotions. Those memories, he kept to himself.

It wasn't until Anton was fourteen, when he got the identity card that all German adults carry, that memories of the Catholic orphanage slipped back into his consciousness. His parents showed Anton his birth certificate, then told him the official East German version of his story, that his natural mother had abandoned him. Anton's relations with his adoptive parents— he came to refer to them as his "stepparents"—soured. The boy felt betrayed, lost. Despite the snapshots of the deep past that had occasionally flashed through his mind, Anton never suspected that the Vosses were anything but his true and only parents. Now, he was angry beyond expression. He wanted to find his real mother and hear her story. How could she have abandoned him? How could she have let all those years go by without the slightest effort to find out if he was even alive? The Vosses made no effort to let Anton in on the truth, but neither did they speak ill of Gabriele. They only wanted everything to be as it had been. For an adolescent who suddenly learned that the certainties in his life were cover stories for a mysterious and forbidden truth, it was too much. One night when he was fifteen, Anton, by then a regular in East Berlin's underground punk scene and something of a renegade in school, got roaring drunk and, filled with liquid courage, poured out his rage at his parents. He would no longer be the good communist son, active in the right political groups at school, parroting back socialist interpretations of novels as his teachers commanded.

Klaus Voss, an alumnus of Hitler Youth who lost a brother in the war, believed in the system with every bone in his body. He and his wife stayed in the Party of Democratic Socialism—successor to the communist Socialist Unity party—for years after unification. Klaus had relatives in high party posts all around the country. To the Vosses, the gift of Anton was no less miraculous than the parting of the Red Sea. The party to which they had given unending support had graciously met their deepest need. The Vosses returned the favor by raising their boy to be a loyal, committed communist. Even after others in the neighborhood let their kids watch western TV, the Vosses refused. (Later, Anton would suspect that their real motive was to assure he saw no western news reports on forced adoptions.)

And now, their son had discovered the outlines of the harsh truth from which they had sought to spare him. By the time Anton was sixteen, he could stand his home no longer. He moved out, quit school, and sank, without a job, into the barely tolerated music underground. The elder Vosses were frightened by their boy's descent into a lifestyle Klaus knew could only end badly, both for Anton and for his parents. The state expected parents to keep their kids in line; those who didn't often suffered at work. Klaus even changed the locks at home in a vain effort to build a barrier between his own life and that of his wayward son. But later, when Anton decided he had to get out of the country, the Vosses accepted reality and did what they could to help his application for an exit visa.

Until he learned about his adoption, Anton thought his only connection in the west was his Aunt Ilse. As it turned out, she was all he needed to find his mother. Suddenly, from out of nowhere, luck and history were conspiring to return some sanity to Gabriele Yonan's life. The son she had last seen peeking over the Berlin Wall, standing on tiptoes to wave at a figure who was supposed to be his mother, reappeared as an adult. Thanks to Böhme, Gabriele had her boy's new name, and thus a phone number. She picked up the phone one evening in late 1987, dialed, and heard a man's voice. "Voss," he said.

"*Hallo,*" Gabriele said, and she told him who she was.

"*Hallo du,*" Anton answered.

"How should I answer that?" Gabriele recalled thinking. "And I said, 'Say Mama to me.'"

Her boy called her Mama. She called him Toti, short for Aristoteles.

Three times a week, they would talk, sometimes for hours, she detailing what she had done to bring him home, he telling his life story. "It was so strange to hear someone with my voice, who had the same pivotal experiences in reading, who used the same phrases and had similar humor," Anton said. "We had four or five months of getting to know each other purely by phone, up to six hours at a time. It was fascinating at the beginning. She had endured such loneliness."

Through Wolfgang Vogel, the East Berlin lawyer who won fame and fortune setting up east-west spy swaps, Anton, now of legal age, sought permission to leave the country and reunite his family. It was 1988, and the repressive machinery of East Germany was slowing down, rusting over. Anton got his visa. On May 3, he and his girlfriend went west. Anton moved into the Yonans' flat, a delicately decorated place with a pink and white sitting room, classical silhouettes and antique string instruments mounted over the bookcases.

The reunion was strained. Anton quickly realized the west was much more alien than he had expected. He felt as though he belonged nowhere, a sense that would hang over him for years to come. And in only a few days, he concluded that he and his real mother were at once too alike and too different for comfort. They both had expectations that could never be fulfilled. As much as she wanted to uncover a mother-son relationship paved over by two decades of lies and harsh political realities, Gabriele realized Anton was not the man she would have raised. She wanted her son to learn her love of music, take on her passion for learning, soak up her facility for language. But the man she met, an angular, working-class guy who came with low-rent girlfriend and tacky clothes, was an unschooled machinist, nice enough, but, as Gabriele angrily told herself, an intellectually stunted prole. Who had done this to her child? Who had the right? Who had the nerve?

Anton saw a bitter, even hateful woman. At times, he thought her lust for vengeance was so deep, so real that he could see her taking a pistol to the east to search out the bureaucrats who had stolen her child. Anton bristled at his mother's constant comments about wonderful David, her other son. "Your brother is a violin wonder," she would say. "What about you?"

Anton would tell her about the illegal rock concerts he had helped organize in the east, about the thick files the Stasi kept on him and his band, about the thieves and car dealers, punks and skinheads, actors and musicians who were his friends and fellow misfits in a society that insisted on conformity. Gabriele didn't hear a word of it. "He just tells these stories because he wants to be like me," she said. "He wasn't a dissident, he was a rebellious adolescent. He and his little gang were buying Russian soldiers' equipment and selling it in the west." She answered his stories with tales of the "real dissidents" she knew in her last years in the East.

Anton's school records show he played the piano, but only for one year, in 1974. "I had thought maybe he would be a pianist," Gabriele said. "But the parents there were so stupid. They fed him and housed him, but otherwise, they mostly left him alone."

David Yonan, who crossed over to the east to visit Anton several times before his half-brother came west, challenged his mother's critical attitude. He was thrilled to have an older brother. "Education is not everything," he said. Even as sparks flew between Anton and Gabriele, Anton and David, eight years apart in age, grew close, despite—or perhaps because of—their mother's invidious comparisons.

Gabriele withdrew. She could not hide her disappointment. "When I got him, he was a machinist, a construction worker, a window cleaner," she said. "He was wild. It's not easy to love a child who looks like this. Really, it's not the same thing as having a small child grow up." She held up a photo of Anton looking dour, even a bit surly. His hair is unkempt, his eyes mistrustful.

Anton took the examination for university study and began a course in dentistry. But he and his "physical mother," as he referred to her, could not find common ground. "It was like a foreign world, with its own way of life," Anton said. "My brother practiced his violin eight hours a day. My physical mother thought my girlfriend of the time was no good." After a couple of months, Anton moved out. "I feel like I'm between a rock and a hard place," he said. "Between my physical mother, who got me out, whom I feel a duty toward, and my parents, to whom I simply feel more bound."

It took some months, but eventually Gabriele stopped calling her son Toti, and managed to blurt out the name Anton. That, she realized, was who he had become. Anton brought to the west childhood photos in which he wore clothes Gabriele had sent east all those years ago. The boy never knew the source of the coveted western clothing. "Anton doesn't have these nineteen years of victim in him," Gabriele said. "He didn't have a bad childhood. He had what a child needs. He only feels wronged in retrospect. And really, the fact that I was in the west helped him get out of East Germany. I was his way to freedom."

At times, Gabriele was more charitable. "Everybody says how intelligent he is. I was very disappointed at first. And then you find a reality you can live with. Intelligence can differ. Maybe his intelligence did not become very clear to me right away. I went out with him once with Mrs. Mauritz [the biological mother in another forced adoption case.] And she called me later and said, 'You are so lucky. My son is in a homeless shelter.' Many people told me, 'Why are you criticizing him? He is a young, normal and intelligent man.' It is more my problem than his, I know that. When I was sick, he called me so many times and I did not call back. I don't know. I am his mother, but there is a gap which I cannot fill."

Even after Anton moved out, Gabriele was demanding. She insisted he visit every week for dinner. He would not. She knew grown children often didn't do that anymore in western Germany, but still, she was hurt. When he did show up, once every few months, she angrily rejected him. She could not stand Anton's intolerance, his comments about Turks or "the Moslem onslaught." "I try to get over it with my intellect," she said. "In reality, nobody gets back his child. In reality, the system has won."

After he moved out, Anton kept his distance from both his families. He worked as a DJ at West Berlin discos, but could never recreate the feeling of community he had in the eastern music scene. Over time, he realized that while Gabriele thought she had kept her son at the center of her life all those years, she had actually lived with a fixed, idealized notion of what that toddler had become. Anton watched families of other forced adoptions and knew that his was the best case, perhaps the only one where the child maintained relations—however strained—with both sets of parents. Still, he was miserable. For two years, Anton and Gabriele did not speak. Eventually, mother and son resumed contact, if sporadically. There was even a birthday celebration that brought the Vosses and the Yonans together, peaceably.

It was not their first meeting: Soon after the Wall fell, Gabriele had visited the Vosses, who served her coffee, cake and a peace offer. The atmosphere was, as diplomats say, cordial. The Vosses said they had done their best for the boy. They urged Gabriele not to seek revenge. Gabriele, who said she could not berate the people her son considers his parents, was controlled, even friendly.

"You can't go back," Klaus Voss said.

"No," Gabriele said. "But I can find the people responsible for this."

Anton had rekindled relations with his adoptive parents; they told one another of their guilt, the pain of losing what they all agreed had been a pretty damn good family. Klaus Voss told Anton about the hurt of losing both his only child and, for the second time in his years, the system, the life he had believed in. The revolution came too late for the elder Voss: He would, most likely, never work again.

Living with a new girlfriend in a tiny two-room apartment in the western part of the city, Anton, by then twenty-six, enjoyed the leisurely pace of a western student. He dressed in black—jeans, sweatshirt, boots. He and his girl shared a mattress on the floor. A huge bowl was filled with Gauloises cigarette stubs and ashes. The walls were covered with bookcases (Stalin, Engels, Dostoevsky, Umberto Eco, Charles Bukowski) and black and white photos of Aryan nudes, a man and woman reaching up toward a dark, cloudy sky. On good days, Anton tried to put his fractured life together. Once, he sought out his natural father, who owned a Greek restaurant in Berlin. Anton ate dinner, watched the unsuspecting Nikos, and then— somewhat angrily, he admitted—approached the stunned, terrified father, who refused to speak to the young man who claimed to be his son. Later, Anton knew he'd blown the opportunity.

Sometimes, Anton could joke about his life ("I'm a form of twins research"), but he was a troubled young man. He tried cutting himself off from easterners. He wanted so badly to assimilate into the west. But it didn't happen. He couldn't get the east out of his system. He retained his legal address there. He talked about the inferiority complex he and other Ossis felt. It was a feeling of disconnection that infected easterners wherever they lived, east or west. Anton's smooth, gentle face was often distorted by a self-pitying pout I had seen on so many Ossis' faces. Older generations were worse hit, but it was the difficulty young people had in adapting to the new life that was most affecting.

Even though the government was gone for good, its paper trail seemed eternal. Anton, like so many millions of easterners, became obsessed with the Stasi's account of his life, a five-hundred-page, two-volume diary that informers and agents had compiled of his last years in the east. His closest friends, he learned later, wrote down for the Stasi every detail of Anton's plans to flee west, his every political utterance, his every mention of Gabriele. The Stasi noted Anton's style of conversation, the strength of his fingers, his offhand comments to friends. Anton had read his file once, but was not permitted to copy it. For months after that first visit to the reading room at the Stasi archives—the Room of Tears, it was called, because few emerged dry-eyed from hours poring over betrayals by dearest friends and family—Anton ran over the material in his mind. He had to get his hands on those pages again. Somehow, the Stasi's version of Anton Voss was at least as important to him as his own.

Gabriele, too, lived through her documents. After Anton's first year in the west, Gabriele saw him only occasionally. But she had her files every day. In a back room of her small apartment, Gabriele kept the thick catalogues of her search, her endless ordeal. She stayed up late reading through the records that a sympathetic eastern Berlin politician gave her, trying to fill the emptiness and answer the questions that had kept her awake so many nights for so many years. Caked over with the distant, impersonal language of totalitarianism, these papers were her only replacement for the years of mothering East Germany had stolen from her. "The documents give answers," she said.

From her papers, Gabriele learned that Klaus Voss had been a group leader for the Stasi. And she found out that the Vosses had known since 1969 that Anton's real mother wanted her son back. Against her own judgment, Gabriele told all of that, every detail, to her son. "I knew he needed his lies for himself to live," she said. "They were his parents. If I were a good mother, I would let him have that. But I am hurt, too, and I want Anton to accept that the Vosses knew the truth from the start. He knows that I know, and I know that he knows."

Gabriele had fantasies of tearing through the streets, Charles Bronson–style, mowing down officials who had stolen her boy away, or condoned it, or failed to help her find him. Armed with her documents, she set out to exact some kind of justice. She returned to the sources she had tapped for information all those years ago. She called the Catholic orphanage to find out more about those murky first months after her son had vanished. But the nun who had responded to Gabriele's letter back in 1972 said she remembered nothing.

Gabriele went to the office of Eva Krebs, the East Berlin youth official who had signed the papers seeking Aristoteles' adoption. Krebs had retired, but a helpful clerk gave Gabriele her home address. On the first visit, Krebs' husband sent Gabriele away. The next morning, Gabriele found the retiree stepping out of her house and striding briskly down a narrow footpath toward a busy street. Yonan had one minute and fifty-six seconds to speak to Krebs before the woman made it to the street and walked away. This is what she said:

"You must speak to me. I have no other chance."

"No," Krebs said, staring ahead, her face frozen in a slight, polite smile. "I am terribly sorry."

"I am a mother," Gabriele resumed, waving a finger at Krebs. "I waited seventeen years for my child. And you signed this." She held out the adoption papers Krebs had signed. "You can tell me who stopped the little one from getting permission to go west. You must say it now. That I demand from you. We have to talk about this. And then I will tell you what has become of my child. I got back a window cleaner. And I have another son, who has become something completely different. All of it—you must clear it up. I wrote you letters in those days. They've been found now in my files. Letters as a mother, from woman to woman. You read those letters and still, you allowed this judgment to be made."

Gabriele paused, waited for a response. "You don't want to say anything now."

Krebs turned slightly toward this voice from the distant past, replied, "I have nothing to say," and kept on walking.

"But you must say something," Gabriele insisted. "You've seen now what has become of your country, where you stayed behind. This was about children. You knew. You could have said, precisely, exactly, that since 1969 I wanted my child. You could have said 'I am responsible for this and see it differently.' You were the caretaker. I've waited twenty years and now I want an answer from you, why you did this to me. And that you must tell me. You're silent now, but we will find a way for you to talk, a totally legal way."

Eva Krebs walked off, a pensioner in a new land, pursued by a single sheet she signed in a country that no longer existed.

Three years after Anton moved west, Gabriele was at home late one night when she got a phone call. There was a delay, as if the call was coming from far away. The man's voice threw her back twenty years. "Hello, Puschi," he said. No one had called her that in decades. "I am Hofmann. Remember, Frankfurt, Weberstrasse 16." The Stasi interrogator, the one who had found her in hiding and threatened her just before Aristoteles was taken. This time, he had another message. "The government is not interested in your investigations," he said. "Stop digging around, stop messing with the past."

Gabriele hung up and reported the call to the police. "The Stasi people are still out there," she said, "and they are afraid now. These people and the people who took my son, like in the Third Reich, were not important people. They had only a small amount of power, but they used it in the most inhuman way, like the concentration camp guards who made Jewish people suffer. I want these people to go on trial, I want these East Germans to say why they could do this. I want a show trial. No blood will run. But these people cannot live like everything is blue skies."

There would be no trial, no more confrontations. Gabriele had neither the money nor, in the end, the vengefulness necessary for such an ordeal. Anton and Gabriele, like all the victims of forced adoptions, were left to find peace with their own pasts. In many, if not most, cases, the brief, emotional reunions that took place in the first months after the Wall fell were only intervals of providence. Too much time had passed. Wounds were too deep. Children returned to the families they had known, or simply went off on their own, too pained, too confused to embrace either set of parents. Gabriele found herself always pushing Anton away as much as she wanted to pull him close. She would slip and call him David. She'd fail to return his calls. She'd look askance at his girlfriends, malign his choice of studies, belittle his naïveté. "David is cosmopolitan," she said. "Anton, with his primitive language, talks about the Turks. I say, 'Anton, your father is Greek!' In Anton, there is a fascistic element. If he were not related, I would not have contact with him. He has not become a member of this western society."

And yet Gabriele worried terribly about Anton, about the loneliness and disaffection so many easterners lived with in the west. Gabriele was hurt that Anton showed no interest in going through her files with her. He didn't respond when she offered to help him get a copy of his Stasi files. She did not know that Anton had approached me on several occasions seeking exactly that kind of help. (I got him a couple of contacts, but he followed up only sporadically.)

Three years after she had tracked down Eva Krebs, Gabriele had calmed. "I was a hunter looking for pieces of a mosaic," she said of all those years of searching. "Now, if somebody offered me a chance to go to Chile to confront the Honeckers, I would do it, just for fun. But really, there is no more left to do. I am not really satisfied. What happens between Anton and me is a story of two people now."

With only strands of memory and the mysteries of DNA to bind them, parent and child drifted into separate lives. "Why?" Gabriele asked. Her fingers nervously played with the straight black hair she kept piled into a tight bun. "All these years I kept my long hair so maybe he could recognize me one day. I had a beautiful, bright two-year-old boy. And then I met someone who is twenty years old. There is no child anymore. Future, past and present are always entwined. But that chapter is finished. Now I see my life, as Brecht would say, as an optimistic tragedy."

16

Back in the Middle Again

The eternal yesterday threatens to suffocate our country's every future.
—Konrad Weiss, *filmmaker, former East German revolutionary, former member of the Bundestag*

No one on this earth has the right to relieve these people of the burden of their murder. —Heinz Galinski, *the late chairman of the German Jewish community*

HER HANDS WERE rubbed raw from digging, her cheeks reddened by the wind. In the dirt, two feet below the surface, Nadja März found stones of the past. The letters engraved on the broken stones were Hebrew on one side, German on the other. As the days passed, Nadja and the others pieced together the stones and cemented them to the graves over which they had stood for centuries. On a small, shaded rise over weed-filled fields, twenty-eight Germans toiled in a ravaged Jewish cemetery in Szprotawa, Poland, putting the pieces back together, one by one.

Nadja März was seventeen, a German from Bavaria. Until this day, she had never met a Jew. Mauricy Kailer was eighty, a Jew from Austria and the Soviet Union and Poland and Nazi Germany and the resistance and the camps and Poland again. He had met more Germans than he cared to remember. Kailer and three other elders from Zery, the nearest town where any Jews survived, gingerly stepped off a Volkswagen bus and walked through the weeds into the afternoon cool of the Szprotawa cemetery.

"I found a gravestone with a number on it—5608," Nadja excitedly told Kailer. "What does that mean? Is it a code?"

"It is the year," Kailer said. "It is the Jewish calendar."

Her parents were against the trip. Too dangerous, they told Nadja. Poles who don't like Germans, neo-Nazis on the rampage against history—a lot of people might not like the sight of young Germans restoring decency to Jewish graves. "The future is formed by the past," Nadja told her parents. "I had to do something. I'm so afraid of what might happen again." She signed up to travel to Poland with Action Reconciliation, a group of German volunteers who do good deeds in Poland, Israel, the United States and anywhere else where people were wronged this century by Germans.

Kailer came because he was invited and because the Germans promised to restore the long-forgotten, overgrown graveyard. "About two hundred people from my family were killed," Kailer said. "My mother. All eight siblings. My wife, my child. I went to war, came back and my child was gone. It is as it is. The Nazis were here. Good Germans, too. These Germans come now and they want to pay for the sins of the parents. Atonement, they call it." Kailer was the most sprightly and clear-voiced of the remaining handful of Jewish elders in this part of Poland, a region that was once the Silesian province of Germany. Kailer was a storyteller who wrote for the dying readership of the *Jewish Word,* the Yiddish-Polish biweekly. He lived to tell his stories, to those who already knew, and to people such as these young Germans, those who should hear.

Nadja approached Kailer again, staring down at the graveyard dirt. "Do you think it's good we do this?" she asked, her thin voice wavering slightly.

"Very good," the old Jew replied in German. "Beautiful."

That night, they sat in a large circle in a dark room at Szprotawa's run-down orphanage, twenty-eight Germans of all ages and four aged Jews. "We're trying to be factual and clear in our meeting with the past," said Wolfgang Erler, a museum archivist in Berlin who brought his wife and children to Poland for the week. "We want to learn about you and tell you who we are."

On the coffee table sat a copy of *The History of the Jewish People,* a pamphlet published by Germany's Federal Center for Political Education. The Germans had done their homework. They made two trips to Szprotawa to set up the visit. They drew maps of the cemetery and documented its ruin, collecting photos and old records in looseleaf binders. They met with the mayor and the town council and spent a day sprucing up the ramshackle municipal hospital. They arrived ready to work, with tools, tight schedules and charts listing each person's tasks. "We are here to atone," Erler told Szprotawa's mayor. "We are critical people, political people who believe we can only deal with the new conditions in Europe if we know and understand the past."

The mayor stared in silence. He asked what German government agency was sending these do-gooders here. None, came the answer. What are your orders? the mayor asked. None, came the answer. "It's too abstract for them," Erler said later. "It's a totally new experience, to think individuals would just decide to do this, without being told to by the government. But we feel a responsibility to Poles and Jews. It's a unity to me. The Poles separate the two, but that's not my problem."

The evening session began with a long, awkward silence. The Germans asked the Jews to introduce themselves, and Kailer told a bit of his own story, interspersed with the tale of a German woman who in 1938 refused a Nazi bureaucrat's command that she leave her Jewish husband. The couple was forced to close their shop and leave their home. The woman, a Christian, was forced to wear the yellow Star of David. After reciting his own story, Kailer put the best face on Zery's Jewish population of "almost a hundred." He spoke optimistically about the community's young people, which turned out to mean anyone under seventy. More than 10,000 of the 15,000 Jews remaining in Poland were seventy-eight or older. "We are the last of the Mohicans," he said.

The room fell silent. The Germans did not know what to ask, what to say. During a break, Barbara Schultze, a fifty-year-old art teacher from Berlin, tried to explain, to herself and to me, why she and the others could not find the questions they had rehearsed so often in their minds. "My parents were Nazis," she said. "I'm here as a kind of reparation for what my parents did. As Prussians and Nazis, they were educated in Jew-hating. They hate the Poles. They told me not to come here. They said the Poles would steal my car. I fight with my parents all the time about these things. I guess I have a love-hate relationship with my parents. I wanted to do this for me, and for my parents. I never met a Jew before. But I feel helpless with them. I don't know what to say to them. I'm ashamed. I don't want to be just the rich German coming here to help. But I do want to help. I don't know what to say— I'm, we're, well, we're not normally so reserved."

When she was younger, Schultze used to pump her parents for details of what they had known in the Nazi years. "You must have known something about Kristallnacht," she would say. "You must have seen the destroyed Jewish shops, homes and synagogues." No, they would say, they knew nothing. Schultze knew there was a synagogue in her parents' village. But she could draw nothing from her father. He never spoke about the war. He barely answered the most basic questions. "He's learned nothing from history," his daughter said. "He's repressed everything."

Back inside, Schultze, emboldened to ask something, leaned over to Kailer: "Is there anything we can do to help you?"

"We don't need anything anymore," he replied, in a gentle but firm voice. "We're old now."

Schultze remained silent the rest of the night. Later, when I asked what she really wanted from the Jews, she said, "I don't know. Absolution, maybe."

Another of the Germans, Hilde Keilinghaus, had no family past to rue, yet she felt guilty nonetheless. "Even if I was born after the war, I see those same attitudes in myself, things we just seem to inhale," she said. "It's inside us, the way we think about Jews and Poles, about what they look like, how they smell. And now to meet these old people here." Before coming to Szprotawa, Keilinghaus and her friends talked at length about the Holocaust and their own families. She wondered whether she had the right to pry into the old Jews' wounds, to ask about their experiences under the Nazis. She decided that she would ask instead about something they might have in common—children. She approached Kailer.

"And he told me. Killed in concentration camp. And stop—I was helpless. I didn't know what to say. I'd thought since they were about my parents' age, they'd have children born after the war. I didn't think it would be that answer."

Again and again, when the room fell silent, the Germans tried to jump-start the conversation by going around the circle formally introducing themselves to their Jewish guests. Each time they started, the effort faltered, as the Germans debated among themselves whether the exercise served any purpose.

Torsten Schramm, the trip's organizer, said, "We want to tell you who we are."

Kailer interrupted with a wave of his hand: "We know you already. We know, we see what you are doing. That's enough for us."

Schramm charged ahead nonetheless. "My father was an SS man, and that is a reason why I work very intensively on the German past. That's why I wrote a book about the German resistance and my search for Germans who had a heart even in that time."

Again and again, the Germans tried to explain themselves. The Jews initiated no conversation. They had no questions. The Germans wanted a dialogue. The Jews had come to bear witness, to speak for those who were stilled.

After another silence, Schramm turned to Kailer. "It is very hard for me to be hopeful," the German said. "Can you help us? Where do you get the strength to believe in good people after everything you've suffered?"

Kailer answered with a memory of his mother. "She always said, 'Lose money, lose nothing. Lose heart, lose everything.' "

"A lot of people tell us we're doing the wrong thing," Schramm said, "that we should stop staring into the past and just look forward."

"You must never forget," Kailer replied, "never stop looking back."

It hurts to look back, for Germans as for Poles and Jews. It was Torsten who had first gotten me interested in Action Reconciliation. Like so many Germans involved in atonement work, he was the child of a Nazi, an SS man who participated in the invasion of Norway and later worked in the German parliament. The elder Schramm refused to discuss his past with his son. But Torsten studied the Nazi years and his father's past, gathering all the details he could and interviewing his father's friends. When Torsten presented his father with a small book, a history of his war—an exploration as much as an indictment—the father held his silence. The son, wracked by what he knew and what he didn't, sought resolution elsewhere. He devoted his career to peace work, and decided it would be wrong to bring children into a world in which people like his own father had done what they did. It took Torsten more than two decades to get beyond that rage and shame, to accept finally that he was not responsible for his father. By the time he decided he might indeed want a child, he was not likely to have one. And so Torsten worked with other young Germans, hoping they might reach some level of comfort and understanding earlier in life.

The oldest among the visiting Germans, Inge Lehmann-Böhm, was a native. Her hometown was called Sprottau then, a Silesian city home to few, if any, Poles. Lehmann-Böhm initiated this project, inviting Action Reconciliation to salvage the Jewish cemetery. She was the only German visitor who sought neither absolution nor liberation from the sins of the elders. "Eventually, we must have some distance from those times," she said. "You can't keep looking back. You need distance for healing." Lehmann-Böhm, seventy, left Sprottau with her family in early 1945, steps ahead of the Red Army, then on its final victory sweep toward Berlin. For thirty years, she did not see her parents' house. More recently, she has returned to the now-Polish city sixteen times.

In the cemetery, she met Kailer. Their conversation was stilted. "We still have a Jewish cemetery in Zery," Kailer said.

"The old one?" Lehmann-Böhme asked.

"From the old one, nothing remains."

The German woman tightened her lips and looked away. After a few seconds, she tried again, telling of her family's friend, Herr Hirsch, who maintained to the end that the Nazis would never come after him because although he was Jewish, he was a twice-decorated German officer. " 'We are

German patriots,' " she recalled him saying. Then, after Kristallnacht, he fled, "to China, I think—can that be?"

"So it was," Kailer said. "Another tragedy."

For a moment, the two seemed to find common ground. "I'm not at home here anymore," Lehmann-Böhme offered. "Just a visitor."

"Like when I go back to Lemberg [Lvov] now," Kailer said. "I'm a visitor there. My mother was born there, but I am a visitor."

But then silence fell over them again, and the German, shifting uncomfortably from foot to foot, felt compelled to explain herself. "I've always admired your firm beliefs, how the people of the Mosaic belief kept to their religion. This cemetery is your last stand, there's eternity here." A long pause. "I wanted to do something, you know."

Kailer nodded. "But there will be no new burials here, nevermore."

Lehmann-Böhm stared into a faraway space. She waited for the old man to go. "I'm not proud of being German," she said after Kailer had walked on. "I'm not ashamed of it either. But why am I not allowed to talk about my relatives who were killed? This right-wing violence in Germany now is terrible, but no one talks about German families who were burned by foreigners." In the last weeks of World War II, sixty-five German soldiers were killed in a battle at Sprottau. No marker honors their lives. Lehmann-Böhme knew where their bodies were buried, because the site was spotted with wooden crosses until 1953, when they were removed in an act of anti-German spite.

The clot of people on the windswept hill just outside Szprotawa's center did not go unnoticed. One day, an old Polish couple approached the cemetery, hoping to find the answer to a question they had been too fearful to ask for forty-eight years. In 1941, when Germans began forcing Polish Jews into ghettos, Nazi soldiers would quash rumblings of rebellion by dragging a few recalcitrant Jews into the town squares and shooting them. In one town in Galicia, a Jewish butcher named Josef Fleischerfarb knew he had to act fast. His wife had already been condemned to death by SS men. He took his two daughters to his Polish neighbors, Karol and Sawa Michalin, and begged them to take his girls and hide them for the war's duration. The Michalins agreed to provide refuge for one child. They said they did not have enough food to handle two. They took three-year-old Malvina Fleischerfarb as their own and called her "Malka."

In 1945, at war's end, a Russian man who said he was Malka's uncle arrived and retrieved the girl. The Michalins never again heard from her, or of her. For half a century, the Polish farmer and his wife, long since moved to Szprotawa, told no one about their lost Malka. Now, they asked the Germans working at the Jewish cemetery if they could help. The Germans told the couple to come to the orphanage, where they would be meeting with people from the Jewish community. So in the middle of their difficult session that night, the Germans and Jews looked up to see a bent, sun-browned Polish peasant and his firm, silent wife step into the room. Torsten Schramm had driven out to the countryside to pick up the Michalins. Outside her farmhouse, Sawa Michalin warned Schramm not to talk about the Jewish girl in the open countryside. "Come talk in the dining room," she said. "Don't let the neighbors hear. They don't know we did this."

At the orphanage, Karol Michalin held his cloth cap so tightly, it almost disappeared into his fist. In the safety of Germans and Jews, Michalin sat next to Mauricy Kailer and told his story. A translator delivered highlights to the rapt Germans sitting around the circle. They watched as Michalin drew from his inside coat pocket two limp shreds of yellowed paper. One, a long sheet filled in by the hurried hand of Josef Fleischerfarb, promised that if his daughter survived the war, the couple who took her in should be rewarded with Fleischerfarb's ten fields and his house. The other evidence was a torn scrap, a makeshift receipt for a seven-year-old girl, signed cryptically by Dr. Bill, the uncle from Russia, the end of the paper trail. Germans and Jews gathered around the documents. Kailer agreed to write to Israeli archives in search of details of young Malka's fate. He said: "This paper can be something or it can be nothing. It has names and addresses, but who knows if it leads anywhere. We don't know who Dr. Bill is, where, what country. We can only try." There was much shaking of hands and the Michalins left, hope, however thin, stretched across their faces.

At evening's end, the Germans serenaded the Jews with a chorus of "Sholom Aleichem," and the three old men and one old woman went home. "Very nice people," said Moses Grin, chairman of the regional Jewish community. "They want to feel they are better than their parents. They must be. But you know, I had enough of Germans a long time ago."

The Germans stayed up halfway to morning, singing "500 Miles," "Michael Row Your Boat Ashore," and a catalogue of folk songs designed to bring tears to the eyes and a glow to the night. Two days later, they headed home to Berlin and Bavaria, leaving behind repaired gravestones, a new fence at the city hospital, some toys for the Polish orphans. Like the Poles and the Jews they met, the Germans returned to the loneliness of what shaped them, the legacies of their lands, the memories that would not be erased.

At the moment the reunification of Germany was consecrated, Helmut Kohl, fresh from winning Mikhail Gorbachev's consent to the demise of East Germany, raised his glass and offered a toast "to Germany." When the west-

ern German writer Patrick Süskind saw the chancellor's gesture, he realized he had never before heard a German offer cheers to his country. He
couldn't help it, he knew it was not right, but all Süskind could think of in
that moment was Auschwitz.

The burden of being German is different for each person, but it weighs
upon those who accept the past as well as upon those who deny it, on young
and old, across the political spectrum. On the left, the weight of the past often creates an overwhelming sadness, a helpless, collective sigh of anguish.
Thomas Mann, in a 1945 speech to the U.S. Congress, said that Germans
"condemn themselves—[a] character trait that cannot be discounted." On
the right, there is a different edge, a simultaneous sense of threat and being
threatened. Germany, said Wolfgang Schäuble, parliamentary leader of the
Christian Democrats, is a "difficult Fatherland," a place in urgent need of
national pride and national identity, hungry for a self-confidence that is a
"precondition for tolerance toward foreigners and minorities." The German
sense of national self is still based on tainted bonds of blood and race; tolerance, to many, seems not a natural obligation, but a luxury that can be delayed. The old definition of a German has yet to be replaced, even now, even
after the postwar cocoon has opened and Germany finds itself once more its
own sovereign.

When being German was too much to bear, many West Germans tried to
be something else. The outside world called West Germany simply "Germany." But many Germans couldn't handle that. They invented a distinction
between the old, Nazi Germany and the place they lived, which they called
"the Federal Republic." As often as not, they left out the "of Germany" part.
They created a postwar life that was whatever Nazi life had not been. Parents tried to dress and raise their children differently. Language changed.
Life became more American. TV and democracy and an economic boom
made the nightmare seem distant, dim. The Germans became the reliable
ally, the well-behaved, quiet, pliant state perfectly situated to bear the
brunt of the Soviet attack, whenever it would come. In our eyes at least, they
had become more or less normal.

But when the impossible happened and Germany reunited, West Germans realized that what had passed for normalcy had been anything but.
After four decades of coddling and molding by Americans, Germans returned to the uncomfortable but dramatic position they had lived with for
generations—back in the middle again, in the center of Europe, geographi-
cally, politically, economically. This Germany was a troubled country,
slowly waking to painful structural problems. Internally, it was so divided it
could hardly muster the energy to look beyond its borders. Germany's task
is unique. When else has a country had to undertake such enormous social

and economic reconstruction without a war, without the benefit of the shared sense of purpose, the common miseries and hopes that arise in the aftermath of battle?

Germany was no longer on the military frontline, but had become a new kind of frontline state—facing a turbulent region of economic chaos, political uncertainty and unpredictable mass migration. And yet abroad, Germany's allies had a quiver full of new demands. Be more responsible, the Americans said. Bail us out, the Russians said. Germans are trapped in an unforgiving complex of no-win situations. They cannot express national self-interest without being accused of nationalism. They cannot respond to foreign calls to join allies in military operations without risking accusations of a new German militarism. They cannot take on responsibility for helping the struggling nations of eastern and central Europe without sparking talk of a new German hegemony. They are imprisoned by their past.

It is tempting to blame this on foreigners. Horst Teltschik, Kohl's national security adviser during the unification years, warned at our first meeting in 1989 that the greatest danger Germany faced came not from the Soviet Union or East Germany, but from the western allies, whose mistrust grew more palpable and painful daily. "If you do not trust us, you will strengthen the radicals in our country," he said. "You have people like Safire," meaning the *New York Times* columnist William Safire, "who dangerously feeds our radicals every week." Despite public talk of partnership and trust, Germany and its western allies remained like wary school-yard antagonists forced by circumstance to team up against a common enemy.

The subcarrier of suspicion about Germany among its allies grew busier as east-west tensions relaxed. The realities of the Cold War and anticommunism had produced an etiquette in which western leaders could openly express doubts, even prejudices toward Japan, but had to smother questions about Germany in a saccharine gleam of cheery words and painted smiles. Hardly any country seems immune from lurking suspicion of the Germans: a correspondent for one of Japan's largest newspapers asked me to lunch in Berlin to let off steam about his failed efforts to persuade his editors in Tokyo that the Germans were not rearming for battle. Denmark's foreign minister told me his countrymen initially voted down the Maastricht plan for European unification largely because they believed it was a Trojan horse camouflaging a German takeover of the continent. And a Russian diplomat named Victor Grinin served me tea and pronounced his country's vision of good economic ties to Germany, but soon dropped his voice and added: "Of course, we cannot overlook the ingrained Nazi attitudes. All the neighbors are fearful, even if they do not say so publicly. You Americans will never understand the impact on Europe of German wars in this century. Not just my generation, but the next as well, will never be able to trust them."

Nervousness about Germany is not a trivial relic of a fifty-year-old war. Germany's new frontline position will force the country to adopt a foreign policy more finely tuned to its unique geographical and strategic position. Inevitably, Germany's interests will diverge from our own, often in minor ways, but eventually on crucial issues as well.

America's task as an ally is to hold back on the temptation to ask the Germans to act their size, hold off on pressing them to join international military missions, stop relying on their generous contributions to support stability in the former East Bloc—in a sense, extend Germany's postwar protection to give the country time to rebuild the east, to begin the difficult task of retrenching an overextended social welfare system, and to redis-cover or re-create whatever binds Germans east and west.

The alternative is dangerous. Suspicion quickly becomes mutual, and it is always corrosive. Few in Germany's political class—the elites of govern-ment, media, business and academia—harbor illusions about what the rest of the world thinks of their country. I always developed a pit in my stomach when German friends described how they introduced themselves as Euro-peans when traveling abroad, or how they struggled to shed accents that sounded too much like a Hollywood version of the evil German. I recalled the days when, as a young backpacker drifting through Europe, I met Amer-icans who sewed Canadian flag patches onto their packs in vain hopes of fooling terrorists or other anti-Americans. But that hapless bit of disguise was meant solely for external consumption; the camouflaged Americans were usually only reaffirmed in their patriotism. Translated to pop psychol-ogy, their slogan was "If you hate me, I must be OK." Germans hiding be-hind the European flag had no such recourse to self-confidence. Rather, they would confess, sometimes in voices grown shaky with anguish, that they took encounters with the outside world to mean "You probably hate me, you might be right, and I don't know who I am."

Exasperated, many seek to lift restrictions imposed by the past. From Helmut Kohl to the pages of the country's establishment newspapers, pleas for a clean slate grow ever more passionate. In Jerusalem in 1994, I heard Günther Gillessen, a leading editor of the *Frankfurter Allgemeine Zeitung* and a university professor, present an eloquent but shocking argument to a gathering of Germans, Israelis and American Jews: To lift the shame that blankets Germany, we must let go of the Holocaust, quit efforts at collective mourning or atoning, and create "a new taboo" against photographic or film representations of the Holocaust. Steven Spielberg's *Schindler's List* had just opened in Germany, drawing a million viewers in less than two months,

Washington's Holocaust Memorial Museum was nearing its first anniversary, and Gillessen wanted this train halted and hauled back to the yard.

"Memory should be permitted to sink in the sediment of time," he said. "These awful crimes should not be permitted to become the pivot of our lives or the lives of our children. . . . However harsh it may sound or difficult it may be to accept, the Shoah is a closed event, but its victims are to be mourned. The second and third generations should be spared from slipping into this morass." Like the victims, "the victimizers were also people like us." Gillessen rejected the notion that the Holocaust was a unique event, saying, "Relativization is the historian's business. . . . It is a blessing and not a curse that human nature is apt to forget." If he had not already stunned his audience into slack-jawed silence, Gillessen threw in a slam against "the usefulness of the idea of a multicultural society" and said that the Holocaust was not essentially different from other organized mass killings carried out in the name of one utopian idea or another.

A few Americans in the audience of scholars, diplomats and journalists nearly walked out during Gillessen's speech. Instead, they stayed and reacted with baffled rage. I had been asked to comment on Gillessen's remarks. But the text I held in my hands was no longer relevant. Gillessen's speech was a morally troubling call for repression. He had bolstered his argument for forgetting with citations from Catholic theology. But what is religion, I said, if not an institutional, ritualized attempt to recall? We create institutions—museums, religions, literature—to remind us of what we have done wrong and what wrong has been done to us, what we have lost and what could have been. Memory is what we are collectively. No matter how we might want to wish it away, or try to suppress it, it returns. The children, even the grandchildren of Holocaust survivors, have unusually high suicide rates. The past does not vanish. "It happened in your country, Dr. Gillessen," said Yehuda Bauer, perhaps Israel's foremost scholar of the Holocaust. "For the first time in human history, people were murdered because they were born. Your society, like mine, won't get anywhere unless it confronts what happened." Time is slipping away, I told Gillessen: This is the last generation of Germans who can create Holocaust memorials and face the Nazi past with any hope that their efforts might reflect the truth of those who were there.

The German audiences who flocked to see *Schindler's List* were mostly young people, hungry to see the very images Gillessen would ban. Millions of Germans seemed eager to collect evidence against the ritual phrases they had heard from grandparents, aunts and uncles: "We couldn't do anything," or "I didn't know anything." Even the generation just reaching adulthood, the first with no direct connection to the Holocaust, wanted to know. They did not want to be blamed for something they did not do, but many did want to understand.

Edgar Reitz, the director whose epic *Heimat* laid out in simple, banal detail how ordinary villagers became Nazis, told me that to his filmmaker's eye, "memory is more important than history." Memory is the magical blend of the rational and the subjective. It is what counts. Shreds of remembrance and convenience become intertwined with time. What remains passes for truth. There is indeed a human tendency toward forgetting, but some things remain fixed in our minds, whether we want them there or not. No matter what Germans may rationally desire, no matter how much they may yearn for the normalcy other nations take for granted, Hitler, as Reitz said, "is always in our heads. He is dead half a century, and he is with us every day." A soccer game between the British and German teams in Berlin is canceled because it was set for April 20, Hitler's birthday, and the danger of neo-Nazi violence was too great to permit the game. A young Christian Democrat with limited political experience seeks a spot on the party's national board of directors, arguing that he deserves the post because he is Jewish. Germany half a century after Hitler is rife with taboos, wary of its own shadow. The generations that followed cannot be spared, whether they wish to be or not.

They can seek out the past, like Nadja März and the others who devote themselves to Action Reconciliation. It is painful work, fraught with the danger of self-pity and hopelessness. But it can heal and redeem. Alternatively, the next generations can seek to hide and repress, like Gillessen. Finally, young Germans can follow neither path, choosing to pretend to be oblivious. The number of visitors to the concentration camp memorial at Dachau plummeted from 933,000 in 1990 to 591,000 in 1993. When I visited the memorial, Barbara Distel, its longtime director, could find no good reason for the decline. She shook her head. "No," she said, "I can see no reason for optimism."

Behind the widespread desire for a fresh start, many Germans harbor deep doubts about themselves. They speak euphemistically of "old compulsions" and "old ways." Too often, discussions and interviews would end on a note of despair, with a plea for someone, somehow to save the Germans from themselves. At times, when I found myself standing before the charred ruins of someone's house, smelling the stale embers, the ripe stench of intolerance, I took that plea literally. But its meaning is not literal. It is a cry from the past, a shout of memory, a call for the help that everyone owes the other. No one has the right to lift the German yoke, now, later, ever. But Germans have the right to move ahead with honest memory, to embrace the burden of the past as their own.

NOTES ON SOURCES

MOST OF THIS book is based on my own interviews and observations in Germany between September 1989 and May 1994. Unless otherwise noted in the text or these notes, quotations are from interviews I conducted either as a reporter for the *Washington Post* or expressly for this book, or from public statements. Portions of this text have appeared in another form in the *Post*. All names are real, except in chapter 15, where I use the pseudonyms Klaus, Petra, and Anton Voss at the family's request.

1. Fault Lines

The government list of banned videos, movies and games is updated regularly and published as *BPS-Report* by Nomos Publishing, Baden-Baden. The quotation from Margarete Mitscherlich is from an interview published in *Bordbuch* magazine, February 1992.

I am grateful to my successor as *Post* correspondent in Berlin, Rick Atkinson, and to Heiko Gebhardt of *Stern* magazine for updating Anna Rosmus' activities. Michael Verhoeven, director of the film *The Nasty Girl*, provided additional details and insights.

Joachim Fest's biography, *Hitler*, richly details how Nazism forced Germans out of their private, inner lives and into the public realm that the regime could control. Hans Bräutigam described the impact of German privacy laws on medical research in *Die Zeit*, April 13, 1990. Ingrid Hoffmann and Hanne Sievert of the German League for the Child provided background on attitudes toward children. The study of young women's attitudes toward childbearing was conducted by researchers at Cologne University. In conversations and in his numerous writings, Jochen Thies, foreign editor of *Die Welt*, inspired my thinking on elites in Germany.

2. Verboten

A paper by Christian Joppke of Georgetown University's Center for German and European Studies contributed to my thinking on Germany's consensus system. Examples of the emphasis placed on stability and order in German political campaigns were displayed in Munich's Stadtmuseum in 1994 at an exhibit called "Munich: Capital of the Movement."

For their contributions to this chapter, thanks also to colleagues and friends Matt Frei, Bret Haan, Joe Joffe, Ferd Protzman, Tammy Jones, Danny Benjamin, Karen Breslau, John Eisenhammer, Robin Gedye, Luca Romano and Daniel Dagan.

3. The Bloody Flag

Writing in the journal *Deutschland Archiv*, Rainer Zitelmann suggested that the paucity of serious research on the phenomenon of German self-loathing and antipathy to the idea of nationhood stems from the fact that German intellectuals are the primary adherents to the antinational philosophy. "Researchers consider an issue to be in need of explanation only if is alien to them," Zitelmann wrote. But there is extensive survey data on the identity question, and countless forests have been felled to produce the essays and articles that fill the German press on this issue. As with many such topics, I found that Germans who had spent a significant amount of time abroad were far more open about their country's troubled relationship with itself than were those who had led more provincial lives.

Stephanie Wahl was particularly helpful on identity questions, as were Claus Leggewie, Tom Kielinger, Jörn Böhme, and Heinrich Bortfeldt. Werner Hoyer, Karsten Voigt and Admiral Ulrich Weisser guided me through the thickets of the German military and its struggle to find new purpose.

4. Helmut Kohl and the Lust for Normalcy

For details of the chancellor's policies, motivations and strategies, as well as helpful analysis, I am grateful to Kohl's former chief adviser on foreign affairs, Horst Teltschik; his successor, Peter Hartmann; Michael Backhaus of *Stern* magazine; Michael Wolffsohn of the Bundeswehr University; Michael Stürmer of the Foundation for Science and Policy near Munich; Wolfgang Gibowski of the Federal Press Office; Hans-Henning Horstmann of the Federal President's Office; Theo Sommer and Robert Leicht at *Die Zeit;* and several Chancellery aides who prefer not to be named. John Vinocur, John Kornblum and Teltschik helped develop the normalcy theme.

The account of Kohl's early years comes from his own published writings, as well as from a 1985 biography, *Helmut Kohl,* by Werner Filmer and Heribert Schwan; and from a 1980 volume with the same name by Konrad Müller and Peter Scholl-Latour. The phrase "golden handcuffs," describing the west's postoccupation restrictions on German policy, was coined by Timothy Garton Ash in his seminal work on Ostpolitik, *In Europe's Name.*

5. The Ossietzky School

In addition to my several visits to the school, I depended on the extraordinary knowledge of Jörg von Studnitz, a senior member of West Germany's last diplomatic representation in East Berlin. Interviews with Klaus Montag, an East German social scientist; Kurt Masur, conductor of the Leipzig Gewandhaus Orchestra; and Alfonse Wonneberg, a professor at East Berlin's Hochschule für Musik, helped considerably.

The failure of East German dissidents to break out of the country's ingenious system of co-option and repression has been the subject of considerable academic research. Manfred Stassen of the American Institute for Contemporary German Studies speaks of the "mediocrity of the country in the middle," a sense that Germans east and west alike were unable to develop a creative and effective leadership or oppositional class, in part because of their countries' stunted role in the Cold War world. Whether Germany's postunity position in the middle of Europe will prompt the growth of elites willing to lead and challenge the status quo will depend heavily on the nation's ability to define itself beyond ethnicity, themes taken up in later chapters.

Kurt Masur's statement that the government decision not to prosecute him was "legally contestable" was made in an interview with the German magazine *Extra.*

6. First Train Out

The Hotz family kindly let me into their home again and again over the years. They were my guides to a foreign place, but we also became friends. Thanks also to Undine and Kurt-Peter Schmidt, who shared their home with me so many times.

7. Wall-Mart

The best German reporters wrote stories and displayed pictures that captured the euphoria of the immediate post-Wall period, as well as the disappointments that followed. But I found German editors in both parts of the country unwilling to accept evidence that the psychological and spiritual gap between east and west was going to be harder to bridge than Bonn politicians had expected or hoped. There was often a striking difference between the tone of what I read in the German press and what my foreign colleagues and I found in our reporting ventures around the country. That stems in large part from the overwhelming emphasis the German press places on "official" news, coverage of events in Bonn, often to the exclusion of tracing the lives of ordinary Germans around the country. A couple of years after unification, the two versions of events merged into a reasonable consensus, but it took the shocks of neo-Nazi violence, deep popular disaffection with politics, and striking evidence of structural economic problems to bring the German media to realize that the troubles with unification had to be viewed from below as well as from above. All of this is to explain why I rely heavily in these chapters on the experiences of "ordinary" Germans to illustrate larger social and political forces.

Nonetheless, I am indebted to my colleagues in the German press, particularly at the best weeklies: *Der Spiegel, Wochenpost, Die Zeit,* and *Stern.* The accounts of easterners' dreams about the Wall are culled from a *Wochenpost* feature that appeared November 5, 1992. The *Wochenpost*'s editor, Matthias Greffreth—and members of his uniquely mixed staff—were helpful on a host of east-west issues.

A footnote to the section on dreams: Günter Schabowski, for many years editor in chief of *Neues Deutschland,* official organ of the communist party, is the man who, on November 9, 1989, took a small slip of paper out of his pocket and read to a news conference: "Starting immediately, private trips abroad may be applied for without any special reason. Permits will be granted promptly." Years later, Schabowski would contend that he and the Politburo knew exactly what they were doing—opening the border with West Germany. At the time, Schabowski seemed bewildered by his own words. Whatever the truth, the Wall opened that evening, thanks to Schabowski's vague words, massing crowds who would not take no for an answer, and sympathetic guards who could not find anyone to issue an official position.

Schabowski's emotionless reading of his slip of paper quickly became an image repeated so often on German TV that it would be seared into the public consciousness, like Nixon's "I am not a crook" or Bush's "Read my lips." Schabowski himself spent nearly three years unemployed before finding a job as a layout man at a small-town newspaper in western Germany. Three years after his famous announcement, Schabowski was asked whether he ever dreamt about the Wall or that press conference. His response was quick and icy: "I never dream."

I interviewed Bärbel Bohley five times between 1989 and 1993. Several of her friends were also helpful, as was Molly Andrews, a political sociologist who helped clarify my approach to the citizens' movements and the continuing debate over what role easterners should play in the reunited country.

Stephanie Wahl's thoughts on identity, authoritarianism and the traumas of history influenced several chapters, including this one. Kurt Kasch, Deutsche Bank's man in Berlin; Norbert Walter, chief of Deutsche Bank Research in Frankfurt; and Kurt Biedenkopf, the avuncular professor and most benevolent of the western carpetbaggers in the east, were guides to the German economy. I am especially thankful to Kasch for a series of lunches at which he patiently tutored me on everything from interest rates to the economics of deindustrialization.

8. Survivors

Egon Zeidler and his wife Brigitte put up with my irregular pattern of impromptu visits for four years. Somehow, Egon always managed to drop what he was doing, pull out a bottle of eastern sour cherry juice from his dwindling stockpile (the bottler had gone under because he did not have the automatic filling equipment to satisfy his customers' new demand for twist-off caps instead of bottle caps), and spend a few (or a great many) hours telling me about his life. I am indebted also to the other members of the Zeidler clan who told me their favorite Egon stories.

The best and most persistent reporting about Eduard von Schnitzler's last days as moderator of *Black Channel* was written by Anne McElvoy in the *Times* of London. McElvoy, the best of the Berlin press corps, collected some of the quotations I have repeated from Schnitzler's commentaries.

9. Carpetbaggers and Scallywags

Several lawyers, including Wolfgang Probandt in the west and Petra Eichenberg and Dietrich Burk in the east, helped me understand the intricacies of the property claims issue. The head of the Nonnenwerth School, Rolf Vorderwülbecke, not only invited me to talk to his students about unification and everything else but also, with his wife Marita, welcomed us to Bonn in grand style.

Discussions with novelist Peter Schneider, sociologist Irene Runge, historian Heinrich Bortfeldt, and Hans-Peter Stihl, professor of media studies at Berlin's Technical University, gave me insight into the gap between Ossis and Wessis. Wolfgang Bernhardt's comments appeared in an essay he wrote for the *Frankfurter Allgemeine Zeitung*. Details of the western takeover of eastern broadcasting came from a paper presented by Maryellen Boyle of the University of Pennsylvania at the German Studies Association convention in 1993. Poll figures in this chapter are taken from *Der Spiegel*, issue 3, 1993, and subsequent issues. Nearly identical findings were reported later in 1993 by Elisabeth Nölle-Neumann in the *Frankfurter Allgemeine Zeitung*.

10. Germans and Jews

Michael Wolfssohn's criticism of the Berlin exhibition "Patterns of Jewish Life" appeared in the Berlin daily, *Der Tagesspiegel*. The Nazi party's warning cards issued to members who sought care from Jewish physicians are kept at the Nazi War Documents Center in Berlin. The American scientist who found ignorance about Jews in Berlin was Nathan Sznaider, who described his experiences in an article in *Die Zeit* in November 1992. Irene Runge opened doors for me in the eastern Berlin Jewish community.

Jürgen Elsässer, author of *Antisemitism—the Old Face of the New Germany* (Dietz Verlag, Berlin, 1992), alerted me to the Hans Klein quotation, the characterization of Gysi, and the Berlin court ruling on Jewish citizenship. The Interior Ministry's form for recording nose shapes was discovered by *Germany Alert*, the newsletter published by record producer Jack Rieley and east German rap singer Jens Müller ("J.").

Ignatz Bubis sat down with me on several occasions; the late Heinz Galinski deigned to answer a few questions once, but stormed out in a rage when I asked about his critics in the Jewish community. The sociologist Claus Leggewie offered useful insights on the roots of anti-Semitic violence in the postunity period.

Historian Julius Schoeps provided figures on the backgrounds of Jews living in Germany. Tatyana Korol was my ever-cheerful guide to the Soviet Jewish refugee community in Berlin.

11. A German Pendulum: Father and Son

Michael Schmidt, a freelance journalist in Germany, worked with me on some of my interviews with Ewald Althans. Swedish Television, and particularly producer Brigitte Karlstrom, supported some of that work. Some background information on Ewald Althans and Ernst Zündel was originally obtained by Graeme Atkinson, who covers the German neo-Nazi scene for *Searchlight*, a British antifascist magazine. The Federal Office for the Protection of the Constitution provided background material on Althans. *Denying the Holocaust*, by Deborah Lipstadt of Emory University (New York: Free Press, 1993), details connections between David Irving, Robert Faurisson and other figures in the deniers movement. Except in the two instances in the chapter where credit is given to Winfried Bonengel's film *Profession: Neo-Nazi,* all quotations from members of the Althans family are from interviews with the author.

12. Fire and Ash

Numerous studies by the German government and by independent academics have sought to produce a profile of right-wing radicals. The conclusions cited here are an amalgam of results from reports by the Family and Youth Ministry in Bonn, and by sociologists at the Free University in Berlin and at Frankfurt University.

Former Secretary of State George Shultz's memoir, *Turmoil and Triumph* (New York: Scribners, 1993), recounts Kohl's decision not to invite Reagan to any concentration camp, but rather to push the president into a visit to the cemetery where Waffen-SS men were buried. Shultz was forbidden by the State Department from reprinting the text of Kohl's "extraordinary" Dear Ron letter to Reagan. State told Shultz the German government objected to publication of the letter.

Marita Schieferdecker-Adolph, commissioner for foreigners in Dresden, provided details on the neo-Nazi and student scenes in that city, and guided me on several visits. The study of western Berlin students was made in 1992 by sociologist Siegfried Grundmann.

13. Ausländer

Statistics on the Turkish community's role in Germany come from the Federal Commissioner for Foreigners in Bonn, the Center for Turkish Studies at Essen University, and the Turkish Embassy in Bonn. The citation from Bahman Nirumand comes from an article in *Die Zeit,* September 25, 1992. The ruling on Ahi Sema Issever's application to study in the United States was made by Wolfgang Börnsen, the legislator in charge of exchange programs.

Some details of Nazi racial classification laws are taken from Klaus Bade's book *Germans Abroad—Foreigners in Germany* (Munich: C. H. Beck, 1992). Figures on the number of immigrants Germany may need in coming years are taken from separate studies by the Institute for German Economics and sociologist Helmut Wittchow of the University of Marburg. The quotation from Heinz Kühn on fear of foreigners was cited by Hans-Dieter Schwind in an article in the *Frankfurter Allgemeine Zeitung* of June 24, 1993. The Christian Democratic position on integration of foreigners was in *Ausländische Arbeitnehmer,* 1977, cited in "The Civil Rights of West

Germany's Migrants," by Peter O'Brien of Kalamazoo College, in the journal *German Politics and Society*.

The government explanation for its decision to grant citizenship to ethnic Germans is quoted from two statements issued by the Federal Press Office on February 3, 1993, and June 28, 1993. Both were written by Henning Wegener, the office's deputy director for external affairs. The Roma National Congress in Hamburg provided court opinions and other citations of anti-Gypsy sentiment.

14. "How Ugly Are We Really?"

The account of the decision to stage the Berlin demonstration on behalf of foreigners is based on interviews with two senior advisers to Kohl who attended many of the meetings on the issue and one adviser who discussed the matter directly with the chancellor. Members of parliament and President Richard von Weizsäcker's staff also provided details. The quotation from Kohl about ethnic strife in Europe and America is from a June 1993 speech in the Bundestag. The quotation from Gordon Craig appeared in an interview in the *Süddeutsche Zeitung*, March 25, 1993. The tourism survey question came from a poll conducted for the German National Tourism Authority. The Thatcher group's list of German characteristics is from a summary of the March 1990 meeting written by the prime minister's foreign policy adviser, Charles Powell.

The quotation from Uthmann is in the *Frankfurter Allgemeine Zeitung* of November 17, 1992. The *Spiegel* reference to Rosenthal is in the edition of December 7, 1992, among others.

The American view of Germans as patriotic and trustworthy, but anti-Semitic and susceptible to extremism, is contained in an extensive opinion survey commissioned by the Chancellor's Office in 1993. The quotations in the account of my appointment as journalist in residence at the German Studies Institute are from memos written by the principals in the controversy.

15. Lost and Found

The woman Nikos Kapogiannis brought to see Gabriele was identified as a CIA agent in East German Stasi documents. East German police records, corroborated by interviews with U.S. officials, tell the story of the battle between U.S. intelligence and the Stasi for Nikos' cooperation.

Ilse Böhme and Gabriele Yonan provided the account of Böhme's 1976 visit to the Vosses.

In 1990, Markus Zimmermann, a young East Berlin city councilman in the last days of the country's existence, found files in a windowless, locked cellar room at the Education Ministry—Margot Honecker's fiefdom—proving that in his neighborhood of East Berlin alone, during the 1970s and '80s, East Germany put 150 children up for adoption against their parents' wishes. The records Zimmermann provided helped document the forced-adoption policy and its impact on several thousand families. The East German Justice Ministry, also in its final weeks, wrote to Gabriele Yonan claiming that forced adoptions were legal and, in most cases, approved by the natural parents. A state secretary wrote to Yonan, "Only a small number of cases, about 100 to 200 a year, involved 'replacement of consent for adoption,' " the bureaucratic Newspeak term for adoption without consent.

Anton Voss, like his mother and others involved in the Yonan story, generously sat for extended interviews. A few of the quotations from Anton are from an interview he gave to Spiegel TV in 1991. The street confrontation between Gabriele Yonan and Eva Krebs was videotaped by Spiegel TV, which made the recording available to me. Details of the East German forced-adoption policy and its impact on parents and children are also found in a 1993 report of the Berlin Senate Committee on Youth and Family, issued by Senator Thomas Krüger.

16. Back in the Middle Again

The quotation from Konrad Weiss appeared in a column he wrote in *Der Spiegel,* issue 45, 1993. Heinz Galinski's comment came in an address delivered at the Wannsee House in Berlin, May 1990. Patrick Süskind related his reaction to the Kohl toast in an essay in *Der Spiegel* in 1990. Wolfgang Schäuble's comments were made in a speech at the Brookings Institution, Washington, D.C., March 1994.

Günther Gillessen's speech was delivered in March 1994 at a conference of the American Jewish Committee and the Atlantik Brücke in Jerusalem.

ACKNOWLEDGMENTS

I HAD THE great luxury of spending four years exploring Germany, wandering where I wished, poking into whatever issues intrigued me. For that rare opportunity, I am indebted to the *Washington Post*, and especially to Michael Getler, for his trust, and for his belief that there is little better preparation for foreign correspondence than writing about schools, pols and street life in a big city. Len Downie, Bob Kaiser and Don Graham have been kind and tolerant bosses; they and Tom Wilkinson made it possible for me to take time away from the paper to write this book.

A few friends read some or all of the manuscript and provided thoughtful criticism: Daniel Benjamin, Catarina Bannier, Peter Slevin, Charles Varon, Steve Reiss, and, especially, Jody Goodman, who slogged through even the roughest of drafts and always made things better.

Wherever I went in Germany, I found people remarkably helpful, in chance encounters, in government and business, and among my colleagues. Many of my most generous sources are acknowledged in the Notes on Sources. In addition, I thank:

In Berlin, in and around the press ghetto on Grolmanstrasse, Charles Lane, Jonathan Kaufman and Barbara Howard, Ed Serotta, Thom Shanker and Lisa Gordinier. The remarkable Ute Hübner was researcher, librarian, organizer, sleuth, guide to all things German, and, with husband Gerd Kotlorz, friend. Eleni Kirkas and Lorraine Leisten were lifelines to Berlin while I lived in Bonn. Gabrielle Öttinger and Peter Gollwitzer were generous friends. Molly Andrews brought to Berlin her ideas and a welcome dose of the Andrews family spirit.

In the former capital on the Rhine, I am grateful for the insights and kindnesses of Stephanie Wahl, Wolfgang Gibowski, Thomas Kielinger, Ulrike Brandlin, Carl-Heinrich Frauens, Angelika Volle, Sabine Ebel and the late Enno von Löwenstern. The Bonn gang shared great times and ideas: Rowena and Robin Gedye, Kirstan Marnane, Luca Romano, Jennifer and Michael Meyer, Tammy Jones, Jochen and Brigitte Thies, Karen Breslau and Ferd Protzman. Lolita Klavins ran the *Post*'s Bonn bureau for many years with a good heart and a deep well of knowledge. Steve Vogel was the *Post*'s essential connection in Bonn. In Paris, the editors of the *Interna-*

tional Herald Tribune treated me as one of their own and gave my stories a terrific ride for four years. Particular thanks to John Vinocur, who knows what it's like to write tough stories about Germany, and the entire Europe desk crew.

In the United States, I am grateful to the American Institute for Contemporary German Studies for its hospitality, and to founding director Robert Gerald Livingston and research associate Manfred Stassen for taking me in. Thanks also to the Foreign Policy Institute, which gave me a place to write for several months, and to the extraordinary Katherine Reese.

My agent, Amanda Urban, believed in this book even before its conception. I am grateful for her verve and intelligence. Alice Mayhew has an extraordinary knack of coming up with the right idea at the most opportune moment—the gift of a great editor. Thanks also to Alice's assistant at Simon and Schuster, Sarah Baker, who was both editor and my guide through the thicket of the publishing world.

Great teachers stand behind anyone who tries to write. I thank Tek Young Lin, Richard Warren, John McPhee, Gene Miller and Gene Weingarten.

Charlie Varon and Myra Levy, Joel Achenbach and Mary Stapp, David Remnick and Esther Fein, Sherry Sprague and Gary Guzy, Teresa McHenry, Philip Goodman and Evelyn Goodman made sure we never felt too far from home. They even visited Bonn. As did my parents, Harwood and Helene Fisher, and my brother, Saul, whose love and support know no bounds.

This book is for Jody, for all her light; and for Bonn's finest act of magic, Julia.

—Washington, D.C.
January 1995

INDEX

Abelein, Fritz, 27
abortion rights, 160
Abs, Hermann, 31
Academy Awards, 209–10
Ackermann, Eduard, 190
Action Reconciliation, 231, 312, 315, 322
Adenauer, Konrad, 80, 90, 92, 95, 165
    Konrad Adenauer Foundation, 78, 286
adoptions, forced, 293, 298–310
airlines, smoking regulations on, 53
Albers, Frau (landlady), 20, 47
Albertinium, 73
Alliance '90, 196
Althans, Bela Ewald, 12, 225–28, 231–37, 246
Althans, Ewald, 228–29, 231
Althans, Florian, 231, 237
Althans, Günter, 12, 225–31, 237
Althans, Ingrid, 225, 231, 237
American Institute for Contemporary German Studies, 285–86
anarchists, 64, 274, 275–76
Antifascist Protective Barrier, see Berlin Wall
anti-Semitism:
    in church administration, 214
    laws against, 28, 223
    literature of, 232
    of neo-Nazis, 235, 244
    official traces of, 213–14, 217
    Persian Gulf War and, 73
    philo-Semitism vs., 206–10
    as political tool, 216–17
    polls on, 210–11, 214, 218
    in public speech, 214–16
    see also Jews
Arafat, Yasir, 73
ARD, 192, 259
Armstrong, Neil, 190
Arslan, Yeliz, 258

Aryanization, 190–91
asylum laws, 245, 254, 264, 266–67, 270–71
Aunt Emma shops, 174
Aurich, Eberhard, 118
Auschwitz, 37, 89
Ausländer, 257
authority, authoritarianism:
    generational shift and, 61–62, 64
    German need for, 61, 64–65, 168
    New Forum philosophy opposed to, 150
    repressive child-rearing and, 76
    social distance linked to, 55
    welfare state vs., 63
auto industry, 159
Autonomen, 275–76
auto traffic, 45, 49, 50, 51, 54, 75, 178
Avalon, 208, 209
Axen, Hermann, 189

Bahr, Egon, 9–10
Barry, Marion, 262
Basic Law, German, 71, 80, 261
bathroom breaks, 50
Bauer, Yehuda, 321
Baum, Bruno, 190
BBC, 165
Becker, Manfred, 158, 159
Beier, Peter, 207
Benz, Wolfgang, 77–78, 187
Berlin:
    anarchist riots organized in, 64
    immigrant population of, 265
    Jewish population of, 223
    Marzahn development in, 248
    1953 people's uprising in, 122, 171
    proforeigner demonstration in, 274, 275–76
    street name changes in, 190–91
Berlin Documents Center, 266

Berlin Wall:
    construction of, 122, 128, 148
    as cultural barrier, 10–11, 108
    East German history texts on, 122
    fall of, 9–10, 41, 142–44, 148
    in nightmares of East Germans, 148–49
    protests near, 109–10
    sale of chunks from, 143
Bernhardt, Wolfgang, 187
Bertelsmann, 282
bicycle laws, 50, 51
Biedenkopf, Kurt, 159–60
Biermann, Wolf, 66, 115–16, 295
Bild, 53
Biolek, Alfred, 203
biomedical research, 29, 31
birth rates:
    East German, 160
    of German Turks, 255
    immigration as compensation for, 261
    West German, 30
Bismarck, Otto von, 77
Bitburg, military cemetery at, 92–93, 246
Black Channel, 163, 164, 166, 167, 168,
    300
blacks, overt racism toward, 249, 261–62
Boam, Lee, 57
Bohl, Friedrich, 53, 63, 282
Bohley, Bärbel, 12, 109, 149–55
Böhme, Ilse, 301, 303
Bonengel, Winfried, 236
Bonn government, East German estrange-
    ment from, 181–82
Bontana, Ergun, 257
Bortfeldt, Heinrich, 188–90
Bosnia, civil war in, 80, 94
Brandenburg Gate, 87, 128, 142–43
Brandt, Willy, 80–81, 92, 185, 301
Brauner, Artur, 209–10
Brecht, Bertolt, 168, 310
Breuel, Birgit, 185
Brezhnev Doctrine, 127
Brie, Michael, 188
broadcasting authorities, 48–49, 191–92
Brown, H. Rap, 150
Bubis, Ignatz, 203, 215–20, 276
Buchenwald, 41–42, 184
Budapest, East German refugees in, 128
Buell & Liedtke, 212

building industry, 57
Bulgaria, East German escapes to, 294,
    296–97
Bundestag:
    asylum guarantee revoked by, 264
    charismatic leaders lacking in, 83
    East German representatives in, 152,
        164, 194, 195, 196
    former communists elected to, 164
    security precautions taken for, 264
Bundeswehr, 77, 80, 81
Burda, Hubert, 192
Burth, Jürg, 22–23
Bush, George, 72, 79, 94–95, 196, 274,
    283, 286
Busse, Stefanie, 145

Cabaret, 88
capitalism, inequalities of, 169
Carnegie, Dale, 157
Carpentier, Jan, 120
Carrell, Rudi, 125, 262
Castle, The (Kafka), 255
Catherine II (the Great), Empress of
    Russia, 266
Ceauşescu, Nicolae, 269, 270
censorship, of Nazi materials, 21–22
Charles VI, Holy Roman Emperor, 267
child care, 137, 195
    mandatory lessons on, 48
    repressive methods of, 76
    working women and, 195
children:
    antipathy toward, 30
    bicycle-riding licenses required for, 50
    day care for, *see* child care
    forced adoption of, 293, 298–310
    government approval of names for, 49, 50
    school hours for, 51, 160
China, People's Republic of, Tiananmen
    Square protests in, 113, 122
Christian Democratic Union:
    in elections of 1990, 147, 148
    in elections of 1994, 99
    in first East German elections, 147, 148
    on immigration issue, 263–64
    Kohl's alliance with, 91, 98
    leadership within, 98
    Ossis in, 195

reunification program of, 147
right flank of, 246
stability promoted by, 46, 246
on street name changes, 190
Christian Jewish Cooperation Societies, 207
Christian Social Union, 72
Christo, 288
CIA, 116, 283, 295
citizenship:
    for East German refugees, 134
    ethnic basis for, 71, 256, 265–66, 281
    1848 debate on, 264–65
    for foreign residents, 255, 266
    of German Jews, 217, 218–20, 222
    Nazi criteria for, 266
City Museum, 20
Clausewitz, Karl von, 77
Clinton, Bill, 283, 287
closing-hours rules, 50–51, 57–58, 160, 174
coal industry, employment cuts in, 160
Cohen, Richard, 279
Cohn-Bendit, Daniel, 72
Comedian Harmonists, 42
communism, revival of interest in, 164
computer technology, resistance to, 55–56
concentration camps:
    communist victims of, 41–42, 184, 190
    development project planned at, 213
    Kohl's visit to, 89
    public education on, 41–42, 139
    refugee camps vs., 22
    right-wing violence at memorials in, 97, 238, 245–46, 254, 274
    slave laborers from, 35, 37
    visitor rates at, 322
    war crimes trials on, 35–36
    Zyklon B gas used in, 164, 235
Congress, U.S., 215
consensus system, 60–61
constitution:
    asylum guarantees in, 245, 264
    on military involvement, 80
    after reunification, 71
consumerism, western, 134, 137, 139, 144, 146–47, 154
Costa-Gavras, Constantin, 208
Craig, Gordon, 277
credit cards, resistance to use of, 46, 56

crime rates, 263, 281
criminal justice system, 29
Croatia, European recognition of, 79, 94
customer service, 44, 56, 57–58, 158–59, 184–85
Czechoslovakia:
    East German emigration routes through, 127, 129, 130, 131–32
    1989 revolution in, 69
    Prague Spring rebellion in, 296

Dachau, concentration camp memorial at, 254, 322
Dahrendorf, Sir Ralf, 59, 60
Dalk, Detlef, 181
Däubler-Gmelin, Herta, 50
day care, 137, 195
Day X, 146
Death of Dresden, The (Lachnit), 73
de Maizière, Lothar, 148, 195
democracy, national commitment to, 77–78, 220
Democracy Now, 22
Democracy Wall, 122
deportation, terminology of, 280
Deutsche Alternative, 242
Deutsche Bank, 31, 56
Deutsche mark:
    East German switch to, 144, 146
    economic symbolism of, 71, 74, 100
"Deutschland, Deutschland über Alles," 67, 68, 170
DIN, 57
disabled persons, 51–52
Distel, Barbara, 322
Dobiey, Burkhardt, 152
Dreher, Herr (shop manager), 242
Dresden:
    Kohl's public appearance in, 85–88
    neo-Nazis in, 252–53
    wartime bombing of, 73
Dreyer, Gisela, 298, 302
driver's licenses, 50
DT-64, 191–92

eastern Germany, post-reunification, *see* Germany, Federal Republic of, eastern
East Germany, *see* German Democratic Republic

East/West cultural differences:
    in automobile traffic, 178
    consumerism and, 134, 137, 139, 144,
        146–47, 154, 174, 175
    desire for preservation of, 152–53, 154
    in dialects, 185
    in education, 121, 122, 123, 139, 183
    employment standards altered due to,
        182–83
    exploitation of, 157, 174
    growing recognition of, 186, 187
    jokes about, 184–85, 186
    media efforts on, 191–94
    on Nazi past, 121, 122, 182
    in personal initiative, 183, 184, 185, 194
    in social relationships, 54–55, 137, 138,
        139, 154, 155–56, 176
    training centers on, 156–59
    in work attitudes, 135, 158–59, 185
    younger generation on, 183, 185
Ebel, Sabine, 291
economic issues:
    consensus system and, 60
    consumerism, 134, 137, 139, 144,
        146–47, 154
    national pride linked to, 71, 74
    reunification costs, 74–75, 108, 181
    small business, 169–76
    socialism within market economy,
        28–29, 159, 167
    social welfare system, 58–60, 62–63
    technological progress and, 56–57
    transition to market economy, 159–60,
        169–70, 173–75, 186
    unemployment, 139, 145, 155, 159,
        160–61, 173, 187, 241
education system:
    East-West differences in, 121, 122, 123,
        139, 183
    elitist vs. egalitarian, 30–31
    half-day schedules for, 51, 160
    and Nazi past, 121, 122
    religion in, 139
Eichmann, Adolf, 26
Einem, Karl von, 191
Einstein, Albert, 204
elections:
    East German, 22, 110, 126–27, 146,
        147–48, 194–95

    former communists in, 194
    of 1990, 22, 88–89, 146, 147–48
    of 1994, 44, 98–99, 154–55, 194, 248
    stability as campaign promise in, 44, 46
    western campaign tactics in, 147–48
elitism, 30–31
Engholm, Björn, 264
environmental issues:
    in East Germany, 145
    technological progress and, 57
Eppler, Erhard, 70, 215
Erbe, Hannelore, 47
Ercan, Kadir, 259–60
Erhard, Ludwig, 54, 186
Erler, Wolfgang, 312–13
Europa, Europa, 209–10
European Community, 69
    currency union for, 71
    flag of, 17–18, 69
    German power within, 93, 94, 278, 319
    national independence vs., 71
    official languages of, 93
    tariff regulation and, 57
    Yugoslavian dissolution and, 94
European Parliament, 154
Evangelical Church, 214, 230

Face of War, The (Gellhorn), 19
Fahr, Margitta, 281–82
fairness, antimodernism and, 57–58
I. G. Farben, 37, 164
Fassbinder, Rainer Werner, 219
Faurisson, Robert, 227
FDJ, *see* Free German Youth
Federal Center for Political Education, 312
Federal Commission for Foreigners, 259
Federal Office for the Examination of
        Youth-Endangering Publications, 21
Federal Press Office, 279, 280–81, 285
feminist movement, 160
Fest, Joachim, 29
Five Wise Men, 61
flag displays, 17–18, 68–69
Fleischerfarb, Josef, 316, 317
Fleischerfarb, Malvina (Malka), 316–17
foreign aid, 78–79
foreigners, attacks on, 238–48
    government responses to, 89, 97, 241–42,
        245–48, 261, 262, 273–76, 282

law enforcement and, 240
mainstream support for, 240, 241
Neo-Nazism and, 225, 244
as political strategy, 216–17
reunification and, 239–40
Rostock fires as, 238, 240–41, 244
statistics on, 239, 240, 242
volunteer security efforts against, 253
foreign residents:
asylum laws and, 245, 254, 264,
    266–67, 270–71
children of, 256–57, 258
deportation of, 266–67
German Turks, 255–62
as guest workers, 201, 257–58
Gypsies, 241, 242, 256, 266–72, 280, 281
national identity issues for, 256–57
as political issue, 97, 246–47, 253–54,
    260–61, 263–64
racist attitudes toward, 261–62
reunification as setback for, 260
second-class status of, 256, 259, 260–61
terminology changes for, 257–58
see also immigration
Forner, Rainer, 109, 110–11, 121, 122, 123
Francke, Egon, 301
Frauenkirche, 85, 87
Frederick II (the Great), King of Prussia,
    73, 77, 78, 94
Free Democratic Party, 62, 156
attitude of, toward Jews, 215, 217
East German revolution heralded by, 144
in elections of 1994, 99
Freedom Party, 232
Free German Workers' Party, 233
Free German Youth *(Freie Deutsche Jugend)*
    (FDJ), 116, 117, 118, 121, 157, 229,
    249, 252
Freud, Sigmund, 75, 204
Frey, Gerhard, 31–32
Friedrich, Andrea, 179–80
Friedrich, Rainer, 179, 180
Führer, Christian, 129
Funcke, Liselotte, 247
Furtwängler, Wilhelm, 113

Gaffer, Michael, 122
Galinski, Heinz, 216, 311
gambling, 145, 146

Gandhi, Mohandas K., 235
Gansel, Norbert, 82–83
garbage regulations, 47–48
Garz, Klaus, 144
Gastarbeiter (guest workers), 201, 257–58
Gauck, Joachim, 152
Gedye, Robin, 281
Gellhorn, Martha, 19
Gencary, Ahmet, 257
General-Anzeiger (Bonn), 17
genetic research, 29, 31
Genscher, Hans-Dietrich, 55, 78, 94, 95,
    131–32, 145, 186
Georgi, Frank, 157
Gerecke, Annerose, 110–11, 121
Gerlach, Klaus-Dieter, 155–56
German Democratic Republic (GDR) (East
    Germany):
antiwestern propaganda in, 163, 164,
    165–66
attitudes on Holocaust in, 41–42, 121,
    122, 184, 213
borders closed by, 171–72
churches closed in, 140
coded speech used in, 130
collapse of, 107–24, 127–30, 238–39
educational system in, 108–11, 120–23,
    293–94
effectiveness of repression in, 111
elections rigged in, 110, 126
emigration to West Germany from,
    131–35, 144
escape routes from, 127, 128–33, 151,
    230, 294, 296–97
establishment of, 168
family businesses nationalized in, 171
forced adoptions in, 293, 298–310
foreign workers in, 201
intellectuals' cooperation with, 111–14
Jews in government posts of, 189
last communist prime minister of, 118
media reflections of dissatisfaction in,
    116, 118–20
national identity of, 70
New Forum movement in, 149–52, 154
1953 Berlin uprising in, 122, 171
official termination of, 146
party elite's privileges in, 107, 112–13,
    116, 117, 126, 171, 172, 177, 229–30

German Democratic Republic (GDR) (East Germany) *(cont.)*
  paternalistic state in, 134
  peacefulness of revolution in, 238–39
  persecution for ideological divergence in, 126–27
  private real-estate ownership in, 178
  psychiatric practice in, 75
  psychic impact of repression in, 75–76
  restricted frontier zone of, 144
  retail businesses in, 134, 171, 172
  sale of dissidents to west by, 108, 111, 129, 151
  security of welfare state in, 114–15
  sex discrimination in, 150
  socialist school curriculum in, 108–9, 110–11, 120, 121, 122, 123
  standards of living in, 114–15
  student dissent in, 107–11, 116–18, 121, 122–24
  urban planning in, 75
  voting required in, 126–27
  western goods restricted in, 134
  western-owned real estate in, 178
  women's peace initiative in, 150–51
  youth groups in, 116–17
  see also Germany, Federal Republic of, eastern
German Historical Museum, 20–21
German Press Association, 260
German-Soviet Friendship Society, 117, 229
Germany, Federal Republic of:
  antifascist youth groups in, 231
  antimodernist views in, 55–58
  asylum seekers in, 239, 240
  citizenship standards in, 71, 256, 265–66, 281
  consensus system eroded in, 60–64
  constitution of, 71, 80, 245
  eastern, *see* Germany, Federal Republic of, eastern
  East German emigrants accepted by, 131–35, 144
  economy of, 9, 56–57, 58–63, 71, 74, 187
  foreign population of, 255, 263; *see also* foreigners, attacks on; foreign residents
  industrial subsidies in, 56–57, 159, 167
  international opinion on, 273–74, 275, 276–88, 319–20

  Jewish population in, 203–24
  military involvements of, 79–82, 168, 319
  national identity defined for, 70, 318
  Nazi materials banned in, 20–22, 223, 232, 233, 236–37, 281
  Polish border of, 93, 94–96
  political stability in, 44, 46
  population decline in, 261
  postwar denazification programs in, 187
  privacy issues and, 28, 29, 48, 63
  public image of, 28–29, 273–88
  reliance on regulations in, 44–55
  religion in, 139, 214
  reparations payments and, 39, 95, 268–69
  repudiation of Nazi culture in, 28–31, 63
  socialist aspects of, 28–29, 159, 167
  speech and press restrictions in, 21–22, 28, 223, 232, 233, 236–37, 281
  tourists from, 51–53
  war crimes prosecutions in, 31–36, 40
  welfare system in, 28–29, 58–60, 62–63
Germany, Federal Republic of, eastern (formerly German Democratic Republic):
  administrative changes in, 136
  deindustrialization of, 156, 186
  economic conditions in, 137, 139, 147, 155, 156, 159–60, 173, 186–87
  elections in, 22, 146, 147–48, 154–55
  environmental issues in, 145
  former Stasi informants in, 153, 188, 195
  Lost Generation in, 155, 156, 189–90
  marriage and birth rates in, 160
  media control in, 146, 191–94
  national identity for, 75–77, 152–53, 186, 190–94
  nostalgia for communist regime in, 164
  political debate in, 149–50, 152–53, 154
  population of, 201
  press policies revised in, 146
  property reclaimed in, 166–67, 178–81
  real estate development in, 139–40, 213
  retail businesses in, 139, 147, 169–70, 173–74, 175–76
  retaliation against former communists in, 145, 166, 167, 184, 187–90
  retraining efforts in, 157–59
  right-wing violence in, 238–42

second-class status of, 192, 196, 197
sense of disorientation felt in, 76,
    155–57, 181, 239
street names changed in, 190–91
teachers fired in, 123, 137, 188–90
unemployment in, 139, 145, 155, 159,
    160–61, 173, 187, 241
Wessi visits to, 178–80, 182, 183–85, 193
western condescension toward, 181,
    182–87, 193
women workers in, 160–61, 195–96
see also German Democratic Republic
German Youth Education Enterprise, 233
"Germany Song" (Hoffmann von Fallers-
    leben), 68
Germlish, 147
Gibowski, Wolfgang, 74–75, 197, 245–46, 253
Gillessen, Günther, 287, 320–21, 322
glasnost, 108, 109, 110
Gödert, Herr (landlord), 10
Goebbels, Joseph, 22, 23, 83, 227, 232,
    244, 278
Goethe, Johann Wolfgang von, 69, 261
Gorbachev, Mikhail, 88, 108, 109, 110, 113,
    119, 127, 128, 130, 317
Grand Hotel, 142
Grass, Günter, 78
Green movement, 57
Greffreth, Matthias, 193
Grin, Moses, 317
Grinin, Victor, 319–20
Gropius-Bau, 206
Gross, Johannes, 277
guest workers *(Gastarbeiter)*, 201, 257–58
Gulf War (1991), 63, 73, 79–80, 81, 82,
    168, 223, 253
Gypsies:
    begging by, 241, 267, 268, 269
    cultural life of, 271–72
    deportations of, 256, 266–67, 268, 270,
        271, 280, 281
    Nazi persecution of, 267, 268–69, 272
    prejudices against, 241, 242, 267–69
    Romanian repression of, 267, 269–71
Gysi, Gregor, 215

Haake, George, 147
Haan, Bret, 215
Haase, Günther, 185

Haase, Horst, 144
Hager, Kurt, 108
Halle, tunnel market in, 75
Hamburger, Franz, 269
Hardt, Ulrich, 77
Hartmann, Peter, 245
Hasert, Raul, 122
Havel, Vaclav, 111, 114
Havemann, Robert, 295
Haydn, Franz Joseph, 67, 68
Haydn, Hermann, 27
Heiden, Sven, 241
Heidner, Franz, 27
Heimat, 204–5, 322
Heitmann, Steffen, 41, 96, 263
Heller, H. P., 27
Here Is Germany, 283
Herzog, Roman, 32, 70
Hess, Rudolf, 232
Heuwagen, Marianne, 247
Heym, Stefan, 111
Himmler, Heinrich, 24
Hinrichshagen, refugee Gypsies sent to,
    241–42
Hitler, Adolf:
    absence of references to, 19, 279
    background of, 227
    boyhood home of, 24, 25
    British rhetoric on, 278
    charismatic leadership of, 83, 84
    Germans as victims of, 24
    Jewish extermination planned by, 206
    motherhood promoted by, 30
    neo-Nazi reverence for, 226, 227, 232,
        234, 235, 236, 237, 250, 252, 322
    order imposed by, 44, 253
    photographic portraits of, 20, 288
    public spectacle emphasized by, 29
    racial identity promoted by, 70
    rise of, 164–65, 279
    in school curriculum, 139
    taboo about, 19, 20, 21, 22, 25, 322
Hitler Youth, 117, 170, 229
Hobbes, Thomas, 263
Höbel, Peter, 53
Hoffman, Abbie, 150
Hoffmann, Heinrich, 20
Hoffmann von Fallersleben, August Hein-
    rich, 68

Holland, Agnieszka, 210
Holocaust:
    atonement efforts and, 311–17
    denials of, 34, 226, 227, 232, 235, 236,
       237
    East German attitudes on, 41–42, 93,
       121, 122, 184, 213
    films on, 321–22
    as identity issue, 223–24, 320–22
    in school curriculum, 121, 122
    war crimes prosecutions and, 31–40
Holocaust Memorial Museum, 286–87,
    321
home-building industry, 57
Homicide, 211
Honecker, Erich, 107, 116, 120, 248
    background of, 113, 168, 189
    on Berlin Wall, 125
    dissident criticisms of, 114, 151
    on East German emigration, 108, 119,
       120, 132
    ideological rigidity of, 108, 109, 116,
       118
    Masur as favorite of, 111
    removal of, 112, 146, 149, 188
    successor to, 110
Honecker, Margot, 108, 110, 300
Horn, Gyula, 128–29
Hotz, Ekkehard and Elke, 12, 125–28, 188
    antigovernment views developed by,
       126–27
    East German return of, 136–40
    emigration of, 128, 130–34
    western life tried by, 134–36
Hotz, Katja, 131
Hotz, Mareika, 138
Hotz, Mirko, 130–31, 134
Hotz, Philipp, 131
housing:
    for foreign refugees, 22, 239
    for guest workers, 201, 239
    outmoded technology for, 57
    postreunification property claims and,
       166–67, 178–81
    for Soviet Jewish immigrants, 222–23
Hoyer, Werner, 62, 156
Hoyerswerda, foreigners assaulted in, 239
Hübner, Frank, 242
Hughes, Thomas, 285

Hungary:
    dissidents in, 151
    East German refugees in, 127, 128–29, 151
Huntscha, Hans Joachim, 215

"If Angels Travel," 204
immigration:
    asylum laws and, 245, 254, 264,
       266–67, 270–71
    history of, 69–70, 264–65
    limitations for, 247, 253–54
    neo-Nazi rhetoric on, 227, 234, 244,
       247–48, 249
    refugee cash allowances and, 242
    shape of nose noted on forms for, 213
    of Soviet Jews, 222–23
    see also foreign residents
Inability to Mourn, The (Mitscherlich), 24
Inner Leadership Academy, 77
international affairs, German role in,
       78–82, 89, 93–94
Intershop, 134
Irving, David, 227, 236
Israel:
    German Jewish emigration encouraged
       by, 220, 222
    German visitors to, 42, 204, 207, 209, 231
    Law of Return in, 281
    neo-Nazi rhetoric on, 235
    Palestinian conflict with, 230–31
Issever, Ahi Sema, 260

Jabotey, Cherno, 259
Jagger, Mick, 147
Jahnke, Horst, 146
Jewish Cultural Association, 217
Jewish Museum, 224
Jews, 203–24
    antiforeigner violence and, 216–19
    cemeteries of, 203, 212–13, 311–12, 316
    church attitudes on, 214
    citizenship of, 217, 218–20, 222
    community leaders of, 215–16
    emigration considerations for, 219–21
    German ignorance about, 42, 211, 213,
       214, 215, 218, 311
    idealized images of, 209–10
    intermarriage with, 214
    memories suppressed by, 33–34, 38–40

military exemption for, 222
museum exhibitions on, 19, 205–6, 238
neo-Nazi rhetoric on, 235
philo-Semitic attitudes toward, 206–10
population levels of, 206–7, 215, 220,
    222–23
power attributed to, 214–15, 235, 246
reconciliation efforts and, 27–28, 207,
    208, 212, 231, 238, 311–17
Russian/Soviet, 204, 222–23
television depictions of, 204–5, 212–13
war crimes prosecutions and, 31–36, 40
see also anti-Semitism
John, Barbara, 261
Johnson, Lyndon, 98
jokes, 184–85, 186, 258
journalism:
    authoritative views in, 63–64
    foreign, 273–88
    after reunification, 192–93

KaDeWe, 50–51
Kafka, Franz, 255
Kahane, Annetta, 222–23
Kailer, Mauricy, 311–12, 313, 314–17
Kanther, Manfred, 96
Kapogiannis, Nikolas, 294–95, 300, 306
Karajan, Herbert von, 113
Käs, Christian, 263
Kasch, Kurt, 74
Keilinghaus, Hilde, 314
Kemna, Friedhelm, 17
Khomeini, Ayatollah Ruhollah, 234
Kielinger, Thomas, 41
Kimmitt, Robert, 283
Kinder, Kirche, Küche (KKK), 195
Kinderfeindlichkeit, 30
Kinkel, Klaus, 80, 274, 277
Kippe, Andreas, 54
Klavins, Lolita, 48
Klein, Hans, 215
Klein, Robert, 27–28
Kleinmann, Luisa, 35
Klemperer, Otto, 204
Kohl, Hans, 91
Kohl, Helmut:
    antiforeigner sentiment and, 89, 97,
        245–47, 261, 273–75, 282
    Auschwitz visited by, 89

background of, 90–91, 96
East German disenchantment with, 176
East German refugees and, 22, 129
economic policies of, 56–57, 59, 71, 89,
    97, 155, 159, 186–87
European union and, 71
foreign opinion and, 274, 276, 278
on future of Europe, 100–101
German press on, 60–61
on German public image, 273–78, 282
on international role of Germany, 78–79,
    80, 89, 93–94
Jewish issues and, 93, 212, 215, 245–
    246
on national anthem, 68, 100
on national identity, 73, 80, 88, 90–91
in 1990 election campaign, 88–89, 95,
    147, 148, 155
in 1994 election campaign, 98–99
normalcy as political goal of, 92–93, 99
ordered progress promoted by, 46–47
patriotism of, 88, 96, 317–18
physical appearance of, 88, 89, 91
Polish border recognition and, 93,
    94–96
political career of, 85–90, 91–92,
    95–96, 98–99, 246
presidential candidate supported by, 41,
    96, 263
at proforeigner demonstration, 276
public appearance in Dresden, 85–88
reunification process and, 46–47, 56–57,
    86–88, 89, 93, 96–97, 100–101, 143,
    146, 147, 239
speed limits opposed by, 54
staff for, 53, 57, 63, 245, 246, 319
street name changes backed by, 190
successor generation vs., 82, 83, 98
territorial borders and, 93, 94–96, 167
U.S. relations with, 93, 94–95, 97–98
war dead honored by, 92–93, 99–100
on women's issues, 195–96
Kohl, Walter, 92
Kohl government:
    cabinet for, 195, 196
    on domestic military presence, 74
    on East German development, 186
    German patriotism studied for, 72
    on Holocaust memorials, 287

Kohl government *(cont.)*
  on immigration issues, 74–75, 90, 97,
    253–54, 260–61, 264, 268
  international image and, 273–77, 282,
    285
  property claims policies of, 181
  on right-wing radicalism, 243, 273–76
  tabloid press and, 192, 193
Kollwitz, Käthe, 99
Krämer, Willi, 232
Krebs, Eva, 299, 307–8, 309
Krenz, Carsten, 110, 111
Krenz, Egon, 110
Krickstein, Aaron, 214
Kristallnacht, 19, 41, 83, 205, 316
K-10, 144
Kühn, Heinz, 263
Kühn, Volker, 23
Kühnen, Michael, 233, 243, 244
Kupfer, Lothar, 240
Kuss, Cornelia, 183

Lachnit, Wilhelm, 73
Lafontaine, Oskar, 88
Lane, Charles, 242, 281
Langerbeck, Georg, 118, 120
language, formality of, 54–55
Lautzbach, Wilhelm, 54
lawn mowers, restrictions on use of, 47
leadership, postwar ambivalence toward,
    83–84, 91
legal system, constitutional basis for, 71
Leggewie, Claus, 247–48
Lehmann-Böhm, Inge, 315
Lehmann-Grube, Hinrich, 156–57
Leipzig:
  property claims disputes in, 180
  weekly candlelight demonstrations in,
    129–30
Leisch, Marie-Lu, 66–67
Lenin, V. I., 132
Lerman, Miles, 286
Leuchter, Fred, 227
Levinson, Barry, 208
Libeskind, Daniel, 224
Liebknecht, Karl, 151
Linsmayer, Eleonore, 182–83
Livingston, Robert Gerald, 285–86
Lob, Wolfgang, 214

Losansky, Frank, 147
Lost Generation, 155, 156, 189–90
Löwe, Rüdiger, 182
Lufthansa, 53, 159
Lutheran Church, 75, 117, 151
Luxemburg, Rosa, 151

Maaz, Hans-Joachim, 75–76
maiden names, 49–50
Makulla, Annette, 147
Mamet, David, 211
Mann, Golo, 248
Mann, Thomas, 58, 318
Maras, Sevda, 256–57
market economy:
  socialism within, 28–29, 159, 167
  transition to, 159–60, 169–70, 173–75,
    186
Maron, Monika, 44
marriage rates, 160
März, Nadja, 311–12, 322
Marzahn, 248–49
Masur, Kurt, 111–14
Mathiopoulos, Margarita, 188
Maunz, Theodor, 31–32
Maximoff, Mateo, 271
medical culture, 62
Mein Kampf (Hitler), 21, 139, 223, 232
Mercedes, 159
Merkel, Angela, 195–96
Mertes, Michael, 57
Meves, Christa, 30
Meyer, Edith, 179
Michalin, Karol, 316–17
Michalin, Sawa, 316–17
military:
  budget constraints on, 82
  international coalitions of, 79–80, 81, 93
  Jewish exemption from, 222
  postreunification merger of, 77
  public reluctance toward, 81, 82
  women in, 150–51
Millner, Max, 36
Mitscherlich, Margarete, 24
Mitterrand, François, 92
Mitzlaff, Winfried, 158
Modrow, Hans, 87, 118, 143, 194
monetary merger, 144, 146
Morr, Hubertus von, 287

motherhood:
    fertility research and, 29
    forced adoptions and, 293, 298–310
    Nazi promotion of, 29–30
    work and, 58, 160, 195–96
Mueller-Stahl, Armin, 208–9
Müller-Westernhagen, Marius, 66
Münch, Walter, 184
Murdoch, Rupert, 192
Music Box, 208
My Parents' Home (Kohl), 91

names, government regulations on, 49–50
Nasty Girl, The, 25, 27
national identity:
    artistic expression of, 66–67
    authoritarianism and, 76, 168
    democratic government and, 77–78
    economic pride and, 71, 74
    emotional connections removed from,
        71–72
    flag displays and, 17–18, 68–69
    of foreign residents, 256–57
    German anthem and, 67, 68
    global involvements and, 78–82
    Holocaust and, 223–24
    initial establishment of, 68, 69–70, 265
    international opinion and, 273–88, 318–19
    militarism and, 70, 73–74, 80
    negative definitions of, 70, 108, 224,
        265, 318
    political leadership and, 82–84
    for postrevolution East Germans, 70,
        75–77, 152–53, 186, 190–94
    victim status and, 24, 73
National List, 243
National People's Army, 77, 122, 126, 145,
    229
nationhood, nationalism vs., 68
NATO (North Atlantic Treaty Organization),
    81, 122, 284
Navon, Benjamin, 210
"Nazi, The," 21
Nazis, Nazism:
    as burden in family history, 208, 291,
        313, 315
    censorship of materials on, 20–22, 223,
        232, 233, 236–37, 281
    citizenship rules of, 266
    controversial terminology linked to, 22,
        280
    dissociation from, 19–22, 25–31, 41–42,
        63
    East German school curriculum on, 121,
        122
    euphemistic references to, 17, 22
    exposure of town history of, 24–28
    Gypsy victims of, 267, 268–69, 272
    intergenerational questions on, 24, 208,
        229, 291, 313, 315
    lack of art exhibits on, 19, 20–21
    large families promoted under, 29–30
    military discipline under, 170–71
    in museum exhibitions, 19–21
    national anthem and, 67, 68, 100
    popular music associated with, 22–24
    postwar German life as repudiation of,
        28–31
    reparations claimed for damages of, 39,
        95, 268–69
    street names aryanized by, 190–91
    war crimes prosecutions and, 31–36, 40
neo-Nazis, neo-Nazism:
    as adolescent rebellion, 226
    antiforeigner agenda of, 225, 244
    anti-Semitism of, 235, 244
    benign reactions to, 252–53
    Berlin club for, 248–52
    childhood experiences of, 226, 228,
        231–33, 243
    demonstrations in opposition to, 274,
        275–76
    domestic intelligence on, 227, 233, 237,
        243
    East German development of, 139
    financial backing for, 226, 234, 250
    foreign opinion and, 273, 278, 279, 282
    German public image and, 26, 273–76
    girlfriends of, 251
    government censorship and, 22, 233,
        236, 243
    Hitler revered by, 226, 227, 232, 233,
        234, 235, 236, 237, 243, 250, 252
    Holocaust denial and, 226, 227, 232,
        235, 236, 237
    homosexual, 233
    immigration opposed by, 227, 234, 244,
        247–48, 249

neo-Nazis, neo-Nazism *(cont.)*
  leaders of, 233–37, 242–44
  media coverage on, 227, 236, 242–43,
      273, 278, 279
  Ossi vs. Wessi, 243–44
  prosecution of, 233, 236–37, 243
  social worker's reform efforts for, 250–
      251
  victim status cultivated by, 236–37, 244
Neue Wache, 99–100
Neue Zeit, 194
New Forum, 129, 149–55, 194
Newiger, Monika, 123
newspapers:
  East-West differences and, 192–94
  foreign, 273–88
news reporting, authoritarianism and,
      63–64
New York Times, 215, 279
Nicolescu, Ion, 270–71
Niffgen, Renata, 183
Nirumand, Bahman, 260
noise regulation, 47, 51
Nonnenwerth School, 183
Nooteboom, Cees, 277

Object Green, 171
Oder-Neisse line, 94
Öhme, Joachim, 158
Olympic Games, 23, 186
1199, 119–20
Oranienburg, postsocialist life in, 136–38
Örland, Irmela, 214
Carl Ossietzky School, 107–9, 110–11, 114,
      121–24
Ossi Park, 157

Pagel, Dietmar, 255
Palace of Tears, 157
Palestinians, 73, 230–31
Pampers, advertisement for, 186
Party Control Commission, 126
Party of Democratic Socialism, 124, 148,
      168, 194
Passau, Nazi history suppressed in, 25–28
patriotism, resistance to, 72
pedestrian traffic, 45, 51, 75
Peer, Charlotte, 142–43
Perel, Salomon, 209, 210

Perger, Werner, 260
Perot, H. Ross, 61
Persian Gulf War (1991), 63, 73, 79–80, 81,
      82, 168, 223, 253
Hector Peterson School, 255, 256–57
Philip Morris, 145
physicians:
  as authority figures, 62
  Jewish, 208
Pinkelpause, 50
Pink Floyd, 109
Pleitgen, Fritz, 264
Poland:
  dissidents in, 151
  East German emigrants in, 127
  German border with, 93, 94–96
  reconciliation effort at Jewish cemetery
      in, 311–17
Polat, Nilgun, 257
"policy community," U.S., 284
politeness, 44–45, 158–59
politics:
  of consensus system, 60–61
  disaffection with, 61
  Ossi-Wessi relations in, 156, 194–96
  postwar generation in, 82–84
  of symbolism, 88, 275
  western campaign tactics in, 147–48
Politikverdrossenheit, 61
Pordzik, Wolfgang, 286–87
postal workers, breaks mandated for, 50
Pot of Color, A, 116
Prague Spring, 296
privacy issues, 28, 29, 48, 63
Profession: Neo-Nazi, 227, 236
property claims, 166–67, 178–81
Przemysl, Jews evacuated from, 34–35, 36,
      37
Püschel, Aristoteles (Anton Voss), 294,
      295, 296, 298–300, 301–10
Püschel, Gabriele, *see* Yonan, Gabriele
      Püschel

Quayle, J. Danforth, 63–64

Rabattgesetz, 58
racism, 241, 242, 249, 261–62, 267–69
  see also anti-Semitism; foreigners,
      attacks on

radio broadcasting:
    license fees for, 48–49
    western control of, 191–92
Rangsdorf, 177–80
Rauch, Renata, 149
Ravensbrück, 213, 254
Reagan, Ronald, 92–93, 246
Reconstruction, 196–97
Red Channel—Poor Germany (Schnitzler),
    167
Reich, Jens, 151
Reichstag, Christo's wrapping of, 288
Reitz, Edgar, 322
religion:
    church anti-Semitism and, 214
    government information forms on, 48
    in public education, 139
Remer, Otto, 232
Republican party, 246, 263
Republikflucht, 126, 132, 171
research, biomedical, 29, 31
retail sector:
    closing hours specified for, 50–51,
        57–58, 160, 174
    credit cards resisted for, 46, 56
    customer service in, 44, 50–51
    discounting regulated in, 58
    in East Germany, 134, 139, 147, 169–
        176
    street vendors in, 75, 263
retraining, 157–59
reunification:
    armies merged after, 77
    attacks on foreigners and, 239–40
    confrontational politics and, 84
    development efforts and, 159, 213
    dominance of western culture after, 178,
        190–92, 194, 197
    economic issues and, 74–75, 105,
        159–60, 181
    German international position after,
        78–82
    initial popularity of, 115–16
    market-economy transition and, 159–60,
        169–70, 173–75, 186
    of monetary system, 144, 146
    national identity affected by, 70–71,
        76–79
    pace of, 145–46

    power increased by, 145
    property claims activated after, 166–67,
        178–81
    psychological impact of, 155–57, 181
    skepticism prior to, 9–10
    television sitcoms on, 77
    U.S. Reconstruction vs., 196–97
    victimization issues and, 73
Rexrodt, Günter, 55
Ridley, Nicholas, 278
rights of way, 51
Ritter, Bruno, 32–41
Ritter, Inge, 39
Ritter, Monika, 32
Rogins, Lardly, 52
Romania, Gypsies persecuted in, 267,
    269–71
Room of Tears, 307
Roosevelt, Franklin D., 83
Roots (Wurzel), 249–52
Rosenberg, Alfred, 232
Rosenkranz, Stefanie, 54
Rosenthal, A. M., 279
Rosmus, Anna, 24–28
Rostock, refugee apartments burned in,
    238, 240–42, 244
Ruback, Mike, 249
Rühe, Volker, 263

Sachsenhausen, 41–42, 97, 238, 245–46,
    274
Safire, William, 279, 319
St. Nikolai Church, 129
salary parity, 187
Samtleben, Gurdana, 147
Schanz, Joachim, 275
Schäuble, Wolfgang, 74, 318
Scheffler, Mark, 196
Schiffauer, Werner, 61
Schikorr, Detlef, 69
Schiller, Friedrich von, 112
Schindler's List, 288, 320–21
Schlagkamp, Franz-Dieter, 215–16
Schmalz-Jacobsen, Cornelia, 247, 276
Schmidt, Helmut, 71, 72
Schmidt, Hermann, 26
Schmidt, Karlheinz, 203
Schmidt, Monika, 123
Schmidt, Undine, 291

Schnitzler, Georg von, 164
Schnitzler, Karl-Eduard von, 162–69, 300
Schnoor, Herbert, 83, 268
Scholl-Latour, Peter, 95–96
Schönhuber, Franz, 97, 246
Schöps, Julius, 205
Schramm, Torsten, 314–15, 317
Schultze, Barbara, 313–14
Schumacher, Hanns, 79, 281
Schuster, Paul, 271
Schwammberger, Josef, 32–36, 40
Schwilk, Michael, 193
scientific research, 29, 31
security, desire for, 83, 246
SED (Socialist Unity Party), 112
Sen, Faruk, 259
Senst, Axel, 156
Serbia, Bosnian war with, 94
Serotta, Edward, 211
service businesses, 158–59
Service for Germany, 229
Sewering, Hans, 31
shopping hours, 50–51, 57–58, 160, 174
Sievering, Katharina, 67
Silbermann, Alphons, 221
Sinti, 267
Slovenia, European recognition of, 79, 94
smoking regulations, 53
Sobczynski, Katrin, 72
Social Democratic Party:
    aversion to power in, 82, 83
    in elections of 1990, 88
    in elections of 1994, 99
    on immigration issues, 245, 264
    patriotic emotionalism eschewed by, 72
    Republican appeal to, 246
    Tuscany Faction of, 83
socialism, West German market system
        and, 28–29, 159, 167
Socialist Unity Party (SED), 112
Society for Sports and Technology, 117
Solidarity, 115
Sommer, Theo, 182
Soviet Union:
    Brezhnev Doctrine abandoned by, 127
    East German control and, 108, 109–10,
        111, 127
    Hungarian independence from, 127, 128
    Jewish emigration from, 204, 222–23

speed limits, lack of, 54
Speer, Albert, 19
Spielberg, Steven, 320
Sprick, Marina, 72
Sputnik, 109
Staatsschutz, 281–82
Stahl, Karl-Heinz, 63–64
Stalingrad, 24
Stasi:
    archives of, 152, 307
    dissidents persecuted by, 127, 151, 172,
        295–96
    informants for, 41, 108, 111, 153, 188,
        195, 215, 295
    refugee trains menaced by, 132–33
    theme park depictions of, 157
    youthful cynicism noted by, 118
Stassen, Manfred, 285
sterilization, 160
Stolpe, Manfred, 41, 153, 215
street names, alteration of, 190–91
street vendors, 75, 263
Streibl, Max, 275
Streim, Alfred, 31
successor generation, 82–84
Sudhoff, Jürgen, 128–33
suicide rates, 181
Super!, 167, 192–93
supermarket chains, 169, 174, 175
Süskind, Patrick, 318
synagogues:
    reconstruction of, 205, 212, 221
    security measures for, 221, 222
Szprotawa, Jewish cemetery in, 311–12,
        316

tabloid press, 192–93
Tamaz, Franz, 241
Tapetenfabrik, 66
Tautz-Wiessner, Gisela, 158–59
technological innovation, resistance to,
        55–57
television:
    communist antiwestern propaganda on,
        163, 164, 166
    East German political dissatisfaction re-
        flected on, 116, 118–20
    German Jews depicted on, 204–5,
        212–13

license fees for, 48–49
minorities on, 259
news reporting on, 63
reunification sitcoms on, 77
western impact on East Germans
  through, 120, 125
Teltschik, Horst, 78, 93, 96, 319
Thatcher, Margaret, 278
Thies, Jochen, 42, 62, 71
Thies, Nora, 42
Third Reich, *see* Nazis, Nazism
Third Way, 149
Tiananmen Square, protests at, 122
Tisch, Harry, 119
Trabants, 141, 184
trade, nontariff barriers to, 57
traffic safety, 45, 49, 51, 54, 75, 178
trash, regulations on, 47–48
Treuhand, 156, 185
Turks, German, 255–62
Tuscany Faction, 83

Uhrlau, Ernst, 247
Ulbricht, Walter, 114, 166, 168
unemployment, 139, 145, 155, 159, 160–61,
  173, 187, 241
unification, *see* reunification
United Nations:
  High Commissioner for Refugees, 264
  military actions of, 80, 93
  on protection of Gypsies, 264, 268
  Security Council members of, 94
Uthmann, Jörg von, 279

Verhoeven, Michael, 25
victimization, 24, 73
Vogel, Wolfgang, 129, 130, 132, 303
Voigt, Jutta, 148–49
Voigt, Karsten, 72, 79
Volga Germans, 266
Volk, 61, 265
Volkskammer, 165
Volkswagen, 159
Volle, Angelika, 182
Voss, Anton (Aristoteles Püschel), 294,
  295, 296, 298–300, 301–10
Voss, Klaus, 299–303, 306, 307
Voss, Petra, 299–303
Voss, Werner, 191

Wahl, Stephanie, 59
Waigel, Theo, 72, 187
Waldheim, Kurt, 94, 246
Walesa, Lech, 111, 114
Wall in the Head, 186
Walters, Vernon, 95
war crimes, prosecutions for, 31–36, 40
Washington Post, 9, 17, 52, 279, 280, 285
Wegener, Henning, 280–81, 285
Wehrmacht, courts-martial by, 171
Weill, Kurt, 204
Weiss, Konrad, 311
Weizsäcker, Richard von, 236
  on impact of Nazi past, 93, 291
  on international role for Germany, 81
  on national identity issues, 68, 74
  proforeigner efforts shown by, 97, 245,
    258, 262, 274, 275–76
  on right-wing violence, 262
  structural changes advocated by, 58,
    61
  successor to, 96
  on Turks in Germany, 258, 262
Welde, Sabina, 144
Welt, Die, 41, 62
West Germany, *see* Germany, Federal
  Republic of
Widera, Hans, 241
Wieczorek, Michael, 249–52
Wieczorek-Zeul, Heidemarie, 50
Wiesel, Elie, 279
Wieseltier, Leon, 287
Wiesenthal, Simon, 26, 35, 36
Wilf, Yael, 214
Wilhelm I, King of Prussia, 73
Willemson, Roger, 210
Williams, Arthur, 38, 39
Willmann, Helmut, 81
Wirtz, Jakob, 112
Wochenpost, 193
Wolf, Christa, 111
Wolfssohn, Michael, 206
Wollenberger, Vera, 110, 196
women:
  in government positions, 150
  on military involvement, 150–51
  in workforce, 58, 160–61, 195–96
Women of the SS, 21
Worch, Christian, 243–44, 246

workers:
   benefits for, 59, 62–63
   mothers as, 58, 160, 195–96
   Ossi vs. Wessi, 55, 135, 158–59, 182–83,
      185
   social distance among, 55
   strict schedules for, 50–51, 57–58
   unemployment and, 139, 145, 155, 159,
      160–61, 173, 187, 241
Wössner, Mark, 282
Wurzel (Roots), 249–52

Yonan, David, 301, 304, 309
Yonan, Gabriele Püschel, 293–310
   A. Voss's adoption and, 12, 298–302
   A. Voss's relationship with, 303–10
   escape made by, 295–98

marriages of, 294–95, 300, 301
Young Pioneers, 116
Yugoslavia, dissolution of, 79, 94

Zank, Robert, 21
ZDF, 204, 259
Zeidler, Brigitte, 169, 170, 171, 172, 174, 176
Zeidler, Egon, 12, 162, 163, 169–76
Ziebura, Katherine, 208
Zimmermann, Markus, 116–18
Zimmermann, Monika, 193–94
Zirzow, Antje, 143
Zirzow, Ruth, 143
Zitelmann, Rainer, 41
Zorn, John, 66
Zündel, Ernst, 234
Zyklon B, 164, 235

ABOUT THE AUTHOR

MARC FISHER WAS bureau chief for the *Washington Post* in Bonn and Berlin from 1989 until 1993. In 1993, he won the Overseas Press Club Award for best interpretation of foreign news. He is currently a staff writer for the Style section of the *Washington Post* and lives in Washington, D.C., with his wife and daughter.

28 ~~~~ DAYS

DATE DUE

DEC 2 8 1995		
MAR 2 6 1996		
JUL 1 3 1996		
AUG 2 1996		
SEP 9 1996 WITHDRAWN		
SEP 2 3 1996		
OCT 4 1996		
DEC 1 4 1996		
JAN 4 1997		
JAN 1 8 1997		